Multi-Track Recording
For Musicians

Multi-Track Recording

For Musicians

A volume in the Keyboard magazine library for electronic musicians

By **Brent Hurtig**

With a contribution by J.D. Sharp

A **Keyboard** magazine book
GPI Publications, Cupertino, California

Alfred Publishing Co., Inc.
16380 Roscoe Blvd., P.O. Box 10003, Van Nuys, CA 91410-0003

GPI BOOKS

Director
Alan Rinzler

Art Director
Paul Haggard

General Manager
Judie Eremo

Art Assistant
Robert Stockwell Jr.

Assistant
Marjean Wall

GPI PUBLICATIONS

President/Publisher
Jim Crockett

Executive Vice President
Don Menn

Corporate Art Director
Wales Christian Ledgerwood

Production
Cheryl Matthews (Director)
Joyce Phillips (Assistant Director)
Andrew Gordon, Gail M. Hall, Joe Verri

Typesetting
Leslie K. Bartz (Director)
Pat Gates, June Ramirez

Order Processing
Rekha Shah
Lynne Whitlach

Photo Credits

Cover: Paul Haggard

Interior: Page viii, 25 (top left), 32 (bottom), 57, 68, 75, 76 (left), 77 (top), 86 (top), 87, 104, 118, 126, Paul Haggard; 16, 25 (right), 30, 32 (top left), 36, 45 (bottom), 76 (right), 80, Warren Hukill; 15, 69, Spectral Music (N.Y.C.); 79 (top), 129 (right), Bettman Archive; 128 (bottom), Jim Hatlo; 84, Steve Rubin. All others courtesy of the manufacturers.

Diagrams: Page 80 (bottom), Barbara Popolow and Rick Eberly; 87 (right), Brent Hurtig; 100, Alan Wald; all others Rick Eberly.

Hurtig, Brent.
    Multi-Track Recording For Musicians.

    (Keyboard magazine library for electronic musicians)
    "A Keyboard magazine book."
    1. Sound—recording and reproduction. 2. Magnetic recorders and recording.
I. Sharp, J. D. II. Title. III. Series.
TK7881.4.H87   1988   621.389'32   88-7685

Alfred Publishing Co., Inc.
16380 Roscoe Blvd., P.O. Box 10003, Van Nuys, CA 91410-0003

ISBN: 0-88284-355-9
Item Number 2608

CONTENTS

INTRODUCTION

Creative expression is what music is all about. As musicians we cup sparks of creativity in our hands, and hope to coax them into flame.

Until the early part of the twentieth century, sounds would come and go, to be appreciated by only those who heard them at the time. Today, the miracle of recording has changed all of this, and allows us to re-experience music any time and anywhere, long after it has been performed. The 1950s' breakthrough of multi-track recording—the ability to record and overdub music one part at a time—brought us to another stage. And the 1980s' development of MIDI—the Musical Instrument Digital Interface—has brought us even further. Today's technology allows musicians, working alone or together in a studio or even a living room, to create elaborate, high-quality recordings. Even more astonishing, much of this gear is relatively affordable.

With such power, however, we face a new challenge: Aside from being musicians, we must be engineers, technicians, and to some degree, computer scientists. In other words, it's a brave new world out there, with phenomenal degrees of technology to master, or at least understand. That's why this book exists.

MULTI-TRACK RECORDING FOR MUSICIANS is designed to be a comprehensive overview for beginners and intermediates—as well as an invaluable reference for the professional. Since music technology is constantly evolving, the emphasis for this book is on the "hows" and "whys" of multi-track recording, instead of rote instructions. Its aim is to teach *understanding*, so that, for instance, when you compare a small ministudio with a full-blown professional mixer, you'll appreciate their basic similarities, rather than be overwhelmed by their differences. Feel free to pick and choose different sections of this book as they interest you, or as they apply to your own setup, and enjoy the amazing process of multi-track recording. It's my hope that MULTI-TRACK RECORDING FOR MUSICIANS will help you capture your own creativity, from spark to flame.

Brent Hurtig

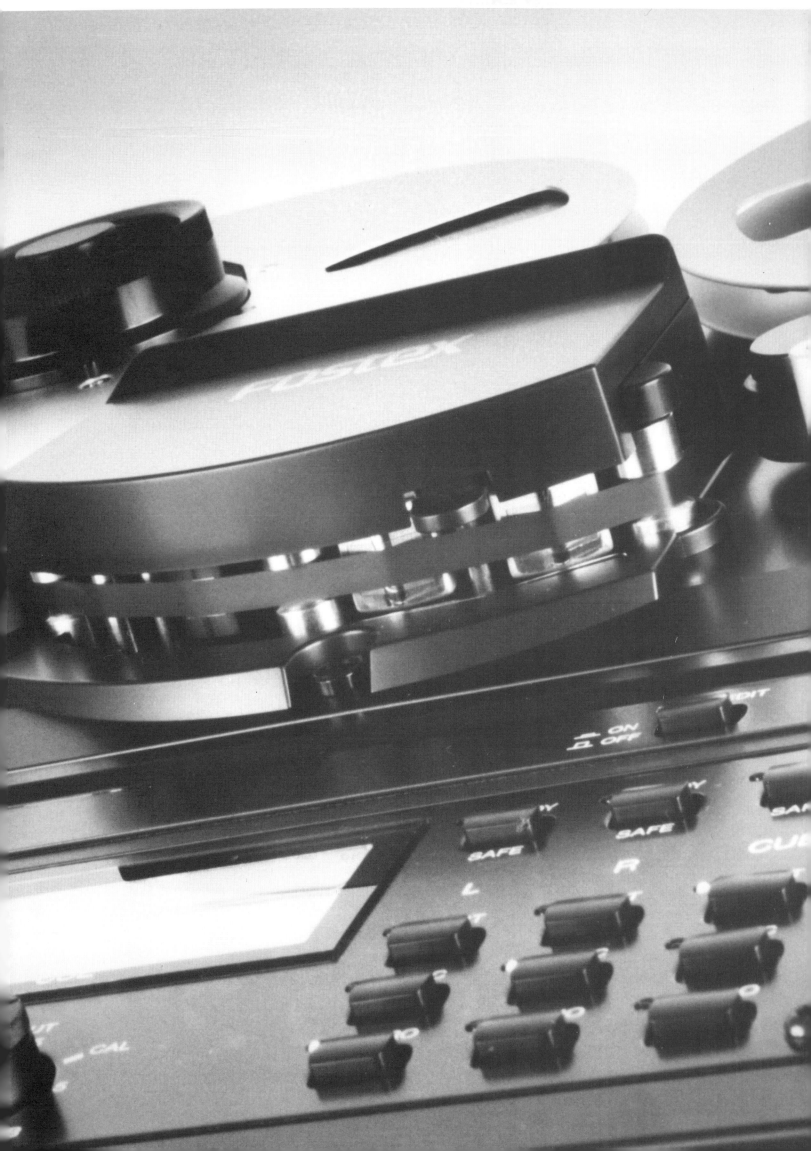

Part I: Fundamental Concepts

For every musician who records a song in a home or professional studio, a wealth and history of technical knowledge exists which allows that recording to take place. And today, while it's *not* necessary to know exactly how and why every step of the recording process works, knowing some of the fundamental concepts of sound and recording can greatly enhance your creativity. The more you choose to understand about recording music, the less mysterious it becomes—and the greater your creative options.

Some of this basic material may get a bit technical, and some of it you may know. Feel free to pick and choose; hopefully the terminology and concepts will help you to produce better recordings. So take your time—and most of all, have fun—as we learn about sound and recording. . .

Sound is a word we use to refer to vibrations that we're able to hear. By examining the nature of sound vibrations, we'll be able to understand the concepts of:

- frequency
- sound waves and pressure
- the audio spectrum
- pitch

and several other important terms which are used in multi-track recording. These concepts may seem a bit theoretical, but much of what follows is essential for understanding everything from proper microphone placement to adjusting levels.

Vibrations are everywhere, from the movement of a bee's wings to a truck rolling by on the street. Some vibrations which can't be heard can still be felt—as anyone who's experienced an earthquake will appreciate. And then there are vibrations which our senses cannot detect, such as radio frequencies.

We're able to describe audible vibrations in terms of how loud they sound, whether they are 'high' or 'low' in pitch, and in terms of the character (timbre) of sound, such as 'harsh,' 'bell-like,' 'clean,' and other subjective adjectives. Let's take a look at the components of sound which distinguish one from another.

Frequency

Vibrations travel through space—air or solid—in the form of *waves*. Imagine what happens when a pebble is dropped into a pond. From where the pebble enters the water (the *source*), ripples, or small waves, form and spread in all directions. Each ripple travels in *cycles*: One complete wave motion, start to peak to trough to start position again, is one cycle.

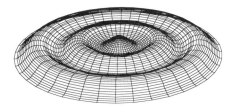

Figure 1.1 Like ripples in a pond, sound travels in waves.

The speed at which a wave completes a cycle is known as its *frequency*. This frequency is expressed as *cycles per second* (*cps*), or more commonly, *Hertz* (*Hz*), named after the German physicist who first described audible vibrations as sound waves.

Sound Waves And Pressure

When something vibrates in air it creates a series of wave cycles. With each cycle, the air particles will move back and forth, alternately raising and lowering air pressure.

Think of the bee's wings. The wings move back and forth, or *oscillate*, creating waves in the air. If it's your average-size bee, the wings may oscillate at 250 times per

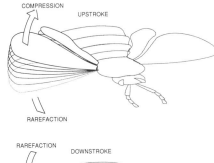

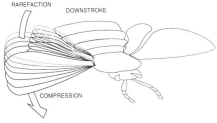

Figure 1.2 Sound waves are created by compression and rarefaction of air.

second. In other words, the *frequency* of the bee's wings is 250 Hz.

As the wing moves out from the body, it *compresses* the air being pushed away, increasing the air pressure of those particles. The air behind the wings decompresses, or *rarefies*. When the wings return, they compress and rarefy air particles in the opposite direction as before. As we can see in the diagrams, these pressure changes create sound waves. In the case of the bee, the waves travel through the air at 250 Hz and reach our ears. At that point, the ear drum, and eventually in turn cilia (tiny hairs in the inner ear), are stimulated 250 times per second, and our brain interprets this stimulation as *sound*.

The Audio Spectrum

The frequency range of human hearing is approximately 20 Hz to 20,000 Hz (20,000 Hz can be expressed as 20 *kiloHertz*, or 20 *kHz*). That is, our ears can detect pressure changes in the air between the rates of 20 Hz to 20 kHz. If something is vibrating at a rate of 20 Hz to 20 kHz, it's creating sound waves, and it can be heard. We call this range the *audio spectrum*.

This range varies, depending upon one's gender and age. Generally females can hear higher—closer towards 20 kHz—as do younger people. Typical hearing for a middle-aged male might be something like 20 Hz to 14 kHz.

Pitch And Frequency Range

When the shape of a sound wave follows a regularly-recurring pattern rather than a random shape, we can say it has a pitch. That is, when a sound source has a specific or dominant frequency at which it's creating sound waves, we can hear a specific pitch. When a sound source is capable of creating (or responding to) more than one pitch, we can say it has a frequency range. Here are some examples of various pitches and ranges:

- The lowest note on a piano is 27.5 Hz, and

the highest is 4186 Hz; thus, the frequency range of a piano's note is 27.5 to 4186 Hz.
- The frequency range of the notes of a guitar is 82.41 Hz (low *E*) to 1046.5 Hz (high *C*); a bass guitar's notes range from 41.2 to 523.25 Hz.
- Concert Pitch—the pitch to which orchestras tune—is 440 Hz, the *A* above Middle *C* on the piano. That's why it's also known as *A-440*. Many orchestras take exceptions to this: For example, the Dresden Symphony tunes to *A-443*, and the Boston Symphony Orchestra has tuned as high as *A-445*!
- The human voice has a range of approximately 80 to 1200 Hz.
- The low buzzing sound that you can hear in an old guitar amp is the frequency of the AC power: 60 Hz (50 Hz outside of North America). The high-pitched tone which emanates from a TV and drives some people crazy: 15,734 Hz.

Frequencies which exist below and above our range of hearing are known respectively as infrasonic and ultrasonic. FM-band radio frequencies emanate from antennae at a range of 88.5 to 108.5 *megaHertz* (million Hertz!); an earthquake can produce frequencies of 5 Hz and lower. And yes, animals have different hearing ranges from humans: Fido's silent dog whistle is usually 25 kHz, and blue whales can communicate at 5 Hz.

In music, a change of an *octave* is an exact doubling or halving of frequency. For example, *A* one octave above *A-440* is 880 Hz, and the *A* one octave lower is 220 Hz.

Wavelength

Anyone who's listened to short-wave radio has heard the term *wavelength*. This is simply another way of measuring frequency, though instead of measuring cycles per second, the actual physical length of the cycle is measured.

Here's an interesting formula:

$$\lambda = V \div F$$

[λ= Wavelength in feet (or meters); V= Velocity of sound in feet (or meters) per second; F= Frequency in Hertz (cycles per second).]

The velocity of sound depends upon the ambient air temperature, but we can average it to be 1,100 feet/second, or 335 meters/second. Using this simple formula, we can figure out that Fido's 25 kHz whistle sound has an individual cycle wavelength of about 1/2" (1.3 cm). Some other sample wavelengths:

- 440 Hz concert pitch = 2.5' (0.76 m).
- Low *E*, bass guitar = 26.7' (8.13 m).
- 5 Hz blue whale call = 220' (67 m)!

* * * *

So far we've learned that:

- Vibrations in the air create sound waves

by changing air pressure.
- Sound waves have cycles, and the frequency of these cycles determines the pitch that we hear when the waves reach our ears.
- A sound's frequency is measured in cycles per second, or Hertz; it can also be physically measured as a wavelength.
- The frequency range of human hearing is known as the audio spectrum.

There are four other important concepts to learn about components of sound waves:

- The *amplitude* of a sound wave determines how loud it sounds to us.
- The *decibel* is the measure of amplitude.
- Sound waves have different *phase* cycles.
- The *timbre* of a particular sound wave—that is, the shape of its cycles—is what makes it sound different from another sound wave.

Amplitude

When we draw a sound wave, we're actually creating a diagram of pressure changes. A peak of the wave represents a compression of air particles, and a trough represents rarefaction. Simply, the greater the distance between peaks and troughs, the greater the *amplitude* of the wave.

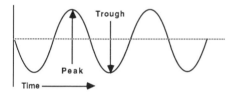

Figure 1.3 The degree of air pressure changes determines the amplitude of a sound.

Amplitude describes the loudness, or volume, of sound. Just as bigger waves crash on the beach with more 'force' than smaller waves, bigger sound waves stimulate our eardrums and cilia with greater force than smaller waves, and sound 'louder' to us. A sound wave which has a greater volume than another sound wave is said to have a greater *sound pressure level* (SPL). This SPL is expressed in terms of decibels.

The Decibel

In this book, we are going to learn about several different types of *decibel* scales. They describe relative levels: sometimes the power levels of audio/electrical circuits, sometimes meter readings of those circuits, and so on.

Decibels are commonly used to express sound pressure levels. With this scale a decibel can be referred to as a *dBA*, or more commonly (though less accurately) as just a *dB*. The 'B' is capitalized, by the way, as a hommage to Alexander Graham Bell, the father of the telephone and other sound-related devices.

Sound pressure is measured on a scale from 0 dB (the threshold of human hearing) to about 140 dB (blown eardrums and general mayhem). But this isn't your average type of scale. For example, the ambient noise in a supermarket may measure about 60 decibels, and a loud rock concert may measure 120 dB. Does this mean your typical rock concert is twice as loud as a supermarket? In fact, no—120 dB is actually *1,000 times louder* (in terms of sound pressure) than 60 dB! In fact, a change of just 10 dB represents a doubling of apparent volume, at least to the 'average' ear.

Here's a few more points to keep in mind when discussing sound pressure levels and decibels. First of all, to the 'average' ear, changes of a little as 1 dB are detectible—though some people with otherwise fine hearing require a change as great as 3 dB in order to preceive a difference.

The other point refers back to the fact that for most people, if one sound is 10 dB greater than another, it's twice as loud. That's correct, but only if the two sounds are the same frequency. That's because our ears are less sensitive—especially at relatively quiet levels—to frequencies below 500 Hz and above 7 kHz or so.

An example: Let's say we play a really high note on a guitar, about 1000 Hz, at a quiet level of about 60 dB. In order for the lowest E string at 80 Hz to sound just as loud to our ears, we need to play it at about 70 dB. This difference becomes less the louder we play. Of course, none of us run around measuring how loud in dB we play individual notes, but we do compensate naturally as we play quietly. In fact, the 'loudness' control found on many stereos takes these sensitivities into account, by boosting the low and high frequencies at low listening levels. You may, incidentally, run across something known as the *Fletcher-Munson curves*: This is a chart used by audio design engineers, which shows relative loudness of different frequencies at different listening levels. For the most part, fortunately, we don't need to worry about these frequency differences: When sound levels are expresed, it's usually an average of all frequencies.

Phase

Just as ocean waves rise to crests and fall to troughs, so do sound waves. When two identical sound waves rise and fall at the same time and place, they are *in phase*; when they rise and fall at different times, they are *out of phase*.

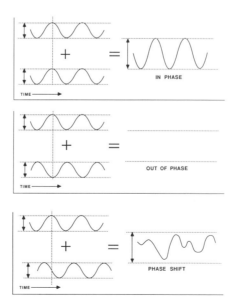

Figure 1.4 Phase addition and cancellation.

In sound (as with water), when waves arrive at a person's ears or a microphone, they add together. Because of this, two identical sound waves which are perfectly in phase will add together to create a *composite* wave which is twice as loud. Two waves which are slightly out of phase have the effect of partially cancelling each other out, however. Audibly, when two waveforms are out of phase with each other, the cancellations create a composite wave with 'holes' in the frequency range. These holes can make the sound seem 'thin,' and can make the source of the sound seem as if it's shifting from side to side. (We'll examine this shifting effect further ahead on page 52).

Finally, if two identical waves which are perfectly 180 degrees out of phase arrive at the same time, they will cancel each other completely, and no sound will be heard!

Timbre And Waveforms

A flute and a saxophone are both able to play a Middle C note—what makes their sound character, their *timbre*, so different from each other?

The answer to that question could fill a book (and has). For our purposes, a simplified overview will help us understand timbre, and conclude our introduction to sound.

Most notes, from an instrument or voice, have one frequency which is the loudest—that's known as the *fundamental* frequency, and it's that frequency which we hear as a note's pitch.

With musical instruments, as with almost all natural sounds, the fundamental frequency is accompanied by *harmonics*, or *overtones*. These are other frequencies which can be heard—usually at a quieter level—along with the fundamental. These additional frequencies all add together with the fundamental to create a more complex waveform than would be produced by just the fundamental. Their number and relative levels shape the sound's timbre.

Here's another way to look at this: As we've learned, the frequency of a wave determines its pitch. Now we're going to see how the shape of a wave determines its timbre. Let's consider a mathematically 'perfect' wave:

Figure 1.5 A mathematically 'perfect' sine wave.

This wave has smooth, consistent, and evenly-spaced peaks and troughs. It's known as a perfect or ideal wave because it has no irregularities; technically, a sound wave that looks like this is known as a *sine wave*. It's possible to create the sound of a sine wave using a synthesizer or audio test equipment. It's also possible to hear a close approximation of a sine wave with a tuning fork and even a flute. These are instruments which produce almost perfect vibrations.

Figure 1.6 shows a plot of the tuning fork's sound wave. When we plot a sound wave in this manner, we can call it a *waveform*. This term is used a lot, not only by recording engineers, but also by musicians who describe the sounds of synthesizers and other instruments in terms of waveforms.

Since different sound sources vibrate 'imperfectly,' waveforms other than the sine wave exist, and have a different sound char-

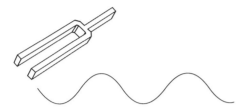

Figure 1.6 If we could plot the waveform of a tuning fork, it would resemble a sine wave.

acter from the 'pure' sine wave. There are many reasons why sources have distinct vibration characteristics. If the source is an instrument, everything from its construction material, to its size, to the way it's played contributes to the waveform.

Aside from the sine wave, some other mathematical waveforms are shown in Figure 1.7.

Those of you with synthesizers may in fact have some of these waveforms within your instrument. If so, and if you're unfamiliar with these sounds, call them up on the synthesizer and compare their timbre. While a sine waveform has a pure, flute-like tone, a square wave has a 'warmer,' reed-like tone, such as that of a clarinet. Triangle and sawtooth waves are more complex, and have 'harsher' tones, such as that of a saxophone. But the *primary*, or *fundamental*, waveform of a sound is only one component of a sound's overall, or *composite* waveform.

A composite waveform can become extremely complex. *Overtones*, or *harmonics*

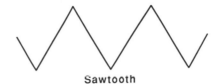

Sawtooth

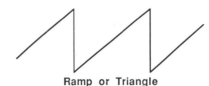

Ramp or Triangle

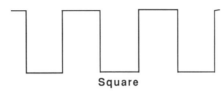

Square

Figure 1.7 Some other simple waveforms, as are commonly found onboard many analog synthesizers.

(such as all the extra tones that can be heard when a gong is struck), serve to define an individual waveform. If two different instruments are played together at the same time, our ears sum together their waveforms.

In this manner, the music of an entire orchestra could be represented as one highly complex waveform at any given time. Figure 1.8 shows a diagram of a complex waveform. It's a single piano note, and it's represented three-dimensionally to show all the overtones.

Up to now, we've been talking about waveforms as sounds travelling through air.

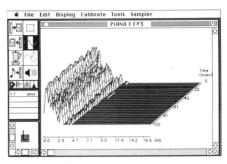

Figure 1.8 Digidesign's Apple Macintosh-based Sound Designer program analyzes the waveform of sound samples. This shows a single piano note, with all of its overtones. The number, relative amplitude, and pitch of the overtones over time all combine to help shape a sound's timbre.

When we record and play back sound, though, we're dealing with electrical waveforms. The three-dimensional waveform shown in Figure 1.8 has been generated by a computer, and it's electronic representation of an acoustic waveform. We'll learn more about the relationship between sound and electricity in the coming pages, and we'll learn more about how we hear sound starting on page 48.

* * * *

At this point, we now have an understanding of the basics of sound. While most recording engineers seldom refer to sound in terms of vibration and pressure, it's useful to be aware of how sound is created, how it travels, and how we hear it.

Many of the other terms we've covered, such as frequency response, the decibel, amplitude, and more, will be used throughout this book. Our basic understanding of what these mean and why they're used will be a good foundation for the next chapter, when we look at how recording works. □

CHAPTER 2: MAGNETIC RECORDING

In this chapter, we're going to learn some of the basic theory which makes multi-track recording possible. This includes:

- How sound is converted to electricity.
- How the electrical signal is stored on magnetic tape.
- Playing back the recorded signal.

We'll also take a look at:

- The transducer.
- Some fundamentals of electricity.
- The early development of multi-track recording.

Let's examine what most of us who make our own recorded music take for granted—the fascinating process of magnetic recording.

Transducers: Converting Sound To Electricity

Take a thin sheet of paper, hold it tightly with two hands up in front of your mouth, and talk into it. (Sure, it may seem a little

weird, but this is in the name of *science!*) What do your fingers feel?

If you've talked loud enough, you should have felt the paper vibrating with your speech. Now, sing a single note, "aahhh"-style. The paper should vibrate more consistently than when talking. In fact, if you recall what we learned in Chapter One, you'll realize that the paper is vibrating at the same rate—at the same fundamental *frequency*—as the note you're singing.

What's the point of this exercise? To see how sound can be converted to a physical vibration—this is a necessary step in the conversion of sound to electricity.

It's this process that Leon Scott de Martinville observed in 1857, when he invented the precursor of Thomas Edison's phonograph. De Martinville used a scribe, attached to a sound-sensitive diaphragm, to etch sound waveforms onto a cylinder coated with lamp black. It wasn't until 1877 that Edison created a device that was able to read back recorded waveforms (on a wax-coated cylinder), and reconvert them to sound.

Both de Martinville's and Edison's inven-

tions created mechanical representations of sound. In the modern recording world,

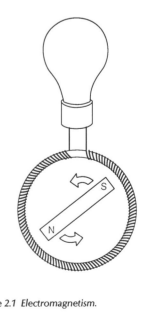

Figure 2.1 Electromagnetism.

however, sound is seldom recorded directly to a mechanical medium. Rather, electricity plays an important role, as we'll see next.

The Transducer. A device which converts one form of energy into another is known as a *transducer*. We use transducers in the process of converting sound energy into electrical energy. Most of us should remember an experiment from elementary school: When a permanent magnet is moved within a coil of wire, electricity is generated (see Figure 2.1). This is a function of *electromagnetism*.

Operating under the same principal of electromagnetism, when a coil of wire is moved within the magnetic field of a permanent magnet, electricity is also generated. This is one way a microphone can pick up sound and convert it to electricity. A basic dynamic microphone consists of a diaphragm, around the back of which is wound a coil of wire (known as the *moving*

those which come with Walkman-type tape players, will operate as crude mikes, since the cones are light and sensitive.

Transducers are also used in the studio to convert electrical signals to electromagnetic signals—which can in turn be stored and played back from magnetic tape. All tape recorders have an *erase head*, a *record head*, and a *play head* (or sometimes a combination record/play head). We'll learn more about these special transducers in the coming pages.

Magnetic Tape

The earliest magnetic tape recorders were developed by the German company AEG in 1935. Prior to that, there were magnetic recorders, but they didn't use tape at all. They were known as wire, or steel-band recorders, since the recording was made onto a steel wire. The wire was able to hold only a crude recording, however, and mag-

Notice in Figure 2.3 how the particles are on only one surface of the tape? When people talk about 'flipping over a tape,' they're really talking about *reversing* a tape. For example, when a cassette tape is 'flipped,' just the housing of the cassette is turned over—the same tape surface faces the heads, and the playback or recording happens in a different direction.

Bias, Equalization, And Tape Types. Have you seen controls on tape recorders labeled *bias adjust* and *tape equalization*, or cassette tapes labelled *normal* or *high bias*? These controls and tape types refer to two processes which are used to improve the performance of magnetic tape: *bias* and *tape equalization*.

During the recording process, the tape's magnetic particles have a tendency to resist alignment. They would just as soon stay randomly oriented, and have a natural tendency when forced, to 'more or less' align, yielding a poor recording. To compensate for this problem, and the resulting nasty distortion and dynamic range limitations which accompany it, tape recorders record a high-frequency inaudible tone known as *bias*. By recording this very strong, but inaudible signal, the particles are 'excited' out of their state of rest, and are more amenable to being oriented by the audible-range signal from the record head. This bias tone, usually in the range of 80-150 kHz, orients, or biases, the magnetic particles in a way which ensures optimum performance between the tape and the machine.

Biasing was discovered by accident during the early development of the tape recorder; one of the electrical components malfunctioned, but the resulting recording was vastly superior to previous attempts. Biasing works by 'tricking' the magnetic particles on the tape into behaving as if a much stronger signal was forcing them to align than exists in the standard recording signal.

The benefits of injecting this ultra-high frequency into the record signal include:

- Reduced distortion, resulting in a 'cleaner' sounding signal, as well as more *headroom* to record higher signals without distortion.
- More even frequency response, especially in the higher and lower ends of the recorder's frequency spectrum.

When technicians and engineers adjust the bias of a tape recorder, they are adjusting the amount of bias signal to be mixed with the audible signal. Biasing is necessary with any tape recorder to achieve optimum results with the tape being used.

In addition to bias, another modification of both recorded and played back signals is called *equalization*. This is different from tone equalization (which we'll look at on page 43). Rather, record and playback equalization (EQ) are used to optimize the accuracy and range of the frequency response of the tape recorder. The basic idea is as follows: When left to its own devices, the recording process has a tendency to create recordings with poor high frequency response and not-so-great low frequency response. Without an EQ circuit, a tape recording would sound very 'muffled' in the high end.

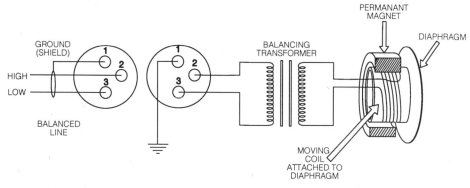

Figure 2.2 The inside workings of a dynamic microphone. Sound strikes the diaphragm, which in turn generates an electrical signal. (We'll examine the function of the 'balanced line' ahead on page 23.)

coil). This moving coil is mounted so that it's surrounded by a permanent magnet (see Figure 2.2).

As sound waves strike the diaphragm, it moves in a way which corresponds to the waveform of the sound, just like the paper you held to your lips a minute ago. In turn, the coil moves within the magnetic field, and generates an electrical signal—as the sound waves vary, so do the electrical *voltages* leaving the mike.

In the case of a basic loudspeaker, the process works in the exact reverse of a dynamic microphone—and the two are almost the same design. An electrical signal passes through the electromagnetic coil mounted within the field of the permanent magnet, which makes the coil move. As the coil moves it causes the cone (analogous to the microphone's diaphragm) to move, generating sound waves.

An electrical signal has to be *amplified* in order to be played back through a loudspeaker. The microphone's diaphragm is very sensitive, and responds to very quiet sound waves. In order for the loudspeaker to recreate even quiet sound waves, however, quite a bit of force is required to move the cone. An *amplifier* is used to create this force. A microphone could theoretically be used as a loudspeaker, but it lacks the ability to move a lot of air—and hence get loud. A loudspeaker could be used as a microphone, but with most speakers the cone is so stiff that it is insensitive to all but the loudest of sound waves.

A pair of headphones is in fact a pair of small loudspeakers; some designs, such as

netic tape was created as a superior recording medium. This tape was originally a magnetic paste which was cured onto paper and acetate backings. Modern magnetic tape also uses a magnetic paste, or *coating*, but uses a strong mylar tape backing.

The actual recording takes place in the coating of the tape. This coating is essentially made of microscopic rust (iron oxide) particles, which can be magnetized. These oxide particles are oriented completely at random when the tape is unrecorded, or 'blank.' It's the ability of the tape heads to realign these particles which allows a recording to take place. As the heads generate the realigning signals, the tape particles align in a manner which is *analogous* to the signal. That is, the particles align in ways which look like the electro-magnetic signals; this is why this type of recording is known as *analog* recording.

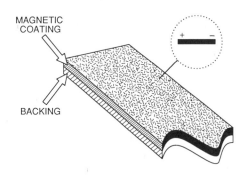

Figure 2.3 Magnetic tape.

The EQ circuit works in two stages. The first stage is known as *pre-emphasis*, which boosts the high frequencies when they are recorded. Then, on playback, those same frequencies are *de-emphasized*, creating a normal-sounding recording.

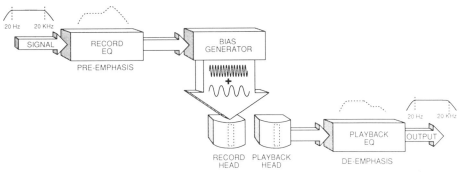

Figure 2.4 *Equalization and bias are critical steps in the recording process. They overcome magnetic tape's inherent limitations, and allow tape recorders to deliver near-perfect frequency response, with minimal distortion and increased headroom.*

Internal bias and EQ adjustments are factory-set on all tape recorders. While most musicians manage all right without ever thinking about them, the proper setting, or *calibration*, of bias and EQ is critical: Calibration of your equipment can make a huge difference in performance, since the settings are very dependent on the type of tape being used, and can drift out of calibration. Consequently, it's a really good idea to have a qualified technician readjust the settings when you purchase your tape machine, and when you change tape brands—whether it's an inexpensive 4-track or a world-class 24-track. (Many professionals recalibrate their machines with each new roll of tape!)

Most consumer cassette decks have external bias and EQ switches, known as *tape type* switches—they're the switches labeled 'CrO$_2$' (or 'High'), 'Metal,' and 'Normal.' These three switches represent the most common types of cassette tape. Normal bias tapes are the least expensive to produce, and while they deliver very good frequency performance, usually they are noisier than other types of tape. Chromium dioxide (CrO$_2$) tapes are quiet, but are more costly than normal tapes. Finally, metal tapes deliver the best all-round performance, though they are the most expensive of the three formulations.

Multi-track cassette recorder/mixers, almost without exception, are factory-calibrated for high bias CrO$_2$ tapes, such as TDK SA, Maxell UDXLII, and other brands. Use the factory-recommended tape for best performance, unless you have your machine re-calibrated.

In open-reel tape, there aren't the same distinct categories as are found with cassette tapes. Rather, the various manufacturers—including Ampex, 3M (Scotch), Agfa, and BASF—have all worked independently to develop their own tapes. Generally, an open-reel tape recorder needs to be recalibrated every time a different type of tape is used. Unlike consumer cassette decks, there are no standard settings to allow simple switch readjustments. (There are some expensive machines which allow you to program the tape type settings, but you won't find those machines in your typical home studio.)

As with 4-track recorder/mixers, most manufacturers of open-reel machines do tend to have a recommended tape choice, and they factory-adjust the machine to that tape. And while there is no true standard, there is one *de facto* standard which seems to have come about. Ampex 456 (also known as Grand Master) became very popular by the late 1970s, and compatible formulations have been developed by 3M (Scotch 226), as well as Agfa (469)—it's possible to interchange 226, 469, and 456 without having to recalibrate. Both Ampex 457 and 3M 227 are also compatible with the 456 standard, though they are thinner tapes designed to give longer playing time.

Width, Speed, And Thickness. We've already mentioned that tape is available in different formats, and many of you may know that tape can run at different speeds. Magnetic tape is found in widths from 1/8" (the Phillips Microcassette and cassette) to 2" (for 24 and 32-track work). Typical home multi-track machines range from 4-track cassette to 1/2" or 1" 16-track open-reel (a discussion of the various multi-track formats begins on page 12).

Speeds of tape (the speed at which the tape moves past the heads during playback or recording) are from 11/16 inches per second (ips) on some cassette machines to 30 ips on some open-reel decks. The cassette standard is 1⅞ ips, though a lot of the multi-track cassette machines operate at double speed, 3¾ ips. Most of the open-reel personal multi-track machines operate at 15 ips; a few run at 7½ ips, and 30 ips is generally reserved for professional machines.

Why do these various machines use different tape widths and speeds? Why are there 1/2", 1" and 2" 16-tracks, for example? The reason is that tape width relates to the 'quality potential' of a tape machine. Generally, for a given number of side-by-side tracks, the wider the tape the better the results.

Similarly, the quality-potential increases with tape speed. Simply, wider and faster-travelling tape has the advantage of being able to spread a magnetic signal over a greater number of magnetic particles.

More particles for recording a signal is analogous to film resolution. A fine-grain film, with more light-sensitive particles per given area, delivers a better resolution than coarse-grain film.

Theoretical advantages of wider tape and higher-speed tape recording include:

- A greater signal level in comparison to the tape hiss. This comparison is known as the *signal-to-noise ratio*.
- Better low-end frequency response. As we'll see shortly, magnetic heads have *gaps*, and it's at these gaps that the recording takes place (there's one gap for every track on each head). The wider head gap of heads used with wider tape allows a longer wavelength (lower-frequency) signal to be recorded.
- Less *crosstalk* between tape tracks. Multi-track heads have multiple gaps, and there's more space in between the gaps with wider heads—compared to narrower heads with the same number of tracks. A lower crosstalk level means less likelihood that one gap's signal will interfere with or be picked up by an adjacent gap.
- Lower risk of *drop-out*. Drop-out occurs when particles of the tape's coating come off, causing the sound to lapse momentarily during playback. A wide- and fast-recorded track, with a greater number of magnetic particles than a narrower and slower-recorded track, means that lost oxide particles are less likely to ruin an entire portion of a track.

Of course, it can be quite expensive to use wider tape at higher speeds (a 1/2" 2500' reel of tape costs about one third the same length of 1" tape). Fortunately, recorder technology has increased so dramatically over years past that, for example, a modern 1/2" 8-track sounds in many respects better than a 1" 8-track of ten years ago. So don't worry too much about tape width—chances are *any* new machine you own or may be considering will perform most adequately for any personal recording.

Also to be considered is the *thickness* of the tape. Thickness is measured in *mils* (thousands of an inch): Open-reel tape is either 1.5 or 1.0 mil thick; cassette tape is typically less than 0.5 mil thick. To give you an idea of how *thin* that thickness is, cassette tape with a 0.5 mil specification would have to be layered 2000 times to make up an inch. Considering how thin tape is, and all the back and forth shuttling it goes through, it's remarkably strong!

This thickness has a direct bearing upon the recording/playing time of a tape. Obviously, if we have two 7½" rolls of tape, and one is 1.0 mil and the other 1.5 mil tape, the thinner tape will run longer. The disadvantage of thinner tape is that it is more prone to stretching, as well as *print-through*—which is where magnetic particles from one layer of tape can transfer magnetic energy to an adjacent layer. This print-through can sometimes be heard, and we'll learn how to minimize it on page 87.

The Tape Heads

The tape heads are the only *electronic* components of the tape recorder which touch the tape. All tape heads are transducers, serving as the translators between electrical and magnetic signals.

The Record Head. By now, you should have a clear enough concept of electromagnetic signals to appreciate just how clever the design of a tape head is. Take a look at Figure 2.5. When the signal reaches the head, it passes through windings around a permanent magnet. At one end of the magnet—where the head meets the tape—

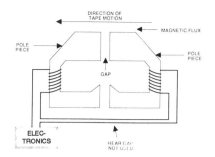

Figure 2.5 Cross-section of a record head (overhead view).

there's a *gap* in the design of the head. As we mentioned earlier, tape heads have a gap for every track. For example, a single-gap, or *full-track* head is designed to record and playback a single track; a 16-track head has 16 individual gaps, all sandwiched next to each other.

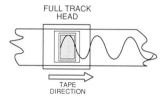

Figure 2.6a A full-track head has a single gap.

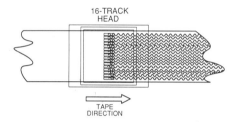

Figure 2.6b Multi-track heads have multiple gaps.

A magnetic field is created at this gap which varies as the electrical signal reaching the head varies. When the tape passes by, all those magnetic particles on the tape (which were previously at random) are aligned by the magnetic activity happening at the gap. And there it is: a recording!

The Playback Head. Depending on the manufacturer, the playback head is either very similar or identical to the record head in design; not surprising since its purpose is to function in a reverse manner to the record head. When blank tape passes by the playback head no signal is detected, because of the randomness of the tape particles. (The head is actually able to detect a pattern in the randomness—we hear it as tape hiss—but this is not a signal *per se*.)

When the particles have been aligned by a recording, however, they recreate a magnetic field at the gap of the playback head. This field, in turn, becomes an electrical signal in the coils of the head, which can be amplified and ultimately played back through a loudspeaker.

The Erase Head. The erase head is also designed like a record head—except that it records in such a way that the tape particles are randomly realigned, just like blank tape!

The Headstack. Figure 2.7 shows us a 3-head headstack. The order of heads in a headstack, in terms of which head the tape sees first, is always as follows:

1. Erase Head.
2. Record Head.
3. Playback Head.

This order, easy to remember as 'ERP,' makes sense. When we record over a previously-recorded tape, the tape is actually erased before it's recorded, and finally we play it back.

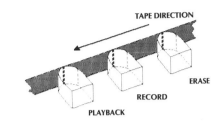

Figure 2.7 From right to left, we see the erase, record, and play heads.

2- Vs. 3-head Design. Up to this point, we've been describing 3-head machines, with three discrete heads. Most tape decks which have all three heads as separate units allow you to listen to the recording *while* it's being made. This feature is useful for ensuring that a recording is actually taking place. It also allows a technician to be able to hear the results of adjustments to the recorder while the recording is being made. Three-head decks are often quite expensive, and aren't necessary for most applications. In fact, all 4-track recorder/mixers, and many musician-affordable open-reel tape recorders are of a less expensive 2-head design.

With 2-head machines, the record and playback heads are combined as one head. The gaps of a combination record/play head function in record or playback mode, depending upon the settings of the tape recorder. There are a few disadvantages to a 2-head design. For one, they don't allow you to listen to the actual track you're recording while it's being recorded. Another disadvantage is that technicians have to rewind and listen to the results of adjustments, instead of hearing them while recording. Otherwise, however, there are no serious disadvantages to 2-head machines.

Alignment. As you may have guessed, proper alignment of the heads is necessary for good performance. The gaps must mate to the tape with the proper angle.

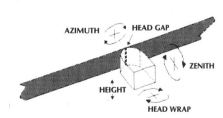

Figure 2.8 Alignment.

Alignment is a tricky process, and requires proper equipment and training. Just as proper calibration of bias and EQ levels can help optimize the performance of your recorder, so can head alignment. Your heads should be aligned when you purchase your machine; thereafter it's a good idea to have them aligned at least once or twice a year, or every 100 hours of use.

Recording Formats
Monaural And Stereo

The first machines available were *monaural* decks, followed by *stereo* decks. By learning about these two formats, we'll gain better insight into how multi-track formats work.

Full-Track. Until the early '60s, almost all magnetic recording took place on 1/4" *full-track* tape recorders. They make recordings across the full width of the tape, and once a recording is made, no further tracks can be added without erasing the original track. (The term *track* refers to the path of a gap's recording on tape; *full-track* describes the *tape-head format* of the machine.)

Half-Track Stereo. In the mid-'50s, *half-track* recording was developed in response to the growing consumer acceptance of stereo LP (Long Playing) disks. The idea was pretty simple: Take a tape recorder, and build the heads in such a way that there were *two* gaps, side by side, with a *guard band* in between to separate the signals. Then two channels, or tracks, of recording could take place, providing a stereo recording. It's called 'half-track' because each track of recording takes up half the tape's width.

In fact, the half-track's evolutionary precursor was *dual-track* monaural, first introduced in 1949. Unlike half-track, where two tracks are recorded by a single 2-gap record head, dual-track used two record heads next to each other, each with a gap that covered one-half of the tape. Following the record heads were two playback heads, each picking up half the tape. With dual-track a consumer could record on one half of the tape, in mono, then turn the tape over and record on the other side. Dual-track is virtually obsolete, though one hold-out is the mono cassette recorder, which uses half of the cassette's 1/8" width to record each mono side, and has a single record/playback head.

Half-track has been the professional stereo standard to this day. Since two tracks can be recorded at once on a half-track, it's often referred to as a 2-track. This term can be a bit confusing, since any machine which is designed to record two tracks at once can also be called a 2-track. Other 2-track machines which are not half-track include the stereo cassette deck and quarter-track open-reel, as we'll see in a moment.

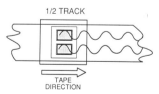

Figure 2.9 Half-track heads record two tracks in one direction.

It was the creation of the dual and half-track formats which made multi-track possible. Since more than one track could be recorded onto a single width of tape, machines were introduced which allowed the tracks to be recorded at separate times.

There are a number of different machines used today for stereo recording, including DAT (digital audio tape) recorders, Hi-Fi video tape, and more.

Quarter-Track Stereo. Given the audio cassette's popularity, quarter-track stereo is probably the world's most common track format.

We just learned that a half-track recording has each track recorded on half the tape; as you may have guessed, with a quarter-track recording each track occupies a quarter of the tape's width. Quarter-track recording was developed in the late 1950s to allow a stereo open-reel tape to be played in two directions; that is, when the tape was finished on one side, it could be 'flipped over' and played on the 'other side.' (Remember, 'flipped over' means the tape is being played in the opposite direction, since the recording takes place on only one surface.)

Does this sound like a cassette yet? Take a look at Figure 2.10: This shows the four tracks found on a quarter-track recording, two in each direction.

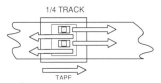

Figure 2.10 Quarter-track heads record two tracks in either direction.

Most home consumer stereo reel-to-reel decks use a quarter-track head design, as do all of the home, car, Walkman, and other non-multi-track stereo cassette decks.

It's easy to confuse the terms 4-track and quarter-track, by the way. True, a tape recorded on both sides on a quarter-track machine has four tracks going across the tape, though in two different directions—which is different from a 4-track recording (as we'll learn about shortly). But remember, here we're discussing tape-*head* formats. The quarter-track is in fact a 2-track stereo machine, with only two gaps, each covering a quarter-width of the tape. The 4-track has four gaps, each covering a quarter-width of the tape.

* * * *

So far, we've learned about the following head formats:

- Full track mono.
- Half-track stereo (along with dual track mono).
- Quarter-track stereo.

All of these formats are designed to make a single-pass recording—a finished product in one pass of the tape, without 'overdubs.' Most important to us, perhaps, the design of the dual-track head paved the way for multi-track, since it allowed more than one track of recording to take place on a single width of tape. □

CHAPTER 3: BASIC MULTI-TRACK RECORDING

Today, when we think of multi-track recording and music, we usually think of the ability to *overdub* different musical parts on different tracks. Modern-day overdubbing is when:

1. One track of music is recorded.
2. The tape is rewound, and the original track replayed.
3. Successive tracks are recorded, or overdubbed, on the same tape, without erasing and in *synchronization* with the original music track.

This is the way in which one or two musicians can layer many musical parts. Two things made this modern day technique possible. One was the impetus of musician Les Paul, and the other was a post-World War II technological development.

In 1949 the Ampex Corporation in California created the Model 200 dual-track (see the previous section on half-track recording). Along with enthusiastic consumers who recorded music on both sides of a tape, the U.S. armed forces employed 200s to record test data. These dual-track machines were modified so that the two record heads could record simultaneously. By doing this, one machine, for example, could record the data for *both* a rocket's fuel consumption and air speed.

This military application of the dual-track tape recorder was so successful that a year later, in 1950, Ampex introduced the Model 500, with four tracks on 1/4" tape—the world's first true multi-track. Just two years later they developed a 7-track version of the 500, also for data recording. The 500 was *not* designed, however, to do overdubbing; it could only record all of its tracks *at once*. But the heads were all 'in-line' design, which is to say that all four or seven tracks were recorded by one head and played back by another head. To do this, the Ampex engineers had developed the means to build a single-unit, *multi-gap* head.

Ironically, the multi-gap head—the technology which would allow multi-track overdubbing—was created three years before anyone had the idea of using a multi-track recorder for music.

Until the 1952 advent of multi-track recorded music, all of music recording had been either recorded directly to disk, or on full-track mono tape. Bing Crosby (who was the first to use video tape in the late 1950s) purchased the first magnetic recorder for music recording in 1948, a full-track Model 200.

Now let's take a look at the person who ultimately thought of using a multi-track recorder for music, and some of the creative things he was doing before 1952.

Well-known as a musician and inventor since the mid-'30s, guitarist Les Paul is personally responsible for numerous technological advances in music. Les Paul was the first musician to popularize the solidbody electric guitar, and thousands of people worldwide own the Gibson Les Paul guitar.

There are two recording techniques attributed to Les Paul, both in use today. We've already mentioned multi-track overdubbing. The other technique, *sound-on-sound*, helped lead Paul to the multi-track process.

Sound-On-Sound

In the mid-'30s, Les Paul experimented with disk recording lathes (the machines which 'cut' records), and found himself recording disks with a rhythm guitar part, then playing a lead guitar part along with the disk. Before long, he developed a technique which would allow allow him to overdub, first using disks, and later tape.

Disk-To-Disk, And Tape-To-Tape. In 1945, Paul developed the technique of sound-on-sound (SOS), which was to be used on a number of his hits with guitarist/vocalist Mary Ford. On their Number One hit *How High The Moon* [Capitol, 6004], he and Ford alone recorded 27 musical parts, all overdubbed one-by-one!

SOS with the disk-to-disk method worked for Paul in the following way:

1. The first part, rhythm guitar, is recorded on disk.
2. The first disk is played back, and the bass guitar part is played. The output of Turntable #1 is mixed with the bass guitar output using a simple mixer, and these two signals are recorded to disk on TT #2.
3. This second disk, with rhythm and bass guitar, is played back, and a lead guitar part is overdubbed. The lead's output is mixed with the output of the second disk, and all three parts are recorded onto a new disk on TT #1. The original disk is not used again, unless a mistake is made and the process needs to be started over.
4. Now we have a third disk on TT #1 with rhythm, bass, and lead guitar. At this point the vocals could be overdubbed, mixing the output of TT #1 with the mike, and recording it all onto TT #2.

And so on. For tape-to-tape SOS, this technique can work exactly the same way with two tape recorders—although instead of cutting new disks as the mix progresses, the same tapes can be used and re-recorded over. Theoretically, this process can go on indefinitely.

There are three major drawbacks to SOS. The first is that the noise level can build up very quickly. When the first disk is played back, its noise is recorded onto the second disk. When the second disk is played back and recorded onto the third disk, not only is there the first record's noise, but also the new noise from the second disk. Using tapes instead of disks, the noise problem remains.

In case you're wondering how Les Paul recorded 27 parts and still managed to have a huge hit *without* an absurd amount of noise, he recorded the least important parts first—background vocals and guitar har-

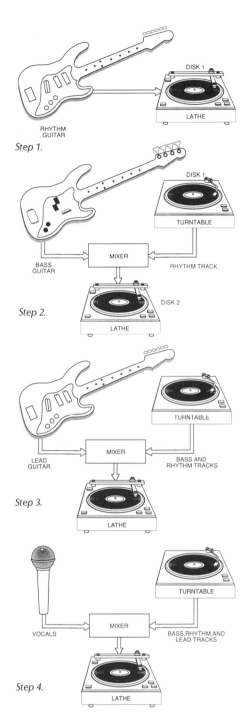

Step 1.

Step 2.

Step 3.

Step 4.

Figure 3.1 Four tracks created by sound-on-sound, using one conventional turntable and one disk-cutting (lathe) turntable.

monies. That way, the most important parts—lead guitar and lead vocal—could be recorded at the end of the SOS process, with the least amount of hiss built in.

When using disks instead of tape, there's a second drawback: If a mistake is made in an overdub, the record upon which the previous disk and the live overdubbed part are recorded has to be scrapped.

And finally, the third disadvantage is that the relative levels of the parts cannot be changed after they are recorded. In other words, ten overdubs into the process you can't go back and make the second overdub louder in relation to the other parts, without starting over.

Single Machine SOS. In 1948, Les Paul, tired of using disks to do his overdubbing, realized that there was a way that the SOS technique could be used with just a single tape machine. Again, the idea was simple,

but profound.

We recall the order of tape heads: erase, record, and play. Les Paul thought of putting a fourth head just in front of the erase head; this fourth head would function as another playback head.

He called this fourth head a *preview* head. Imagine recording a first musical part to tape, such as a rhythm guitar. When this recording is played back, a preview head can listen to it before it reaches the erase head. So the following can take place:

1. The output of the preview head feeds a simple mixer, which may be built into the tape recorder. The originally recorded part, such as a rhythm guitar, is played back, and is listened to via the preview head.
2. The next instrument/microphone to be overdubbed, such as a lead guitar, also feeds the mixer, and is played in time with the rhythm part.
3. The output of the mixer, with both the original rhythm and now the lead guitars is fed to the input section of the tape recorder, and recorded by the record head.
4. Now there's both a lead and a rhythm part on the tape, and the next part can consequently be overdubbed in exactly the same manner.

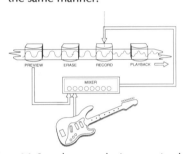

Figure 3.2 Sound-on-sound using a preview head.

Single machine SOS was a general improvement over tape-to-tape SOS, for the main reason that only one machine was needed to overdub, and the process was all the faster. It still left a few things to be desired, however. Since just one roll of tape was being used, if a mistake occurred the entire recording would have to be scrapped. Noise was successively added, as with tape-to-tape and disk-to-disk SOS. And levels could still not be adjusted after an overdub was recorded.

All of these difficulties were soon to disappear, when Les Paul thought of all those rolls of military data spinning around on 7-track Ampex Model 500s.

Track Synchronization

The first multi-track recorders such as the 4- (and later 7-) track military recorders of the early '50s, recorded all tracks at once. To use a multi-track machine for music overdubbing, however, Les Paul realized that the machine would have to be able *to record and play back tracks at the same time.* That is, in order to overdub a new musical track, the musician would have to be able to hear any previous tracks while recording the new track.

Sounds straightforward enough. In order for it to work, however, something known as *synchronization,* or *sync,* needs to take place. We're going to see and use that

word in a variety of applications later in this book: Here we're talking about *track synchronization.*

All multi-track machines used for music today have track synchronization. It's this technology which allows a prerecorded track to be played back *in sync* with a track being recorded.

Figure 3.3 shows us what happens when a multi-track doesn't have sync between the tracks:

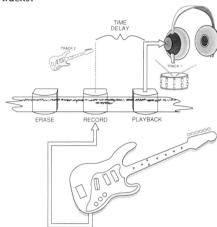

Figure 3.3 Without sync, we hear tracks from the playback head, but record them to the record head, resulting in an audible delay when both are played back.

As we can see, the second track is recorded after the previous track. When the two tracks are played back together, the first track reaches the playback head first, and consequently there's a *time lag* between the two tracks—making the tracks *out of sync* with each other. This time lag is the time it takes for the tape to travel between the record head and the playback head.

If we tried recording a third track, we'd be heading for real chaos, since first we'd hear track 1, followed by track 2. If we used track 1 as the musical cue, track 3 would be recorded at the same time as track 2; if we listened to track 2's playback as the musical cue, track 3 would be recorded even further along the tape.

To address this problem, Ampex (in response to Les Paul's request) developed what they called *Sel-Sync.* It enabled the record head to perform *simultaneously* as a record and playback head. That is, using switches, tracks which were previously recorded could be played back through the record head while overdubbing, instead of

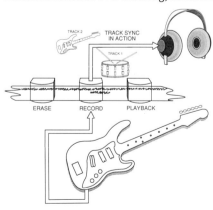

Figure 3.4 Track sync to the rescue: The record head functions as both a record and playback head during overdubs.

the playback head. With this system, over-dubbed tracks are recorded onto tape at the same place as the previous tracks are played back, and there's no time lag—the tracks are played back *in sync*.

2-Head Vs. 3-Head Track Synchronization. Not so long ago, all multi-track machines with track synchronization had three heads. Most personal multi-track machines these days, however, are 2-head design.

The demands of personal recording are usually less than professional applications. Because of this, 2-head tape recorders are often fine, and save considerable equipment expense. For this reason, all multi-track cassette 'ministudios' are 2-head design, along with a growing number of 8-and 16-track open-reel machines.

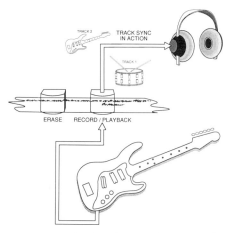

Figure 3.5 Two-head machines work in sync mode automatically.

With a 2-head machine, since the record and play heads are already one in the same, track sync already exists with no switching difficulty—as we can see from Figure 3.5.

Multi-Track Meets Music

The first multi-track for music, conceived by and delivered to Les Paul, was unofficially known as the Ampex 300-8. The unit is still in use by Paul to this day, and has some unique features—for one, Paul has designed a remote control for it which fits into his guitar.

Compared to some of today's equipment, this first 8-track is of behemothic proportions: over 2 meters (6 feet) high, about 200 kilograms (440 pounds), and built like a tank. This was not a commercially-

produced machine, however, and only four were built—for as revolutionary as it was, multi-track recording didn't take the world by storm. For example, by the mid-'50s Ampex had sorted out the bugs in Les Paul's machine. But it wasn't until 1967 that a machine with more than 4-tracks was available on the market, when Ampex delivered the MM-1000, with 16 tracks on 2" tape.

In between 1952 and 1967, several other manufacturers entered the multi-track arena, including Crown and Studer, from the USA and Switzerland respectively. But as we mentioned, the music industry was very slow to respond to the capabilities of multi-track: In the early '60s people such as George Martin (producer of The Beatles) were multi-tracking with 2- and 3-track 1/4" machines. As many people know, *Sargent Pepper's Lonely Hearts Club Band* was recorded by Martin using just a 4-track Studer. While it's incredible to hear what Martin was able to do with four tracks, it's odd to realize that Les Paul's 300-8 had been made 15 years earlier!

In any event, the professional world eventually did catch onto the 2" 16-track format, and soon the 2" 24-track standard. With this, it wasn't long before Ampex's MM-1000 was joined by other 16- and 24-track machines from Studer, 3M (USA), and MCI (USA).

Following the wide acceptance of multi-track recorders, new possibilities arose for the single musician. Stevie Wonder and Todd Rundgren were two of the better-known pop musicians who chose to play and overdub all of the instruments on albums they produced in the early '70s. Mike Oldfield's *Tubular Bells* album of 1973 [Virgin Records, PE34116] proved to be another one-man showcase of modern overdubbing, and further opened people's ears to the possibilities of multi-tracking. On that album, the ambitious 20-year-old Englishman played virtually all the instruments, among them piano, glockenspiel, organ, bass, acoustic and electric guitars, timpani, percussion, and of course, tubular bells. *Tubular Bells* was a portent of today—with the advent of sampling keyboards and drum machines, many of us are multi-tracking multi-'instrumentalists' ourselves.

By the mid-1980s, the professional market had changed considerably, with Ampex and 3M having left the audio machine business. Studer and MCI (now Sony/MCI) are currently joined by Otari

(Japan), Soundcraft (UK), and several others, all marketing in the high-end professional direction.

The Birth Of Semi-Pro Recording. In the 1970s, multi-track split into two directions. The professional world adopted 16- and 24-track formats. The other direction was initiated by a company known as TEAC, the first company to address the 'semi-pro' market. TEAC's idea was that there were thousands of musicians who would like to be recording themselves in their own studios—without the expense and time restrictions of a 'professional' facility. Their early-'70s market entry, the TEAC 3340, was a 4-track, 3-head open-reel machine which enjoyed great success.

TEAC soon found competition from Dokorder, Sony, JVC, Akai, and a few other Japanese companies producing open-reel 4-tracks. TEAC formed a more upmarket-oriented division, Tascam, and produced in 1975 the world's first 1/2" 8-track, the Model 70. Continuing as a market leader, TEAC went on to create the Model 144 in 1980, a 4-track cassette recorder with a built-in 4-channel mixer.

With this product, the dream of a portable home studio could become realized for the cost of a day or two in a professional studio. In addition, by having a mixer built into the tape recorder, the perceived complexity of the recording process was greatly reduced. The 144, which became known as a 'PortaStudio,' heralded the modern age of low-cost home recording for musicians.

In 1980, several ex-TEAC personnel formed a company known as Fostex. They introduced their version of a recorder/mixer 'ministudio' (the model 250), as well as an 8-track recorder which used 1/4" tape (the model A-8). Rather than 'semi-pro,' Fostex called their approach 'personal multi-track recording.'

* * * *

In this chapter, we learned about the technologies which make modern multi-track recording possible:

● Multi-gap heads.
● Sound-on-sound overdubbing.
● Track synchronization.
● Les Paul's first 8-track.

Next, we'll take an overview of the various approaches to creating a contemporary *personal* recording studio. □

To anyone who's witnessed the development of multi-track recording, the equipment that's available now is just incredible. What used to take up an entire room and cost tens of thousands of dollars can now fit onto a desk top and cost several hundred dollars. On top of that, current equipment often outperforms its larger and more costly predecessors.

Today thanks to the personal studio, the composer has the luxury of being able to experiment however much he or she desires. With the power of MIDI (which we'll look at on page 106), one can 'pre-produce' music, hearing different parts played any desired way, and prepare at home before entering an expensive studio or rehearsing with other musicians. The concept of the one-man (or woman) orchestra has come to fruition.

Approaches To Personal Recording

While there are lots of ways to equip a personal multi-track studio, many musicians struggle with choosing between two fundamental approaches:

- The first is to use a 'ministudio'-type unit, with tape recorder and mixer integrated in one housing. This all-in-one approach is usually a 4-track cassette recorder combined with a 4- to 8-input mixer, though currently there are both 8-and 12-track recorder/mixers from a couple of manufacturers (using 1/4" open-reel tape or special 1/2" cassettes). A ministudio is convenient: No connections are required between the mixer and the recorder sections, and many are small enough to move easily—some even run on batteries!
- The other approach is to use an independent tape recorder and mixer, which these days usually means an 8-track studio and beyond. While it costs more, many musicians appreciate the added flexibility of a component system in this style.

For some musicians, bigger is definitely not better; a small, self-contained 4-track can sound very good, be portable, be easy to operate, and cost less than a week's wages. On the other hand, an open-reel system with a separate mixer has the potential to make better-sounding recordings, as well as provide greater flexibility in terms of adding accessories, accommodating more instruments, and recording more tracks.

How Many Tracks?

If you have a 4-track recorder, it follows that you can record up to four independent tracks of music. With an 8-track you can record eight independent tracks, and so on. There are, however, a couple of ways to record many more musical parts than you have tape tracks. Keep in mind these following techniques—you may need fewer tape tracks than you think!

MIDI And 'Virtual Tracks.' With multi-

track machines offering anywhere from four to 32 tracks, there's obviously a lot from which to choose. For most personal studios, cost considerations dictate something in the range of four to 16 tracks.

A huge advantage for those of us starting out in personal recording, has been the advent of MIDI (the Musical Instrument Digital Interface). MIDI is a digital communication system for keyboard, guitar, and wind synthesizers, along with drum machines, samplers, effects devices, and more. As we'll cover in detail starting on page 106, there are devices known as *sequencers*, which function like tapeless tape recorders for recording and playing back information from MIDI-based instruments. Using a sequencer, it's possible to 'drive' up to 16 or more synthesizers or other instruments, plus a drum machine, all from one magnetic tape track!

Here's the concept: Sequencers, along with drum machines and other devices, can be *tape synchronized* to one track of a multi-track recorder, In this way, their parts can play along with whatever 'normal' tracks are recorded on the multi-track. These additional musical parts are known as *virtual tracks*, since they behave, for the most part, like tracks recorded on the tape machine.

While current sequencers won't record lengthy vocal and other microphone-dependent tracks, they will record all MIDIed electronic keyboard and drum parts (including synthesized bass). With virtual tracks taken care of by a sequencer (which is controlled from a single tape track)—or even with just a tape-synced drum machine—perhaps three to seven 'regular' magnetic tracks are enough, to record acoustic and electric guitars, and a vocal part.

What all of this boils down to is that many musicians who used to dream of a 16-track are now content with an 8-track, or even a 4-track. The one catch is that if you have a lot of virtual tracks, you're going to need a mixer with a lot of inputs to mix both your MIDI instruments and tape tracks. But enough about MIDI for now; have a glance at the MIDI section if you're in the process of deciding upon your set-up, to help you evaluate how much of your recording workload could be handled by a MIDI sequencer.

Bouncing For Additional Tracks. Aside from MIDI sequencing, another way to gain 'extra' tracks is to *bounce* tracks together. Bouncing (also known as *ping-ponging*) is the technique of merging tracks together. Let's say you had a 4-track and had recorded a bass on track 1, a vocal on track 2, and a drum part on track 3. It's possible to bounce those three tracks together onto track 4, so that tracks 1, 2, and 3 are free to be recorded on once again.

The trade-offs of bouncing are signal degradation and the lack of being able to control individual instrument levels once they're bounced—much the same questions Les Paul had to contend with. See page 92 for more information.

The Bare Essentials

Aside from the two fundamental approaches of equipping your studio (ministudio or components), and the questions of MIDI virtual tracks, bouncing, and how many tape tracks, you'll also need to decide how much in the way of extras you'll be adding to your studio.

It doesn't take a lot of equipment these days to make multi-track recordings. Many people view their multi-track as a kind of musical sketchbook, and work alone with an instrument, a voice, a mike, a playback system (headphones or speakers), and perhaps a rhythm machine of some sort.

If your budget or current needs are most satisfied with this approach, you may not create a commercial product, but you may achieve some very satisfactory results.

Beyond The Essentials

For a lot of people, a minimalist songwriting tool isn't enough—and there's a lot of equipment out there which goes way beyond the basics.

A more elaborate multi-track setup could include any or all of the following types of equipment, which will be discussed at length later in this book.

Signal Processing. Many signal processors are *outboard gear*, which refers to all devices independent (outboard) of the mixer. Most mixers do have some kind of signal processing built-in, however, and a growing future trend will be to incorporate more and more integral signal processing.

In this catch-all we have three major categories:

- *Equalizers (EQs)*, which alter the tone of—*equalize (EQ)*—the signal.
- *Spatial effects*, which change the 'time' and types of 'spaces' in which we perceive sounds to occur. Such effects include *reverberation* (or just plain *reverb*), *echo* or *delay*, and others. Spatial effects devices often can do a number of 'special' effects as well, such as *flanging, chorusing, pitch-shifting*, and much more. Spatial effects can increase both the realism and the surrealism of a recording.
- *Dynamic-controlling devices.* These include *compressors, gates*, and other units which affect a signal's *dynamics*, or changes in amplitude.

Mixdown Tape Recorder. When the multi-track recording is completed, a *mixdown* must be made in order for the recording to be played back on other systems. This mixdown—with all the tracks at their appropriate levels and with their correct tones and special effects—is made onto a 2-track machine. The traditional personal 2-tracks have been a regular cassette deck or an open-reel half-track. Now, with the advent of DAT (Digital Audio Tape) recorders, as well as VHS and Beta Hi-Fi video cassette recorders, there are some affordable and wonderful-sounding options.

Patch Bay. If a mixer is the 'Command Central' in a multi-track system, a patch bay is the 'Master Switchboard,' determining where signals come and go. Devices connected to the bay, such as outboard gear, can be *patched-in* to a mixer by using *patch cables*.

MIDI/Virtual Track System. As we've mentioned, the personal studio can have its capabilities greatly enhanced with a sequencer or drum machine. In addition there is a growing trend today for MIDI-ized mixers and effects. These can offer automated control of levels, EQ, and more.

Video Synchronization. By syncing a multi-track recorder to a video deck, a composer or producer can work quickly and effectively with a video tape, for sound-

Multi-Track Recording Formats

All kinds of equipment and formats are vying for a share of the home multi-track market. The 4-track cassette recorder/mixer ministudio is very popular, and can cost from under $300.00 to over $2000.00. Some of the better-known machines are made by TEAC, Fostex, Akai, Yamaha, Vesta Fire, AMR, and Audio-Technica. Features and capabilities can vary tremendously, and in the coming chapters we'll examine the various components to consider. Also popular in personal studio applications are:

- An 8-track cassette recorder from Tascam.
- 1/4" 8-track machines from Fostex.
- A 1/4" 8-track recorder/mixer ministudio from Tascam.
- 1/2" 8-tracks from Otari and Tascam.
- 1/2" 12-track cassette recorders and recorder/mixers from Akai.
- 1/2" 16-track machines from Fostex, Tascam, Studio Magnetics, and ACES.
- 1" 16-tracks from Otari, Tascam, and ITAM.

There are several formats which are generally restricted to commercial studio applications, because of cost. These include:

- 1" 8-track recorders from Otari, Studer, Sony/MCI, Soundcraft, and Scully.
- 2" 16-, 24-, and 32-track machines from Otari, Studer, Sony/MCI, Soundcraft, Tascam, Stephens, ACES, and Studio Magnetics. Previous models were made by 3M and Ampex.
- Various multi-track *digital* tape formats, such as 8 millimeter 12-track (by Akai), 1" 24-track (by Sony), and 1" 32-track (by Mitsubishi and Otari, and discontinued by 3M). These machines do use magnetic tape, though the signals they record are streams of data, and not direct electrical representations of waveforms (which we'll examine on page 124). Ranging in cost from more than the average automobile to more than the average home, these are not to be found in your average personal studio!

Clearly, sooner or later we'll all have digital recording devices, though they may not use magnetic tape (as we'll learn about on page 124).

track, sound effects, jingle, and other 'audio post-production' work. We'll take a brief look at the world of synchronization starting on page 110.

Your Studio

Deciding *what* equipment you'll be using in your studio is one matter—deciding *where* you'll use that equipment is another. Depending upon individual needs, your personal studio can be located in a bedroom, its own professional setting, or anywhere in between.

How Many Rooms? The traditional professional recording studio consists of two rooms: a *control room*, and a *studio*, or *live room*. The control room is the domain of the engineer and producer, whereas the studio room is where you'll find the musicians. The control room also houses the mixing console, tape recorders, effects, and just about every other bit of gear, except for the microphones and instruments, which are usually in the studio room.

The control and studio rooms are acoustically separate: Sounds produced in either room can't be heard in the other. The control room does look out to the studio, however, through multi-paned glass. While some studio rooms are just large enough for five or six musicians and their instruments, many can accommodate an entire orchestra. Traditional control rooms are usually smaller than the studio room, often just large enough for those five or six musicians to sit and listen to their finished performance.

In addition, the traditional recording studio often has a third, acoustically separate room, the *isolation booth*. The isolation booth is at best large enough to hold a drum set, though many such booths are just big enough to hold one or two announcers.

The two- or three-room professional studio was developed for some very sound reasons. If microphones are being used for the session, a separate control room allows the engineer to listen through speakers

without fear of feedback or causing a 'spill-over' of previously recorded tracks into the mikes. Two rooms also allow the engineer and producer to converse—and the tape machines to make noise—without being picked up by the mikes. If the musicians are playing very loudly, even the best headphones wouldn't allow an engineer to hear very well without being acoustically isolated from the live music. Furthermore, a better mood is often established between musicians if they can play together without 'observers' in the same room.

In modern professional and personal recording sessions, however, many of these points no longer apply. For one, many contemporary sessions don't even use mikes, except for perhaps a single vocal or acoustic guitar overdub. Most synthesizer, drum machine, bass, and other tracks are recorded direct to tape without amplifiers, allowing the engineer to listen at whatever level he or she wishes. And—particularly in the personal studio—it's common for the single musician to record and overdub tracks alone, rather than with a group or even an engineer.

For these and other reasons, traditional studio designs are becoming less common. In fact, there are a slew of professional studios that have huge control rooms, capable of holding racks of keyboards, computer stations, musicians, and more. These studios may have a large isolation booth for vocal and acoustic instrument overdubs, but often no live room.

Since the advent of MIDI in 1983, and even earlier, most home recordists have found that a one-room design is more efficient for recording primarily electronic music. If you have to play engineer and musician, it's a lot more convenient to play your instrument as you sit near your recording gear, without having to get up and run into another room once you've pressed 'record.'

Of course, two rooms may still make sense for either a professional or private

Figure 4.1 New Age composer Michael Stearns in his home studio. Among other gear, from left to right, we see a TAC Scorpion 32-input mixer, and Otari MTR-90 24-track, an Otari MTR-12 4-track, a Serge modular synthesizer, an Apple Macintosh Plus computer, and the 24-track remote and autolocator.

studio if two or more people are working together—with at least one as an engineer—and if they plan to record a lot of microphone tracks. Otherwise, today's ideal personal studio is a one-room affair, with perhaps some type of isolation booth.

Further Choices. After deciding on the number of rooms, there are other questions to ask yourself:

- Do I need complete acoustic isolation, either from noisy surroundings or to appease neighbors?
- How much space do I need for my gear, whatever gear I plan to add, and anyone else I may work with?
- Do I plan to 'go commercial,' and be open to outside clients who may have to traipse around my laundry to reach the studio? Is the neighborhood zoned for a commercial enterprise?
- Is acoustical perfection critical to my work? Am I going to produce a finished product, demo tapes, or just song-sketches?
- If it's a garage or backyard shack, does it have AC power, and is it completely weatherproof and burglar-proof? Is this space covered by my homeowner's or tenant's insurance?
- Do I want to be able to leave the equipment set up all the time, or am I happy with setting it up each time I work and putting it away when finished?
- Am I willing to build a great space, or would I just as soon set up anywhere and roll tape as soon as possible?

The answers to these and other questions will not only determine what kind of studio space you put together—they may determine the quality of your work, how frequently you get to record, and possibly how much money your studio can earn.

Acoustic Treatment. What if you have acoustic isolation problems, and find yourself recording unwanted truck sounds, birds, horns, or any other real-life distractions? Or what if your neighbors are less than thrilled with the sounds of your heavy metal kazoo solo when it's 3:00 a.m.? Unless all of your tracks are recorded directly without mikes, and all your listening is by headphones, your studio may need some *acoustic treatment*.

There are two basic reasons—and many different ways—to acoustically treat a room. One reason is to provide *acoustic isolation*—between different rooms, from outside noises, or even between different instrumentalists or vocalists. The other reason is to improve the acoustics of the recording environment, both for recording and listening to tracks.

Acoustic isolation can range from a heavy sleeping bag thrown over an outside window, to a completely isolated space. The amount of external noise with which you have to contend or are willing to endure will prescribe how much isolation is needed.

True isolation is an expensive proposition, and is beyond the scope of this book. To give you a taste of what it's about, though, here's the idea: An acoustically isolated room is in fact a room within a room. For one, the floors are usually *floated*, by pouring a concrete floor, then building another floor on top of the concrete. Ideal-

ly, that second floor is also concrete, and floats above the original floor on top of large rubber *doughnuts*. In this way, there is a *dead* air space between the two, and it serves as an effective sound trap. In similar ways, inner walls are floated with large rubber grommets off the outer walls, and the inner ceiling is suspended from the top ceiling by specialized spring or rubber hangers. Wherever two inner surfaces (such as a wall and ceiling) meet, there is further isolation with caulking, foam, fiberglas mattings, and other materials.

Why are these rooms so elaborately isolated? Why not use lots of acoustical foam, drapes, or other sound absorbers? The fact is that sound absorbers such as drapes and the like only serve to reduce *high* frequency sounds. Lower frequency sounds with their longer wavelengths—such as a bass guitar or a kick drum—need an actual air space to be *trapped*, or stopped. If you've lived in an apartment block and ever heard your neighbor's stereo, chances are you've heard kick drum and basses, and not cymbals. If you need to reduce such low frequency sounds from inside or outside your studio, acoustical foam or tiling won't help you one bit—you'll likely need to create air spaces between your walls or ceilings. Or to build a floating floor.

On page 48, we're going to learn some important fundamentals of *acoustics*—the way sounds behave in a space. One concept that's important to studio design is the fact that sound waves reflect off surfaces. We'll also learn that in order to prevent an accentuation of low frequencies, an ideal studio has no parallel surfaces. That's why professional studios have ceilings angled in relation to the floor and also odd wall angles.

If you choose to build or modify your space, an indispensable reference is a book by Jeff Cooper, called *Building A Recording Studio*. There are many different approaches to design that one can take, and this book will help you through the nuts and bolts—literally! And if you plan to do a lot of con-

struction, it's really worth taking your plans to a professional acoustical consultant. A good consultant may not be cheap, but even a few hours with one can save you a lot of grief.

Most of us recording at home don't go to the elaborate steps of building an acoustically isolated studio, or creating non-parallel surfaces. There are some easy things we can do, however, to improve the overall quality of sound within our workspace.

For reasons we'll learn more about starting on page 48, hard and smooth walls—of concrete, wood, or other such surfaces—reflect more high frequency sound than soft walls—those with drapes, acoustical foam, or other materials. That's why hard walls are usually called *reflective*, and soft walls are *absorbent*. A reflective room is called a *live*- or *wet*-sounding room, and a non-reflective room is acoustically *dead* or *dry*. Assuming none of us live in a concrete tube or an anechoic chamber (a special testing room with no reflections), the rooms in which we set up our gear will be live or dead to varying degrees.

Up until the early 1980s, most people sought as dead a sound as possible—the home studio of the 1970s typically was lined with fiberglass matting, carpeting, and so on. The idea, as is held by a minority of people today, was that any desired *ambience* or acoustical life should be added electronically, since ambience can be easily added but not subtracted. This applies to microphone recordings, and not tracks which are recorded directly from a synthesizer or other electronic instrument.

Today it's widely felt that there's nothing wrong with recording some room ambience when using a mike; should a very dry recording be desired, an isolation booth can be used. For those of us with a live-sounding bedroom for a recording space, there's no reason why a closet stuffed full of absorbent clothing couldn't be used as a makeshift isolation booth. What this boils down to is that it's not necessary to line your walls with

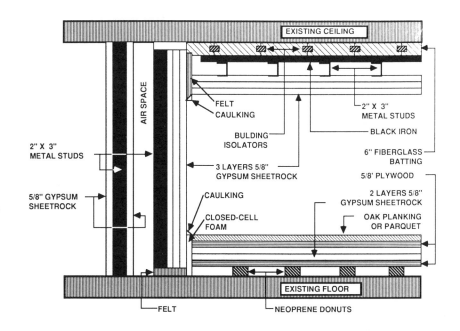

Figure 4.2 *A cross-section of a 'floating' room. By physically isolating all surfaces from each other, noises can be kept in or out of the room.*

blankets, fiberglass, teddy bears, and anything else that's soft and absorbent—assuming unwanted noise is under control.

There are some things that can be done to reduce the reflectivity of a very live room, however, and many of us have to resort to some variation of the following approaches. In general, the theme is to use absorbent materials to break up the reflectivity of surfaces. For example, windows—being very hard and smooth—can be 'controlled' with drapes.

Perhaps the ideal anti-reflection wall treatment is Sonex, a specialized foam, as pictured in Figure 4.3. Its multi-faceted surface literally breaks up sound waves, much as ocean waves break up on a rocky shore. Another effective wall covering is called Tectum, and is made by U.S. Gypsum. Both Sonex and Tectum come in sheets, and can be mounted to fit a space. Keep in mind that to control reflectivity it's not necessary to cover all surfaces completely—a few sheets of Sonex randomly spaced can do wonders.

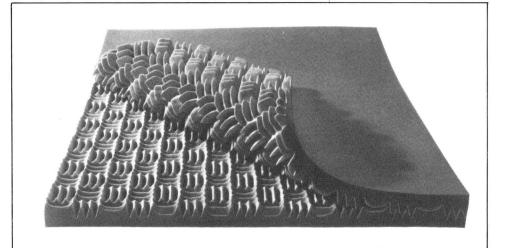

Figure 4.3 Sonex acoustic foam is used to reduce reflections; it's particularly effective at mid- to high-frequencies.

Mounting either Sonex or Tectum on frames suspended from wall studs can create a trap of sorts, which will help control some lower frequencies. They can also be mounted on movable frames, which are called *goboes* (see Figure 4.4). Goboes are also excellent devices for controlling leakage between instruments, when recording more than one instrument live, such as a piano and a drum kit. A gobo placed between the two can minimize the chances of the piano's mike picking up the drums and vice versa.

Most normal rooms have *resonant* frequencies. These are the frequencies at which the entire room or portions of the room can vibrate *sympathetically* with sound. Next time you're in the shower, try singing different notes, up and down scales. Listen for certain notes which may sound markedly louder than others; there may be only one note which stands out. When you find that note, you've found a resonant frequency for the shower or bathroom.

In the same way, all rooms have resonant frequencies, usually most pronounced in the low frequencies. Excessively resonant low frequencies must be *trapped* by acoustic cavities that are *tuned* to the offending frequencies. This is the *only* effective way to reduce excessive low frequencies. The idea

is to identify the offending frequencies, and using the formula described on page 2, their actual wavelengths are calculated. Then, once a soundwave's size is know, an appropriate trap can be built. Building a trap is well described in Cooper's book. Some companies, such as ASC/TubeTrap, offer self-contained bass traps.

How can you tell if you have a reflectivity or low frequency problem, and how can you identify the problem frequencies? There is equipment which can measure such problems, though it's expensive even to rent, and can be difficult to use or interpret (we do discuss this gear on page 74). Many musicians settle for evaluating their rooms subjectively.

For example, reflectivity can be a problem either when recording with mikes, or when playing back through speakers. When recording with mikes, and listening back with headphones, does the recording tend to sound 'muddy,' or incoherent? If the bass levels on your mixer are normal, and your

miking technique is good, you may have a room problem. Or if you're listening to playback, and things sound fine through headphones but jumbled and 'boomy' through the speakers, that may be another sign of reflectivity problems. Once you develop an ear you'll be able to judge rooms just by listening to them, though accurate analysis can only be performed using special equipment.

You may encounter the term *LEDE*. This refers to a popular professional studio design, and is licensed by Chips Davis, a well-known studio designer. LEDE stands for *live-end, dead-end*, and refers to the two opposite ends of the control room. Davis' thesis is that room listening is optimized if the monitor speaker end of the room is acoustically dead, and the opposite end is live. His process requires very careful evaluation of the space available, and often incorporates *diffusers* to break up reflections at the live end. Many people agree with his approach, and find LEDE rooms to be very consistent-sounding, and very 'listenable.' You may wish to experiment on your own with this approach; while you won't create a true LEDE room without a Davis design, you may come up with a sound you like.

Placing The Equipment. Monitor speaker placement is critical, for reasons we'll look at on page 74. Consequently, if you're not building a 'properly treated' room, the speakers' optimum location in a room may suggest the placement for all the rest of your equipment.

It's also important to organize your equipment in a way that coordinates with your work. For example, if you record lots of guitar tracks, but rarely use your keyboard, perhaps your keyboard can be placed far enough away from the mixer or recorder/mixer so that your guitars can be close at hand. Similarly, a remote control for your tape recorder may be really handy for those occasional keyboard tracks.

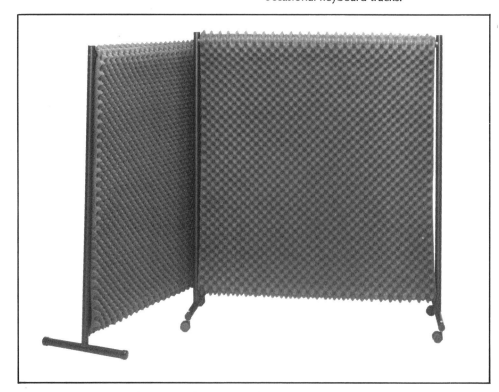

Figure 4.4 Shown are two goboes from Tubecraft, covered with Acoustifoam, a material similar in its applications to Sonex.

Signal processors such as reverbs, delays, equalizers—as well as MIDI'd sound modules and even some mixers and tape recorders—are ideally housed in a *rack*. Racks are available from many different manufacturers, or you can build your own. Rack mount equipment is based on a standard width of 19". A *single-space* height is 1¾", and most rack mount gear is based on multiples of that space: 1¾", 3½", and so forth.

AC Power. Unless you're using a battery-powered ministudio exclusively with acoustic instruments, wherever your equipment is located, it needs AC (mains) power. An ideal source is a well-wired, 3-prong grounded outlet. From your outlets, you can run one or more power strips to accommodate your gear. Cheap molded extension cords may be asking for trouble, and a multi-outlet 'octopus' is definitely bad news. Your AC power is important, and potentially dangerous if run through poor cabling.

MIDI gear is microprocessor-based; that is, your typical modern synthesizer is actually a computer in disguise. If you've used computers, you may have had the bad for-tune to find out first hand that they're very intolerant of voltage fluctuations, even to the point of losing data during as short a power loss or surge as 20 milliseconds—which can happen anytime, anywhere. If you're using MIDI gear, or especially if you're using a computer in your studio, at very minimum you should have *surge protectors*, which are a special kind of power strip designed to protect the AC line from brief, potentially-harmful voltage spikes. In areas with poor power you may also want a *voltage regulator*, to maintain constant voltage.

Finally, if you're really paranoid about your data, or find that writing electronic music in the throes of an electrical storm is your idea of musical inspiration, you'll want a *UPS*—an uninterruptible power supply. One of these several hundred dollar boxes will supply constant and regulated power to a computer or whatever. With built-in batteries, they'll even supply power for about 10 or 20 minutes after a complete power outage, which is plenty of time to save your work to disk or tape and wait for the normal power to return.

On page 81 we'll examine how to ground your gear in a way which will minimize potential radio interference with your equipment.

* * * *

Equipping—or even building a studio—can be an open-ended affair. We've discussed everything from a 'bare-bones' approach to a full-blown professional set-up. And while many people opt for something in the middle, even a very uncomplicated 4-track system can benefit from some basic signal processing, such as a reverb. Similarly, an extra bit of acoustic treatment can make the difference between a 'basement' tape and a professional-sounding product. Expanding your set-up beyond the essentials can yield higher quality results, and let you have a lot more fun in the meantime.

In the next section we'll take a detailed look at some of the equipment you'll be using in your studio—along with a few technical basics to help you further understand the process of multi-track recording.

Figure 14.5 *The Sandbox, in Fairfield County, Connecticut. This studio has a very large control room, designed for intensive MIDI work. From left to right we see a Studer A820 2-track, two Macintosh Plus computers, an E-mu SP-12 sampler/drum machine, a Roland SBX-80 sync box, racks o' signal processing gear, and a Yamaha KX88 keyboard controller. From the far corner we continue with an E-mu Emulator II sampler, an Oberheim Matrix 12 synth, an Oberheim OB8 synth, a Kurzweil 250 expander module, a Fairlight CMI Series III, two Otari MTR90-II 24-tracks, an Otari remote and autolocator, and a Neve Series V mixing console, on top of which is a Necam 96 moving fader automation controller.*

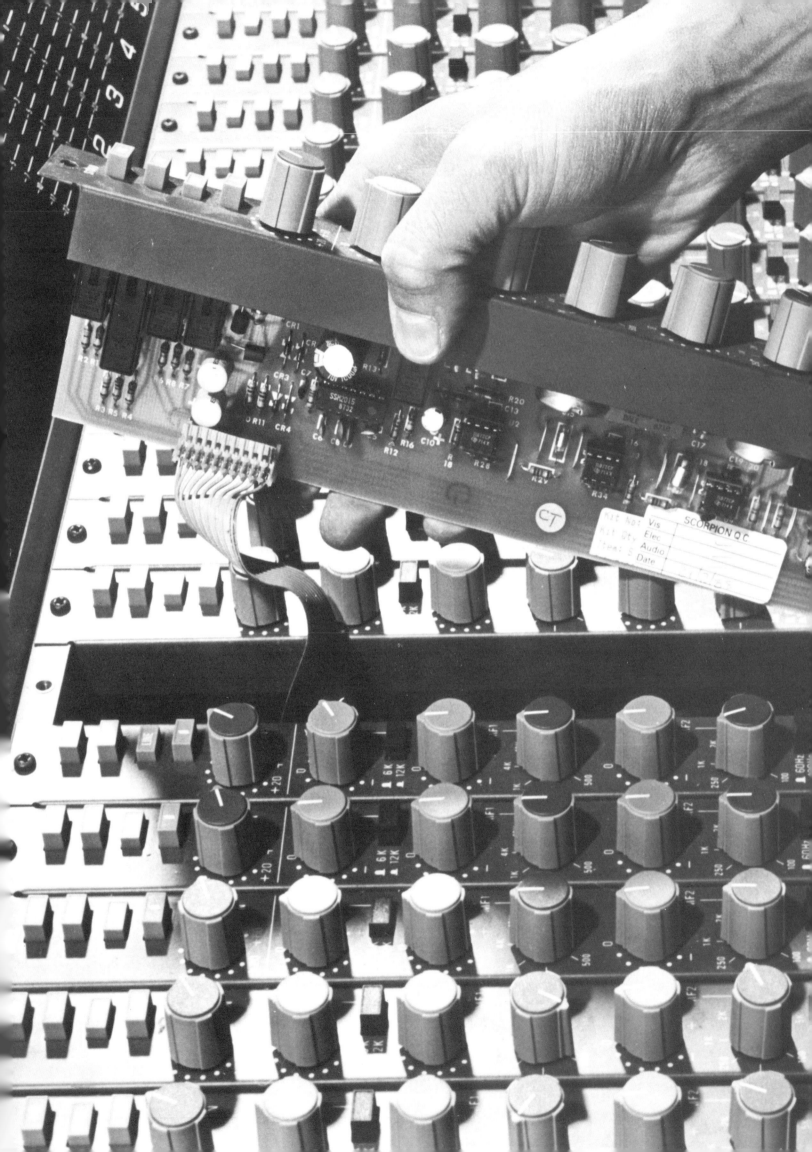

Part II: Understanding Your Equipment

So far, we've been concentrating on the theory of recording and sound. Now let's take a look at the equipment required to make multi-track recordings.

A few years back, this might have been a less complicated part: Almost everyone doing multi-track at home used an open-reel 4-track tape recorder with a rudimentary built-in mixer, or perhaps a simple outboard mixer. Today, however, there is a plethora of equipment, generally high in performance and relatively low in cost.

Throughout this discussion of equipment, we'll try to address multi-track recording *in general*. For this reason, there will often be several ways listed of doing things, and different descriptions of the *specific* components found on various types of equipment. In this manner, the information will be pertinent not only for your present equipment, but also for any personal recording setup you may acquire down the road. If it interests you, take a look at how some of the equipment you don't own operates; learning about other equipment can give you all sorts of clues and insights into how to get the most from your own gear.

Before we discuss the actual equipment used in multi-track recording, let's look at some of the basic terminology we'll encounter. It's not necessary to know all of the following technical information, and if it gets a bit heavy, you can skip ahead to page 85. When it comes time to hooking up or operating your equipment in the best way, however, use the upcoming pages as a reference if you encounter difficulties.

CHAPTER 5: TECHNICAL BASICS

Have you ever picked up a 'spec sheet' for the latest technological wonder, hoping to learn something new—only to be greeted by a sexy-looking photo of the device and a maze of incomprehensible terms like "Nominal Level: +4 dBm, switchable to –10 dBV," and so on?

This sort of 'techno-speak' is rampant in most product literature, and while it may seem incomprehensible, the truth is that it's useful. Once you understand specs, you'll be much better equipped to compare equipment and make informed purchasing decisions.

What if you don't care about spec sheets? After all, it's not always necessary to understand equipment specifications and related terminology—especially if you're following the bare-bones, ministudio approach. As a musician and a recording engineer, however, there are a number of technical difficulties you may encounter. You may be recording an acoustic guitar one day, for example, and hear a gruesomely distorted signal. A friend might bring over her microphone, and it may not work when plugged into your setup. Or you may wonder why many of your recordings are too noisy. Hopefully, the following few pages will help you understand the causes of some of these quandaries, and allow you to be better equipped to solve them.

What follows is a rundown of important general technical concepts and specifications. Most can be applied to any recording gear. Some equipment, such as tape recorders and speakers, have their own standards of specification, which are covered in their respective sections of this book. If the going gets a bit too technical, don't worry about understanding everything—feel free to move on, or to return to this section down the road, as needed.

Basic Electricity

As we learned on page 2, sound is a flow of vibrations through the air. These vibrations are an example of sound energy. Electricity is another type of energy, involving the flow of electrons through a conductive material, such as a wire. Since a lot of what we're dealing with has to do with electricity, the following terms will give you a foundation for concepts we'll cover later in this section.

Circuit. A conductive course through which electrons flow is known as a *circuit*. If it helps you, think of a circuit as a race track. The circuit must be closed in order for the electrons to flow, just as a race track must be 'closed' for racers to complete their laps. A switch can *break* the circuit.

Voltage. *Voltage* is the force which causes electrons to move around a circuit. When something is capable of expending energy, such as a race car which can go from standstill to 100 mph, that object has an *energy potential*. When an electrical circuit or device, such as a battery, is capable of expending energy, we can say there exists an *electrical* or *voltage potential*. *Volts* are

the units we use to express that potential energy in electrical circuits.

Resistance. When something is in the circuit which causes work to be done by the circuit, such as a light bulb or an electric motor, it's said to introduce *resistance* to the circuit. Resistance is measured in *ohms* (Ω). You might think of resistance as the drag of a race car's weight—which the engine's horsepower has to keep moving. (Don't confuse resistance with *impedance*, which is also measured in ohms. We'll tackle impedance starting on page 22.)

Current. Measured in *amperes*, or just *amps*, the *current* is the amount of electricity—electrical energy—moving through a circuit. When something with a low resistance is in a circuit, it 'draws' a high amount of current. (It's like an engine's torque.)

Wattage. The 'power,' or amount of work that can be performed by an electrical circuit is measured in *watts*, as the power of a race car is measured in horsepower. Wattage is the product of a circuit's voltage multiplied by a circuit's current. For example, a 110 volt circuit drawing 10 amps is performing 1100 watts worth of work.

Ground. All electrical circuits must have a *ground* to which voltage and current can flow. Forget about the race car; Ben Franklin's lightning rod is the best analogy here. A ground can be an actual connection to earth, or it can be what's known as a *virtual ground*, where there's actually no earth connection, but rather a common ground for all electrical components within a device. As we all know, touching an electrical device while standing in water is a risky undertaking—that's because we can act as a path for the electricity to flow to the water, and the water can act as a path to ground! (Actually, laboratory-pure deionized water is a poor conductor, but that's not the water most of us encounter.) We'll learn more about grounds and audio on page 82.

Signal Levels And The Decibel

Understanding how signal levels and decibels interrelate is important in order to know:

- How to interconnect different types of equipment.
- How to read meters and use them effectively.
- How to create better-sounding recordings.

On page 3, we learned that sound is measured in decibels (dBs). What happens to sound when it becomes an electrical signal? How do we measure the levels of electrical signals?

It so happens that the decibel makes a convenient scale of measurement for electrical signals. Open-air sound is measured by using a very sensitive microphone, which converts the sound to an electrical signal of varying degrees; those variations are then measured and represented in terms of decibels. This leads us right to another ques-

tion: If we're measuring the actual electrical signal, why not represent it in volts or watts, rather than dBs?

Here's why: dBs are a convenient scale for measuring large changes in level. If we measure changes in level with volts, let's say, then a doubling of level would mean a doubling of volts, a tripling of level would mean a tripling of volts, and so on. This type of relationship is known as a *linear-scale* relationship, where a single unit of change in level is expressed as a single unit change in volts. With a linear scale such as this, large changes in level are expressed as large numbers of volts—this can get cumbersome, as we'll see in a moment.

We also learned earlier that a change of 10 dB represents an audible doubling of level. This type of relationship between dBs and level is a *non-linear* (also called *geometric* or *logarithmic*) relationship; the idea is that small changes in dBs can represent large changes in watts or other electronic measurements.

For example, 1 dB is just above the virtual threshold of hearing (which is 0 dB), and a jet plane in close proximity measures at about 130 dB (a deafening level). As John Woram points out in his excellent technical reference, *The Recording Studio Manual*, the jet plane is in fact 10,000,000,000,000 (10^{13}) times as loud as the threshold of hearing, when measured by linear mathematical methods. The decibel allows us to express this gargantuan difference as just a change of 130 dB!

Thanks to this handy system, we musicians can get by using dBs to measure everything from volume levels to signal strength and relative levels of recorded tracks.

The dB issue isn't cut and dried, however—there are actually four major scales of dBs. It may be useful to know the difference between them, particularly if you intend to be using professionally-oriented equipment with personal recording and hi-fi gear. The four common types of dBs you'll encounter on spec sheets, meters, and more are the *dBA*, the *dBm*, the *dBV*, and the *dBv* (also known as the *dBu*).

dBA. When talking about sound pressure levels and relative amplitudes of sounds, a decibel is measured as a *dBA*—but most people just use the word 'dB.' (It's also slightly misleading but very common to speak of the three following types of dBs in terms of 'dB,' rather than 'dBm' and so on.)

dBm. Most high-end professional and broadcast equipment measures its *line levels* on a scale known as dBm, and typically, such equipment uses input and output signals which operate at a line level known as +4 dBm. What does this mean?

The term 'line level' refers to a general operating level *between* equipment, such as between a tape recorder and a mixer.

The term 'dBm' refers to a scale which references decibels to milliwatts (thousandths of a watt). One milliwatt is equivalent to a signal of 0.775 volts being fed into a *600 ohm load*. (The 600 ohm load could be a

18   Understanding Your Equipment

tape recorder input, for example. 600 ohms is a reference to *impedance*, which we'll examine shortly. A lot of this knowledge is very much interlinked, but for now, think of that 600 ohms as something which receives a signal and puts it to work, such as that tape recorder input.)

You've probably seen meters labelled 'VU meter.' *VU* stands for 'volume units,' and it's a common scale. This scale is similar to the level meters found on most home hi-fi cassette decks, that have scales which run from '-20' up to '+3' or so. Now, armed with all this information, we can find out what +4 dBm means. As we just learned,

0 dBm = 0.775 volts (into 600 ohms).

On professional and broadcast equipment, when a VU meter reads '0,' it means that a +4 dBm signal is being received. In other words,

0 VU = +4 dBm = 1.23 volts (into 600 ohms).

Because a 0 VU reading is equivalent to a +4 dBm level, when a VU meter on a pro piece of gear reads '+3,' it's receiving a +7 dBm signal, and when it reads '-5' it's receiving a -1 dBm signal. Note that '-' is only a term relative to the 0.775 volts reference: a -1 dBm signal is still a positive voltage value.

dBV. Most 'semi-pro' personal recording equipment, and virtually all home hi-fi gear, operates at signal levels known as *-10 dBV*. If this suggests to you that +4 dBm professional and -10 dBV personal gear operate at different levels, you're right!

Basically, -10 dBV gear operates at a lower level than +4 dBm gear. This means that a signal coming from a -10 dBV device is usually at too low a level to be received optimally by a +4dBm device. Similarly, a signal from a +4dBm device will usually *overload* a -10 dBV device, because the former's signal is too strong for the latter unit to receive without distortion.

What is the dBV scale, and how does it differ from the dBm scale? The dBV scale is referenced to voltage only, such that 0 dBV = 1 volt (there's no 600 ohm description). Why the different scale? The original dBm scale was developed when most audio equipment was built to 600 ohm specifications. For a variety of reasons such designs are expensive, and today's home and personal recording equipment often operates at different impedance ratings. Consequently the dBV scale was created—useful for technicians, something confusing for musicians.

As we just learned, with the dBV scale, 0 dBV = 1 volt. In a manner similar to the +4 dBm scale, when a VU meter for a -10 dBV device reads "0," it means a -10 dBV signal is being received. That is:

0 VU = -10 dBV = 0.316 volts.

A reading of '+3' on the VU meter would mean a signal of -7 dBV was being received, and a reading of '-5' would indicate an input signal of -15 dBV.

Note that because *different scales* are used, there isn't a 14 dB difference in level between -10 and +4 gear. Functionally, there is approximately an 11.8 dBV difference in level between most -10 dBV and +4 dBm gear.

This comparison of dBm and dBV levels will solicit grumbles from most electrical engineers—they would tend to say that we're comparing apples and oranges. But since many people *do* mix and match the equipment, it's useful for us to express some average difference. Bear in mind that we're talking about operating levels *between* equipment. Many people think that -10 and +4 gear record different levels on tape, and that's not so!

dBv, or **dBu**. It's less common for musicians to run across things rated in dBv (also called dBu—the term we'll use—to avoid confusion with dBV). The dBu scale was designed to create a correlation between levels from -10 devices and +4 devices. It operates independently of impedance, and is set up so that 0 dBv = 0.775 volts. With this scale, a -10 signal is exactly 14 dBu less than a +4 signal.

Equipment Levels

So far, all the levels we've been discussing are line levels, which as we learned are the standard operating levels between audio equipment such as mixers, tape recorders, and signal processing gear. There are in fact a total of four types of levels that we'll encounter in the world of home recording. These are, in increasing relative signal strength, or *gain*:

- Microphone level.
- Instrument level.
- Line level.
- Speaker level.

Let's begin with line levels, and how they may be something you need to consider when assembling your studio's equipment.

Line Level. We've seen that *not all equipment operates at the same line level.* Specifically, most equipment designed for professional or broadcast environments operates at a line level of +4 dBm, and most equipment designed for home recording or hi-fi use operates at -10 dBV (actually, some broadcast gear operates at +8 dBm levels, but we needn't worry about it). In practice, this means that +4 signals are a lot higher than -10 signals.

What does this mean to the average home recordist? In many cases, nothing. If all the equipment is from one manufacturer, such as Fostex or Tascam, or is oriented to

home recording, everything should operate at the same -10 dBV levels; conversely, professionally-oriented gear from different manufacturers should operate at the same +4 dBm levels. If, however, different equipment is being mixed and matched, it's often important to make sure everything is at the same operating level, whether that's -10 or +4.

One common trend is for manufacturers to try and make their equipment compatible to *both* -10 and +4 levels, normally by means of a switch either inside or on the outside of the gear. The switch is usually labelled '-10 / +4,' though sometimes the +4 setting is substituted with a '0 dBm' setting, which is close enough to +4 dBm for most applications. If it so happens that the bulk of your gear, including tape recorder and mixer, can operate at +4 dBm, that setting is preferable to a -10 dBV setting. The reason is that a stronger signal is more likely to mask the sound of noise and other interference as it travels through the cables.

Consult the manuals and consult with your dealer, to ensure compatibility. In many cases, +4 equipment can be modified or adjusted to operate at a lower level (it's much more difficult and costly to modify -10 to operate at a higher level). As a final resort, in case of mismatch, there are -10 to +4 (and +4 to -10) level matching devices available, from Valley Audio, Rane, Fostex, and several other manufacturers.

Microphone Level. Rather than line level, mikes operate at a much lower level known as microphone level. Remembering our discussion from page 5, a microphone is a small transducer. They generate relatively little electricity, however, even when screaming into one. Because of this, mikes are usually among the lowest-level devices in home recording. (If you use a phonograph, the levels coming out of the pickup/stylus assembly are even lower, though that level is amplified by a *preamp* up to -10 dBV before it leaves the turntable.)

The typical output of a microphone is in the range of -60 up to -20 dBV. There are a few exceptions that can operate as high as +4 dBm levels, but these are expensive and rare.

When the mike's signal reaches the mixer, it encounters a microphone *preamp*. This is a small amplifier, which raises the gain of the signal up to -10 or +4,

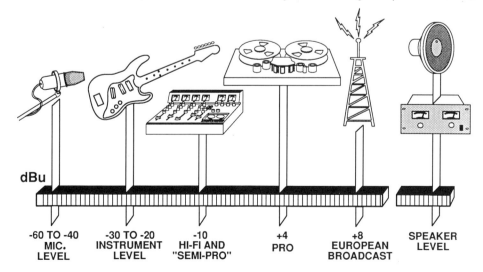

dBu						
-60 TO -40 MIC. LEVEL	-30 TO -20 INSTRUMENT LEVEL	-10 HI-FI AND "SEMI-PRO"	+4 PRO	+8 EUROPEAN BROADCAST	SPEAKER LEVEL

Figure 5.1 A chart of relative signal levels, on the dBu scale.

depending upon the operating level of the mixer.

Instrument Level. The signal levels from electronic instruments can vary quite a bit. The output levels from an electric guitar are usually in the range of –30 to –20 dBV; this range is a vague description of what engineers call *instrument level*.

Most home recording mixers or recorder/mixers are capable of receiving an instrument level directly. Many professional-oriented consoles are designed to receive mike or line levels only, and consequently, a small box known as a *direct box* (or *D.I.*, for direct input or injection) is needed to lower an instrument to microphone levels. Electro-acoustic keyboards (such as a Fender Rhodes) operate at instrument levels.

Synthesizers are capable of delivering line levels anywhere from –30 up to 0 or even +4, allowing them to interface directly to all mixing consoles.

Speaker Level. This refers to anything designed to operate at the output level of a power amplifier; in practice, this means either loudspeakers or accessories such as speaker selectors (for multiple sets of speakers). This level can be very high, even approaching 50 volts or more.

When compared to a typical home mixer, which is designed to receive levels of 0.316 volts, it's easy to see why it's a cardinal sin to plug the output of a power amplifier into *any* line level input! The results of such a mismatch are at best the most horrifically nasty sound you've ever heard; and at worst, a 'fried' input, complete with fire and mayhem.

Distortion

Think of a distorted sound. If nothing comes to mind, imagine a small, cheap, hand-held transistor radio, playing music at full-blast. What you'd hear would be much quieter than a quality stereo at really high 'party levels,' but would sound much more offensive, because of all the *distortion*. A small transistor radio isn't a requisite for distortion, though—no matter how fine our recording gear, we have to beware of unwanted distortion, know what causes it, and know how to minimize it.

In its pure sense, audio distortion occurs anytime a signal's waveform is changed. In the real world, audio waveforms do change slightly as they pass through various stages of equipment and through a speaker. What counts is distortion we can hear.

In the case of our cheap transistor radio, we'd likely be able to hear two kinds of distortion. First of all, we could hear the *speaker* distortion: The cone of the loudspeaker has limits to its physical *excursion* (how far it can travel). If it receives a signal so strong that it's required to exceed its excursion, distortion results, since it's no longer able to faithfully reproduce the signal. What we hear is a 'gritty,' 'dirty' sound.

The second kind of distortion we'd be able to hear from that transistor radio is *electronic* distortion. What is electronic distortion?

Signals pass through circuits, as we know. Electronic distortion occurs when a circuit is unable to accommodate the level of a signal passing through, and can occur in subtle ways. Let's imagine an electronic

waveform (Figure 5.2)—we could think of this as being the output of a synthesizer. In normal operation, with proper levels, the synth's signal falls well within the capabilities of a mixer's line level input. In this case, let's say that the *nominal* (or optimum) line level of the mixer is –10 dBV. If the highest line level that mixer can receive without distortion is –2 dBV, we could say that the mixer's line input has a *headroom* of 8 dB. As long as the output of the synth is less than –2 dBV, no problems. But if we turn its level up to +2 dBV, we've turned up too high: We exceed the headroom of the input, and the signal distorts. The higher the input level, the more distortion we can hear.

Another term for distortion is *clipping*. We can see why in Figure 5.2: When the signal distorts, the top of its waveform is 'clipped.' When engineers talk about clipped signals, though, they're usually talking about very audible distortion.

Distortion is measured in terms of percentage; that is, the percentage amount of distorted signal compared to the 'clean' undistorted signal.

There are many forms of electronic distortion. The two most common forms—usually listed on most spec sheets—are:

- *Harmonic* distortion.
- *Intermodulation* distortion.

Harmonic Distortion. The best-known form of electronic distortion is harmonic distortion, and it's the least nasty form. Also called *THD* (Total Harmonic Distortion, or Third Harmonic Distortion), it's the amount of the *third harmonic* of a signal created by a clipping situation. For those of you not already versed in some music theory, for example, the third harmonic of a C note is E. It so happens that clipping can induce this type of harmonic to a signal.

Because it produces a musically harmonious distortion, THD is a desired effect in some circumstances. Vacuum tubes (valves) are well known for being able to produce a good deal of THD when driven to overload. For example, all those great-sounding, raunchy, Marshall guitar amps get their distinctive sound by producing *lots* of THD; distortion footpedals do the same type of thing using special transistor circuits.

Aside from this effect, however, and despite its musicality, THD is not usually desirable—it can ruin the clean sound of an acoustic guitar, piano, or even vocal track.

Distortion is measured as a percentage: How much of the overall signal, in percentage terms, is distorted? Most people can hear THD levels of 1% or greater, and a few 'golden eared' individuals can sense THD levels of less than 0.5%. But as long as the equipment is being operated at the proper levels, THD is rarely a problem in home recording: Most gear has THD levels of less than 0.08%.

Intermodulation Distortion. Aside from THD, another common form of electronic distortion is *intermodulation* distortion (*IMD*)—sometimes known as *transient intermodulation distortion (TIMD)*. IMD is a much less musical form of distortion, when compared to THD, since the harmonics it induces are random frequencies, and the sound is much more grating. Transistors are prime culprits for IMD, which is one reason why many guitarists who prefer a "warm THD" sound prefer tube amps. Our ears are

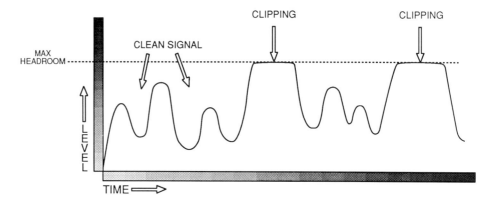

Figure 5.2 When analog audio signals exceed their headroom, clipping of the waveform can occur, resulting in audible distortion.

much less tolerant of IMD, because of its general unpleasantness; in general, IM levels of less than 0.05% are required for high audio performance.

Other Electronic Distortions. Electronic distortion can appear in many forms other than THD and IMD—too many to list here, in fact. There are, however, two you may encounter. . . .

One common, though usually overlooked, form is that of *phase* distortion. (This shouldn't be confused with Casio's Phase Distortion synthesis method, though they are related to some degree.)

Earlier, we learned that when two identical waveforms arrive slightly out of phase (out of time) with each other, some frequencies are cancelled, and the sound can be 'thin' or sound like it's shifting around. This happens with 'live' sounds, as well as electronic signals. Phase cancellation can come about whenever microphones are used. Otherwise, it so happens that recording gear can induce phase distortion, which are cancellations due to equipment misalignment, malfunction, or basic design. In practice, even the best multi-track tape recorders induce some phase distortion. Since phase distortion is a fact of life, there's little for the home recordist to do about it, aside from making sure all equipment is up to its optimum performance.

Aside from THD and IMD, a common form of electronic distortion is *electromagnetic*, or *tape saturation*, distortion.

Tape saturation occurs when magnetic

tape receives a signal too strong to record properly, and the result is a loss of high frequencies. Some engineers actually like the sound of saturation, since it can make signals sound 'compressed,' or 'squashed.' The classic, 'punchy' drum sound, for example, is a result of recording the drum tracks at slightly too high a level, perhaps a peak meter reading of '+6' or so. Much higher though, and the high frequencies begin to drop steeply.

Signal-To-Noise

Often abbreviated as *S/N*, a signal-to-noise ratio is the measurement of how much *signal* can be heard in relationship to how much *noise* can be heard. The measurement is in good old dBs (most of the time). Whenever we record or whatever gear we use, the higher the S/N ratio, the better.

As we send audio signals back and forth between our instruments and recording gear, and even as we route signals within one piece of gear (such as a mixer), we're always forced to play a kind of level game. If too much level is fed from one *source* to another *destination* (such as a mixer to a tape deck), we get distortion. So it might seem that the best way to avoid distortion is to use very low-level signals. The problem with that approach is that, while you'll avoid distortion, your S/N will deteriorate.

Without noise reduction, many cassette tape players reproduce a lot of tape hiss. Please look at Figure 5.3. What we see here is the level of noise (hiss) that exists on a piece of magnetic tape. This type of inherent noise, whether tape hiss or electronic noise, is known as a *noise floor*. When we record a signal to the tape, our goal is to record that signal as loud as possible without distorting; the purpose of this is to maximize the signal-to-noise ratio, so that the signal 'covers up' a maximum of hiss. As we can see, if the recorded signal's gain drops too low, it begins to approach the noise floor, so that upon playback the hiss would sound very loud in relationship to the signal.

level is than the signal level, in any given device. The larger the dB figure, the better the S/N. For our purposes, a minimum S/N ratio rating for a tape recorder would be about 45 dB. This means that the noise floor of the tape recorder would be 45 dB quieter than any signal recorded at maximum level. A really good recorder, with an excellent noise reduction system, might register a S/N ratio of 75 to 90 dB.

For other equipment, including digital tape recorders, mixers, signal processors, and so on, today's standards are much higher. With this type of equipment, we should look for signal-to-noise ratios of 85 dB or greater; a CD player, for example, has a S/N ratio of 90 dB or greater. At signal-to-noise ratios that high, noise is effectively inaudible.

Another term for signal-to-noise is *dynamic range*. We could, for example, say that a CD player has a dynamic range of 90 dB. This refers to the useful range, in decibels, of sounds that can be recorded above the noise floor. Yet another term is *equivalent input noise* (EIN), which often is used when rating the S/N ratios of gear. When measuring EIN, an *equivalent circuit* is used, to simulate a microphone, line input, or other real-world device in use with the gear being tested.

Level Meters

How do we avoid distortion? How do we maximize signal-to-noise ratios in our equipment? Assuming our gear is in good working order and that there are no gross level mismatches (*i.e.*: +4 to –10 mismatches), an important way of avoiding distortion is to use our ears—with careful attention, it's possible to hear distortion before and after recording signals.

We can also avoid distortion and noise by watching our levels as we send signals back and forth. By using *level* meters to record as high as possible without distortion, we can minimize the noise we hear.

Meters come in several different styles.

mechanical meter with a single LED *peak* indicator. All of these styles are gradiated with *Volume Unit* (VU) readings. '0 VU' is generally considered an optimum input level; the typical meter range is from –20 or –40 up to +3 or +6 VU. At levels above 0 VU, there is possible input distortion, though many people get satisfactory results at higher levels. We say "possible" because different equipment has different degrees of headroom; it may be with your equipment that signal levels can reach +3 or higher on the meter before any distortion can be heard. As you become more experienced, you'll find that your ears are an excellent tool for avoiding distortion.

Meter Ballistics. The ways in which meters respond to their incoming signals is known as a meter's *ballistics*. Any of the three meter styles listed above can be found with one of the following ballistics.

The first, and most common of these is known as *averaging*, or VU (Volume Units) ballistics. A meter with averaging ballistics will respond to overall, or average, changes in gain. Averaging meters are effective for watching overall levels to guard against overloading. They don't respond instantaneously to quick signal peaks, however, and sometimes a quick peak is all that is needed to induce distortion.

The second most common meter ballistic is known as *peak-reading*. A peak-reading meter responds to instantaneous changes in levels, and is very useful for observing unwanted peaks which could cause distortion. Peak-reading meters are usually LED bargraph-style because a bargraph can display peaks much more quickly than a mechanical needle, which has to physically move, and that takes extra time.

The disadvantage of peak-style meters is that they tend to fluctuate up and down scale so quickly that it's very difficult to gauge the average signal levels. Because of this, a hybrid type of meter ballistics was developed, known as *peak-reading, average-decay*. This type, found in both analog and bargraph styles, *rises* in response to signal peaks with much the same speed as a peak-reading meter, but *decays* with an averaging speed, so that there are not such rapid fluctuations between peaks and lower-level signals.

Finally, as mentioned above, one common style is to use a hybrid analog meter with a single LED. With this design, the analog meter has VU ballistics, and the single LED responds strictly to instantaneous peaks.

Crosstalk

When signals from one circuit 'bleed through' and can be detected in other nearby circuits, the unwanted effect is known as electronic *crosstalk*. Crosstalk is similar to signal-to-noise, in that it's an unwanted signal that interferes with the desired signal; instead of hiss or other noise, however, crosstalk is an unwanted audio signal. When the crosstalk gets too high in level and becomes audible, it can ruin a good recording.

Crosstalk is common with tape recorders. Let's say you record a bass guitar on track 1 of your 4-track. If you listen just to the adjacent track 2 and can hear some of the bass guitar faintly 'bleeding' or 'leaking' from

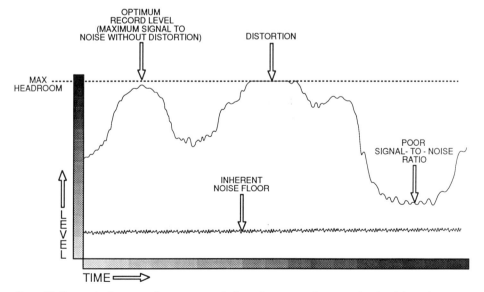

Figure 5.3 *Our goal, when recording to tape—or in fact, whenever passing an analog signal through any device—is to keep the signal low enough to avoid distortion, and high enough to mask tape hiss or other noise.*

A signal-to-noise ratio represents how much louder a signal is, in terms of dBs, than a given noise floor. Conversely, we could think of this as how much quieter the noise

The traditional *mechanical* meter uses a moving needle to indicate levels, though bargraph-style *LED* meters are growing in popularity. A common hybrid design is a

track 1, you're hearing crosstalk. If you then re-recorded the bass guitar on track 1, you'd be stuck with hearing a bit of the original bass track on track 2. This type of crosstalk can also be heard between adjacent channels of mixers and amplifiers, and other gear with more than one audio circuit.

Crosstalk, like signal-to-noise, is measured in dBs, and the higher the number of dBs, the greater the ratio between the wanted audio signal and the unwanted crosstalking signal. In other words, more dBs is better. An acceptable level of crosstalk for tape recorders is at minimum about 40 dB; 50 dB to 60 dB are excellent figures. For mixers and other gear, figures of 50 to 70 dB are desirable.

There's not an awful lot that can be done to minimize electronic crosstalk, assuming that tape heads and other components are aligned and working properly. In fact, in the real world, even professional gear suffers from some crosstalk. If tape crosstalk becomes objectionable, it may help to lower the recorded levels, though the drawback to that is poorer signal-to-noise response for that track. Cymbals, bass guitars, and other instruments that stand out at the high or low extremes of the frequency band are most prone to causing crosstalk problems, since there aren't other similar-frequency instruments to 'mask' them. For example, a tambourine would be more prone to being heard on an adjacent guitar track than another guitar would be.

Frequency Response

Frequency response is a measurement of a device's frequency range, and how accurately it records, reproduces, or transmits a given range of frequencies. For example, a tape recorder with poor 'high-end' frequency response would be one that reduced higher frequencies, such as those above 10 kHz, and it would tend to sound muffled. Similarly, a speaker with excessive mid-range response would be one that overly accentuated the mid-frequencies, perhaps those from 500 to 1500 Hz, causing a 'middy,' or 'honking' sort of sound (to use some engineering lingo).

The goal for most tape recorder, mixer, and other equipment designers is to create gear with *flat* frequency response—gear that's capable of recording, reproducing, or transmitting audio signals without inducing any frequency changes to the signals entering the device. Unwanted changes in response are known as *colorations*.

Why the term 'flat'? Response changes are measured in dBs. If a device alters a particular frequency by raising it 2 dB, that change can be graphed. If a device doesn't alter frequencies, its frequency response graph would look flat. Take a look at Figure 5.4a.

As we can see in Figure 5.4b, the flat signal of 20 Hz to 20 kHz entering the device has had its frequency response altered. Since none of the changes are greater than 3 dB, we can say that the device has a frequency response of 20 Hz to 20 kHz, ± 3 dB. Of course, not all gear aims for flat response. Equalizers, for example, are useful because they *can* alter frequency response. Still, most gear aims to reproduce sound as flat, or *accurately*, as possible.

It's not uncommon, with mixers or amplifiers, to see responses such as 20 Hz to 50 kHz, ± 1 dB. While this is obviously an excellent spec, most experts would say that it's no better in real-world terms than a 20 Hz to 20 kHz spec. There are a few audiophiles (also kindly known as 'tweaks') who claim that good response well beyond the upper range of human hearing is important to capture all the nuances of music—that if those inaudible frequencies are missing, their absence can have a detrimental effect on lower harmonically-related frequencies. To some degree they may be right, but the quest of such performance is beyond most musicians' budgets.

Finally, when comparing frequency response specs, it's important to consider the '±' spec. A spec of ± 3 dB means that there's a variability of 6 dB in total, which is quite large, though acceptable. Typically you should see variations from 0 to 3 dB; beware of specs that have a greater variation.

Impedance

Earlier we spoke of a '600 ohm load.' This describes *impedance*. Many musicians and audiophiles have come across 'low- and high-impedance microphones,' '8 ohm speakers,' and other references to impedance. Some common conceptions are that low-impedance is the professional standard, and that impedance is the same as resistance—are these conceptions correct, and what are 'ohms,' 'impedance,' and a 'load'?

When a device opposes a circuit's electrical current, that device is inducing *resistance* to the circuit. When a light bulb is introduced to an electrical circuit, for example, it creates a resistance to that circuit's current, and that resistance is manifested as light and heat. With the exception of the new world of superconductivity, where electrical circuits can conduct electricity without any resistance, all electrical circuits have a resistance to them. When there is no resistance to a circuit, it's *short-circuited* and the system fails, since the energy in the circuit is 'all dressed up' with nowhere to go. Most of us associate short-circuits with blown fuses, fire, and general mayhem—now we know why.

Resistance is measured in ohms (Ω); the higher the ohmage, the higher the resistance.

Impedance is in some ways similar to resistance. For one, it is also measured in ohms, and for another, it also represents an opposition to a circuit. The big difference is that impedance varies with frequency, whereas resistance stays the same regardless of the frequencies being passed through the circuit.

Let's think of it this way: A light bulb and a speaker are similar in their opposition to a current; the bulb produces light and heat, and the speaker produces sound as well as some heat. A small light bulb might introduce a 250 Ω resistance. Its resistance will be 250 Ω regardless of the strength or frequency of the current passing through it. A typical loudspeaker might have a nominal impedance of 8 Ω. In use, though, its impedance could vary from 50 Ω (with very high frequency material), all the way down to 2 Ω or less with very low frequency signals. This frequency-dependent variation of ohmage ratings is a type of *reactance*, and a proper impedance rating considers both resistance and reactance.

In terms of real-world applications, a loudspeaker with an 8 Ω rating introduces more opposition to an amplifier's output than a 4 Ω speaker—thus, a 4 Ω speaker will allow an amplifier to put out more power (in terms of watts) than an 8 Ω speaker. If you've read spec sheets for amplifiers, you may have noticed under the category of 'Output Power' something like '50 watts per channel @ 8 Ω, 70 watts per channel @ 4 Ω.'

So why not have 1 Ω or even 1/2 Ω speakers—wouldn't that yield lots more power from amplifiers? In fact, such speakers *would* yield more power, but that extra power wouldn't last for very long before the amplifier self-destructed or shut down. When there's little or no opposition to an amplifier's output, there's nothing to dissipate all the power it's producing. Con-

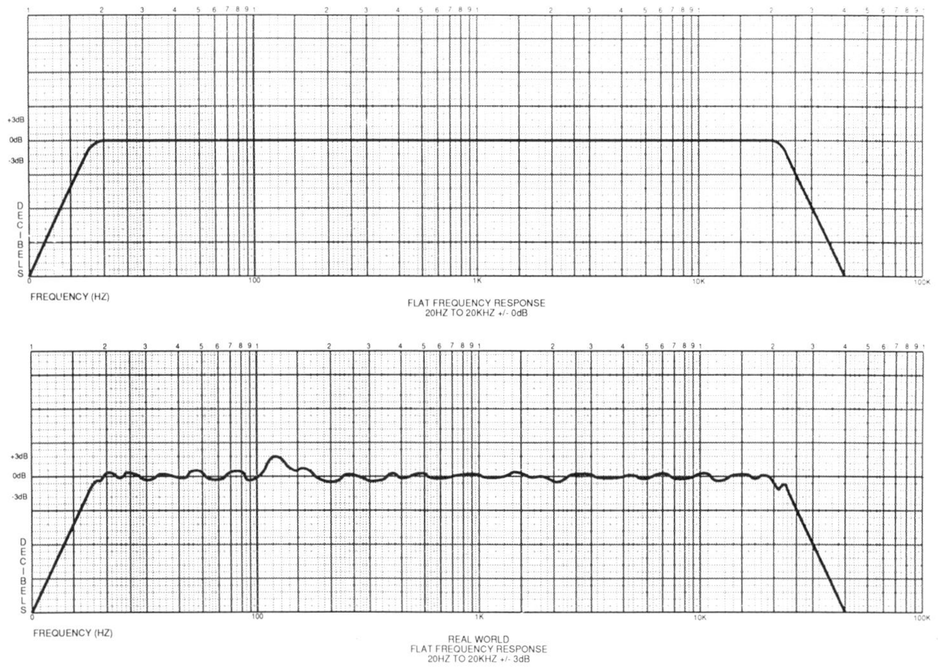

FREQUENCY (HZ)

FLAT FREQUENCY RESPONSE
20HZ TO 20KHZ +/- 0dB

FREQUENCY (HZ)

REAL WORLD
FLAT FREQUENCY RESPONSE
20HZ TO 20KHZ +/- 3dB

Figures 5.4a, 5.4b Pefectly 'flat' frequency response (top) is rarely attainable. The lower diagram shows the typical frequency response of a quality analog tape recorder. The 3 dB rise around 130 Hz represents the recorder's 'headbump,' which is an inherent design trade-off for flatter response in the high frequencies.

sequently, the amp overheats and shuts down from having created so much current much like a short-circuit. It used to be that if you turned up an amp without having a speaker attached, meltdown was guaranteed. Today's amps are designed to avoid overheating by switching themselves off.

This unhappy example of malfunction can occur in situations other than amp/speaker setups. In fact, in the world of audio, any *source*—such as an amp, instrument, microphone, mixer output, and so on—must see some type of *load*—such as a speaker, mixer input, amp input, etc.—to work properly. Sources have outputs, which have output impedances, and loads have inputs, which have input impedances. As a general rule of thumb, the load impedance should be equal to or greater than the source impedance. Impedance, by the way, can also be referred to as Z, as in *low-Z* and *high-Z* (low- and high-impedance).

To bring us back to the real world, let's look at the type of source and load impedances we musicians are likely to encounter.

Line Impedances. There are two camps of line impedances, high-Z and low-Z. As we'll see, a lot of equipment falls into both camps. Remember these are line impedances—microphones are a different kettle of fish, as we'll see below.

Much personal recording gear (including most products by Fostex, Tascam, and others) operates at –10 dBV levels, and has high-Z line inputs and outputs. By high-Z, we're talking about input (load) impedances of 10 to 150 kΩ (thousand ohms) or greater, and output (source) impedances of 2 to 10 kΩ.

These devices are limited to output cable lengths of less than 10 to 15 meters (33 to 50 feet); that's because they are more susceptible to losses of high-frequency information, and other problems induced by *cable capacitance* (discussed on page 78). If you've ever tried running a cassette deck through some super-long cable and have heard muffled cymbals, dull-sounding guitars, and the like, you've heard this problem.

Professional and broadcast-oriented recording equipment (which usually operates at +4 or +8 dBm levels) can have *either* low-Z or high-Z line inputs, though high-Z are most common. Professional equipment almost always has low-Z line outputs. In this case, low-Z input impedances are usually 600 Ω, and high-Z input impedances are 10 to 25 kΩ. Low-Z output impedances range from about 50 to 600 Ω.

In practice, most of the 'enlightened' manufacturers of consoles design high-Z line inputs for their professional consoles, because these inputs will accept either low- or high-Z source impedances. A few broadcast-oriented companies, such as UREI and Ward-Beck, offer 600 Ω low-Z inputs as standard—but as musicians, unless you've been picking up some obscure ex-military or radio station bargains, you shouldn't run across low-Z line inputs.

Low source (output) impedance signals are much less affected by cable capacitance, and are capable of running through hundreds of meters of cabling without frequency problems. Nonetheless, they can still pick up interference if not *balanced*, as we'll see below.

Microphone Impedances. High-Z mic-

rophones typically have an output impedance of about 2 to 10 kΩ, and low-Z mikes range anywhere from 50 to 600 Ω, with somewhere around 250 Ω as the norm. High-Z mikes are often distinguished by 1/4", guitar-type plugs. Low-Z mikes usually have 3-prong, XLR-type connectors.

High-Z mike inputs are distinguished by 1/4" jacks, and have an impedance of 10 kΩ or greater. Low-Z mike inputs typically have 3-pin XLR connectors, and have a load impedance of 150 to 2000 Ω (600 Ω is average for recording gear).

In practice, most home recordists use low-Z mikes, which are fine since they'll work perfectly in low impedance mike inputs and reasonably well in high impedance inputs. Because mike levels are so low to begin with, though, many people prefer to use a *transformer* when running a low-Z mike into a high-Z input. A low-to-high-Z transformer—a small cylinder-like device which plugs into the mike's cable—will help maximize the mike's performance.

High-Z mikes, on the other hand, will work fine in high-Z inputs, but won't work properly at all in low-Z inputs—they sound distorted and low in level. All in all they're lousy performers when not used with a high-to-low-Z transformer. In addition, most high-Z mikes on the market today tend to be poorer performers than low-Z mikes. So even if you have a ministudio-type recorder/mixer with high-Z 1/4" inputs, you may prefer to select a low-Z mike and use a transformer. More about this on page 62, when we look at microphones.

As with line signals, low-Z mikes are capable of very long cable lengths; high-Z mikes are best restricted to cable lengths of less than 6.5 meters (20 feet).

A Rule Of Thumb. When considering questions of impedance, there's a handy rule of thumb you can use:

Low into high will fly,
high into low won't go!

With this in mind, let's sum up what we need to remember about impedance when choosing and hooking up our recording gear:

- Low-Z source (output) impedances *will work* when fed into high-Z load (input) impedances; high-Z sources *will not* work properly into low-Z loads. In general, you don't have to worry about line impedances, except to remember that high-Z sources can depreciate in quality when run through long cables.
- A transformer is *not* necessary to use a low-Z mike in a high-Z mike input, though it can optimize the mike's performance. A transformer should be used with a high-Z mike being fed into a low-Z mike input.

Unbalanced Vs. Balanced

All analog audio equipment is either *unbalanced* or *balanced* in its design. These terms refer to the way the signals are conducted within and between audio components. A balanced circuit is one which is designed to minimize noise interference by using two circuits, or *conductors* (plus a ground circuit), to carry the audio signal. These two circuits 'balance' each other to

reduce noise. Unbalanced circuits are less expensive to build, since they use a single conductor (plus ground), but are more prone to noise interference.

Does this mean in all cases that balanced gear is necessarily better than unbalanced? Does owning unbalanced gear mean that you'll be plagued by noise and other sonic rubbish?

The answer to both of those questions is a definite "Not necessarily!" There are ways of connecting your equipment which are designed to minimize the chances of *RFI* (radio frequency interference), *ground loops*, and other unwanted noise which can affect both balanced and unbalanced gear. We'll examine those ways starting on page 81.

Typical unbalanced –10 dBV home recording and hi-fi gear is connected with 2-conductor cabling and connectors, using 1/4" 'phone' plugs and jacks (named for the standard connector design used in telephone switchboards). Similar 2-conductor cables with RCA plugs are also common (see page 75). Two small conductor wires are used in 2-conductor cables to carry the electrical signals. One is known as the *hot*, or *positive* (+), conductor; the other is the *ground* conductor.

A cable can be a pretty good antenna for picking up radio stations, CB and police radios, and all sorts of other sources of RFI which are in the air around us. Granted, the mixers, signal processors, and other devices into which we plug cables aren't radios—but they are amplifiers, and low-level RFI (which is typically at –80 up to –30 dB levels) can be picked up by the cables, amplified, and heard by us. The longer the cable, and the lower the audio signal passing through it, the greater the chances of RFI. Because of this, 2-conductor cables usually use the ground wire as a *shield*. The ground wire is twisted and wrapped around the inner hot conductor, and it literally shields it from most RFI. Still, some RFI can pass through.

How Balancing Works. Balanced circuits are designed to 'erase' RFI electronically. They accomplish this in a rather clever way.

Most professionally-oriented +4 and +8 dBm gear has balanced inputs and outputs, using 3-conductor cabling and connectors. The most common connectors are 3-pin XLR (or 'Cannon') plugs and jacks, as well as 3-conductor 1/4" phone plugs and jacks (similar to stereo headphone connectors).

In the balanced circuit, there is the hot (+, or *in-phase*) signal, the *cold* (–, or *out-of-phase*) signal, and the ground (shield) conductor. Both the hot and cold signals are audio signals; the difference between the two is that the cold signal is 180 degrees out of phase with the hot signal. To understand the importance of why these signals are out of phase with each other, let's recall our knowledge of signal phase:

- When two identical, in-phase signals are added together, the summed result is a boosted signal.
- When two identical signals are 180 degrees out of phase with each other, they cancel each other when added together, and no signal is heard.

When hot and cold signals pass through their cabling, they are susceptible to induced noise even though they are both shielded by the ground wire. This noise is the same phase in both the hot and cold conductors, though the actual audio signals remain out of phase.

When the balanced signal reaches an input to a balanced device, there is a circuit at that input which electronically reverses the phase of the cold signal. Then the hot and cold signals—which are now in phase with each other—are added together. The two results of performing this trick are:

- The cancellation of now out-of-phase signals (the RFI).
- The boosting now in-phase signals (the audio carried by both the hot and cold conductors).

In practice, this usually works very well, assuming that everything connected is properly balanced and all cables are well shielded. But even balanced equipment is subject to unwanted noise—we'll examine this further ahead on page 81.

Microphone levels are very low in strength, as we know, and are most prone to letting us hear RFI when amplified. Consequently, many mixers designed for personal recording have balanced mike inputs (even though all of their line ins and outs may be unbalanced).

Mixing and matching balanced and unbalanced gear is sometimes problematic, though it can be done. There are two pri-

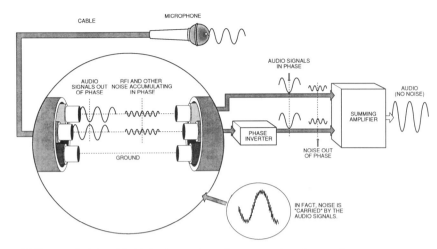

Figure 5.5 The wonderful world of balancing, as shown between a microphone and a mixer input.

mary trade-offs when you connect a balanced device to an unbalanced device: First, the signal may drop about 3 dB in level. Secondly, the circuit between the two devices becomes unbalanced, and all the benefits of balancing are cast to sea. If you can live with these two problems, then no worries, mate. (Since balanced gear is almost always at +4 levels, and unbalanced gear is usually –10, be sure you don't wind up with level-matching problems.)

The interface between balanced and unbalanced gear is usually facilitated by wiring the cold conductor of the balanced cable to ground—some gear is designed to connect 'transparently,' however, and needs no special modifications. Of course, there are various outboard devices which not only balance or unbalance signals, but also match signals levels.

*   *   *   *

We've covered quite a lot of territory in this chapter! Hopefully this technical tutorial will be a useful reference to you as you get deeper into the jungle of recording lingo and concepts. Now let's consider the heart of your studio: The multi-track tape recorder. □

CHAPTER 6: THE TAPE RECORDER

Back in Chapter Two, we learned a few generalizations about tape recorders. We also learned some very specific information about tape heads, and how they can record and play back information stored on magnetic tape. Now we'll go beyond theory, and concentrate on the controls and components of recorders, and their functions.

If you own a multi-track tape recorder, it may be part of an integrated recorder/mixer 'ministudio' (such as a 4- or 12-track cassette), or it may be an independent multi-track recorder, with a separate mixer. In this next section, we'll cover information which will apply to almost any multi-track recorder. If you are using an integrated recorder/mixer, it may be easier to consider your ministudio as two separate sections—a tape recorder and a mixer—that have been permanently connected, or hardwired. Similarly, if you have an independent tape recorder and mixer, yet find the ministudio concept easier to grasp, think of your two units as an all-in-one, with the connection between the two sections made of loose cables, instead of 'hard' wires.

All tape recorders can be broken down into two separate sections, the transport and electronics. The transport is what controls the physical movement of the tape, and the electronics are responsible for all signals entering, leaving, and within the tape machine.

Tape Transport Components

The transport is the system of motors, guides, and other components which move the tape. Cassette and open-reel transports are in fact quite similar to each other. The difference is basically that a cassette is a shell for the tape, and requires no threading of the tape across the heads—since the tape is already attached to both 'reels' within the shell. With that in mind, many transport components are comparable between the two formats.

Take-Up And Supply Reels. These are used to wind and rewind the tape. For cassettes, the take-up and supply sides of the tape are respectively the right and left hubs inside the plastic shell. Open reels sit on what are known as reel platters (also known as reel tables). Hubs and platters are in turn driven by take-up and supply motors (sometimes one motor with a gear). During the play mode, the take-up motor winds the tape slowly onto its reel; in fast-forward the take-up motor kicks into high speed, and winds the tape quickly.

On many open-reel machines, the supply motor supplies a slight amount of back tension to the tape during the play mode; that is, it creates a drag on the tape by holding the tape back slightly, resulting in a smoother, more even tape supply. Otherwise, the supply motor is normally not on, except when the transport is in rewind

mode. At this point, the motor winds the tape quickly back onto the supply reel. The reel holders are used, yes, to hold the reels on the platters.

Depending upon the machine, open-reel multi-tracks are usually designed to operate with 7" or 10.5" maximum-diameter reels (a few of the more professional machines can use reels as large as 12" or even 14", for extended playing time). Some machines, such as the Otari MX-80, allow you to select the reel size, in order to optimize the torque (strength) of the motors when winding and minimize the risk of stretching or otherwise damaging the tape.

Capstan And Pinch-Roller. The capstan and pinch roller move the tape past the heads when recording or playing back. The capstan—either direct-driven or belt-driven by the capstan motor—spins at a constant speed. On some machines it is switched on when tape is loaded, on others the capstan runs all the time.

When play or record modes are engaged, the pinch roller (sometimes called the puck), moves and gently squeezes the tape between itself and the capstan. At this point the capstan is able to move the tape, which is pulled along by the take-up reel. On a cassette transport, the capstan fits in through a hole in the cassette shell, and the pinch-roller and take-up motor function as on an open-reel. Most professional ma-

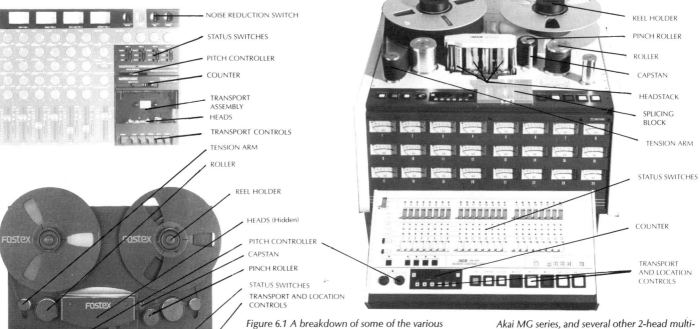

NOISE REDUCTION SWITCH
STATUS SWITCHES
PITCH CONTROLLER
COUNTER
TRANSPORT ASSEMBLY
HEADS
TRANSPORT CONTROLS
TENSION ARM
ROLLER
REEL HOLDER
HEADS (Hidden)
PITCH CONTROLLER
CAPSTAN
PINCH ROLLER
STATUS SWITCHES
TRANSPORT AND LOCATION CONTROLS

REEL HOLDER
PINCH ROLLER
ROLLER
CAPSTAN
HEADSTACK
SPLICING BLOCK
TENSION ARM
STATUS SWITCHES
COUNTER
TRANSPORT AND LOCATION CONTROLS

COUNTER

Figure 6.1 A breakdown of some of the various components found on tape recorders. At top left we see the Tascam Porta Two 4-track cassette recorder/mixer, with its recorder section highlighted. Its basic design is similar to many other ministudios. Beneath it is the Fostex Model 80 1/4" 8-track recorder. Its operation is quite similar to the Tascam 388 and MS16, the Fostex E-8 and E-16, the

Akai MG series, and several other 2-head multi-track recorders. The Otari MX-80 24-track, at right, is shown with its remote controller. Its basic operation is in fact very similar to most other 3-head tape recorders, including: The Tascam 30, 40, 50, and ATR series; the Otari MX and MTR series; the Studer A series; and the Revox C series.

chines are designed so that the pinch roller is on the oxide side of the tape, with the capstan against the backing of the tape. The Fostex 80, and others (including cassette machines), have an opposite arrangement.

There are a few professional machines on the market, such as the Otari MTR-100, which have a capstan though not a pinch roller. These machines have extremely high-grade, microprocessor-tensioned reel motors, and some people feel that this approach helps avoid physical trauma to the tape's oxide—which can be a source of tape dropouts and result in a loss of portions of the recording.

Tape Guides And Lifters. These are the components which hold the tape on its proper course past the heads. Open-reel machines use various designs to accomplish this; cassette machines use guides along the edges of the heads.

Tape lifters are exclusive to open-reel machines. Normally, in stop or high-speed wind modes, the lifters are engaged, keeping the tape off the surface of the heads. This is to reduce headwear, and also to reduce friction on the tape.

The lifters can be withdrawn by using the *tape lifter defeat*, or *tape cue* switch. In a high speed wind, this allows you to hear, or *cue*, the program material on the tape as it whizzes by the heads. In the stop mode, defeating the lifters allows you to hear the program for editing (see page 101). Many cassette machines have a cue and *review* mode; see below under the descriptions of fast forward and rewind.

Open-reel machines also have *tension arms*: These provide additional tension on the tape while it travels between the reels. Frequently a switch is attached to the right-hand tension arm, which turns the reel motors off when the tape has finished and runs off the reel. This switch can also turn off the capstan motor, when there's no tape threaded. A few machines, most notably those made by Studer/ReVox, use a photo-

sensitive switch to accomplish these functions: As tape passes by the heads it interrupts the beam of light, and keeps the motors on. When the tape runs out, the beam can be sensed and the motors turn off.

The 'auto shut-off' feature of cassette machines works by sensing an increase in either the tension of the tape or of the reel motors—both of which occur when a side of a cassette finishes.

The Headstack. We first encountered the headstack in Chapter Two—and we learned that all recorders have an erase head, a record head, and a play head (or a combination record/play head).

The PortaTwo and the Model 80 pictured above are both 2-head machines, with an erase head and a combination record/play head. The Otari is a 3-head machine, and is capable of monitoring the recording as it's being recorded.

Many open-reel machines have a manually- or automatically-engaged *head shield*. This is designed to prevent stray electro-magnetic signals or impulses from being recorded or played back.

Caution! It's easy, when using a machines with a manually-controlled shield, to forget that it may be covering the heads. Make sure that it's out of the way when threading the tape!

Using The Transport Controls

Transport controls can be either a 'feather-touch' *solenoid* or a *mechanical* 'piano key' design. Solenoid controls use little electrically-activated plungers (solenoids) to change the transport modes, and the mechanical design operates with gears, levers, and other manually-driven components. A cassette machine variation on mechanical transport controls is known as a 'soft-touch' control. This is a light mechanical switch which engages a motor, which in turn moves the heads against the heads.

While we're all familiar with the standard

transport controls of *play*, *stop*, *rewind*, *fast-forward*, and *record*, here are a few tips that will help you achieve optimum performance from your tape transport.

Spare The Capstan. On some tape recorders (open-reel and cassette) the capstan stops turning in stop mode, and in other machines it continues to run. If the capstan in your machine continues to run, you may want to extend the life of the capstan motor by doing one of two things when not using the machine for ten minutes or longer:

- Turn the machine off.
- If it's an open-reel machine, releasing the tension on the tension arms—by adjusting the reels of tape—will trigger a switch on many machines, which turns off the capstan motor.

Watch For Slack. Have you ever had a cassette tape 'eaten' up by a tape recorder, and had to retrieve reams of cassette tape from the inner bowels of a transport? This unhappy ritual of 'feeding the cassette god' is related to two problems. The first is that the heads and pinch roller need to be *cleaned*—this is described on page 86, and should be performed before *every* session.

The second problem is slack tape within the cassette shell. Before inserting a cassette, it's necessary to take up the slack. The procedure is to hold your finger tip or pencil-like device in one hub, while winding the tape taut with another finger tip or 'p.l.d.'.

With open-reel machines, it's also necessary to ensure that there's no excess slack in the tape before engaging play (or any mode). Some machines, such as the very professional Otari MTR-100 or Soundcraft Saturn, have *constant-tension*, and take up the slack automatically. Otherwise, before starting your session, hold one reel still, and pull the tape taut with the other reel.

Cueing The Tape. If your cassette machine has a *cue* mode—usually entered by pressing play along with fast forward—the tape will make contact with the heads as the headstack engages against the tape. This allows you to listen to the tape as it winds. On open-reel machines the tape lifter defeat switch will accomplish the same thing, though the headstack doesn't move; rather, the lifters move the tape against the head. What you're listening to will likely sound like chipmunks in mating season, but it's still useful for finding a place on the tape.

If the cassette machine has a cue function, it likely has a *review* function, which—like cue—engages the record/play head and allows you to hear those mating *rodentia* noises, only in reverse. The lifter defeat is used on an open-reel machine to hear the tape at high-speed rewind.

Be sure to cue the tape only when necessary, since the extra friction can cause tape dropouts, particularly after many passes.

'Toggling.' Some older open-reel machines, such as the TEAC 3440, should be manually slowed down when changing from a high speed wind in fast forward or reverse. This is done by pressing either stop or the opposite control of the direction of the tape. In other words, if the tape is in a high speed rewind, 'toggling' back and forth between stop or fast forward and reverse will slow the tape as you approach the place you wish to stop or play the tape.

The Edit Switch. This switch, found exclusively on many open-reel machines, simply turns off the take-up reel motor. Used for discarding lengths of tape while editing (see page 101), edit is engaged along with the play mode, and causes tape to be sent past the heads and then 'dumped.'

Caution! In some older machines, this switch may also function during fast forward. Beware, unless spooling up 2500' of tape off your studio floor sounds like a nice way to spend an evening!

Speed Selection. Some machines allow you to choose the record/play speed of the tape. On multi-track cassette machines, if there's a choice it's between 1⅞ or 3¾ ips (4.8 or 9.5 cm/s); on open-reel machines oriented towards personal multi-tracking, the choices are usually between 7½ and 15 ips (19 and 38 cm/s). Remember that a tape recorded at one speed must be played back at the same speed, unless you're out for special effects.

Pitch Control. Also known as a *varispeed* or *VSO* (vari-speed oscillator), this allows the tape speed to be varied, usually ±10% maximum. A pitch control can serve a number of purposes:

- The pitch of material being played back can be adjusted in order to match the tuning of a new instrument being added (such as a piano, which would be not so easy to retune for a quick take!).
- The playback speed can be adjusted to match the record speed. When powering a multi-track by battery, the charge can drop over time. The resulting recording, which would be made at slightly too slow a speed, would sound sped up and high in pitch when played back (this will also change the pitch).
- The tempo of the playback can be adjusted to suit one's taste.
- Special effects can be created by changing the pitch while recording or playing back.

Caution! Always remember to return the pitch control to the *off* position when finished, otherwise your next recording could be made at the wrong pitch. (Assuming you played it back at the same speed at which it was recorded, however, the performance could be salvaged.)

The Tape Counter And Autolocator

Nearly every multi-track has some form of tape counter, which keeps track of the position of the tape and can be reset to '0' at the appropriate place—usually the beginning of a song or in the middle of a section you're rehearsing. There are basically two types:

- An *arbitrary counter* is just a series of numbers which roll by, such as '000' to '999.' These can be either mechanical like a car's odometer or electronic in operation with an LED or fluorescent readout. While arbitrary counters provide a reference guide, they don't tell you anything about timing.
- A *real-time counter* tells you, with generally high accuracy, how much time worth of tape—in minutes and seconds—has passed since the '00:00' mark. Real-time counters are almost always electronic.

Memory counters usually have a *zero shut-off* function, which turns the transport off when the tape rewinds to the mark. It's becoming more common to find much more elaborate memory functions, however. Many units can *return* or *search to zero.*

Still other units boast an internal or external *autolocator*, which allows additional memory, or *cue* points to be stored and then sought. Aside from being able to store locations on the tape, autolocation functions include:

- The ability to *shuttle* between any two points. This feature starts the deck playing at point 'A,' then causes the transport to rewind back to point 'A' after it reaches point 'B'—a very handy feature for rehearsing overdubs with segments of music.
- *Auto punch-in and -out.* As we'll learn about on page 91, you can enter and leave the record mode for any given track by 'punching in' and 'punching out' while the tape is running. Some autolocators let you program such points in time.

The rapid drop in price of computer memory has meant that many manufacturers can offer autolocation features built-in to their products. There are some very powerful external autolocators made by Fostex, Otari, Tascam, and others.

Also growing in popularity is an *Edit Decision List* (EDL) computer, or *editor*: These are external computers which carry out extremely complex autolocation functions. EDLs have been around for years in the video world, and as video and audio continue to merge, we should see more of this approach. See page 123 for more on this topic.

Tape Recorder Electronics

Moving tape around is one essential function of a tape recorder. Other essential functions are to receive electronic signals, record them, and play them back. The components involved in these roles comprise the 'electronics' of the tape recorder. True, the reel motors, autolocators, and capstan motors, are electronic components—but since they are involved in the transport of the tape, and not in the actual recording process, they're considered to be part of the mechanical tape transport.

Just as with transport components, not all machines will have all of the following components. Use an owner's manual, if you are comparing this list with your own machine, and it will help you to establish terminology and component discrepancies.

The tape heads, incidentally, are considered to be both electronic and transport components. Having covered them earlier, we'll leave them out of this section.

Noise Reduction Switch. Almost all the recorder/mixers, along with some open-reel multi-track machines, include some form of noise reduction. Noise reduction reduces the tape hiss inherent in magnetic recording. This switch enables or disables the noise reduction circuitry. Some machines also allow the noise reduction on a single track to be defeated, which is most useful when performing tape sync (page 111).

Many open-reel tape recorders are used without noise reduction, or can be used in conjunction with an 'outboard' noise reduction system.

Input Level Controls. These allow the user to modify the recording level of the signal entering the tape deck. On many multi-track machines, such as the Fostex 80 and the Tascam 38, there are only internal fine-adjustment controls for this function, designed for the technician. The Otari MX-80 has these controls accessible from the front of the machine. It also has switches for −10 dBV or +4 dBm operation (see page 19 for an explanation of operating levels).

Most 4-track recorder/mixers don't allow a separate adjustment of the recording level for each track other than what the built-in mixer provides. The AMR MCR-4 4-track cassette recorder and the Audio-Technica RMX-64 recorder/mixer are two notable exceptions to this rule—they allow you to adjust the record level of the individual tracks, independent of the settings of the mixer.

On some 2-track machines, there are two sets of input controls: one for the line input level, and the other set to adjust the input level of microphones.

Output Level Controls. These allow the adjustment of the output level of the tape machine. But as with the input level controls, many machines have only an internal adjustment of the output level.

If you are using a recorder/mixer, don't confuse this with any of the *mixer* output controls on your machine. In fact, there are no recorder/mixers (at time of publication) with external tape output level controls.

Sync Output Level Control. When syncing gear to tape, it can be useful, and sometimes necessary, to adjust the output level of the sync track. A sync output level control is really just a tape track output level control for one track, and the Tascam PortaTwo and Yamaha MTX2 are two ministudios which offer this control.

Level Meters. We learned on page 21

that meters are of several different styles and can have averaging and/or peak ballistics. Whatever the design, your tape recorder's meters are vital for minimizing noise and distortion.

The meters are directly linked to the status switches.

Status Switches. Sometimes called the *mode* or *electronics* switches, the status switches are the controls which determine what's going on at the heads, as well as the input and monitor (or output) stages of the tape recorder.

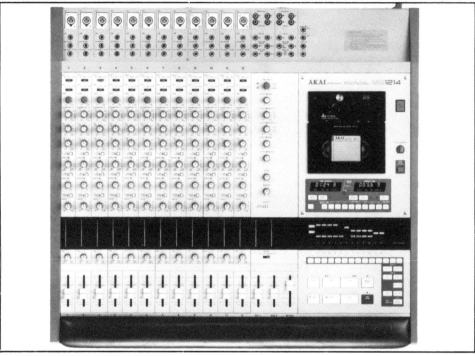

Figure 6.2 *The Akai MG1214 recorder/mixer records 12 audio tracks, one sync track, and one 'control' track (for autolocating) on special 1/2" audio cassettes.*

There are three types of status switches:

- *Mike/line input select* switches.
- *Record enable* switches.
- *Tape monitor mode* switches.

Mike/Line Input Select. Some machines, almost exclusively 2-track open-reel or cassette, have a *mike/line input select* switch. This allows you to chose whether the input to the machine is from a microphone or the line connected to it, usually from a mixer. If your machine has this switch, then a microphone can be connected directly to the tape recorder without a mixer between them. Please note that many recorder/mixers have mike/line switches, though these are for their *mixer* inputs.

None of the contemporary multi-track open-reel machines have mike/line switches. Their only inputs are line inputs, designed to receive a signal from the mixer.

Record Enable. When multi-track recording, in addition to a record transport switch, we need to chose *which* tracks are to be recorded. This is done with the *record enable* switches, and there's one for each track. These switches should be in the *safe* position when a track is being played back normally or in sync. That's track sync, by the way, and not tape sync, which we just discussed—see page 9 and below if you need a refresher on sync mode.

Should you wish to record on a track, the

switch should be in the *ready* position. This doesn't actually start the recording, even if the tape is playing, since the record button has to be 'hit.' On many machines, when the ready mode is engaged an LED will flash, showing that the machine is ready to record a track. When the record button is consequently engaged, the same LED will stay lit, to indicate that a recording is taking place.

All multi-track machines have record enable switches.

Tape Monitor Mode. These switches, one for each channel, allow you to select whether you're listening to the track's input, the track's output, or the track's synced output. We'll explore these options in just a moment.

Not all machines have individual tape monitor mode switches. Many (including all recorder/mixers) select the modes automatically as we'll also learn.

Tape Recorder Monitor Modes

There are three main stages of multi-track recording. They are:

- Recording.
- Overdubbing.
- Playback.

Multi-track recorders have three different *monitor modes* which allow us to hear what's going on during these three different stages. Let's explore this a little further.

In the recording stage, we need to be able to hear the instruments (or microphones) we're recording. In other words, we need to be able to hear the input to any given track or group of tracks we're recording.

In the overdubbing stage, we need to hear the playback of previously recorded tracks, as well as the input to any new tracks we're recording. As we learned back on page 9, those previously recorded tracks must be played back in sync with the new tracks. ('Bouncing,' or 'ping-ponging' tracks

together, is also an overdubbing technique.)

Finally, during the playback stage, all we need is to hear each of the tracks played back from the tape machine. We no longer need to hear any inputs to the tape machine, nor do those tracks need to be in sync with any inputs.

In order to monitor the tape recorder during these three stages, all multi-track recorders are designed to be able to operate in three different monitor modes. They are:

- *Repro* (reproduce) mode. This is for playing back tracks when no recording or overdubbing is taking place, during the playback stage.
- *Sync* (synchronization) mode, sometimes called *sel-rep*, for *selective reproduce*, or *sel-sync*, for *selective sync*. This mode is used to hear previously recorded tracks as they're played back during overdubbing.
- *Input* mode, which is used for any tracks being recorded—whether they are the first tracks to be recorded, or whether they are going to be overdubs with previous tracks.

Let's look at each of these monitor modes, and see how they operate.

Reproduce Mode. This is selected when you want to just listen to a track or group of tracks. There are a few different ways to select this mode, depending upon the tape recorder or recorder/mixer in question. Many recorder/mixers and open-reel multi-tracks *automatically* select repro mode when none of the tracks are record enabled. In other words, if all the record enable switches are set to 'safe,' all the tracks are automatically set to repro mode, and are able to be played back normally. Two-head machines (including recorder/mixers) play back the tracks from the combination record/play head, and 3-head machines use the playback head.

Some tape machines, such as the Otari MX-80, allow you to select repro mode individually for each track. For most musicians' applications, however, automatic selection is just fine.

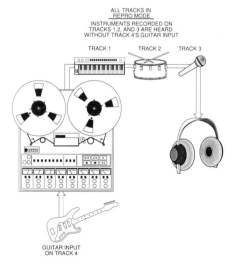

Figure 6.3 *Repro mode.*

Sync Mode. This mode is selected when previously recorded tracks are to be played back in sync with a track or group of tracks about to be overdubbed. (Don't confuse this with 'synchronizing' drum machines and other equipment to the multi-track; we're talking about 'track sync,' which we learned about on page 9.) It's also selected when two or more tracks are being 'bounced' together onto one new track, to make more tracks available. In other words, any time existing tracks must be in sync with a new track, the sync mode must be selected.

On some open-reel multi-track machines, there is an actual 'sync' switch for each channel. On most machines, however—including most recorder/mixers—the sync mode is selected automatically whenever one or more tracks are put into record. Then whichever tracks are *not* in record are played back off the record head in sync with the new tracks being recorded. Synced tracks are played back from either:

- The record head on 3-head machines, or
- The record/play head on 2-head machines and recorder/mixers.

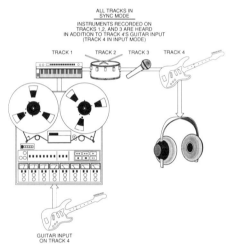

Figure 6.4 *Sync mode.*

Input Mode. Whenever we wish to record a track, we should select input mode for that track. This may get a bit tricky, but here's why: Since the track has yet to exist on tape, we can't hear it by playing back the tape. Consequently, we must listen to the input to that track. For example, let's say we want to record a guitar on track 1. Since we have yet to record that track—which would allow us to play back the track in either sync or repro mode—we are able to hear the guitar by listening to the input to track 1.

We *could* monitor instruments or microphones about to be recorded by listening to their mixer inputs. But there's a problem: Many mixers and recorder/mixers allow us to monitor *either* the inputs to the mixer, *or* the outputs of the tape machine—not both at once. If we only listened to the mixer's inputs, we wouldn't be able to hear any previous recorded tracks—which would prevent us from being able to overdub. So consequently, it's common engineering practice to listen to the outputs of the tape machine. And if we have to listen to the channel outputs of the tape machine, the only way we can hear tracks we're recording or are about to record is to listen to the input to those tracks!

That's why all multi-track machines have an input mode. The input mode allows us to

hear, through the channel outputs of the tape recorder, any new tracks about to be recorded.

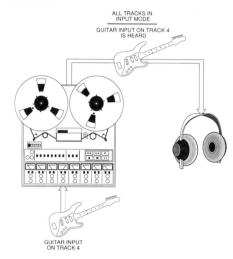

Figure 6.5 *Input mode.*

All recorder/mixers and most open-reel recorders will automatically switch a track to input mode once you switch the track's record enable to 'ready,' and press record on the transport. You needn't press record and play together at this point, if you just want to hear the input. Thus, the source can be heard, in the input mode. Some machines, such as the Otari MkIII-8, have manual switching, as well as a 'standby' mode, which enables automatic switching whenever a track is in 'record ready.'

Monitor Modes In Action. Here's a quick example of how monitor modes might be used during the overdub stage of a typical recording session.

Let's say we're making a 4-track recording. If tracks 1, 2, and 3 have been recorded, and we wish to add a keyboard to track 4, we need to be able to hear the keyboard. This is done by:

1. Listening to the tape machine's outputs (1-4).
2. Putting track 4 into record, which should automatically select input mode for track 4, and automatically select sync mode for tracks 1 to 3.
3. If the machine doesn't have automatic monitor switching, input and sync modes should be manually selected.

Since we're listening to the *input* to track 4, we're able to hear the keyboard source as well as tracks 1, 2, and 3.

When the tape rolls, by pressing play and record together, the keyboard on track 4 can be recorded, and track 1 to 3 can be heard back in perfect sync. Finally, having made a satisfactory recording, all the tracks can be put into the 'record safe' setting. This should automatically switch all tracks to repro mode, allowing all four tracks to be heard. If not, select 'all repro' and you'll be ready for playback.

* * * *

Before we move on to the 2-track mixdown recorder and then the mixing console, let's recap some of the important things we've learned about the tape recorder:

- The transport and transport controls are responsible for the movement of the tape across the heads and back and forth from the reels.
- The electronics pass the signals in and out of the tape recorder, all the way to the heads, where the signals are electromagnetically recorded and played back from the tape.
- All multi-track recorders have similar-functioning status switches, to enable or disable record functions on the different tracks. The tracks of a multi-track recorder are also able to operate in one of three monitor modes: repro, sync, or input.

The 2-Track Mixdown Recorder

When you finish making a multi-track recording, you certainly want to be able to listen to the fruits of your creativity. One way to do this is by playing back the recording through your mixer (or recorder/mixer), and making all the desired adjustments—fading in and out of certain tracks, raising the level of the vocal tracks, panning the guitar solo from left to right, and so on. But what if you wish to play back your recording without having to make continuous adjustments? Or what if you want to create a finished product that someone else can listen to on a cassette deck, open-reel, or even on a phonograph or a CD player?

The solution is to make a *mixdown* of your multi-track tape: The multi-track recording is played back and recorded onto a 2-track stereo mixdown deck, while the tracks are mixed down and all necessary adjustments are made.

There are several different types of machines that can be used as mixdown decks. Perhaps the only trait they share is that they're all 2-track machines—since stereo is the standard medium for almost all music production. The various mixdown formats include:

- Stereo (2-track) cassette.
- Open-reel 2-track.
- Video cassette—both digitally-encoded and 'Hi-Fi Stereo.'
- Digital audio tape (DAT).

Stereo Cassette. A regular cassette is perhaps the most common final product to come out of most personal studios, though it's clear that digital machines are going to be the long-term systems of choice. Nonetheless, a quality cassette deck is relatively inexpensive, and if you give someone a cassette of your work you can rest assured that they'll have something on which to play it back.

Ideally, a mixdown cassette deck should have three heads, so that you can monitor the recording whilst it's being made—but three heads are a luxury, not a necessity. What *is* a necessity is noise reduction. Your cassette deck should have Dolby B, as well as either Dolby C or dbx (we'll discuss noise reduction systems ahead on page 59). All current 2-track cassette machines record at 1⅞ inches per second (ips).

Cassette mixdowns do have their limitations. For one, few cassette decks are able to deliver the kind of quality needed from which to *master* a recording, for LP, CD, or other mass-duplication. Secondly, *editing* a cassette tape by splicing the tape—to re-order songs, alter verses, eliminate un-wanted noise before and after songs, and so forth—is just a bit easier than performing microsurgery on a flea. Tape editing is per-formed with a razor blade and splicing tape, and the 1/8" width of a cassette tape is very tricky to edit. For this reason, many personal recordists, and most professionals, turn to a 2-track open-reel machine for mixdown.

2-Track Open-Reel. While open-reel machines can be quarter- or half-track (as we learned in Chapter Two), the latter offers better performance and is the mixdown standard.

The standard tape speed can be anything from 3¾ ips all the way up to 30 ips; the most common mixdown speed is 15 ips. Some professional studios use Dolby A or Dolby SR for 2-track noise reduction (page 60), but most personal studios can't afford such systems. Finally, some studios use 1/2" 2-track mixdown machines for optimum results, but 1/4" is the standard affordable medium. Don't be confused by all these options: The most common open-reel 2-track mixdown format is 1/4" half-track, at 15 or 30 ips with no noise reduction.

Open-reel machines usually offer better performance than most cassette decks, but their greatest advantage is that it's easy to edit 1/4" open-reel tape. In Chapter Twelve we'll take a look at editing techniques.

Up to this point, we've been talking about analog (non-digital) tape machines. Some professional studios use digital open-reel machines for mixdown, and most offer the advantage of superb sonic performance along with the ability to edit. We'll talk a bit about the digital process further ahead on page 124, but for now it appears that open-reel digital machines may never become popular in personal studios: They're very expensive, and alternate digital formats such as DAT may preclude their mass acceptance.

Digitally-Encoded Video Cassette. In the early 1980s, devices known as *digital proces-sors*—such as the Sony PCM F-1, 501, and the Technics SRV-100—came into the market. These processors are able to con-vert incoming audio signals into digital

Figure 6.6 Otari's MX-55 2-track mastering deck.

Wow And Flutter

Wow and flutter specs refer to audible fluctuations in the travel of the tape. *Wow* is an average of any fluctuations which occur at a low-frequency. Tape which has been stretched has an audible wow, which tends to make recording sound as if the entire pitch of the music being played is rising and falling at a slow rate.

A good example of wow is the type of pitch variations one can hear when a wind-up gramophone begins to slow down. *Flutter* is similar, though it's heard as a rapid pitch variation. If there's audi-ble flutter with a tape deck, a good way to hear it is to listen to a single, sustained piano note. It will tend to waver quickly, rather than sound like a constant, even note.

Wow and flutter are measured as an average percentage, usually to a standard known as *NAB* or *IEC/ANSI* weighted—the letters represent various organizations, and 'weighted' means adjusted to a scale which represents human hearing. If the machine is a two-speed unit, the wow and flutter will be less at the higher speed. A reasonable spec for most cassette trans-ports is +/- 0.1% (peak, or maximum), and most open-reel machines should offer performance of at least +/-0.06%. Less is better.

codes. An affordable storage and playback medium for these codes is a standard 1/2" VHS or Beta video cassette recorder (VCR).

These units record the digital code on the same tracks normally used for the video signal, and they do it with 14-*bit* fidelity (the Sonys are switchable to 16-bit as well). We'll explain 'bits' on page 125, but for now let's say that a 14- or 16-bit digital recording sounds superb, with no added tape hiss, immeasur-able wow and flutter, and so on. These pro-cessors, in conjunction with a VCR, are per-fect for making live 2-track recordings, such as classical music. If you want to mix and match choruses and verses, however, you'll need an open-reel machine—unless you invest a small fortune in a digital editing system.

Finally, there's one other major draw-back with this system: With the advent of DAT machines, production of these en-coders was discontinued.

Hi-Fi Stereo Video Cassette. This can be found in all three formats of video cassette recorders (VCRs): VHS, Beta, and 8 mm. Many musicians have taken to Hi-Fi Stereo recording, particularly with VHS and Beta, as a relatively inexpensive way to make very high quality mixdowns. The VHS and Beta Hi-Fi systems aren't digital, though they sound close; 8 mm Hi-Fi is in fact a type of digital recording, though of fairly low quality—few people are mixing down to 8 mm Hi-Fi.

VHS and Beta Hi-Fi recording takes ad-vantage of the VCR's video head design. VCRs use rotating record and playback heads: By using a rotating head against tape moving in the opposite direction an ap-parent super-high tape speed of over *200 inches per second* is created. In addition, the Hi-Fi process encodes the signal on recording and decodes it on playback, to further improve the sound.

Just as with a digitally-encoded VCR recording, a Hi-Fi recording can't be edited. And because the medium is still analog, copying tapes or using two machines to assemble a finished master tape with the songs in the right order will build up extra hiss. Nonetheless, Hi-Fi Stereo VCRs are much less money than a quality open-reel machine, and sound better than most.

DAT. For the average personal studio, a promising medium is the *DAT—digital audio tape*—format. Also known as *R-DAT*—for *R*otary head DAT—the format seems destined to play large role in the personal recording industry.

A DAT cassette resembles an analog cas-sette, but it's much smaller and has a protec-tive cover over the tape, similar to a video cassette. The heads rotate like VCR heads, and the signal is encoded digitally. In func-tion and performance, a DAT machine is rather like a combined digital processor and VCR, though the medium seems as if it will enjoy much broader support than did the processors.

When the DAT format was announced in 1986, a number of political action groups sprang into action, since, they argued, a DAT machine can make perfect copies of compact disks and thus threaten the record industry. These groups proposed a 'copy-protection system' for the DAT format, but the U.S. National Bureau of Standards effec-tively put an end to copy code protection by revealing audible and operational problems with the scheme.

Long-time observers note that technical progress is a very difficult thing to halt, and that grim predictions which may accom-pany any new development may not always ring true: Television, as one example, was originally viewed as a threat to the Holly-wood motion picture industry—and lobby-ists in the late 1940s worked hard to impede television's acceptance.

Like video tape, DAT can't be physically spliced, though relatively inexpensive video-like editors are on the horizon. Some manufacturers are also discussing the pos-sibilities of *multi-track* DATs. If some none-too-slight technical hurdles can be surmounted, the $300 battery-powered ministudios of the future may be 8-track DAT recorder/mixers!

*　　*　　*

Several years back, when the most popu-lar home recording multi-track tape re-corder was the 4-track Teac 3440S, many people managed without a mixing console, since that tape recorder had a simple mixer built-in. For people working with other machines, it was necessary to build a simple mixer, or shell out a small fortune for a pro-fessional mixer.

The home recording market has expe-rienced some drastic price reductions, however: Many people are able to afford independent recorders and mixers, and even the simplest recorder/mixer mini-studio has a more advanced mixer than was found in the 3440S. In this next chapter, we'll take an in-depth look at the mixer, and gain insights into your specific mixer, whether it's part of a recorder/mixer, or an independent console. □

Often referred to as a mixing *console*, *board*, or *desk*, a mixer by any other name is still a mixer. And true to its name, a mixer's primary function is:

- To combine—or *mix*—audio signals together in a controllable manner, with adjustable input and output levels.

In addition, mixers are used:

- To route the signals as desired, to tape machine inputs, outboard effects devices, monitor amplifiers; from tape machine outputs to headphones, and the like.
- To alter the signals, with built-in equalization, and occasionally other effects.

Whether stand-alone or built-in—as found in an integrated recorder/mixer—your mixer is the key to controlling your recording. Just several years ago, many musicians recording at home worked without mixers, or used the rudimentary mixers included in their open-reel 4-tracks. Nowadays mixers and recorder/mixer ministudios are affordable. And not only do they assist your creative potential—they're a lot of fun to use!

In this section, as throughout this book, the concepts of the mixer will apply to both integrated recorder/mixers and independent mixers. While it is impossible to discuss every available piece of gear, the examples provided should by and large apply to most contemporary mixers.

* * * *

With all its knobs, switches, meters, and other bells and whistles, a mixer may seem intimidating at first. The fact is, however, that it's relatively easy to understand how mixers work, since most mixers are a series of repeating controls. Once you really understand your own mixer, you're capable of understanding many other mixers.

What tends to affect the overall size and intimidation factor of mixers is the number of input channels. Input channels are the sections of a mixer which determine:

- How many input sources (microphones, instruments, etc.) can be accommodated at once.
- How those sources' signals are affected (equalization and effects controls).
- Where the signals are going (to which track or output of the mixer).

Because each of a mixer's inputs are usually the same, if you understand one input, you'll understand them all. For example, let's say you own an 8-channel mixer, with 148 controls total. At first, that may seem like quite a formidable number of buttons, sliders, and knobs to master. But if each one of the eight input channels has 15 controls, once you know the functions of those 15 controls, you'll know 120 of the mixer's 148 controls.

Mixers are *modular* or *non-modular* in design. A modular mixer has individual modules for each of its input channels, so that the electronic components for any individual channel can be removed by pulling the module from the mixer's *mainframe*.

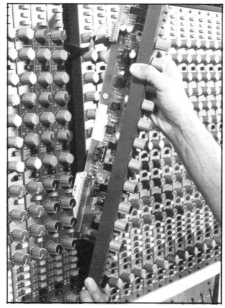

Figure 7.1 An input module of a TAC Scorpion mixer.

The inputs of non-modular mixers are all built into a single chassis. With modular mixers, you have the advantage of being able to remove a faulty input and still run the board. There's a price for such flexibility, however—a modular mixer can cost as much as 40% more than a similarly equipped non-modular mixer. (If you have a modular mixer, be sure to consult your manual before removing a module—it may be necessary to switch off the power to avoid damage, or screws may need to be loosened to release the module.)

A mixer can be specialized for theatre, live concert, film, and other applications. The mixers that interest us, as recording musicians, are specialized for multi-track recording.

In the next few pages we're going to look at some mixer basics, which could apply to any application. Following that, we'll explore those mixers which are designed for multi-track recording. As we'll learn, there are different approaches to building a multi-track mixer—being able to understand how mixers operate in general will help you to master your own mixer.

Mixer Basics

Musicians are often familiar with the fundamentals of mixer design and operation—for many, it comes with the territory of being an all-in-one performer/engineer/roadie/manager. If you have some mixer background, great; you may wish to skip ahead to page 31. If not, or if you could use a bit of brushing-up, the following should serve as a useful reference.

A Simple Mono Mixer. A rudimentary mixer has at least two inputs, each with a *gain*, or volume control, and one output. Let's imagine a very simple mixer, along with a block diagram description of how the signals flow through it (Figure 7.3).

This mixer is quite straightforward, as one can see. There are four inputs, and a single output. This is similar to many mixers designed for live performance. With this type of mixer, for example, up to four keyboards can be mixed together at once, each with individual level control.

Figure 7.2 Soundcraft's 6000 mixer. Generally, large boards have many more things in common with smaller mixers than they have differences. Once you understand the concepts and components discussed in this chapter, you'll be able to understand the basic operation of many mixers—from those found in ministudios, to full-blown professional consoles. The Soundcraft 6000 shown has 24 group outputs (the faders at right), a 24-return 'split' tape monitor (above the groups), and an integral patch bay.

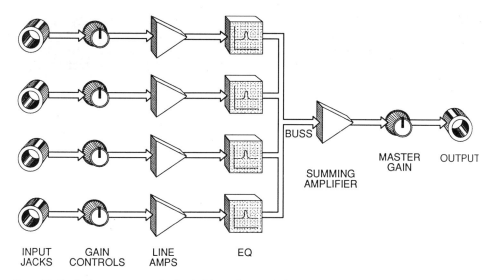

Figure 7.3 The basic components of a simple 4-input, 1-output mixer.

INPUT JACKS   GAIN CONTROLS   LINE AMPS   EQ   BUSS   SUMMING AMPLIFIER   MASTER GAIN   OUTPUT

Most basic mixers include the following components:

- *Input and output jacks*, for all mike-, instrument-, and line-level connections.
- *Channel gain controls*. A gain control (sometimes inaccurately called a volume control) is used to adjust channel levels. A rotary gain control is also known as a *potentiometer*, or *pot*. A straightline sliding pot is usually referred to as a *linear fader*, or just *fader*.
- *Preamps and summing amplifiers*. These are part of the internal circuitry. The preamps (short for *preamplifier*) take a relatively low level signal, such as a microphone, and bring it up to the level of the internal operation of the console. Summing amps are a bit different: They electronically *sum* together signals, and provide an amplified output. Some types of summing amps are also known as *buffer* amps. This output isn't amplified enough to be connected to a loudspeaker, but it does give the signal enough gain to travel moderate distances through cabling to effects, other amplifiers, and the like.
- *Buss*. In electronics, a *buss* (sometimes spelled *bus*) is a wire or circuit to which other circuits are commonly joined. In mixing console lingo, a buss is an output to which signals are sent—usually signals from input channels. Some mixers have output level controls for their busses, though many don't—especially most recorder/mixers. We'll run into busses quite a bit as we explore more advanced mixers.
- *Master gain*. This is the master volume control for all the inputs feeding it, via a buss. When the master gain fader or pot is off, all the inputs are off, and there is no output from the mixer. There are mixers without a master gain—where the output level of the mixer is the total summed level of the buss—but in most real-world applications, a master control of some sort is necessary.

A Simple Stereo Mixer. The previous components and block diagram represent a basic, no frills, 4-input, 1-output mixer. This type of mixer, in engineering lingo, is called a 4x1 mixer (pronounced: *four by one*).

With just a single monaural output this mixer *can't* be used to make a stereo (2-track) or multi-track recording. With a

stereo mixer, however, we have two output channels, and can balance a source between the left or right channels.

If, for example, we wanted to do a live (no overdubs) 2-track recording of a stereo drum machine, an acoustic guitar, and a vocal, we would need a mixer with four inputs and two outputs, as shown in Figure 7.4.

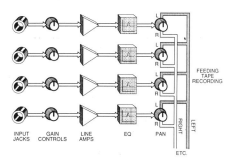

INPUT JACKS   GAIN CONTROLS   LINE AMPS   EQ   PAN   FEEDING TAPE RECORDING   LEFT   RIGHT   ETC.

Figure 7.4 A stereo 4x2 mixer.

In this stereo 4x2 mixer, there are two differences from the 4x1 mixer. The first is two output busses; the second is that there is a *pan* (for 'panorama') control. With a pan control, a signal can be assigned to either or both of the stereo busses, so that we're able to 'place' sounds within an 'environment'—

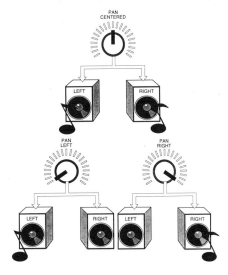

Figure 7.5 The audible effect of a stereo pan control.

a guitar, for example, can be placed mostly on the right channel, and bass in the middle (equally on both channels), and a keyboard can be balanced to the left, to re-create a live listening environment.

The Multi-Track Mixer

The mixers we've described so far are all oriented toward live applications, either for mixing to an amplifier or mixing to a stereo tape recorder. What if we want to record to a multi-track tape recorder? It is possible to do this, in some cases, with a 'live'-oriented console. Many of the early home recordists did so, and were able to achieve remarkable results. Today, however, most of us with personal studios are using mixers *designed* to make multi-track recordings.

The three main sections of a multi-track mixer are:

- *The input section*, including the microphone, line, and signal inputs from effects devices. Aside from gain and pan controls, inputs almost invariably have some type of equalization, as well as sends to *auxiliary* (effects) outputs.
- *The output section*, including the buss and group outputs—which feed the multi-track tape recorder—and the auxiliary outputs—which feed the effects and other devices.
- *The monitor section*—this includes any function related to listening to or observing (with meters) the audio signals. Common controls include headphone and control room speaker volume, along with a means of choosing *what* is being monitored. Most multi-track mixers have within this section a *tape monitor*, which allows one to listen to previously recorded tape tracks while overdubbing, and listen to the tape machine inputs of tracks about to recorded.

These three main sections can be found on virtually all multi-track mixers, from most ministudios to world-class professional consoles. The flexibility offered within each of these categories is what differentiates mixers.

Now let's take a look at some of the individual components you can expect to find on average multi-track mixers.

The Input Section

In Figure 7.7 we see a typical input channel. Of course, what we're seeing is the *top* of the channel, so we can't see any of its input or output connectors. The following is a list of typical input components; most are shown in Figure 7.7. They're all listed in the usual order in which an audio signal flows through an input. Remember to compare your own equipment with the components listed below.

Channel Input Jacks. Some mixers, particularly 4-track ministudios, have a single, unbalanced 1/4″ jack—designed to accommodate microphone, instrument, or line sources.

Better mixers have separate mike and line inputs. In this case, the mike inputs are balanced XLR jacks, and the line inputs are either 1/4″ (balanced or unbalanced), RCA (unbalanced), or more rarely XLR (balanced), jacks. Some mixers may also have a separate 1/4″ or RCA 'tape input' jack.

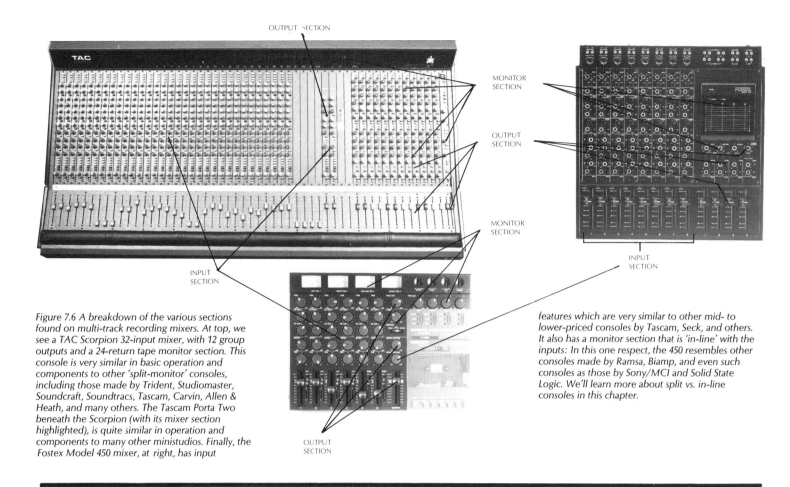

OUTPUT SECTION

MONITOR SECTION

OUTPUT SECTION

MONITOR SECTION

INPUT SECTION

INPUT SECTION

OUTPUT SECTION

Figure 7.6 A breakdown of the various sections found on multi-track recording mixers. At top, we see a TAC Scorpion 32-input mixer, with 12 group outputs and a 24-return tape monitor section. This console is very similar in basic operation and components to other 'split-monitor' consoles, including those made by Trident, Studiomaster, Soundcraft, Soundtracs, Tascam, Carvin, Allen & Heath, and many others. The Tascam Porta Two beneath the Scorpion (with its mixer section highlighted), is quite similar in operation and components to many other ministudios. Finally, the Fostex Model 450 mixer, at right, has input

features which are very similar to other mid- to lower-priced consoles by Tascam, Seck, and others. It also has a monitor section that is 'in-line' with the inputs: In this one respect, the 450 resembles other consoles made by Ramsa, Biamp, and even such consoles as those by Sony/MCI and Solid State Logic. We'll learn more about split vs. in-line consoles in this chapter.

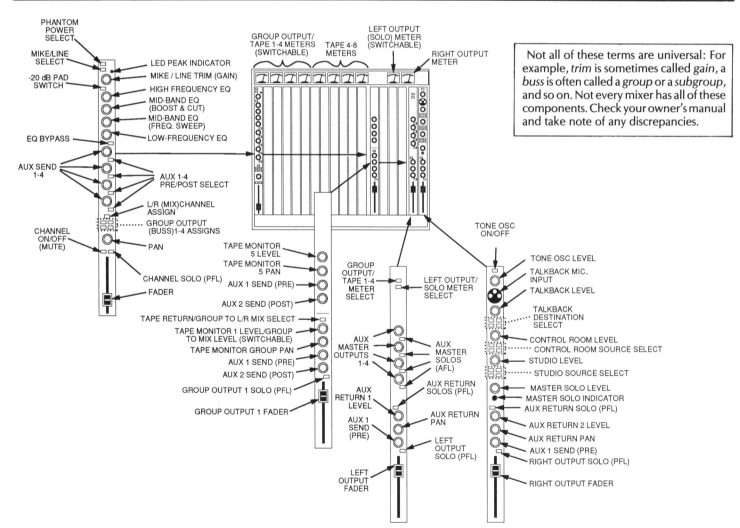

Not all of these terms are universal: For example, trim is sometimes called gain, a buss is often called a group or a subgroup, and so on. Not every mixer has all of these components. Check your owner's manual and take note of any discrepancies.

Figure 7.7 The components of a typical mid-sized mixer. From left to right we see an input module, a group output module (with tape monitor section), and the left and right master output modules. This mixer is a 'split-monitor' design (page 41). If it were an 'in-line' design, the tape monitor returns would be located within each input. With some in-line boards, the group output level controls are also located within each input, as rotary pots.

If the line inputs are designed to accommodate true line levels only, then a *direct box* must be connected to the mike input, if you wish to plug electric guitars and other instrument-level devices into the mixer without a mike. Your owner's manual will tell you if you can plug instruments directly into the line inputs—remember that most synthesizers can produce line levels, and can be plugged into any line input. Refer to page 19 for an explanation of levels, and see page 66 for more on the direct box.

Phantom Power. As we'll learn more about on page 62, condenser microphones need some form of power in order to operate. Found either as individual channel switches or a single master switch, phantom power provides a voltage between 12 and 48 volts DC, and—with few exceptions—cannot harm non-condenser microphones.

Pad. Not found on all consoles, this is a circuit which can be switched in to *pad*, or reduce the sensitivity of the microphone input—usually by 20 dB. Unlike the trim, it is not continuously variable in its effect, though some pads have two or more selectable degrees of effect. Sometimes a pad is labelled 'mic. att.,' for 'microphone attenuation.'

Phase Reverse. Indicated by a 'Ø,' this is found on some of the better recording mixers. This reverses the phase of the input's balanced signal, switching the hot and cold conductors. Phase reverse can correct for microphone mis-wiring, since not all manufacturers abide by the 'pin 2 hot' specification for XLR microphone inputs.

Microphone/Line/Tape Input Select. The input select switch allows you to chose what the source to the input will be. On some mixers, the choice is between the mike/line combined, *or* the tape: With the switch in the 'mike/line' position, the input will receive its signal from both the XLR mike input and the 1/4″ or RCA line input—what's plugged in determines whether or not the source is a mike or a line.

On other mixers—including many of the British consoles—the selection is the microphone input *or* the line input (the latter of which is a combination line/tape). A few consoles allow you to independently select mike, line, or tape.

At least one recorder/mixer, the Tascam Porta 05, selects the 1/4″ mike/line input if anything is plugged into the jack; otherwise it automatically selects the tape tracks as input sources.

Input Trim. Sometimes called the *mike/ line trim*, or *gain*, this control allows the incoming signal to be adjusted, or fine-trimmed, to the proper operating level for the mixer. By adjusting the sensitivity of the input, most any mike/line signal can be accommodated, regardless of the signal's strength. A properly set trim can minimize distortion and maximize the input's signal-to-noise ratio. You can use either an input peak LED or a regular meter to set the trim.

Input Peak LED. Normally, the input's peak LED (light-emitting diode) should just flash at the loudest, or peak, signals from a source. The input peak LED is used to help adjust the trim level.

High-Pass Filter. Found on some of the better consoles. This is a filter which allows only signals of a preset (or sometimes adjustable) frequency *and higher* to pass through

the input. This is very useful for reducing low-frequency rumble, such as handling noise with a microphone.

Channel Mute/Off. This is used to turn off an input. On some boards, *mute* shuts off any *output* signal from the faders; on other boards it turns off the *input* to the fader. Generally, it's preferable to have the former—that way, the faders can't generate noise by being left up. When there is no independent switch, such as on the Fostex 450, a channel can be muted if there is a 'neutral' position for the input select or buss assign switches; many of the less expensive mixers don't have any mute functions.

A few of the better boards allow muting to be done in *mute groups*, where several inputs can be turned on and off as a group—either automated or manually. Chapters Thirteen and Fifteen describe automated muting and how it can help you.

Access Send/Receive, or Insert, Jack. Essentially, this is a pair of connectors which allows you to access the signal in order to *send* it to an outside device and then *receive* it again. Access or insert points are used to insert an effect or some type of signal processing, such as a compressor. When there is a single 1/4″ jack for insert, it's in fact a three-conductor TRS jack (tip-ring-sleeve): With a special cable you can access both the send and receive conductors (see page 76). The insert send level is unaffected by the fader level.

Equalizer (EQ). The equalizer is the tone control section of the input. It can be as simple as a 2-band tone control—bass and treble adjust—or extremely complicated and powerful. It allows you to tailor the tone quality of a recorded sound to suit your taste, in the same manner in which tone controls can be adjusted on a home stereo.

A low-frequency control, for example, can be used to add 'bottom end' to a kick drum, as a high-frequency control can bring out a desired brightness to an acoustic guitar. It can also be used to correct true deficiencies and problems with the source. A more in-depth discussion of equalization can be found on page 43.

An *EQ bypass* switch defeats the EQ section. It's really useful for 'with and without' comparisons of signals being EQ'd.

Fader. This determines the level of the input signal being fed to the outputs. When all the way down, the signal is shut off and not sent to any of the buss or stereo outputs. Faders are either labelled on an arbitrary scale of 0 to 10, or on a scale which represents their effect on the signal's level in terms of dB.

When the fader has a dB scale, ' -∞ ' represents an infinite amount of level *cut*, or attenuation, and the signal is off. At a level such as '+10 dB,' the signal is being boosted, or amplified, by 10 dB. At '0 dB' on the fader scale, the signal is unchanged from the trim control's level (unless there's an EQ boost or cut).

Most boards have a shaded area which represents the fader's optimum level, usually about 3/4 of the way up (around '7' on a fader labelled from one to 10, and '0' on a dB scale). Normally, when recording signals through your mixer, it's best to try and aim for the shaded area of the fader's throw: At that shaded area, the fader is operating at its quietest level. To keep the fader there, one

trick is to adjust your input level with the trim control, providing you don't run into distortion.

Solo. In Italian—the language of music—'solo' means 'alone.' When offered on a mixer, a solo function allows you to monitor, through headphones or speakers, just the soloed channels. This is extremely handy for hearing the EQ or level of a single channel or group of channels, such as a drum set, without having to turn down the level of other channels. Many mixers also have a solo function on some of the outputs, such as the buss and auxiliary outputs.

Solo can also be known as *PFL* (pre-fader level). That means that the channel's fader setting has no affect on its soloed level: You can even solo a channel when its fader is off. Some mixers have *AFL* (after-fader level) soloing, particularly on output faders, in which case the fader level does affect the solo level. Solo is usually a mono signal—the position of the pan control doesn't affect the solo signal. On more professional mixers you can find *solo-in-place*—a stereo solo which follows the pan control.

Ideally, solo systems are completely 'non-destructive,' so that pressing a solo button affects only the monitor, and not the group or stereo outputs.

Auxiliary (Effects, and Cue) Sends. An auxiliary, or *aux* send is a controllable means of sending a channel's signal to an external device. This external device is usually an effect of some kind, such as a reverb or delay, though it can be a power amplifier or other device.

Each aux send usually feeds a corresponding *master aux* output. When labelled as an *effects* send, or *post* (for post-fader), the aux send receives its signal after the fader. Consequently, when the fader goes down, so does the level to the aux send. When labelled as a *cue* send, or *pre* (for pre-fader), the aux send's level is unaffected by the fader's level. Input channels can have from one to eight or more aux sends, and it's common to find both pre- and post-fader aux sends in the same input channel. Aux sends are usually mono (single channel), though stereo sends are popular.

Pre-fader aux sends are typically used to feed a headphone amplifier for other musicians. This enables musicians to hear their own mix of the various signals, regardless of the fader levels feeding a tape recorder or—in the case of live sound—P.A. speakers. For most personal multi-track purposes, a pre-fader aux send is not all that useful. While pre-fader sends are sometimes labelled 'cue,' this shouldn't be confused with *tape cue*, as Tascam calls the *tape monitor* section of its mixers and recorder/mixers (see page 40).

Post-fader aux sends are used typically as effects sends. Pre-fader aux sends can be used as effects sends, but post is preferable, since the amount of effect remains relative to the fader level.

We'll explore further the use of aux sends on page 93.

Pan. The pan control allows the signal to be sent to the left or the right stereo buss. In addition to this simple left/right assign, the pan control can also be used to assign mixer inputs to tape machine inputs via the mixer's buss outputs, as we'll learn on page 37.

Group, or Buss, Output Assign. Known

by a variety of similar names (see "Getting On The Right Buss," this page), a buss is an output to which more than one input can be assigned. A bit further ahead, on page 37 we'll examine how group output busses are used to assign mixer inputs to different tape machine inputs. Multi-track mixers allow you to assign any input to at least two and as many as 64 busses. Most mixers designed for personal recording have from two to eight output busses; most professional mixers have from eight to 24.

The buss or group assigns usually work in conjunction with the pan control. Two-buss mixers—including those found on many ministudios—have just a pan control to assign inputs to busses. Mixers with four or more busses use switches, often in conjunction with the pan control, to assign inputs to busses.

In addition to assignment switches for the available busses, many mixers have an assignment switch for the left/right stereo output buss. When there is no direct stereo assignment, signals are sent to the stereo output buss via busses 1 and 2.

Direct Output. This is a jack at which the signal can be 'tapped,' in order to be sent to a channel of a tape recorder, or to an effect; the fader controls its level. True direct outs are rarely found on recorder/mixers: They may have 'tape out' jacks, but those are *tape* and not *channel* outputs.

Direct Assign. Most recorder/mixer ministudios don't have direct mixer outputs. Instead, such units often have a *direct assign* of each input to its respective tape track (see page 36).

Auxiliary/Effects Return. This is not a normal channel input, and in fact isn't found in the input module. Rather, this is a line-level-only input, designed to receive the output, or *return* of an effects device, such as a digital delay or reverb—and is typically located near the output section of the mixer. Because they are line level, some people use aux returns to receive the signals from drum machines and synthesizers. On some mixers, such as the Fostex 450, the aux returns are labelled as *buss inputs*, with a volume and pan control.

When there is a single aux return pot with *two* aux input jacks (a left and a right), such as on some ministudios, the aux return is actually a *stereo* return. Its two input jacks are fed via the aux return pot to the stereo output buss. The single pot then controls the overall amount of effect. This type of return is designed to receive a stereo effect, such as a stereo reverb or digital delay. If a single aux return pot has a *single* input jack, then it is a *mono return*, and usually has in addition to its gain pot, a pan pot which allows you to determine the stereo placement of the effect. Without a pan pot, a mono return will feed the same level to both the left and right output busses.

Occasionally, an aux return has its own buss assignment, so that the return signal can be routed to any output buss. This is very helpful for sending effects to tape tracks, along with any inputs that may be assigned to the same output buss. On some mixers, the aux returns can become quite elaborate, with EQ, pre-fader aux sends (for a second musician's headphone mix), and more. Such fancy aux returns are practically the same as regular inputs, except they don't

Getting On The Right Buss

Many musicians who have done live sound are familiar with *subgroups*, or just *groups*. These are mixer outputs to which more than one mixer input can be assigned, by means of a *buss*. As we learned, a buss is an output circuit to which signals, such as mixer inputs, are joined. Each group usually has an output fader or pot to control its overall levels.

By using group outputs in live sound, for example, all the background vocals can be assigned to one group, all the keyboards to another group, and all the drums to yet another group. In this manner, the group faders allow an easier means of control: Instead of having to adjust seven faders to control the level of the drums, just one group acts as a master fader for the drums (or two groups, if the drums are in stereo).

Similarly, during recording, when more than one mixer input is to be assigned to a single tape track, a group is used. In some mixers and recorder/mixers, however, it's quite common for such a recording group *not* to have an overall group fader control. In this case, inputs can be grouped together with just an internal summing amp. A fader-less group to which inputs can be assigned is usually just called a buss, or *group buss*. Bear in mind, however, some potential confusion in terminology:

- Recording engineers tend to use either 'buss,' 'subgroup,' 'group,' 'group output,' or 'group buss,' when talking about a group to which inputs can be assigned.
- Stereo busses and auxiliary sends are simply known as 'busses,' or 'outputs,' and not 'groups.'

have a microphone input!

Sync Input. On recorder/mixers, it's a growing trend to have a separate sync input. This is an input designed to receive a sync tone from a drum machine or other device, in order to sync the unit to tape. Usually, it's just a separate input jack with a level control, and it feeds an 'outside track,' such as track 4 (on a 4-track recorder). The sync input bypasses any noise reduction system, to ensure that the sync code is recorded and reproduced as cleanly as possibly. Sync *can* be accomplished without a sync input—see Chapter Fourteen.

Tape Monitor/Buss Output. Most *in-line monitoring* consoles include both these controls in the input section of the mixer, See "Understanding The Tape Monitor" (page 40) for more information.

The Output Section

The output section of a mixer receives most of its signals from the input section. Figure 7.7 shows a typical output section up close. Bear in mind that some output sections are very simple, consisting of not much more than buss and aux output jacks, along with stereo output jacks and level controls. Some can be very elaborate. Compare your

own mixer's features, with your manual as a reference.

Stereo Master Fader(s). This is usually a linear fader, but occasionally is a rotary pot. When there is a *single* fader or pot (and the mixer does have stereo outputs) it's in fact a stereo control—simultaneously controlling the left and right output levels. When there are two separate faders, the left and right levels can be adjusted independently. Depending upon the mixer, the stereo master can receive its signal directly from the input channels, the group outputs, and/or the tape monitor.

In addition to feeding the left/right output jacks, the stereo master also feeds the headphone and/or speaker level controls. On most ministudios, the stereo master also controls the levels to the tape tracks, when recording via the left/right buss (see page 37.)

Mono Master Fader. Found on Ramsa and a few other brands of mixing consoles, the mono master is a sum of the left/right stereo output, and is useful for live P.A. work.

Group, or Buss, Output Faders. Also known as *subgroup* faders, these receive their signals from any inputs which are assigned to them. Group outputs are normally routed, via output jacks, to the tape track inputs (recorder/mixers are hardwired as such without jacks). Buss 1 output normally feeds track 1 input, buss 2 feeds track 2, and so on.

In addition to feeding the output jacks (and/or tape tracks), the groups may feed the stereo master output. On many mixers there is a gain and pan pot for each group— these control the level and pan of that group to the stereo output.

The group faders are usually located on the right-hand side of the console. Many *in-line monitoring* consoles, however, have group output pots located within each channel input. See "Understanding The Tape Monitor" on page 40 for more information.

Auxiliary Send Master(s). These receive their signals from the aux sends of the channel inputs, and control the overall output level of the aux sends. When using an effects device, a common practice is to feed the input of the effect with the master output of a send. In this way, adjusting the aux master

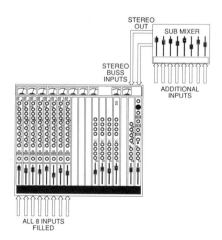

Figure 7.8 If your console lacks stereo or group buss inputs, you can always feed a submixer to one or more regular line inputs.

level will adjust the overall level to the effect.

Some mixers—such as those made by Fostex—don't have aux send master controls. Rather, all of the individual channel aux sends sum together at the aux output jack(s), without an overall master control.

Group and Stereo Buss Inputs. As we'll learn below, a buss input can serve as an aux return, especially if it has gain and pan controls. Otherwise, group and stereo buss input jacks can be used to sum together signals. For example, the stereo output of one mixer can be fed to the stereo bass input jacks of another mixer. In this example, the stereo master fader of the second mixer would control the overall level of both mixers (see Figure 7.8).

Sync Output. This is the output level control, off of tape, for a device *synced* to tape, as described above ("Sync Input") and on page 111.

Talkback Circuit. Usually reserved for the more expensive consoles, this is either a built-in microphone or a microphone socket, which can be routed to the group outputs and/or to the aux sends. With a talkback mike, the engineer can *slate*, or record his or her voice on any or all of the tape tracks, without having to plug a microphone into a regular input.

Talkback mikes can also be used to communicate to other musicians: In larger facilities, when the engineer in the control room talks to musicians in the studio (through headphones or speakers), the talkback mike is being used.

Tone Oscillator. Again, usually found on more upper-end consoles. When selected, it sends a tone (fixed or variable) to the groups. This tone is useful for maintenance as well as troubleshooting. *Caution!* If your mixer has a tone oscillator, ensure that before you turn it on, all outputs from the mixer are turned way down! This dangerous little button has the capacity, if turned on unexpectedly, to destroy tape recorder meters, speakers, headphones—not to mention eardrums! If the oscillator has its own level control, this can be turned down instead, and then gingerly raised to the desired level.

Output Jacks. These can be either XLR, 1/4", or RCA jacks. Their nominal line output level depends upon the individual mixer. Normally, in personal multi-track equipment, the output levels are –10 dBV and are unbalanced. Most other gear uses the +4 dBm balanced professional standard. Some mixers allow you to internally select –10 or +4 levels.

The Monitor Section

The monitor section lets us select what we're going to hear, as well as see signal levels (via meters) from the output section. All but the simplest mixers have some sort of a monitor section—and virtually all multi-track-oriented mixers have at least a few of the following components.

Meters. The meters allow us to monitor visually the output levels of the busses (group and stereo), as well as—on some mixers—the aux send and solo levels. Sometimes, for economy's sake, switches are used to allow us to choose what a meter is monitoring, instead of having individual meters for everything being monitored. On most

recorder/mixers, the meters can switch from monitoring buss levels to monitoring the tape track outputs.

Monitor Level (Headphone And Control Room). These are often separate pots, allowing independent adjustment of headphone and control room speaker levels. On other mixers, this is a single pot, controlling both levels. On some mixers and many recorder mixers, there is no control room or monitor output—in this case the left/right stereo output is used. Professional mixers include a studio-level control.

Monitor Source Select. When there is no select switch for the headphone or speaker monitor, it's safe to assume that it receives its signal from the left/right stereo buss. In this way, whatever is feeding the stereo buss— the group busses, the inputs, the tape monitor, or anything else—feeds the control room and headphone monitor outputs.

Otherwise, the monitor outputs can receive their signals from a wide range of sources, and this can vary from mixer to mixer. In some cases, the control room, headphone, and even studio outputs have independently selectable sources, though this is an unnecessary luxury for most of us working alone. Commonly selectable monitor sources include:

- Left/right stereo buss (sometimes switchable to mono).
- Auxiliary sends.
- Group buss outputs.
- Tape monitor.
- 2-track tape return—which allows one to hear the output of a mixdown deck.

Normally these are selected one at a time, though some mixers allow you to combine monitor sources.

Solo Level. When a mixer has solo facilities, it's common to find a separate solo volume level. It's often accompanied by an LED solo indicator.

Tape Monitor. On page 27 we learned how it was necessary when overdubbing to

be able to hear the output of the tape machine. The tape monitor is actually a special input section of the mixer designed solely to listen to the output of a tape machine. This section shouldn't be confused, by the way, with the tape monitor function found on home stereo receivers.

Most multi-track mixers have tape monitor sections—though not all of them. Some, such as the Audio Technica RMX-64 recorder/mixer, expect you to listen to tape returns through channel inputs, as if they were a line source. But recording life is much more pleasant with a tape monitor. Normally, the tape monitor section is used during the overdubbing portion of the recording process, and the mixer should have as many tape monitor channels as there are tape tracks.

There are two basic types of tape monitors: *In-line monitor*, and *split-monitor*. On page 41, we'll take a close look at these different types of tape monitors and how they're used. Some tape monitor inputs can function as additional line inputs during mixdown—this can be a useful trick. For a description of this, please refer to page 99.

Understanding Mixer/ Tape Recorder Signal Flow

Chances are, if you own a multi-track mixer or recorder/mixer, that you're able to record and overdub tracks with reasonable success—and if what we've learned so far about tape recorders and mixers has answered most of your questions, you may wish to skip ahead to page 42. Should any facet of recording with your mixer have you bewildered, however, or if you'd like to strengthen your understanding of how multi-track mixers work, these next few pages are for you.

Despite differences between mixers, there are some very important similarities. We've learned that most multi-track mixers have three sections in common: the input, output, and monitor sections. Along with these features, there are two signal flow

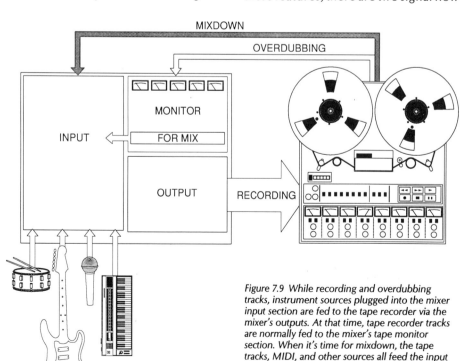

Figure 7.9 While recording and overdubbing tracks, instrument sources plugged into the mixer input section are fed to the tape recorder via the mixer's outputs. At that time, tape recorder tracks are normally fed to the mixer's tape monitor section. When it's time for mixdown, the tape tracks, MIDI, and other sources all feed the input section of mixer—though many mixers allow the tape monitor section to be used as additional line inputs during mixdown.

functions which all multi-track mixers should be able to perform *simultaneously*, in order to make a multi-track recording. These are:

- To route signals, via outputs, to a multi-track tape recorder, in order to record tracks.
- To receive signals from a multi-track tape recorder (in order to hear previously recorded tracks), either through input channels or the mixer's tape monitor section.

To address the first function, multi-track mixers route signals to tape recorders in one of three ways:

- Using the direct outputs/assigns.
- Using the group, or buss, outputs.
- Using a combination of direct and buss outputs.

Most multi-track mixers these days are able to do all three ways of signal routing listed above. There are still quite a few mixers, however, which can only route their signals via one of the first two methods. Let's take a look at how all three of these methods work.

Recording With Direct Outputs Or Assigns

While functionally similar, *direct outputs* are usually found on independent mixers, while *direct assigns* are found on recorder/mixer ministudios.

Direct Outputs. A direct output is an output from a mixer's input channel, and is typically a 1/4″ or RCA jack located near the channel's input jacks. The signal is usually taken post- (after) channel fader and post-EQ, so that as the signal coming out of the direct output is affected by both the EQ and the fader. Direct outputs can be found on many independent mixers designed for multi-track use, though virtually *none* of the ministudios have true direct outputs. (One exception is the Fostex 460.)

When recording with direct outputs, the idea is to connect an input channel's direct output to a tape recorder's input, by means of a cable. This can be done one input at a time, if you're recording only one track at a time, or more conveniently, several cables can be connected. With more than one cable, there's usually a correspondence between the outputs and inputs: Mixer direct output 1 is connected to tape recorder input 1, direct output 2 feeds recorder input 2, and so on.

To find out if your independent multi-track mixer has direct outputs, simply look at the back panel. Near each channel's input connectors, there should be a plug labeled 'direct out' (sometimes it's labelled 'tape out'—but that's different from the 'tape out' found on ministudios—use your owner's manual to be sure).

If there are no such outputs, your mixer is designed to multi-track using group busses only, and you can skip ahead to page 37. Without direct outputs, it may be possible to use an access (insert) send as a direct output—though this signal is usually pre-fader, and would require you to use the trim control to adjust the signal's level.

Direct Assigns. Direct assigns are found exclusively on most recorder/mixers. Simply, it's a switch for each of the tape tracks that assigns corresponding mixer inputs to recorder inputs directly. For example, when 'direct assign' is engaged for track 4, then mixer input channel 4 *directly* feeds track 4. If all the direct assigns are engaged (there is usually one switch for each track), then channel 1 feeds track 1, channel 2 feeds track 2, and so on.

Some 4-track recorder mixers, such as the Fostex X-30 and Tascam Porta 05, are able to record a maximum of just two tracks at once. Such units use their left/right busses to record, and don't have a direct assign mode—you can skip ahead to page 37 if this applies to your multi-track set up.

Most recorder/mixers which are capable of recording all of their tracks simultaneously have some form of direct assignment. One exception: Some ministudios' input

Figure 7.10 Typical input module connectors. Aside from microphone and line inputs, and the send/receive insert jack (page 33), we also see the direct output jack.

channels—including the Audio-Technica RMX-64, the Tascam 246, and Fostex 460—have assignment buttons to *any* of the tracks —*i.e.*: Channel 1 has switches which can assign it to any of the tracks, as does channel 2, etc.. With this arrangement, any tape track can receive *more* than one input—and these are not true direct assigns. Rather, this is a type of buss assign, and is covered on page 37. As a general rule of thumb for recorder/mixers, if each input has assignment switches for each track, then busses rather than direct assigns enable the unit to record all of its tracks simultaneously.

Direct Recording. We mentioned that direct outputs and assigns were functionally similar. This is because both are used in the same way: When *direct recording*, either via direct outputs or assigns, normally the output of mixer channel 1 is fed to track 1, the output of channel 2 feeds track 2, and so forth.

As we can see in Figure 7.11 the direct outputs/assigns feed the tape recorder. Note that in this scheme, no buss outputs

---

Mixer Nomenclature

We've already learned about 4x1 and 4x2 mixers: They are four input mixers, with one and two buss outputs respectively. Manufacturers and engineers can infer quite a bit about any given mixer by this type of description.

For example, a common recording mixer format is 16 x 8 x 8 x 2 x 1. What does this tell us? The breakdown is as follows:

16	x	8	x	8	x	2	x	1
INPUTS		GROUPS		TAPE MONITOR CHANNELS		STEREO OUTPUT		MONO OUTPUT

In general, the first figure is the number of inputs, followed by the number of groups and the number of tape monitor channels. The last figure (or two figures) represents the stereo (and mono) outputs.

Figure 7.11 Recording with direct outputs. With a recorder/mixer, the concept remains the same, though inputs are assigned directly to tape tracks with a 'direct assign' switch.

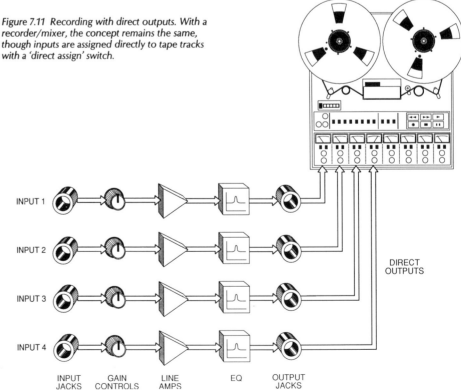

INPUT 1

INPUT 2

INPUT 3

INPUT 4

DIRECT OUTPUTS

INPUT JACKS   GAIN CONTROLS   LINE AMPS   EQ   OUTPUT JACKS

are being used (remember, a buss is a circuit to which more than one input is assigned).

Also bear in mind that if this were a picture of a recorder/mixer, the connect cables would be 'hard-wired' internally to the tape recorder inputs, and electrically connected with a direct assign switch.

Why Use Direct Outputs/Assigns? There are several reasons for recording with direct outputs/assigns. Among them:

- Direct recording with direct outputs/assigns is conceptually a very easy technique. When you want to record on track 1, you plug into input 1, and so on. If a system has either direct outputs connected to tape recorder inputs, or an integrated unit has direct assigns, these connections are the *least* confusing means of assigning mixer inputs to tape tracks.
- Since the signal being assigned to the track is not passing through the extra electronic stage of a buss, the signal may be a bit quieter via the direct method.
- As we'll learn in the next section, when using just busses to record, the number of tracks that one can record simultaneously is limited to the number of busses. By using direct outputs/assigns *in addition* to using the busses, additional tracks can be recorded. This technique is covered in the section "Combined Direct and Buss Output Recording," on page 38.
- Some multi-track mixers, such as the AMR 42, have no true buss outputs, other than a stereo buss out. Such mixers are designed solely to be used in a direct mode when overdubbing.

There are also some disadvantages to direct recording, among them:

- When using only direct outputs/assigns, no more than one input can be assigned to any given track at a time.
- As we'll examine on page 92, tracks cannot be *bounced together* using direct outputs or assigns.
- Plugging into a new input every time you want to record a new track can be quite tedious. For example, if you have one microphone for an acoustic guitar, and are overdubbing three tracks of acoustic guitar, each time you want to record a new track the mike has to be unplugged from one input and plugged into another input.

Recording via busses offers some real solutions to these problems. Let's take a look at some of them. . . .

Recording With Group Busses

In multi-track recording, one way to route mixer inputs to tape recorder inputs is via group buss outputs—these are outputs to which more than one input can be assigned. With some mixers, in fact, it's the *only* way to multi-track record. If you own an independent multi-track mixer or ministudio with buss assignments at each input, this section's for you!

Why are busses, rather than direct outputs, used? As we just learned, with direct recording, each mixer input feeds a corresponding recorder input. A fine arrangement, but as noted above, there are several

disadvantages to direct recording.

For example, what if we had two people who wanted to sing background vocals together, each with his or her own mike, and they were to be recorded together on the same track? Using direct outputs or assigns only, there's no way to assign both mike inputs to the same track input of the tape machine. We need a means of combining mixer inputs together to feed single tape recorder inputs. The solution is to *group* those inputs together by using a group buss. Another reason to use buss outputs is if you wish to record several inputs to two tracks, for stereo recording. For example, four or five microphones on a drum kit could all be recorded to two tracks, by assigning the mike inputs to two buss outputs.

And, in addition to being able to record more than one mixer channel on to a single tape track, busses also allow:

- The bouncing together of tracks (as detailed on page 92).
- The routing of any input to any track. This means that you don't have to replug a microphone/instrument every time a new track is to be recorded.

Depending upon the mixer, inputs are assigned to busses either via *discrete* or *odd/even pairing* assignment.

Discrete Buss Assignment. (This is not to be confused with *direct output/assign*, which, as we know, routes mixer inputs to tape tracks *without* using busses).

Let's look at a 4-buss mixer. With a true 4-buss mixer, any input can be assigned to any one of 4 busses. When a 4-buss mixer has *discrete assignment*, it means that each input has four individual group buss buttons, one for each buss, and that any combination of the busses can be selected. Figure 7.12 shows what a single input—with discrete 4-buss assignment—looks like.

With discrete assignment, it's very easy to assign a mixer input to any tape track. For example, the acoustic guitarist who wants to overdub up to four guitar parts on his or her 4-track can leave the guitar's mike in the same input channel, and just press the appropriate button—1 to 4—to assign the input to each successive track.

As we'll learn next, though, there is a popular alternative to discrete assignment of group busses.

Odd/Even Pairing Buss Assignment. Having discrete, or individual, buss switches for each input can lead to quite a costly mixer. Because of this, it's more common to have a simpler-to-manufacture way of selecting buss assignment. This way, often known as *odd/even pairing*, has half as many buss assign switches as the discrete design, and makes use of the pan control. It still allows you to assign any input to any track, as we'll see.

The simplest type of odd/even pairing buss assignment is found in all stereo mixers. In a 2-buss stereo mixer, when the pan pot is all the way counterclockwise (CCW), the left (buss 1) output is selected; conversely, when the pan pot is clockwise (CW), the right (buss 2) output is selected.

Imagine there is a switch after the pan pot on each of those two busses which allows you to select another buss out. In this manner, when panned CCW, you choose between buss 1 and buss 3, and when panned CW, the choice is either buss 2 or buss 4. Since fewer switches are involved compared to the discrete design, this can save manufacturers and consumers quite a bit of money.

Many mixers and recorder/mixers use this method of grouping inputs. With this design:

- Odd-numbered busses are assigned by panning to the left and choosing which odd-numbered buss is desired.
- Even-numbered busses are assigned by panning to the right and choosing which even-numbered buss is desired.
- An odd- *and* an even-numbered pair of busses can be selected by selecting a paired switch and panning to the center.

While odd/even pairing *does* allow selection of any one buss, only half as many busses can be selected at any one time with

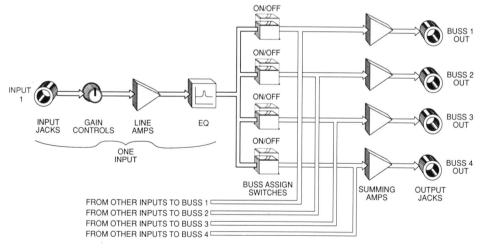

Figure 7.12 Discrete buss asignment allows any input to feed any group buss output, merely by pressing the appropriate switch. Alternately, a pan control can allow for panning between two buss outputs.

this design, compared to the discrete buss select design. That is, a 4-buss mixer with odd/even assign has only two assign buttons or switch positions. Does this matter? Not especially—just ahead we're going to learn a couple of ways to get around the limitations of odd/even pairing, when we look at using direct outputs in conjunction with busses.

To sum up the process of recording with odd/even pairing, let's say we had a single synthesizer plugged into a single input of a

4-buss odd/even pairing mixer, and we wanted to record four successive tracks with the synth. The process of assignment would be as follows:

1. Select the group buss pair 1-2 switch. Turn the pan control all the way CCW to select buss 1. Select track 1 on the tape recorder to 'record ready,' put the recorder into 'record,' and you're off and running.
2. When finished, turn the pan control all the way CW to select buss 2. Make the necessary selections at the tape machine, rewind, and record track 2.
3. Select the group buss pair 3-4. With some mixers or recorder/mixers, the group pair 1-2 switch may have to be disengaged. By panning CCW, the synthesizer can be routed to buss 3 and thus recorded on track 3, with the necessary tape machine selections.
4. Finally, by turning the input's pan control CW, the input's signal is routed to buss 4 and can be recorded on track 4, after putting track 4 into record at the tape recorder.

As can be seen, it's a bit more work than the discrete group buss assign found on some mixers, but for most applications, the odd/even pairing group buss assign works fine.

Combined Direct And Buss Output Recording

There are times, particularly with a 2- or 4-buss mixer, when it's desirable to use *both* the direct and the buss outputs simultaneously. In order to accomplish what we're about to describe, your mixer must have both direct and group buss outputs. If you are using a recorder/mixer ministudio, many allow the use of both the busses and the direct assigns simultaneously—consult your manual to see if it's possible.

One frequent use of combined direct and buss recording is to record more tracks at once than there are busses. A simple example would be the following: Imagine you have an 8-track tape recorder and a 12 x 4 mixer, and want to record simultaneously:

● A stereo drum machine (tracks 1 and 2).
● A stereo synthesizer (tracks 3 and 4).
● A vocal (track 5).

Of course, one way would be to use five of the mixer's direct outputs. Let's say, however, that you want to be able to use all *eight* of the drum machine's outputs in order to equalize individually the percussion voices, and record them all on tracks 1 and 2. Then the drum machine would occupy mixer inputs 1 to 8, leaving inputs 9 and 10 for the synthesizer and input 11 for the vocal microphone. With 11 inputs occupied, we know that there's no way that 11 direct outputs can feed five tape recorder inputs—remember, one direct output feeds one tape machine input.

Similarly, we can't record five independent tracks simultaneously using just four group buss outputs. So what can we do? The solution is to use a combination of direct and buss outputs. This recording could be accomplished in the following manner:

1. Assign inputs 1 to 8 (the drum machine) to busses 1 and 2. Use the pan control to assign the different inputs to either or both of the busses—to create a stereo panorama of the drums. These busses can in turn feed tracks 1 and 2.
2. Assign mixer inputs 9 and 10 (the synthesizer) to busses 3 and 4, and pan the two inputs accordingly. These busses will be routed to tracks 3 and 4 respectively.
3. Take the direct output of input 11 (the microphone), and connect it to the tape recorder's track 5 input.

And *voila!*—by using both the busses and a direct output, we're able to record five tracks with a 4-buss mixer. Since we still had mixer input 12 vacant in the above scenario, by the way, we could have used that input's direct out to record a sixth track, such as another vocalist.

These same concepts could apply to any number of busses—from two to 24 or more.

Recording With Fewer Busses Than Tape Tracks

We recall that when using direct outputs only one mixer input can be assigned to each tape track, and that the solution to that problem is to use a buss. Consequently, we might expect that 4-track studios have 4-buss mixers, 8-track studios have 8-buss mixers, and so on, including 32-buss mixers for 32-track tape recorders.

These days, however, many studios operate with *fewer* group busses than tape tracks. In particular, most 8-track studios use 4-buss mixers, and many 16-track, and even 24-track, studios have 8-buss mixers. And while a few of the recorder/mixer ministudios have as many busses as they do tape tracks, the current trend among ministudio manufacturers is to have a 2-buss mixer design—in fact, the Akai MG1212 and 1214 12-track recorder/mixers operate with just a 2-buss mixer. At first glance, this may seem confusing: Don't studios need to have as many busses as tape tracks? Simply, no.

In the previous section, we saw how we could record five simultaneous tracks on an 8-track, by using all four busses of a 4-buss mixer, and a single direct output. In fact, however, it's not especially common in the personal multi-track world to record more than one or two tracks at once. Consequently, many musicians can get by fine with a 2-buss mixer design.

Remember, a group buss is a means of assigning one or more inputs to a tape track. Because of this, the number of busses needed is *no more* than the number of tracks which will be recorded at any one time—and that number may be even less if your mixer has direct outputs/assigns which can be used at the same time as the busses.

For example, in many professional 24-track sessions, it's unusual to record more than eight tracks at once. Consequently, many 24-track studios are content with 8-buss mixers. If they need to record more than eight tracks at once, they can use direct outputs as well as group busses. Of course for ultimate flexibility, it's wonderful to have as many busses as tape tracks—but you will pay for the convenience of those extra busses.

Assigning Busses To Multiple Tracks.
When recording with busses, it's necessary

to route the busses' outputs to the desired tape tracks. This is done by either 'patching' the cables as necessary, or by wiring them in a special way. Let's say, for example, we were using a 12 x 4 (12-input, 4-buss) mixer. By manually switching the four buss output cables from the first four tape recorder inputs (1 to 4) to the second four (5 to 8), the busses can be routed as required.

A more efficient way, however, to connect the four busses to an 8-track tape recorder is as follows: The four busses can be 'normalled' (as in 'normally connected') to all eight tape machine inputs by 'multing' the busses, as in 'multiple-ing' or splitting the signal (see Figure 7.13 below). In this manner, buss 1 is connected to tape channel inputs 1 and 5, buss 2 feeds recorder inputs 2 and 6, buss 3 feeds recorder inputs 3 and 7, and buss 4 feeds recorder inputs 4 and 8.

With this scheme, note that tracks 4 to 8 are receiving the *same signals* as tracks 1 to 4. Which of the eight tracks are *actually* being recorded is determined by selecting 'record enable' for the appropriate track(s) at the tape recorder status switches.

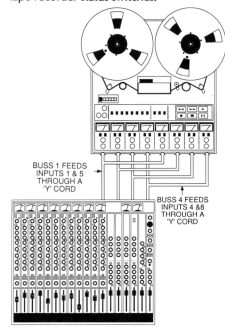

BUSS 1 FEEDS INPUTS 1 & 5 THROUGH A 'Y' CORD

BUSS 4 FEEDS INPUTS 4 &8 THROUGH A 'Y' CORD

Figure 7.13 If group outputs are 'multed' with 'Y' cords, four groups can feed eight tape recorder inputs.

For example, using a 12 x 4 mixer, an 8-track tape recorder, and the four buss outputs of the mixer multed to the eight inputs of the tape machine, the following could take place: With a guitar assigned to buss 1, a synthesizer to buss 2, and the stereo outputs of a drum machine assigned to busses 3 and 4:

● The guitar is actually being sent to inputs 1 and 5 of the recorder.
● The synthesizer is being sent to tape recorder inputs 2 and 6.
● The drum machine is being sent to tape recorder inputs 3 and 4, as well as 7 and 8.

By selecting at the tape machine the appropriate status for record and monitor of each track, we can determine if the guitar is being recorded on track 1 or track 5, and so on. You could conceivably record on *both* of these tracks, but there's very little reason to ever want to do this—unless the track is extremely important, and you want to make a 'safety' track to avoid loss by accidental erasure.

As we said, a number of recorder/mixer ministudios, from 4-track all the way up to 12-track units, have only two busses. When using a recorder/mixer, the buss assignment follows the same normalled assignment as above. For example, with a 6-input, 2-buss, 4-track recorder/mixer:

● An instrument assigned to the left (#1) buss is assigned to both tracks 1 and 3.
● An instrument on the right (#2) buss is assigned to both tracks 2 and 4.

And just as with the open-reel scenario, one chooses which actual track is being recorded at the tape track status buttons. For example, let's say we wanted to record a saxophone on track 3. We would assign the sax's input to the left buss, which would in turn feed tracks 1 and 3. By selecting track 3 to be in record, we would record the sax on track 3, and not track 1. If we wanted to record cousin Izzy playing the zither at the same time we were recording ourselves on sax, and wanted both instruments on track 3, we would assign both the sax and the zither inputs to the left buss, and then put track 3 into record.

With a more complicated recorder/mixer, such as the 12-track, 2-buss Akai MG1214, the story remains the same: The left buss feeds odd-numbered tracks, and the right buss feeds even-numbered tracks.

With recorder/mixers, the busses are *hard-wired* to the tracks. Should an input be assigned to a track by a direct assign switch—rather than a buss—then that switch *breaks* the normalled connection of the buss to the track.

Multing Busses With A Patch Bay. As we mentioned earlier, in an open-reel and separate mixer system, you can use cabling to mult the signal, so that the busses are assigned to various tracks. Instead of cabling, however, it's possible to use a patch bay to route the buss outputs to the appropriate tape recorder inputs.

A patch bay acts as an interconnect for cables. On page 79 we'll be taking a more in-depth look at patch bays and their uses. For now, though, it's worthwhile to examine the process of using a patch bay to route busses to desired tape channel inputs. Figure 7.14 shows in a simple form, how a 4-buss mixer is connected to an 8-track tape recorder.

As we can see, it's quite straightforward. If you look beyond the cables and the patchbay, and just consider the actual signal flow, this routing of busses to track inputs is the same as seen above in Figure 7.13. The patch bay shown is a *normalled* design: That is, the top rows of the bay *normally* feed the bottom row. Without using any patch cords, busses 1 to 4 automatically feed tape recorder inputs 1-4. With a set of four patch

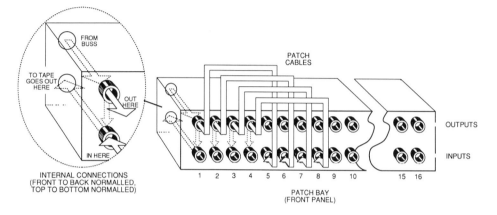

Figure 7.15 With a normalled patch bay, top jacks (outputs) normally feed bottom jacks (inputs), unless something is plugged in the bottom jacks. This shows the front panel view of the patch bay in Figure 7.14.

cords, busses 1 to 4 can be routed to tape recorder inputs 5 to 8.

It's in this manner of buss-to-track assignment that 16-track studios use 8-buss mixers, 24-track studios use 12-buss mixers, and so on. In fact, it's not unheard of to use a 4-buss mixer in a 16-track studio, and as we said, it's somewhat common to find 8-buss mixers in use with 24-track tape machines. For example, the track assigns with an 8-buss mixer and a 24-track recorder are normally as follows:

● Buss 1: Feeds tracks 1, 9, 17.
● Buss 2: Feeds tracks 2, 10, 18.
● Buss 3: Feeds tracks 3, 11, 19.
● Buss 4: Feeds tracks 4, 12, 20.
● Buss 5: Feeds tracks 5, 13, 21.
● Buss 6: Feeds tracks 6, 14, 22.
● Buss 7: Feeds tracks 7, 15, 23.
● Buss 8: Feeds tracks 8, 16, 24.

Once you get the hang of this, you've made a breakthrough that's bound to make life easier if you have a mixer or recorder/mixer with buss outputs. If you can understand the routing as described for an 8-buss mixer with a 24-track tape recorder, you should be able to understand any studio's track assignment routing.

Alternate And Advanced Mixer-To-Tape Routing

We've covered lots of information regarding direct outputs/assigns and group busses, but there are just a few last points to consider before moving on to the tape monitor.

More About Direct Outputs. If you have as many busses as tape tracks, you might not think about using your direct outputs. Here are a few good applications for them:

● When performing live, the busses could be used for live subgrouping of instruments (see page 34), and the direct outputs could be used to feed a multi-track tape recorder for live recording.
● Some people, as mentioned before, prefer to use the direct outputs for critical recording sessions, since the input's signal passes through one less stage of electronics. If you have a mixer or recorder/mixer with both busses and direct outputs, listen for yourself and hear if there's a noticeable difference. In fact, if you're just listening with a single input, the subgroups probably *will* add a noticeable degree of noise. Most people find that during a complete recording, however, with all the parts, the noise is negligible.
● A direct output can be used as an extra effects send, though its level is affected by the channel's fader.

Microprocessor-Controlled Assignment. Some mixers, such as the Allen and Heath CMC and the Soundtracs PC-MIDI series, use microprocessors rather than individual channel buss assignment switches to route inputs to buss outputs. When this is done, it

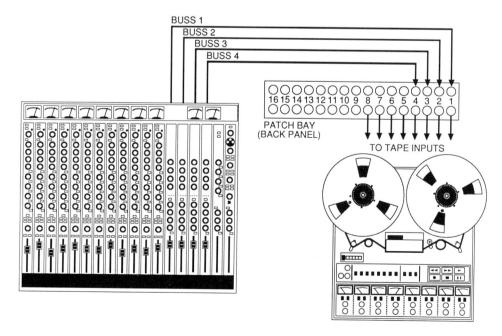

Figure 7.14 This diagram shows the rear panel patch bay connections necessary to allow four groups to feed eight tape inputs. Using front-panel patch cables, as shown in Figure 7.15, the four groups can simultaneously feed all eight inputs, assuming the bay is 'normalled.'

can be become relatively inexpensive to have 8, 16, or even 24 busses, all under computer control. As we'll learn in Chapter Fifteen, such 'intelligent' routing systems can usually be automated.

In time, we can expect to see most mixers under some type of microprocessor control.

Figure 7.16 Allen & Heath's CMC mixers offer microprocessor-controlled buss assignment and MIDI automation. It's not 'split': It's an in-line board, with eight line-only inputs at right.

Switched Buss Outputs. One relatively inexpensive way to have 16 or more busses is to *switch* the buss outputs between output connectors. On the Ramsa WR-T820B, for instance, a switch on each of the eight group output faders determines whether or not the output fader feeds one of the busses 1 to 8, or one of the busses 9 to 16. With this system, up to eight tracks can be recorded at any one time using the busses, though with the group output switches, any mixer input can be assigned to any of 16 tape recorder inputs.

Similar systems can be found on 12-buss mixers by Soundcraft, Amek, and others, which via switches can route any of their twelve groups between tape recorder inputs 1 to 12 or 13 to 24.

This method of assignment, along with more advanced microprocessor-controlled routing devices, will likely mean that more and more busses will be found on increasingly less expensive mixers.

* * * *

Among the things we've covered so far in this chapter are:

- A simple monaural output mixer.
- A stereo, or 2-buss mixer.
- Input, output, and monitor components of mixers.
- Direct output/assign recording.
- Buss output recording.
- Combined direct/buss output recording.

Essentially, we've learned all the basic ways to assign mixer inputs to tape recorder inputs, via the outputs. In this next section, we're going to learn how—and why—the tape monitor is used.

Understanding The Tape Monitor

Once you understand busses, you've

come a long way toward understanding mixers. Once you understand the idea behind the tape monitor—which is a key component for being able to hear tape tracks while recording—you've earned your 'wings!' Not only will you be able to get a lot out of your mixer or recorder/mixer and be better equipped to make great recordings—you'll also be able to understand how most of the world's mixing consoles operate.

This section will apply equally to independent mixer and recorder setups, as well as almost all recorder/mixer ministudios.

Up to this point we've learned how to route the mixer inputs to the tape recorder. There are two ways to receive signals *back* from the tape recorder:

- Through the regular inputs.
- Through the *tape monitor*.

There are four main reasons *why* we want to be able route the tape recorder outputs back to the mixer. These are:

- To mixdown the tracks, at the end of recording.
- To bounce tracks together.
- To hear parts about to be recorded, when they're assigned to tape recorder tracks.
- To hear previously recorded tracks when overdubbing.

As we'll learn more about on page 97 when all the overdubs are finished and it's time to mixdown the multi-track tape to a 2-track master tape, the multi-track tape is played back through the normal line inputs of the mixer. Those inputs are then assigned to the stereo buss output, and that output in turn feeds the 2-track machine. Similarly, the tape recorder outputs are also returned to the mixer's line inputs when bouncing tracks together (as we'll learn about on page 92).

What about during recording and later overdubbing? Well, we still need to hear the tape recorder during those stages, for two reasons:

- Back on page 28 we learned that it is common engineering practice is to listen to the output of the tape machine when

multi-tracking as opposed to the mixer's input channels themselves—in that manner, we hear not only previously recorded tracks (with the machine in repro or sync mode), but we also hear instruments that are about to be recorded on new tracks (by listening to the input to those tracks). Some mixers and recorder/mixers allow you to listen to either the mixer input channels or the output of the tape machine, and not both at the same time. With these, you *must* listen to the tape monitor when overdubbing.
- We have to be able to hear previously recorded tracks in order to be able to overdub along with them.

In essence, the tape monitor is a separate little mixer. The output of the tape recorder feeds the tape monitor section, which in turn feeds the headphone, speaker, and left/right output sections of the mixer.

Why do multi-track mixers have tape monitors? Why can't the regular inputs be used to hear the tape recorder during overdubbing? In fact, inputs *can* be used on some mixers to hear previously recorded tracks. The problem with that arrangement is that you forfeit the use of those inputs for anything *but* listening to the tape tracks.

This may help explain the role of the tape monitor: Let's say we own a 4-input, 4-track recorder/mixer ministudio, and we've recorded three tracks—a vocal, guitar, and a drum part. By switching three of the *mixer's* inputs to 'tape input,' we could listen to those three tracks.

Sounds great, and no problems so far. Now let's say we want to overdub a background vocal and a synthesizer part, at the same time, onto track 4. The vocal mike will occupy one input, and the synthesizer will occupy a second input. Here's where the problems start—we're already using three of the four inputs to hear the previously recorded tracks, but now we need two of those inputs to record the vocal and the synth! How do we get around this problem?

Well, one solution would be to give up listening to one of the previously recorded tracks, so that two of the inputs are used to play back two tracks, and the other two inputs are free to record the new parts. That might work, but it's not very satisfactory. A better solution is to use your mixer's tape monitor, and here's how it works. . . .

If your mixer or recorder/mixer has a tape monitor section, then there should be some level controls labelled 'tape monitor,' 'tape cue,' 'monitor,' 'monmix,' 'aux (tape),' or some similar term. If your mixer has four of these level controls, then you can monitor four tape tracks; if it has eight monitor controls, you can monitor eight tape tracks, and so on. Most recorder/mixers have as many tape monitor channels as they have tape tracks. If you have an independent mixer designed for personal multi-track work, it likely has four, eight, or 16 tape monitor channels—ideally, also as many tape monitor channels as tape tracks. Most professional mixers have 16 to 48 or more tape monitor channels.

When overdubbing, you use these tape monitor channels to listen to the tape recorder. By adjusting the level of the various monitor channels, you can create a *monitor mix*, with the tracks set to whatever relative monitor levels you wish—you can even turn a monitor channel off if you don't want to hear a track.

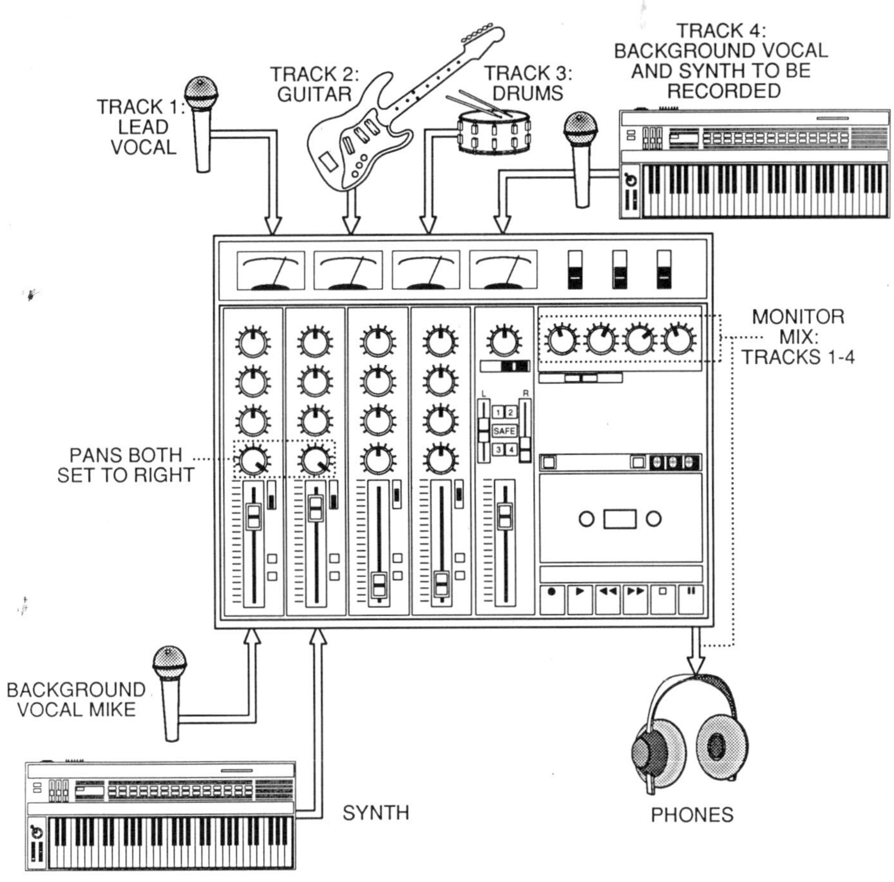

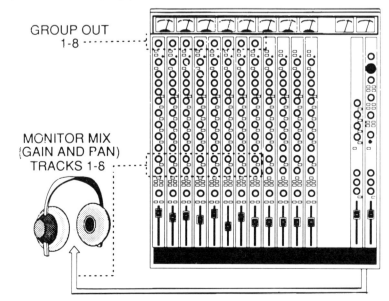

Figure 7.17 While overdubbing, your mixer's tape monitor allows you to listen to prerecorded tracks along with whatever new tracks are being recorded.

stereo position of each track. You could, for example, place the original vocal slightly to the left, the guitar on the right, the drums in

tune the response of the tape monitor inputs.

Split Vs. In-Line Tape Monitors. There are two types of tape monitors:

• When the tape monitor is located in an independent, separate section, 'split away' to the right of the input channels, it's known as a *split monitor*.
• When the tape monitor controls are integrated into the same space as the input channels, we have an *in-line monitor*.

Take a look back at Figure 7.6. Notice how the Scorpion's tape monitor section is a split design? If you look carefully, you'll also notice that the Fostex 450 has an in-line monitor—and that the Tascam PortaTwo is split. (The Fostex's monitors are slightly unusual, in that they can either be aux sends or tape monitors—in the 'tape' position they are tape monitors.)

Functionally, the tape monitors are very similar between these three units. If we want to monitor tape tracks 1, 2, and 3, we simply turn up the levels of tape monitors 1, 2, and 3, regardless of whether the monitor is split or in-line.

Split-monitor consoles, in general, are easier to understand, because the monitor controls are physically separate from the inputs. An in-line monitor design can be a bit more confusing: Let's say you're assigning inputs 1 and 2 to track 4, as we described in Figure 7.17. If you have a split monitor and want to hear the input to track 4, no problem, you just go to tape monitor 4, and turn the level up. If you have an in-line monitor, you do the same, but note that tape monitor 4 is physically located in-line with mixer input 4. This could get more confusing if, let's say, we also had a guitar in mixer input 4, and wanted to assign it to track 1. In this case, you would have mixer inputs 1 and 2 assigned to track 4, and mixer input 4 assigned to track 1. You would find tape monitor 1 (to hear the guitar from mixer input 4) in-line with mixer input 1, and you'd find tape monitor 4 (to hear mixer inputs 1 and 2) in-line with mixer input 4.

The key to understanding tape monitors, and staying on top of the potential confusion, is to remember that *during overdub-*

As we can see above in Figure 7.17 the vocal mike and the synth are plugged into inputs 1 and 2, which are in turn feeding track 4. Inputs 3 and 4 are unused. We can also see that there are four sources feeding the monitor section of the recorder/mixer: the previously-recorded vocal, guitar, and drum tracks, as well as the background vocal and synth tracks which we're about to record. This way we can hear and adjust the four tracks to whatever levels make us comfortable. We may want to hear a lot of drums, just a little guitar, and a moderate amount of the first vocal track. By adjusting their corresponding monitor levels, we can create our own custom monitor mix for this session.

By putting track 4 into 'record ready' (we may also have to press 'record' and possibly 'pause' depending upon the unit), the mixer section will automatically switch to *input monitor* mode for track 4, allowing us to hear the background vocal mike and the synth (we covered input mode back on page 28). Then, by adjusting the monitor level for track 4, we could set a comfortable listening level for the parts we're about to record. Remember, we're not listening directly to the input channels—rather, we're listening to the monitor section.

Most monitor sections, particularly those on independent mixers, have pan controls in addition to level controls. When tape monitors have pan controls, not only can you set the relative levels of tracks for your monitor mix, you can also set the

the center, and the background and synth in the center.

Some advanced mixers offer aux sends from each monitor channels, in addition to the level and pan controls. These aux sends can be used to add effects to tracks while you listen to them, or to create additional monitor mixes for other musicians.

Finally, a few professionally-oriented mixers have equalizers for some or all of their tape monitors, allowing you to fine-

Figure 7.18 With an in-line board, tape monitors returns are located within each input, rather than 'split away' as shown in Figure 7.17.

bing, mixer inputs feed tape tracks, and tape tracks feed tape monitor inputs.

Then, as long as you know how to route mixer inputs to tape tracks (via busses or direct output/assigns), and know which tape monitors to listen to and where to find them, you'll be able to record and to hear whichever tape tracks and inputs you want.

As mentioned earlier, many in-line consoles have their group outputs—as well as their tape monitor controls—located within channel inputs. That is to say, group buss 1 is in-line with input channel 1, group buss 2 is in-line with input channel 2, and so forth. Since each input module is both an input and an output, this is often known as an *I/O* design.

Many split consoles have the advantage of being able to use the tape monitor chan-nels as extra line input channels during mixdown (some in-line consoles can be configured to do this, but not as easily). This technique is described on page 99.

While in-line consoles are a bit trickier to understand, they are physically smaller than equivalent split consoles, and are just as easy to use once you get the hang of them.

* * * *

There is a wide variety of mixers and recorder/mixers on the market, and many of us will undoubtedly graduate to bigger and better mixers as we progress. For these reasons, this chapter has emphasized con-cepts, rather than rote, step-by-step in-structions.

We've seen the three main sections of multi-track mixers: the input, output, and monitor sections. We've covered many of the fundamental components you can expect to find in all of those sections—just remember that the three main sections of multi-track mixers can be found in a wide variety of different physical permutations. These variations can apply to any mixer or recorder/mixer of any size and though some may appear very different from one another, most are functionally similar.

We'll see more of mixers in action in the coming pages. When we start to lay down tracks in Chapter Twelve, be sure to refer back to this section anytime you have a question about mixer terminology or con-cepts. Being able to understand and use your mixer creatively may at times feel like a game—but it needn't remain a puzzle! □

CHAPTER 8: SIGNAL PROCESSING

Signal processing is to the recording engineer as lighting is to the photo-grapher. It allows the subject—music—to be colored and expressed in a variety of ways. Used properly, it can enhance your music and offer more professional-sounding results. But in the same way that the best lighting can be of little help to a photo-grapher with a poor choice of subject, all the latest and greatest signal processing gear is only a tool, and doesn't guarantee good music. In fact, many of the best producers realize that an overkill of effects can ruin a good song.

In any case, the last few years have seen the cost of effects and other signal process-ing gear drop to new lows, and a lot of this gear can be extremely useful to enhancing your music—just as lighting can enhance a photograph's mood. Effects that until a few years ago were reserved for the elite are not only affordable, but many of them are great performers! Used creatively and judiciously, signal processing can help you achieve pro-fessional-sounding results.

Without any kind of signal processing, the sound of everything we recorded would solely be dependent upon:

- The performance of our equipment.
- The sound of the instruments or voices.
- The acoustics of the room in which we recorded or monitored.

With accurate (and costly) equipment and beautiful room acoustics, some music is best recorded without any signal processing or special effects. Classical music, certainly, is one such music which most people prefer to record 'unadulterated.' When recording classical or other acoustic music, micro-phone placement determines how much of the room's natural reverberation is re-corded, and is usually the primary means used to effect the 'color' of the recording. When the equipment is not the most accu-rate, however, and the room isn't Carnegie Hall, we need to consider ways in which we can alter the sound to achieve realistic results. And, more to the point, today's music frequently tries to achieve distinctly non-realistic results. In fact, ever since the introduction of the electric guitar, popular music has used electricity to *modify* sound, creating new sound colors, tones, and spe-cial effects—wailing guitar feedback, cavern-ous-sounding drums, and swirling synthe-sized sonic soundscapes are commonplace to our ears.

Types Of Signal Processors

There are several categories of signal processing equipment which create these and other special effects. The categories include:

- *Equalizers* (EQs), which are used to alter the frequency response—or tone—of a signal.
- *Delays*—used to simulate echoes, in addi-tion to many special effects such as 'flang-ing,' 'phase shifting,' 'chorusing'—all of which use delay functions to create their swirling and shifting 'multi-dimensional' sounds.
- *Reverbs*, which can recreate the natural reverberation of acoustic spaces, such as rooms, concert halls, and even canyons, as well as perform special, 'unnatural' effects.
- *Dynamic controllers*, which control in different ways the amplitude levels of sig-nals. Some dynamic controllers include *compressor/limiters, gates, expanders,* and other devices, and are used to help record with proper levels, reduce noise, and create special effects.
- *Miscellaneous processors*, which include unique devices such as *vocoders* (which allow an instrument to 'play' a voice), *exciters* (which enhance the apparent brightness of music in a way which changes with the music), and other devices.
- *Noise reduction*, which can be built into tape recorders or added as outboard gear, to reduce tape hiss and make for quieter recordings.

Virtually all mixers used for multi-track recording have some type of built-in equali-zation. A few mixers—particularly those oriented for live sound work—have built-in reverbs and delays, and some of the most expensive multi-track mixers have integral dynamic controllers.

Aside from EQ, however, most signal processors are in the form of *outboard* gear—that is, they are not built into the mixer, and are connected as outboard, aux-iliary devices.

Digital Vs. Analog Processing

Pick up any current musicians' maga-zine, and you'll see advertisements for a host of signal processing products. Particularly in the field of reverbs and delays, *the* buzz-word is *digital*. What does this mean when talking about an effect—does an effect have to be digital to be any good?

A true digital effect is one which pro-cesses all of the sound digitally, using a microprocessor (essentially, a computer). With digital effects, the incoming *analog* (non-digital) signal is converted to a series of binary computer-code numbers, called *bits*. By altering the structure of the computer codes, and reconverting the codes back to an analog signal, the sound can be manipu-lated in a number of different ways. This is an ideal method for reverbs, delays, and other devices to operate, since the codes can be stored for recall, and the digital pro-cess introduces no noise to the signal. (More about digital audio on page 124.)

In general, EQs and dynamic-controlling devices are analog, though this is starting to change. With analog gear, the signal is manipulated by altering the actual elec-tronic signal (and not converting it to a digital code). In doing so, some of the analog device's own noise is introduced to the signal—this is the chief drawback of analog processing. Occasionally EQs and other devices are *digitally-controlled*— which does *not* necessarily mean that the sound entering and leaving the device is digitally processed. Digital control means that different signal effect settings can be stored in the device's memory for later recall (just as with true digital effects). This storage/recall facility is ideal for changing the effect within a song, or for comparing different settings.

Just as the vacuum tube has all but succumbed to the transistor, though, analog gear is being gradually replaced by digital gear, not only for storage and recall, but theoretically better and quieter processing. As this happens, the smart shopper may be able to pick up some excellent though unfashionable equipment at bargain prices. Many analog devices—particularly EQs and dynamic processors—sound great, and introduce little discernible noise, distortion, or other sonic rubbish. In fact, there are engineers who prefer some of the older, 'warmer'-sounding (as in more harmonically distorted) equipment, and put it to creative use. With this kind of an approach, no equipment is ever truly obsolete!

Until multi-effect devices are available six at a time for a pittance (which may not be all that far away), most home recordists must prioritize outboard signal processing gear, starting with one or two pieces and adding slowly. In addition to built-in mixer EQ, a reverb unit is usually the first priority for most home recordists trying to achieve a quality sound, followed by a delay or compressor.

One promising trend is the incorporation of *several* effects into one box. While most of these units can only do one effect at a time, some effects boxes are *multi-tasking*, and can perform two or more effects—such as reverb, delay, EQ, and so on—at once!

Whether or not you purchase any outboard signal processors, chances are you already own several processors—the built-in equalizers in your mixer or recorder/mixer. Let's take a look at equalization. . . .

Equalization

All of us have used equalizers (EQs), if only the bass and treble controls of a home stereo. From those two controls, we know that *boosting* (raising the level of) the treble control makes music sound 'brighter.' We also know that *cutting* (lowering the level of) the treble tends to 'dull' or even 'muffle' the sound of music. Similarly, boosting or cutting the bass creates related changes in the tone of the lower frequencies.

In fact, what's going on when we fiddle with these controls is that we're increasing and decreasing the gain of specific frequency bands in the musical spectrum. By plugging an audio signal into an EQ, we can alter its frequency response—and by doing so, we're able to adjust the overall tone of music to suit our own taste.

Equalizers can be used on a single channel of audio, such as a bass guitar or vocal, or they can be used on an entire mix of music (as they are used in home stereos). By altering frequency response, EQs can be used to:

- Make a vocal track sound as if the singer is coming out of a telephone (by cutting all the low frequencies and boosting the upper-mid- frequencies).
- Reduce high-frequency tape noise or record surface noise (by cutting the appropriate high frequencies).
- Help a piano sound much more 'present'

and 'unmuddy' (by cutting the appropriate mid-frequencies).
- Simulate stereo from a monaural instrument (as we'll learn on page 94).

These are just a few of the uses for equalizers. In their most basic applications, EQs can be used to compensate for microphones, speakers, and so on, in order to make an instrument or voice sound more natural—or at least more suited to our taste. In more advanced applications, EQs are used to create special effects such as the ones described above.

In these next few pages we're going to explore EQs and equalization—things may get a bit technical, but in order to truly understand the role of equalizers in recording, it's necessary to understand how they work, and what they do to your music.

Active Vs. Passive. Equalizers are designed with *active* or *passive* circuits. Active EQ circuits are actually very low-power amplifiers which are capable of boosting or cutting specified frequencies; passive EQ circuits are electronic filters designed solely to cut frequencies. For the most part, EQs designed for recording—including outboard and built-into-mixer devices—have active circuits. A common passive circuit is the tone control found on most electric guitars. By turning this control counterclockwise, it 'filters out' high frequencies, making the guitar sound more 'muffled.' Since passive EQ circuits don't use any amplifier stages, they don't require any AC or DC power to operate. Filters are still found in many synthesizers, and filter-only EQs are sometimes used to equalize the frequency response of monitor speakers.

Bands. A simple bass and treble control—such as those found on many recorder/mixers—is known as a *2-band* EQ. The number of bands that an equalizer has refers to the number of segments of the audio spectrum (20 Hz to 20 kHz, approximately) that the EQ is able to effect individually. So a 2-band EQ divides the audio spectrum into just two bands, a 10-band EQ divides it into 10, and so on.

A typical 2-band bass and treble EQ doesn't offer the ability to control sound in a refined manner, since adjusting one frequency tends to affect a broad band of frequencies. Think of trying to use a single treble control on a home stereo to reduce tape hiss or record surface noise: When you do so you also cut out a lot of music in the high-end! Trying to reduce a rumbling noise with just a bass control also cuts out musical information. Consequently, a 2-band EQ can be used to adjust the overall tone of an instrument or a piece of music, but not specific frequencies. We'll learn more about bands a bit further ahead, under "Graphic EQs."

EQ Response Characteristics. Let's consider a simple 3-band EQ, with a bass, a 'midrange,' and a treble control. Figure 8.1 shows us a graph of such an EQ's *response curves*—the lines which represent the range of frequencies which are affected when the EQ's bands are at maximum cut or boost.

What this graph shows us is the range of effect of the three bands, the bass (low frequency) band on the left, the midrange in the middle, and the treble (high frequency) band on the right. The half of each band

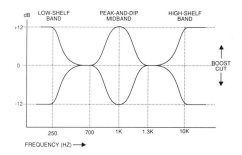

Figure 8.1 *Response curves of a typical 3-band equalizer, with shelving low and high bands, and a peak-and-dip mid-band.*

above the "0 dB" mark shows the maximum range of boost for each band; the half of each band below the "0 dB" mark shows the maximum range of cut.

Notice how the bass and treble bands look different from the midrange band? As with many 2- and 3-band EQs, these low and high frequency bands have a *shelving* response: A *high-shelf* band is one which introduces boost or cut at a *shelf frequency* (also called *hinge frequency*), and then 'flattens out' to boost or cut everything above that frequency to the same degree. Similarly, a *low-shelf* band can boost or cut a shelf frequency, and then flatten out to boost or cut everything *below* that frequency to the same degree.

The midrange band in Figure 8.1 on the other hand, represents a *peak-and-dip* response. Peak-and-dip EQs are exactly as they sound to be: They 'peak' when boosted, and 'dip' when cut, at a *center frequency*—and have a lesser effect on frequencies lower or higher than the center frequency. The center frequency of the midrange band pictured is 1 kHz. As we'll learn about starting on page 45 some EQs allow you to change the center frequencies of one or more bands. For now, though, we're dealing with *fixed-frequency* EQ bands.

Musically, shelving and peak-and-dip bands are quite different from each other. Referring once again to Figure 8.1 take a look at what happens when the high frequency band is cut all the way: All frequencies above 10 kHz or so are cut—and that's why turning down a treble control to reduce hiss at 16 kHz also reduces response around 10 kHz, which can reduce the top end of cymbals and other instruments. Peak-and-dip bands are much more useful for controlling specific instruments or frequencies. A peak-and-dip band centered at 3 kHz, for example, would be able to 'brighten' the sound of a snare drum without boosting hiss.

Shelving EQs do have an important role to play, however, and if used carefully can be quite effective. If a mix is too bright, a high-shelving EQ can be used to lower the overall treble content—it's a lot more straightforward than tying up lots of graphic bands. For these and other reasons, shelving EQs are frequently found not only on recorder/mixers, but also as the high- and low-bands on numerous mixers.

Figure 8.1 also shows us that the amount of boost or cut available from each band is measured in terms of decibels—the typical range of boost and cut is 12 or 15 dB in each direction. The range of control for the bass band in Figure 8.1 can be expressed as *250 Hz (shelving response), ±12 dB*. Remember that every 10 dB is an approximate doubling in apparent volume—so that much of the range of a bass guitar (which is 40 to 440 Hz) will sound louder if we boost a bass control hinged at 250 Hz by 10 dB.

We know now that high-shelf bands affect frequencies above their hinge frequencies, and low-shelf bands affect below their hinges. Peak-and-dip bands, however, affect a limited range of frequencies above or below their center frequencies. For example, we don't boost 1 kHz exclusively when we increase the midrange control. In fact, with the control shown we boost frequencies all the way from 700 to 1300 Hz, though the greatest degree of effect occurs at the center frequency. This range of effect is known as *bandwidth* (page 46). Not all EQs have the same bandwidth for each band, and some EQs allow you to adjust the bandwidth, as we'll learn more about shortly.

* * * *

So far, there are several things we've learned about EQs:

• An EQ can be designed with either active or passive circuits. Active circuits are most common.
• EQs have bands, and each band covers a specified frequency range.
• Bands have shelving or peak-and-dip response curves. Shelving is most common with the highest and lowest bands of 2- or 3-band EQs; those bands are known respectively as high-shelf and low-shelf bands.
• Shelving bands have shelf, or hinge, frequencies at above or below which the EQ can boost or cut.
• Peak-and-dip bands have a center frequency at which the maximum boost or cut takes place.
• When the center or hinge frequency is non-adjustable, the band is a fixed-frequency band.
• Each band can be boosted or cut by a specific number of dBs.
• The frequencies which are affected by boosting or cutting a peak-and-dip EQ band represent its bandwidth.

We've been describing simple 2-and 3-band fixed-frequency EQs up to this point. There are several other types of EQs commonly used in recording, including:

• *Graphic* EQs.
• *Sweep-frequency*, or *semi-parametric* EQs.
• *Parametric* EQs.

Graphic EQs. Graphic EQs are perhaps the most popular type of equalizer, since they are quite easy to use and can be relatively affordable. They are usually single- or dual-channel outboard units, with anywhere from five to 62 fixed-frequency bands per channel—though the most common are 10-, 15-, 27-, and 31-band graphics. Almost all graphic EQs found in the recording world are outboard units.

Most graphic EQs use a series of linear sliders—one for each frequency band of the audio spectrum—to adjust the sound. The sliders are arranged with the lowest frequencies on the left, and the highest frequencies on the right. When adjusted, the various physical settings of these sliders provide a rough graphic representation of which frequencies the EQ is altering, and to what degree. Consequently, they allow you to change signals in a visually-predictive way.

For example, let's say we were listening to a sustained synthesizer chord through a mixer, and the music had a fairly flat frequency response. Now let's say we had a 10-band graphic EQ, and connected it in between the output of the synthesizer and the input to the mixer. Altering the controls of the graphic EQ would produce predictable responses, as seen in Figure 8.2.

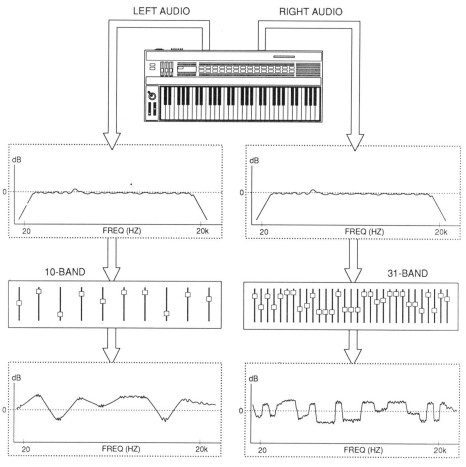

Figure 8.2 Graphic EQs offer a graphic representation of how they affect sound. As we can see, more bands offer greater resolution, and offer greater control over how sound is shaped. (One-third octave EQs are available with anywhere from 27 to 31 bands.)

Figure 8.2 also shows the response curve a 31-band graphic EQ.

Notice that as the number of bands increases, the bandwidth—the plus or minus frequency range of each center frequency—decreases. That's to say, the more bands, the finer the *resolution*, or degree of control. With a 10-band EQ, for example, high-frequency noise around 16 kHz can be controlled with one band of EQ, without affecting musical material around 10 kHz. We couldn't do this with a 2-band EQ because it has less resolution—trying to reduce 16 kHz noise would reduce 10 kHz music content. But with a 31-band EQ, for example, we'd be able to cut down the level of a 16 kHz clicking noise while boosting the uppermost harmonics of a cymbal at 14 kHz—something we couldn't do with a 10-

band graphic.

A 10-band EQ is also known as an *octave* EQ, because its band controls have center frequencies which increase by one octave at a time (a doubling or halving of a frequency is a change of one musical octave). A typical 10-band EQ has its bands centered on *31, 62, 125, 250, 500, 1 k, 2 k, 4 k, 8 k, and 16 k* Hertz. In a similar manner, a 31-band EQ is known as a *one-third* octave EQ, since each center frequency is one-third of an octave apart, and a 15-band EQ is known as a *two-thirds* octave EQ. But what do all of these numbers have to do with *music*?

The answer lies in remembering that music—or more generally, audio—covers an approximate frequency range of 20 Hz to 20 kHz. A single fundamental note of an instrument may have harmonics which go way beyond the fundamental frequency (as we learned on page 4. Being able to cut or boost not only the fundamental but also the harmonics is what allows us to change the *tone quality* of an audio signal. Because a graphic EQ's bands cover most of the audio spectrum, many people use them to shape the overall tone of an instrument or voice. In this manner, many of the bands may stay set at '0 db'—where they aren't affecting the frequencies—while other bands are boost or cut as necessary.

One-third octave graphic EQs are also popular in live sound reinforcement, where feedback can be squelched quickly by cutting the offending frequency. Graphic EQs are often employed in conjunction with a real-time analyzer—as is described ahead on page 74—to adjust the frequency re-

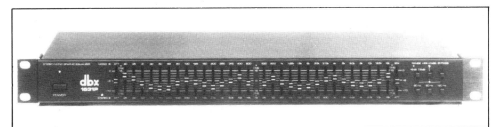

Figure 8.3 dbx's 1531P can function as either a dual channel 15-band EQ, or as a single channel 30-band EQ.

sponse of loudspeakers, so that they perform as accurately as possible in a given room.

There are, by the way, some graphic EQs which aren't really graphics: These fixed-frequency EQs, such as the one-third octave White 802, use rotary instead of linear controls for each band, and can be treated in every way as graphics (except that they don't provide a 'graphic' picture of their effect).

Sweep-Frequency EQs. So far, we've been talking about fixed-frequency EQs, where each band is centered at an unchangeable frequency. The next step up in the hierarchy of EQs is one which allows you to select *which* frequency can be cut or boosted for one or more bands. This is known as a *sweep-frequency* EQ. It's also called a *semi-parametric*, or just plain *sweep* EQ.

There are a few 10-band graphic sweep-frequency EQs on the market, such as the Orban 674A, and they're wonderful, since they provide a graphic visual reference along with a secondary frequency control for each band. For the most part, however, sweep EQs are 2- to 4-band equalizers—built into mixers and recorder/mixers, or outboard—and allow you to adjust the center frequency of one or more of the bands.

A common arrangement with many recorder/mixers is a sweepable 2-band EQ on each input. Even though these are only 2-band EQs, the fact that you can select which center frequency (or hinge frequency, if it's a 2-band sweepable *shelving* EQ) you're cutting or boosting greatly enhances their flexibility.

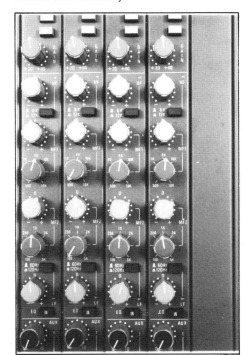

Figure 8.4 The EQ section of a TAC Scorpion mixing console.

Figure 8.4 shows a closeup of the TAC Scorpion's 4-band equalizer. Note that the

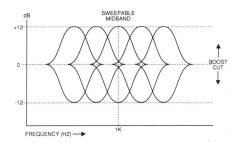

Figure 8.5 A 'sweep mid' control offers a range of cut or boost.

high- and low-frequency bands (which are shelving) each have selectable hinge frequencies. The two mid-bands (both peak-and-dip) can be cut or boosted over a very wide range of frequencies—the upper mid-band can sweep from 500 Hz to 18 kHz, the lower mid from 100 Hz to 5 kHz. This design is known, in insider's lingo, as a '4-band, sweepable mids' EQ.

A sweep EQ can be really handy; the ability to choose *which* frequencies you're

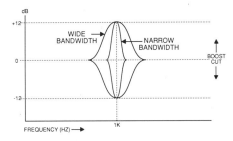

Figure 8.6 Comparative bandwidths.

equalizing provides some pretty powerful tone control. "Basic EQ Tips," on page 47, discusses some things to bear in mind when using EQs, and with a sweep EQ you can take advantage of each of those suggestions.

Parametric EQ. Whereas graphic EQs are useful for general tone modifications and are easy to use, and sweep EQs are common and useful, a true parametric EQ offers unparalleled tone control. As we've learned,

graphic EQs allow you to boost or cut at fixed frequencies and bandwidths; sweep EQs allow you to choose which frequency is being cut or boosted, giving you greater control and flexibility. Parametric EQs, on the other hand, have everything going for them. Each parametric band has three controls which allow you to:

• Select a center frequency for each band.
• Cut and boost on each band.
• Adjust the bandwidth of each band.

Look back at Figure 8.1—and take note of the midrange frequency control's EQ curve. If we could control the bandwidth of just that frequency and band, we could have curves which look like Figure 8.6.

This combination of frequency and bandwidth control allows music to be tailored with a wonderful degree of precision. Unfortunately, all of this control can be difficult to use effectively, and offers a real challenge to the user. For example, when the bandwidth is set to a minimum, it may be impossible to hear the EQ do anything, especially if there's no musical content at the frequency selected!

Specialized Filters. There are four other types of equalization we haven't discussed. All of these are known as filters, since they cut frequencies, though they can be active or passive (again, passive EQs don't require any power to operate).

The most common of these are *high-pass* and *low-pass* filters. Many people are familiar with these controls from their home stereos: The switch marked *subsonic* (or sometimes *low filter*)—which removes low frequency rumble—is actually a high-pass filter. The the switch marked *high filter*—which removes high frequency hiss and the like—is actually a low-pass filter. Confusing but true! In any event, high-pass filters are quite common, as a single switch, in some better consoles. Low-pass, as well as high-pass filters, are frequently found as switches or variable controls in many top consoles as well as outboard EQs.

Here's what they do: High-pass filters are designed to cut out bass frequencies, and let everything *higher* than a certain frequency be heard. They're usually fixed between 60 and 120 Hz or so, though sometimes are variable on better consoles and outboard EQs. High-pass filters have a really steep roll-off (usually 24 dB/octave), designed to minimize any sound below the pass frequency. This type of filter is useful for eliminating all types of unwanted low-frequency noise and rumble, everything from trucks rolling by on the street to a singer's footsteps, which can be picked up by a microphone (via a floor stand). With certain instruments—such as a bass guitar—a high-pass filter can make the sound pretty thin, by

Figure 8.7 This parametric EQ by Orban can function either as a dual-channel 4-band, or single-channel 8-band EQ. It also includes low- and high-pass filters and a fine-tune 'vernier' control for the frequency of each band.

removing all the essential low-end information. Some engineers, however, prefer to engage them all the time (providing they're not adversely affecting the signal).

Low-pass filters let everything *lower* than a selected frequency pass through and be heard. They are most useful for getting rid of excessive high-end noise above 12 kHz or so. A low-pass filter can make things sound dull, though, especially cymbals.

You may run into *notch filters*, which are interesting and useful tools in the studio as well as for live sound. Simply, a notch filter allows you to 'zero in' on a particular frequency and effectively remove it from the signal. We've all been at concerts (or participated in them!) when the grit-your-teeth sound of feedback comes screaming through the speakers, only to be picked up by the microphones again and re-amplified. A notch filter can be used in such a circumstance to find the offending frequency of the feedback and cut it out.

Essentially, a notch filter band is centered at a particular frequency (usually variable) and is able to cut 30 dB or more (up to -∞) at that frequency, by having a curve with super-steep slopes and a very narrow bandwidth. In a recording situation, a notch filter can be used to help reduce the squeak from a piano pedal, a 'boomy' frequency from a kick drum, as well as the North American 60 Hz (or 50 Hz elsewhere) hum which

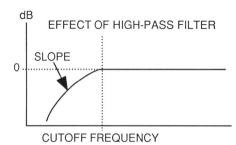

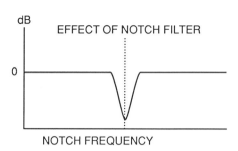

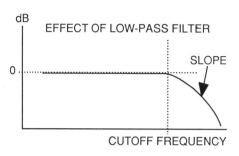

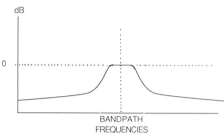

Figures 8.8a, 8.8b, 8.8c, 8.8d Various filter responses.

can find its way onto a tape of otherwise great music (more about this hum starting on page 81). Notch filters are rarely found in consoles: If not a separate piece of outboard gear, they are often found included in a parametric equalizer.

Finally, a *band-pass* filter is more or less the opposite of a notch filter, in that it singles out a particular frequency and attenuates all other frequencies high and low of the chosen one. These are rare to find these days (outside of synthesizers), as their recording applications are limited.

Understanding Bandwidth

As we know, 'bandwidth' refers to the range of frequencies which are effected by an EQ band. In order to use your EQ to its full sonic potential, it's really important to understand your EQ's bandwidth—whether you have simple 2- or 3-band, graphic, sweep, or parametric EQs.

Parametric EQs allow you to vary the bandwidth. Some of the better mixers may have 'quasi-parametric' EQ bands which offer a switch to choose a wide or narrow bandwidth for one or more EQ bands. All other EQ bands are fixed-bandwidth. The term Q, for "quality factor," is used to express an EQ's bandwidth. Many people use 'Q' and 'bandwidth' interchangeably, though they're not necessarily the same term, depending upon who you talk to. Bandwidth is typically expressed in octaves, so that a one-third octave EQ band has a bandwidth of 0.33 octaves. The higher that figure, the wider the bandwidth.

Instead of referring to the entire bandwidth range, Q is a figure which represents a ratio of the center frequency divided by the '3 dB down' frequencies on either side of the center frequency. It's graph time again:

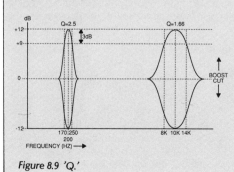

Figure 8.9 'Q.'

In Figure 8.9 we can see two bands of peak-and-dip EQ. The low-frequency band (on the left) has a very *narrow* bandwidth, and the high-frequency band has a very *wide* bandwidth. Take a look at the low-frequency band, and find the frequencies on either side of the center frequency (200 Hz) which are 3 dB down in level from 200 Hz. They are 250 Hz and 170 Hz. Now we can use a formula to calculate the Q:

$$Q = \frac{\text{CENTER FREQUENCY}}{\{\text{HI FREQ} - \text{LO FREQ}\}}$$

[Where "Hi" and "Lo" frequencies are measured at -3 dB down from the center frequency.]

or in other words:

$$Q = \frac{200}{\{250 - 170\}}$$

$$= 2.5$$

So in this case, the Q is 2.5. Try calculating the Q for the high-frequency band. Using the same formula, you should come up with a Q of 1.66. So now we've figured out that—unlike octave representations of bandwidth—the higher the Q number, the narrower the bandwidth.

Parametrics offer variable bandwidths, and the amount of Q that one should select will, of course, depend upon the music one wishes to EQ. Similarly, if you don't own a parametric, knowing the approximate bandwidth of the frequencies you wish to adjust will help you immensely.

For example, let's say we wanted to brighten the sound of an acoustic guitar. A broad boost of its higher harmonics, which might be from 3 to 8 kHz, would be appropriate. With a graphic EQ, this could either be done by boosting bands from 3 to 8 kHz by 1 to 3 dB. With a parametric EQ, you might achieve the same by centering a band at 5500 Hz, setting the band for maximum bandwidth, and boosting appropriately. If, on the other hand, there was a particular frequency which would sound great being boosted (or an offending frequency which begs to be cut), a single graphic band or a narrow Q setting on a parametric would be the appropriate tool to use.

The term *rolloff* (or *slope*), by the way—as indicated in Figure 8.8a—refers to the rate at which the EQ either gains or loses its effect on either side of the center frequency. It's expressed in terms of *dB/octave* (decibels per octave), and helps determine the bandwidth.

When bandwidth is not adjustable, most EQs are designed to be 'musical,' so that their bands cover the frequency ranges which the design engineers consider most effective. Whether fixed or adjustable, however, EQs should have a 'constant-Q' design—so that once set, each band's bandwidth stays the same regardless of the amount of cut or boost. Without this type of design, you'll be affecting a different range of frequencies depending upon how much EQ-action each band is getting.

The most effective way to use a notch or band-pass filter is to set it to maximum cut or boost, then adjust the frequency control. If it's a notch filter and you're using it to eliminate feedback, the feedback should disappear as soon as you dial in the offending frequency.

EQs And Amplitude. One thing to keep in mind when you use EQs is that they can alter the overall level of any signal passing through them.

For example, when you boost any band of EQ, you increase the total level of the track being processed. When a band of EQ is cut, that track's level is also cut. This is perhaps most important to remember with graphic EQs: If every band of a 31-band EQ is boosted 6 dB, then (in theory) an instrument passing through that EQ will sound the same as if it were passing through the EQ with every band set to '0'—except that it will be louder, and there will be more noise in the signal.

The noise factor is an important key: Remember that EQs use amplifiers to boost signals, and even the best of amplifiers introduce noise. You can hear your equalizer's inherent 'self' noise by just listening to it *without* any signal passing through. As certain bands are boosted or cut, you'll be able to hear noise being introduced (or cut) from the system.

Take a look at Figure 8.10. What we have here are two EQs, each with the same EQ settings. The EQ on the bottom is introducing a lot of extra noise, however, since so much extra boosting of the signal is happening—not only are musical frequencies being boosted, but so is noise. The general rule of thumb for using EQs is that usually all the settings should average around zero, as we can see with the EQ on the left.

EQ SET FOR OPTIMUM S/N

EQ SET TOO HIGH FOR OPTIMUM S/N

Figure 8.10

Basic EQ Tips

Equalization is not, in all cases, the best way to control the tone quality of an instrument or voice. As we've learned, active EQs can introduce noise and distortion to your signal. They can also cause subtle phase shifts, which can further degrade your signal. And some of the cheaper models use filters which can actually cause a 'ringing' sound!

For these and other reasons, some engineers prefer to use EQ as a last resort for modifying a tone, and would prefer to re-program a synthesizer or change a mike's placement before using EQ. Related to this, a general rule of thumb to apply to equalization is that *less is more*. This is not only to minimize the sonic problems just mentioned: Too much EQ can create an im-

balanced sound. Subtle use of EQ is often more musically effective than huge 10 dB cuts and boosts all over the spectrum. This minimalist approach can be applied to much of the recording process, in fact, through signal processors to the actual arrangement and production of the music.

Still, equalization remains a powerful tool, and its benefits usually outweigh its drawbacks—particularly if you understand your EQs. Your ears are the best tools for *learning* about EQ, and how to create effective sonic tones. Because of this, the most important tip about EQs (as well as all signal processing gear) is to *experiment*! If you own a graphic EQ, what happens when you boost just one band and cut all the others? If your mixer or recorder/mixer has sweepable bands of EQ, try playing a steady chord (or drum machine pattern, or whatever) through a channel, and listen to the effect of sweeping to different frequencies and cutting or boosting.

As you experiment and listen closely and critically, you'll improve your EQ technique. Listen not only to the effect you are having on the music, but listen for the 'side effects.' If you're equalizing a bass guitar, does boosting around 10 kHz do anything, or does it just add noise? Similarly, does cutting around 500 Hz detract from the 'bottom end' of the bass? Does that depend upon which notes are being played? Remember, most instruments cover a broad range, and just the fundamental notes may cross over several EQ bands.

By using your ears, you'll not only learn which bands and degree of effect are useful to achieve the sound you want with the instruments you're recording, but you'll also learn what's not so useful. Here are some general tips which may help that process:

- **Beware of 'frequency masking.'** An instrument which has been EQ'd to sound great on its own may not always sound so great when it's 'in the mix' with several other instruments. For example, a warm, muted guitar with very little high frequency information might sound wonderful on its own, but may be lost when played back with keyboards and lots of background vocals. This is because our ears make a kind of composite signal of all sounds happening at once. When several instruments emphasize similar frequencies, such as a muted guitar, keyboards, and vocals, those frequencies accumulate, and can become overbearing or cause one instrument to 'mask' another. Be prepared to re-equalize tracks when mixdown time arrives, or better yet, think ahead and try to 'visualize' the frequencies you'll have to contend with when all the tracks are done. This kind of 'frequency inventory' can help you plan appropriate EQ settings.
- **The low end.** Very few loudspeakers are capable of accurate bass reproduction below 40 Hz. So go easy down there—unless your speakers have phenomenal bass response, it will be difficult to equalize, with any accuracy, frequencies much lower than 40 Hz. Those of us with smaller speakers especially may have a tendency to boost bass frequencies—but what winds up sounding good on our little speakers may sound terrible on a larger

pair. The useful low frequencies to pay attention to are from 40 to 250 Hz, where you can find kick drums, keyboards, some vocals, and even the lower registers of a guitar. While some degree of boost can add 'body' to kick drums and male vocals, guitars and other instruments can sound too muddy or boomy if these frequencies are boosted too much.

- **The midrange.** The midrange frequencies (250 Hz to 2 kHz) seem to accumulate an excess amount of information sooner than other frequencies. It's helpful to keep this in mind when building tracks. A piano or guitar, for example, can become quite muddy-sounding if EQ'd with too much midrange. Often a slight cut between 500 and 1200 Hz will help. Don't go overboard, though—it's easy to create a mix that's all 'sizzle' and 'thump,' with too little midrange information, particularly when there are mostly acoustic instruments. The all-important human voice can be found in the midrange, and it's important not to make it too thin by equalizing out the warmth and humanity.
- **The upper-midrange.** Many engineers and producers use the term 'definition'—which can mean a lot of things, but usually refers to the intelligibility, or 'cut' of a particular instrument or voice. The upper-midrange and lower-high-frequency areas of 2 to 6 kHz contain many of the harmonics which, when carefully EQ'd, can improve an instrument's definition. For instance, if you wish to bring the 'snap' of a 'slapped' bass, try boosting around 3 kHz. Many other string instruments in particular, including violins, mandolins, guitars, and the like, have harmonics in this range. Listen carefully—too much boost can make things sound harsh, and too much cut can make a mix sound dull and lifeless.
- **The high end.** The highest frequencies from 6 to 15 kHz (and higher) contain mostly harmonic information, though there are some fundamentals of cymbals, synthesizers, and other instruments residing in this 'top end' of the audio spectrum. Listen closely to each track. Does cutting the high end slightly reduce noise and *not* affect the track? Or does a slight boost add 'life' and 'sparkle' to the sound? Follow your ear, but be careful boosting up here—tape hiss and other noise can benefit more than the music.
- **How's your reference?** Your ears are only as good as the monitor chain. As we'll learn on page 69 it's critical that you use speakers which you can *trust* to deliver a reasonably accurate picture of the sound you're creating. Whenever possible, give yourself 'second opinions' by listening to your music through a car stereo, a portable stereo, or even a friend's stereo. Even in the best studios, a great studio mix can fall apart in a 'real-life' situation.

One common tendency when using EQs in music is to cut the middle frequencies—say those from 500 to 2000 Hz. The audible result with pianos, guitars, and other *mid-range* instruments is that the signal becomes 'cleaner,' with less mid-range 'presence.' For example, Figure 8.11a shows a typical 15-band graphic setting that might work well with a piano:

15-BAND EQ

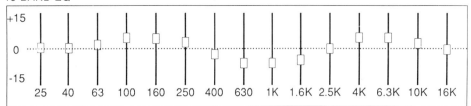

TYPICAL ROCK PIANO SETTING

15-BAND EQ

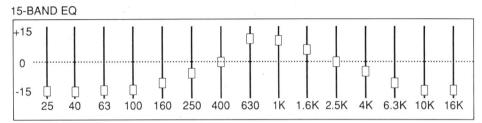

TELEPHONE-CALL SETTING

Figures 8.11a, 8.11b Equalizers can be used for a variety of purposes, from tailoring an instrument's sound, to creating a special effect. Typically, when pianos are heard 'in the mix' with other instruments, they tend to lose definition, since many of their important frequencies are masked by other tracks. Cutting the mids and boosting the lows and upper-mids tends to help many pianos 'cut through' the mix. Similarly, the 'peaky' sound so commonly associated with telephones is in part related to the fact that telephone lines boost mid frequencies—those frequencies where the voice is—in order to provide greater definition. The setting shown mimics that response.

Using the 'graphic' analogy, we can see that the mid-frequencies of 630 and 1000 Hz have been cut by about 6 dB, and some lower and higher frequencies have been boosted. Try to visualize how a piano might sound being equalized in this manner. It should sound brighter and bassier, because of the frequencies we're boosting. Similarly, many of the mid-range tones would be played down, perhaps making the piano sound a bit 'thinner.'

To many people, such a setting makes the piano more intelligible, and gives it more 'cut,' especially when it's recorded with several other instruments. That's because most recordings contain a lot of mid-range frequencies, from vocals to keyboards and guitars—sometimes the recording can benefit by reducing some of these frequencies. For many engineers, however, a much better alternative to having to EQ a piano in this way is to mike it in such a manner that a similar frequency response is achieved.

To demonstrate another application of a graphic, take a look at Figure 8.11b.

Can you visualize what your voice would sound like coming through an EQ with this setting? As we can see, almost all the low end is cut, as is a lot of the upper-high end. In addition, the mid-frequencies are radically boosted. If you have a EQ graphic, try this setting with a vocal—it should sound as if you're singing through a telephone!

No matter what your EQ—a 2-band built into your ministudio, or an elaborate outboard parametric—listen and experiment. Compare other recordings, professional or amateur, with your own. Are the vocals equalized in the same way? Can you tell which frequencies are favored by different producers and engineers with different instruments? Do EQ settings stay the same with the same instruments from song to song, or do they change? Do settings even remain the same within one song?

The answers to these and other ques- tions will describe your recording's 'sound color'—a critical element in your overall artistic statement.

Acoustics And Spatial Effects

Many of the most useful signal process- ing devices on the market are *spatial effects*. Not to be confused with *special effects* (though they can perform them), spatial effects are devices that alter the perceived acoustic space of a sound. These devices can reproduce natural effects, such as *echo*, *delay*, or *reverberation*, or they can create true 'special' effects, such as *flanging* or *chorusing*.

There are quite a few varieties of spatial effects devices, including:

- Delays (including tape, analog, and digital delays), which are used to create single or repeating echoes, as well as flanging and chorusing effects.
- Reverbs, which simulate acoustic spaces such as rooms, halls, and even caverns.
- Phase shifters, as well as independent flangers, and chorus devices, all designed to create specialized, swirling, '3-dimensional' sonic effects.

One common thread linking all of these devices is their ability to *manipulate sound over time*. Sound and time are inextricably linked in our world—to appreciate this, an understanding of the fundamentals of acoustics is necessary, and will help us get the most out of our delays, reverbs, and other spatial effects.

Echoes, Reflections, And Time. *The Grand Canyon. The Swiss Alps. The Taj Mahal.* If we paint a sonic picture of these places in our minds, we can imagine repeti- tive echoes and cavernous sounds, expand- ing a casual yodel into a magical chorus of yodels. These places can do their sonic tricks because the physical shape of their environ- ments cause sound to *reflect* back to its

source. The time that elapses between the original sound and the returning reflected sounds is known as the *delay*. Our ears are remarkable instruments, and as we'll learn, we're capable of hearing astonishingly small delays in sound. Let's take a look at 'real-life' echo and delay, and while we're at it, we'll get in a short lesson on acoustics.

An echo is a repeat of a sound. There are two types of real-life echoes:

- A *single-repeat* echo, which is often called a *slapback* echo by the engineering cogniscenti.
- A *multiple-repeat* echo, also known as a *multiple delay*.

A single echo occurs when a sound is reflected back to its source just once. If you'd like to try some acoustic experiments, and don't live in the Grand Canyon, try this: Find a flat, smooth, hard-surfaced wall, face it head on from a distance of about 10 to 20 meters (about 30 to 70 feet), and clap your hands sharply, just once. If the wall is reflec- tive enough (that is, smooth and hard enough—concrete is ideal), and you've faced it head on (so that the sound of your hand clap will reflect and return to you), you should hear an echo!

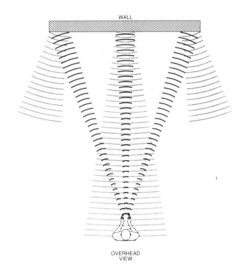

Figure 8.12 Cheap fun with walls.

With a single wall, we'll only hear one echo. After the delayed sound returns to our ears, it carries on past us, and we can no longer hear it.

Next, find two parallel and reflective walls, at least 10 meters apart—ensure that the walls are truly parallel. For now, try and find a space without any connection be- tween the two walls—a path between two concrete buildings is a good choice. Position yourself equidistant between the two walls, let out a mighty clap, and listen to the effect.

If your site selection has been careful, you should hear an *amazing* ricochet sound, as your clap hits a wall, flies back past your ears, hits the opposite wall, flies past your ears, and so on!—until it *decays* to the point at which you can't hear it. With this type of continuous reflection between parallel sur- faces *standing waves* can also occur. When a sound wave keeps reflecting and colliding back upon itself, the resulting 'standing

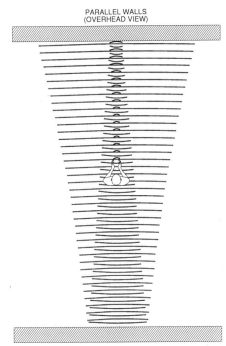

Figure 8.13 Parallel walls can yield repeating reflections, and 'standing' waves.'

wave' is similar to what happens when two water waves collide (see Figure 8.13), with some frequencies cancelling and others adding. These little tests can be as wonderful to hear as the latest studio effect, and they're free—you may even find a great sounding place to record.

Why smooth and hard walls? If a reflective surface is smooth and hard, it will reflect sound in much the same way that a mirror will reflect light. The degree of smoothness describes to what degree the surface *diffuses* the sound, and the hardness describes how *absorbant* the surface is. Many musicians know that drapes, carpeting, and other soft surfaces can be used to help control sound. Such soft surfaces help to control reflections by absorbing higher frequencies, and diffusing reflections.

The nice thing about these tests is that it's easy to visualize what's happening to the sound source. Some experimentation can yield some pretty interesting results. For example, with the single wall, what happens when you move away from the wall? Up to what distance can you still hear an echo? And what happens when you approach that single wall? How close can you get before you know longer hear a distinct echo?

As you may know, sound travels at about 335 meters per second (760 miles per hour) at sea level. It's this relatively slow speed that lets us hear distinct echoes. If you perform the single wall test, you should find that an echo becomes difficult to discern once you get within 9 meters (30 feet) or so. That's because at 9 meters (a round trip of 18 meters), sound takes about 50 milliseconds (abbreviated *ms*, for thousandths of a second) to reach the wall and return to our ears. Sounds which are much less than 50 ms apart from each other in time are no longer discernible as distinct, individual sounds. Because of this, once we hear the initial, unreflected sound of the clap, any echo must take longer than 50 ms to reach us in order to be heard as a separate sound.

When evaluating distance and time, one rule of thumb is that sound travels at a speed of one foot per millisecond; thus, to hear a sound that takes 80 ms to return to its source, position yourself about 40 feet away from the reflective surface.

Reverberation. Our two-wall example above showed us how reflected sounds can be re-reflected. In a case of two parallel walls, the effect is most startling since the reflections are so 'perfect'—that is, smooth and hard parallel walls cause predictable, repeating reflections. In most cases of real-life echo, however, we hear less-than-perfect, *random* echoes, which occur as sounds hit uneven surfaces and reflect in all sorts of directions. Let's take the Taj Mahal, for example.

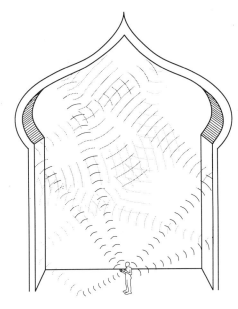

Figure 8.14 Not quite the Taj Mahal, but you get the idea.

As we can see in Figure 8.14, a hand clap in the Taj Mahal is reflected in every which way, with some reflections returning quickly to the source, and others taking much longer. In fact, a hand clap in the center 'sweet spot' of the Taj will echo and *reverberate* for about 30 seconds at night, and 20 seconds in the day (the higher humidity of the day causes quicker decay of the sound).

Notice the word 'reverberate': Repetitive echoes less than 50 ms apart are known as reverberation, or just plain *reverb*.

In a typical concert hall setting, a person in the audience is able to hear many different types of sounds, some directly from the stage, and others reflected.

The *direct sounds* travel to the ear with no perceptible delay (unless it's such a huge hall that there is a time lag, for example, between watching a drum being struck and hearing it). In any event, in almost all cases the direct sounds are *the first to reach the ears*. Basically, whenever a sound source is within line-of-sight, direct sounds will arrive before any reflected sounds.

Immediately following the direct sounds are the *early reflections*. These are usually shorter in time lag than the all-important 50 ms mark, and are not heard as distinct echoes. They typically reach the listener after hitting just one or two reflective surfaces. Following the early reflections are *latter reflections*—known as reverberation—which tend to be further and further apart, in terms of time. Unless the room is cavernous, the latter reflections are sounds which have typically hit three or more surfaces.

In a purely random but highly reflective environment, such as a canyon, these tardy arrivals are able to be heard as distinct echoes. If this were the case in our music settings, however, we would have a tough time being able to listen to music without being distracted by echoes. Giant arenas are generally dreaded as concert venues by sound engineers for this very reason.

Fortunately, most concert venues are designed in such a way that there are no discernibly distinct echoes. That is, the acoustics of the hall have been designed to provide continuous reflections to any part of the hall. Some sounds, certainly, may take one second or longer to reach a listener's ears: If these were the only reflected sounds, they would sound as echoes. But the nature of continuous reflections is that they *mask* the impression of distinct echoes. The continuous arrival of sounds to human ears fools the brain into thinking that they are all one sound, when in fact each reflec-

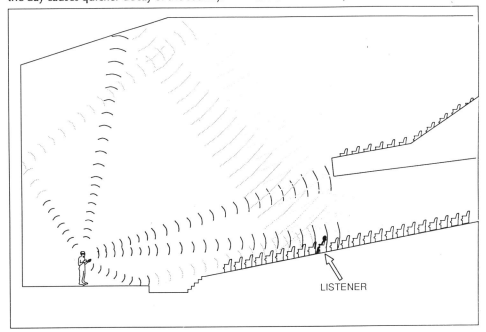

Figure 8.15 In a concert hall, we hear direct—and then reflected— soundwaves.

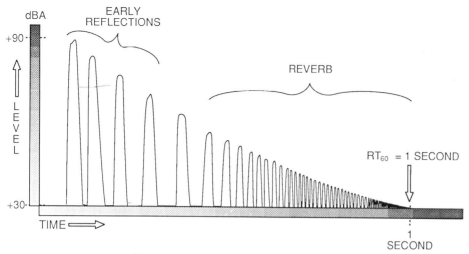

Figure 8.16 *Natural reverb can take from many seconds to less than 10 milliseconds to decay. The point at which the reverberant sound decays 60 dB from its first reflection is known as the RT_{60} level. In this case, we have a decay of 1 second.*

tion is a component of the entire sound.

If this sojourn into the world of acoustics has been interesting so far, keep reading, since there are a few more advanced concepts to cover. If not, you may wish to skip to page 51. All of these concepts, by the way, are useful in order to operate spatial effects most effectively.

Decay And Acoustic Reverberance. We mentioned earlier the word 'decay.' As we know, all sounds (once they're no longer being produced) eventually decay to an inaudible level. This decay occurs because the sound runs out of what's known as *acoustic energy*. The time by which a reflected sound becomes inaudible is known in acoustics lingo as RT_{60}. That term stands for 'reverb time, 60 dB decay,' and comes about from the fact that when a reflected sound has decayed to a level which is 60 dB *below* its original level, it's considered to be inaudible for all practical purposes.

High frequencies reach an RT_{60} level at a *faster* rate than low frequencies—this phenomenon is emphasized when the acoustic space has many highly absorbant surfaces, since those absorbant surfaces affect high frequencies to a greater degree than low frequencies. In addition to reflectivity, long wavelengths travel further than short wavelengths (assuming both were of the initial acoustic energy). Have you ever noticed, when entering a particularly reverberant auditorium or large arena, that the sounds tend to be very 'boomy'—that low frequencies tend to dominate? Well, that's because of this phenomenon of high frequencies having a faster RT_{60} than low frequencies. (This information will all be most useful when we examine reverb units, since there are some reverbs which allow you to have *separate* high and low frequency decay times!)

What are the criteria which determine the reverberance of a space? There are many obscure criteria, all of which make life difficult for acoustic designers, but the main ones are:

- The reflectivity of surfaces.
- The size of the space.
- The angular relationships, or proportions, between surfaces.

Surface reflectivity is in itself affected by

two important factors which we mentioned during our 'echo wall' test. The first is smoothness—how flat is the surface? When a sound hits the surface, will it reflect in an even, predictable way, or will it tend to be diffused and scattered by the unevenness? Generally, the smoother the surface, the more reflective, since an uneven surface tends to break up the sound waves. The second factor of reflectivity is the hardness of the reflective surface: Stand right in front of a mirror, at arm's length, and sing or speak directly at it. Then take a thick towel or blanket, and hold it against the front of the mirror. Sing or speak once again. The difference should be dramatic.

The size of the space is the second important criterion. Basically, if we take a large room and a small room, and construct them of the same reflective materials and proportions, the larger room will be more reverberant. This is simple physics: A larger room has greater distances for sounds to travel between reflective surfaces, and hence, longer delay times of the reflections.

The third criterion of reverberance for a space is the angular relationship between its surfaces—its proportions. Our 'two-wall echo' test allowed us to hear what happens with two perfectly parallel walls: Sounds echo back and forth, causing standing waves, as we saw on page 49. A room with standing waves is acoustically very undesirable, since these waves cause an amplification of whichever frequencies happen to be 'standing.' For this reason, concert halls and professional recording studios are never built with any parallel surfaces. Not only are the walls uneven, but so is the ceiling with the floor.

For non-parallel surfaces, the angles at which they meet are also critical for determining a space's reverberance. In fact, the way sound waves interact with the angular relationships of the surfaces is very much like the way a ball behaves on a snooker table. Because there are so many variables for sound, however (including humidity, the number of people in a hall, and even the type of clothes they are wearing), one would generally be better off betting on the outcome of a snooker game than the sonic outcome of a concert hall design!

These are just a few of the reasons why the study of acoustics is as much of an art as a science. Many older churches and concert

halls have acoustics which far exceed some of the most modern designs. Not that technology hasn't helped—computer models can help designers predict acoustic responses, and scale models can be built to predict the sound of a hall before it's constructed. Recording studios have also benefited greatly from proper acoustic design: It used to be that the 'deader' the studio—that is, the fewer reflections and reverberance—the better. Now, careful designs can allow the professional studio to fine tune both the control room and the studio to a desired and controllable reverberance.

Basic Psychoacoustics. With the exception of the 50 ms and RT_{60} rules, so far we've been talking about the way sound behaves in space—the study of acoustics—and not so much the way we hear things. Psychoacoustics is the study of the way the brain interprets sounds received by the ears. As recording engineers, it's helpful to understand several concepts of psychoacoustics, in order to use your spatial effects gear to its fullest. These concepts include:

- The *precedent* effect.
- The *relative amplitude* of sounds.
- Our ability to *localize* sounds, due to the effects of reverb, precedence, and amplitude on.

Those of us with hearing in both ears have *binaural* hearing, which allows us to locate sounds in terms of dimension: to the left or right, higher or lower, close or far. In the same way that binocular vision allows three-dimensional visual placement of objects, binaural hearing allows three-dimensional placement of sounds.

Binauaral hearing provides several factors to help us locate sound. The most important factor is that, unless a source is directly in front of us, our ears receive sounds at slightly different times. That is, a sound from the left arrives first at our left ear, then our right. The time difference may seem unbelievably small, but our brains are actually capable of perceiving differences as small as 0.5 ms! (This is not to be confused with perceiving *distinct* sounds, which require a time lag of about 50 ms.) This factor is known as the *precedent*, or *Haas* effect, and it's the most important cue we use in real life to place things in a left to right panorama.

If a soundwave arrives at one ear before the other, it's said to reach our two ears slightly *out of phase*. To go back to sound waves, each wave has a changing *phase*. When we represent a wave on a chart, as we saw in Figure 1.3, the portion on the top of the chart covers the first 180 degrees of the wave, and represents the compression of air; the portion of the wave on the underside of the line covers the latter 180 degrees,

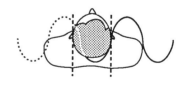

Figure 8.17 *A sound wave (in this example, travelling from right to left) generally reaches one ear before the other ear, after which point the brain uses the phase difference as a location cue.*

and represents the wave during rarefaction (remember these terms?—if not, see page 2).

Figure 8.17 shows the wave reaching our two ears at slightly different phase stages. These shifts can be detected by our ears, and are another cue our ears gives our brain to help us locate sounds. As a matter of fact, phase shifters, flangers, and chorus devices are able to simulate a sound out of phase with itself in a constantly changing manner. In this manner, these devices fool our brains into thinking that the instruments or voice is shifting around in space—which is why flanged and chorused instruments sound so 'spacey' and difficult to 'locate.'

Another psychoacoustic factor is *relative amplitude* of sound sources. If we have two speakers, and each speaker is equidistant from our ears as well as playing the same information, whichever speaker is louder will make us think that the sound is coming from that direction. The louder the speaker, the more the image of the sound will shift in its direction. At first, this may seem a lot like the precedent effect, but in fact it's dif-

tionships between near and distant sounds, our brains are able to produce remarkably accurate perceptions of depth.

So far, we've learned some ways that we localize sound sources from left to right, and from front to back. Our ability to localize *vertical* information is much less understood. Some researchers feel that the shape of the outer ear is the key to understanding vertical sound perception; that the angles at which sounds are reflected into our ear canals by the outside ear cause some high frequency phase shifting, by introducing slight delays between the sounds that reach our ear canals. It's felt that these delays place sounds within the 'up and down.'

With regular stereo loudspeaker reproduction, it's very difficult to create vertical imaging. The popular chorusing effect that's used a lot with guitars and keyboards, however, seems to create some sense of vertical sound movement. This may have something to do with the fact that they cause some higher frequency phase shifting—thus suggesting that time delays *do* play a part in vertical localizing.

DDL. So, without further ado, let's move on to some of these wonderful devices.

Delays

The first artificial delay was created by that early master of the magnetic tape recorder, Les Paul. He found that a single echo could be heard by monitoring the playback head of a 3-head recorder, while also listening to the source being recorded. If the output of that playback head was fed back into the record head, multiple echoes could be heard and recorded.

For many years this and other types of *tape echo* was the only way to create echoes and other delay effects artificially. By varying the speed of the tape, the timing of the echo could be somewhat regulated, and by varying the amount of *feedback* from the playback head back to the record head, the number of repeat echoes could be controlled. Adding more playback heads would yield delays with different times. From the end of the 1960s and into the '70s, many studios had self-contained tape echo units, such as the Maestro Echoplex and the Roland Space Echo.

By the mid-'70s *analog* delays became popular as the first tapeless delays; a number of these are still available as foot pedal devices. In an analog delay, a circuit known as a *bucket brigade* replaces tape. This circuit can electrically store audio signals for adjustable periods of time before playing them back. They're called bucket brigade circuits because they pass the signal along, like a fire brigade passes a bucket of water, until the signal is *tapped* and played back at some point along the line. While more convenient to use than tape delays, and ultimately cheaper, analog delays have a relatively poor signal-to-noise ratio, and poor high-end frequency response. Because of this, many professional engineers continued to use tape as the delay of choice, until the advent of *digital* delays.

First available in 1972, the digital delay (or *DDL*, for *digital delay line*) broke the $1000 barrier and became affordable to smaller studios by the early 1980s. DDLs are usually available for a heck of a lot less money than any of the tape delays, and offer much greater versatility and performance. Most DDLs can perform:

- Single and multiple echoes.
- *Doubling*, which simulates a 'doubled' sound by means of a very short single echo. This can also serve as a simulated stereo effect.
- *Chorusing, flanging,* and other related sounds. There are separate chorus and flanging devices available as foot pedal effects, but most self-contained DDLs offer superior performance and control for these effects.

Some of the more advanced DDLs have additional features, such as:

- Stereo delay effects, by means of two separate delays feeding two separate outputs of the DDL.
- Programmability, which allows the storage and recall of program settings into the unit's memory.
- MIDI control, which allows program changes and other adjustments to be

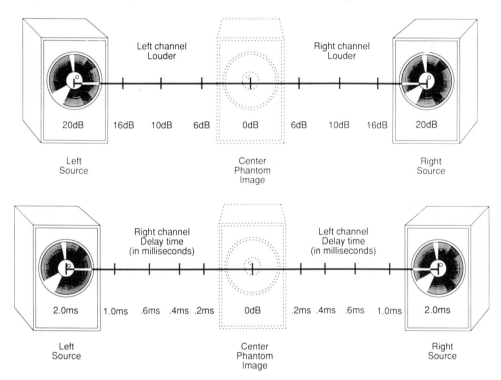

Figures 8.18a, 8.18b When two equidistant speakers play the same information at the same level, we perceive a 'phantom' sound image that's in the center. Should one speaker's sound become quieter or be delayed, we'll perceive an image that shifts towards the other speaker. The delay effect—known as the 'Haas effect'—is something to bear in mind when using a digital delay.

ferent, since (in the example we've given) each ear is receiving the same information at the same time, in phase.

Our ability to psychoacoustically 'place' objects in space is known as *localizing*, or *imaging*. We localize the *depth* of a sound source, or its relative distance from us, by the degree of reverb associated with it, as well as whatever precedent and amplitude effects may be associated with that sound. Think of it this way: A sound source very close to our left ear will sound much louder in our left ear, and there will be a time lag before the sound reaches the right ear. A distant sound, also on the left, may have a more equal amplitude between the left and right ears, though there will also be a time delay for the sound to reach our right ear. By calculating the amplitude/time delay rela-

When we get our hands on some nifty, inexpensive digital reverb, and go about programming it to simulate acoustic spaces, an understanding of acoustics and psychoacoustics will be indispensable. Many of the latest reverbs, even in the $500 range, allow us to control separately the high and low frequency decay rates ($RT_{60}s$), as well as the level of early reflections, the diffusion of the surfaces, and much more. A quality reverb is very useful for creating both natural and unnatural acoustic spaces.

Similarly, the digital delay line (DDL) has become a very important studio tool, not only for echo effects, but chorusing, flanging, and more. Understanding how echoes behave, and at what point they become indiscernible as echoes, is critical information for maximizing your potential with a

made from external MIDI sequencers and instrument controllers (see page 106 for more about this).

- *Sampling* functions, where a digitally-stored audio signal (such as a drum hit or—with some sampling DDLs—a signal as long as a song's chorus) can be held indefinitely and then replayed, or 'triggered,' with a switch or footswitch.

Let's take a look at some of the controls found on various DDLs and examine how they can be used to create some of these effects.

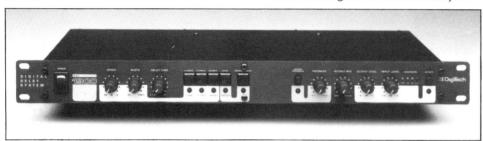

Figure 8.19 The Digitech RDS1900 digital delay offers up to 2 seconds of delay, and can perform chorusing and flanging effects.

DDL Controls

Digital delays use analog-to-digital converters (ADCs) and digital-to-analog converters (DACs), which we will learn more about on page 125. Simply, a DDL uses an ADC to convert incoming audio signals to numbers. These numbers are then held electrically in memory for the desired delay time, after which the DAC reconverts the numbers to sound, which is spit out as a delayed audio signal.

As with any digital processor, it's important to not overload the ADC. The result is usually much worse than the type of overload distortion heard with analog devices, and is best described as digital 'glitching.' Consequently, most DDLs have an *input gain* control and meter. Remember to use the meter to keep the input signal as high as possible (to maximize the signal-to-noise ratio) without glitching or distortion.

Other common input/output (I/O) controls include:

- An *effect bypass* switch. This is useful for comparing the original, or 'dry' signal, with the delayed, or 'wet' signal.
- A *wet/dry* mix control. If an instrument is plugged directly into the effect, this control should be set to your sonic taste, or to 50% for flanging or chorusing. If the unit is connected in an effect send/return loop with a mixer, the mix control is normally set to 100%, so that the only output of the effect is the delayed signal; the balance of the wet and dry signal is then determined at the mixer.
- An *inverse phase* switch puts the wet signal 180 degrees out of phase with the dry signal. Some DDLs have a separate out-of-phase output jack—but beware: When two out-of-phase delayed output signals are summed to mono, they'll cancel each other out. The moral: If your music may wind up in mono (AM radio, TV/video, etc.), don't record in- and out-of-phase signals together!
- Some units have *level matching* switches, to accomodate different level gear (see page 19).

The *delay time* control is often accompanied by a digital readout of the delay setting in milliseconds. The control itself allows you to adjust how much time will elapse between the original sound and any subsequent delayed signals, and is either a ten-key pad (like a telephone, to allow direct programming of the delay), an incremental-adjust (usually two keys, + or –), or a switch/knob arrangement. At minimum, most DDLs offer about 200 ms of delay, though better units can have ten or more seconds of delay memory.

Remembering that the shortest delay we can perceive is about 50 ms, echoes can be created at this setting and up. Below 50 ms, a DDL is used to create chorusing, flanging, and reverberant early reflections.

If you know the tempo of a song, it's possible to calculate 'synchrosonic' delays which fall on the beat. Simply divide 60,000 (the number of milliseconds in one minute) by the tempo (in beats per minute), and you'll have a setting in milliseconds which will yield delays that match the beat.

A *feedback* control adjusts how much of the delayed signal is fed back into the digital delay, in order to create repeating delays. When the feedback control is set at 0, and the delay time is greater than 50 ms, you'll hear just one echo. As you increase the feedback level, you'll hear an increasing number of echoes, which gradually fade out. Through careful adjustment, you can set anywhere from two to 30 or more gradually decaying echoes. A *hold* switch or footswitch will cause an echo to repeat a*d infinitum*, until disengaged.

When the delay time is less than 50 ms, the feedback control is used to adjust the 'intensity' of the chorusing, flanging, or early reflections. The more feedback, the more noticeable the degree of the effect. But be careful with this control: Too much feedback can create a runaway situation, causing a *feedback loop* (similar to microphone feedback), which is both horrible to hear and potentially nasty to your speakers and other equipment.

Most DDLs are able to *modulate* the delayed signal. Modulation is usually heard as a slow, steadily changing sound, and is necessary to create chorusing and flanging effects. To get modulation, DDLs use an adjustable LFO (low frequency oscillator), which varies the delay time by slight but noticeable degrees. The speed with which the modulation takes place is controlled by a *speed* or *rate* control; the depth of the modulation is controlled by a *depth* or *width* control.

Normally, modulation speed is set quite slow. If the speed control is set too high, the effect can become ridiculous—great for

making instruments and vocals sound as if they're 'underwater.' The depth control should be set low if just a subtle flanging or chorusing is desired, and higher for a more intense effect.

Modulation is typically used at delay times of less than 50 ms. If it's used at higher delay time settings, such as 500 ms or more, the effect can be fairly bizarre, with strange pitch bends and the like.

Flanging And Chorusing

Flanging and chorusing are true spatial effects—they cause guitars, keyboards, and other signals seemingly to shift in space and swirl around. Wearing a pair of headphones and listening to a heavily flanged or chorused stereo sound can actually disturb your equilibrium! Whether you use these effects to create a shimmering guitar or a full-bodied bass, the fundamental concept behind them is the delay of time. The actual delays are too fast for us to perceive as distinct echoes: Flanging is in the 0.2 to 20 ms range, and chorusing uses delays of about 15 to 35 ms. The modulation control is the key to creating the effects, however: It introduces a slight shifting of these times, and as our brain tries to follow the shifting it gets confused, causing us to think the sound is moving.

Many guitarists, bassists, and keyboardists use subtle chorusing almost all the time, to 'thicken' their sound and give it some motion. Flanging tends to be more of a special effect, since its intensity can become a bit wearisome, and the effect can make instruments sound a bit thin. Flanging gets its name from an old trick involving tape: If an audio signal is split, and recorded onto two tape decks at the same time, listening to the playback heads of those two decks should in theory let us hear two identical signals. In practice, however, two un-synchronized tape decks will run at slightly different speeds. This speed variation will cause the sound to shift when listening to the two decks, as small and slightly changing delays occur. A popular technique to induce this effect to a further degree was to apply thumb pressure to one of the tape's flanges (metal reels). By 'flanging' in this manner, the time delays would increase—and by varying the pressure, the sweeping, shifting sound would change over time. In the modern DDL, the modulation control replaces the thumb, and the delay time replaces the tape speed variations.

Phase shifting, or phasing, has dropped in popularity since the mid-70s. We've spoken about how changes in a soundwave's phase is known as phase shifting. This is often an undesired sound, caused by misalignment of tape heads, or by poor equipment design. The induced effect of phase shifting sounds very similar to flanging, although it's a bit 'fuller' sounding. Instead of manipulating the timing of delayed signals (as with flanging), phasing manipulates the actual phase of the audio signals. None of the DDLs made are designed to do true phase shifting, but some of the foot pedal phasers, most commonly those by MXR, can still be found.

On some of the more advanced DDLs, the modulation *waveform* is selectable. Normally, the modulation follows a smooth-sweeping sine wave pattern; some DDLs allow you to choose a sawtooth or even square waveform, creating rapid-changing modulation effects, that tend to have a 'full-on,' 'full-off' type of sound. Some better units also have a *clock* input, which allows the speed of the modulation LFO to be controlled independently by a drum machine or sequencer.

Reverbs

Reverberation, as we've seen, is a complex collection of acoustic reflections, which are indiscernible as distinct echoes. Reverb is a common sound in nature and in architectural structures—but until recently it's been very difficult for the home recordist to get a good reverb sound.

People who record classical music in a good concert hall enjoy the benefit of the natural reverberation in the hall. Typically, live classical recording takes place with two microphones some distance from the instruments, so that the sound of the hall is recorded along with the direct sounds of the instruments.

Many commercial recording companies invest in quality studio acoustics, and also record the sound of the studio along with live instruments. Most home and quite a few professional recordings, however, are either made directly—with synthesizers, drum machines, and other sound sources plugged directly into the console—or made with close-miking techniques—where the mike is placed very close to a singer or instrument. Because of direct and close-miked recording, and with many of us forced to be content with the acoustics of a bedroom or garage, there's not a lot of natural room reverberation being recorded these days.

Without natural reverberation, we need to depend upon *artificial* reverberation to give our recordings depth, and the sense of acoustic space. Without any reverb, recordings sound very up-close and 'dry'; while this can be effective with some songs or music styles, many people find reverb-less recordings lifeless, and two-dimensional.

There are four types of artificial reverb devices:

- Acoustic reverb chambers.
- Plate reverbs.
- Spring reverbs.
- Digital reverbs.

Let's take a look at each of these types . . .

Acoustic Reverb Chambers. The idea behind an acoustic reverb chamber is simple: Take a highly reflective room—anything from an elevator shaft, to a long hallway, to a squash court could do the trick—and place inside of it a loudspeaker and a couple of microphones. Feed the speaker with a signal from the mixer (any track or group of tracks to which you want to add reverb) and let that signal reflect around the room. Then pick up that reflected signal with the microphones. Finally, mix this reverberant signal with the original dry signal, and *voila*—artificial reverb.

Reverb chambers have been around since the early days of recording, and a fair number of professional studios still boast some sort of chamber. Assuming one has the gear and the room, there's no reason why a home studio couldn't have its own chamber. Fortunately, for the apartment dwellers and others among us, there are several other, more versatile, ways of getting artificial reverb, all of which are self-contained.

Plate Reverbs. Even in this day of digital-mania, some of the most coveted reverb units are plate reverbs.

Like the chamber, a plate works on the idea of broadcasting a dry signal, delaying it, and picking it up again. But instead of a room, a large, thin, metal plate is used; instead of a speaker, a transducer (like a small speaker) is used to broadcast. The plate's dimensions can be anywhere from 0.5 meter x 1m (1.5' x 3') up to 3m x 4m (9' x 12'). The broadcast transducer is located at one end of the plate. The transducer receives the signal to be processed from the mixer, and as it vibrates, it causes the plate to vibrate. When this happens, all sorts of random vibrations travel throughout the plate, until they are eventually picked up by a couple of contact transducers, and fed back to the mixing console.

Most plates have a mechanical means of 'damping' the vibrations of the plate, which allows you to adjust the decay time. Typical decays are quite short, less than a second, though some of the larger plates can provide several seconds of reverb.

The 'plate sound' is a classic reverb sound, popular for drums: very 'tight,' and bright sounding, with a quick decay. The frequency response of most plates is wonderful, covering the complete audio spectrum. In fact, many professionals look for a great simulated plate sound when they audition the latest digital reverbs.

The disadvantages of plates include their size, as well as their susceptibility to picking up external noises (the plate is very sensitive, and can act like a giant microphone). Because of the latter, plates must be isolated from external sounds, including loudspeakers. This means either mixing with headphones, or placing the plate in another room.

Plates, moreover, have the same limitations as reverb chambers and spring reverbs: They sound the way they sound, and not much variation is available. Plates can and should be tuned, but even the least expensive digital reverb has more variations in sound. Nevertheless, if you have the space, there are some good buys out there in the way of used plates, as the digital revolution plows onward. In fact, building your own plate used to be a popular engineer's pastime—it's not all that hard, and it can be quite inexpensive.

Plates are still commercially available, from Echoplate/Studio Technologies, and other manufacturers. The finest of these plates, such as those made in Germany by EMT, have plates made of thin gold foil, can set you back several thousand dollars, but sound great.

Spring Reverbs. Until recently, spring reverbs were the mainstay of affordable reverb devices. Still found in guitar amplifiers, spring reverbs can be quite fine for many applications. The technical concept remains roughly the same as rooms and plates: dry sound amplified and delayed, then picked up. Instead of a plate, however, two or more springs are used to induce the delay (a single spring would tend to resonate on a particular frequency).

At one end of the springs, a transducer applies the dry signal, which travels up and down, bouncing around the springs. The wet signal is picked up by one or two transducers at the opposite ends. Unlike rooms and many plates, spring reverbs usually have some type of dry/wet mix control, so that the output of the reverb can be adjusted between an unprocessed/processed mix. Most springs are mono, though some have stereo outputs, which improve the realism of the reverb signal.

Some of the best spring reverbs are made by AKG and employ a mechanical damping system for the springs, so that the decay time can be adjusted. Many springs have built-in EQ sections, so that the tone of the reverberated signal can be adjusted. At their best, even inexpensive spring reverbs can sound very good with vocal and other non-percussive sounds. They offer smooth and even decay, and excellent frequency response. At their worst—with drums and other sharply percussive instruments—springs can sound horrid, unless used very carefully. The reason is that when the spring receives a signal which has too much 'attack,' the spring is overdriven, and produces a metallic 'boing' sound. With drums and other such instruments, the levels must be carefully adjusted, and the dry signal should be EQ'd to reduce the punchiest frequencies.

Spring reverbs are also susceptible to outside noise and vibrations, though to a much lesser degree than plate reverbs.

The future of the spring reverb is not especially bright. There are already digital reverbs which far surpass the performance of springs, offer many more sounds, and cost less. All the same, if you already own a spring, or are able to get one cheap as a secondary or tertiary unit, great. Used sparingly and carefully, springs can provide satisfying performance, particularly with vocals, woodwinds, and guitars.

Digital Reverbs. Imagine this: It's 1978, and you're an engineer at a top L.A. studio. Everything is state-of-the-art, from the automated mixing console to the 24-track, right on down to the gold-foil EMT plate reverb, the acoustic reverb chamber, and the AKG spring reverb. Then one day a large, heavy box arrives, brought by a factory representative from Lexicon, a company in Massachusetts. Inside, you're told, is a new reverb unit, the Lexicon 224—a *digital* reverb unit. . . .

. . . The rep explains how there are no moving parts, no plates, no springs, nothing. Just lots of integrated circuits, like the Lexicon PCM 41 DDL in your rack. He tells you how the incoming analog audio signal is converted to a series of digital codes, which can then be manipulated in a bunch of different ways, and then reconverted to an analog signal for playback. All very nice, but what do reverberant manipulated numbers sound like? The rep plugs it in, you connect it up to the mixing console, put on a multitrack tape, and turn up the control room listening level. Remote control in hand, the rep selects a 'Plate' setting, and you listen to it . . .

. . . Sounds nice, almost as good as the EMT, but the EMT costs half the price. While you keep this to yourself, the rep selects 'Hall.' All of a sudden, your drum tracks sound as if they're in a giant concert hall, a much bigger sound than you were ever able to get from the acoustic chamber, let alone the plate or spring. You watch as the rep asks you how big, in cubic meters, you'd like the hall to be! As he moves the controls from a large hall to a small chamber, the reverb begins to collapse into itself, as the simulated walls get closer, creating an intimate yet very alive sound. Before you can express your amazement, he asks you what sort of high frequency decay you'd like, and how many early reflections. But his questions fly past you, as you start to concentrate on ways to sell this *wunderbox* to your boss. *Hmm, maybe if we sell both the plate and the spring, the studio may be able to cough up the 12 grand this thing costs . . .*

It's still possible to spend upwards of $10,000 on a digital reverb, but what's more amazing is that for well under $500, you can get one which in many ways *outperforms* the first digital reverbs. Clearly, digital reverbs are here to stay, and they are undoubtedly the reverb of choice for the personal recording studio.

The digital domain offers the ideal way of manipulating audio signals. Armed with a thorough understanding of psychoacoustics, the digital reverb designers create *algorithms*—mathematical formulae, which are used for manipulating the digital information to simulate both real and surreal acoustic spaces.

As with digital delays, digital reverbs can create numerous different effects, all available with the touch of a switch. In their simplest incarnation, they offer the choice of several different settings, from simulated plates to large halls, as well as a few special effects which we'll examine shortly. The Alesis MicroVerb II is a good example of this type of reverb, with 16 different presets accessible via a front-panel knob, and stereo outputs.

between a number of different settings, including plates, halls, small rooms, and several special effects. In addition, various parameters of these sounds can be altered such as decay times (for both high and low frequencies), the number and level of the simulated early reflections, as well as predelay and other settings.

Digital Reverb Controls

Unlike DDLs, very few digital reverbs share the same parameter controls. The formulae used to create artificial digital reverb are much more complex than those used for delays. Because of this, manufacturers choose different ways of changing similar functions.

Some reverbs are dual-channel devices. These units allow you to select completely different parameters for each of their two channels. For example, with the Ibanez SDR 1000+, you can have a simulated plate sound on one channel, and a large hall on the other. This Ibanez unit, in fact, can perform delay functions on one channel while performing reverb on the other. This dual-channel function shouldn't be confused with stereo operation—many digital reverbs have stereo inputs and outputs, but only one processing mode can be selected at a time, and that same effect is applied equally to the left and right stereo channels.

Here's a listing of commonly-found digital reverb parameter controls.

Input And Output Level Control, Input Level Meter, And Wet/Dry Mix. Just as on the DDL, these allow the user to adjust the signal levels coming into and leaving the reverb. Some units, such as the Lexicon 200, allow for separate Left/Right input and output level adjustments.

Pre-Delay. As we learned back on page 49 (Figure 8.15), in most real-life settings—such as a concert hall—the direct (dry and unreflected) signal is the first to reach a listener's ears. Following this direct signal, after some delay, are the early reflections, then the reverberant signals. A pre-delay control is a means of controlling the length of time which passes between the dry signal

times with song tempo is given on page 52.

Room Type. The room type describes how many reflections take place, how complex those reflections are, and other similar functions. This allows you to select the basic reverb sound: The simulated 'room' in fact, can sound like anything from a small casket to a plate reverb, from a mid-sized room to the Grand Canyon. When designers of digital reverbs sit down at the drawing board (or design computer), it's this area which will take up most of their mathematical musings —as they create the room algorithms which ultimately lead to the reverb's distinctive sounds. Most digital reverbs offer anywhere from two to 30 or more different room types. Dual-channel units will allow you to choose one or two of these rooms at a time, while most stereo units limit you to one room type at once.

The room type is an important choice when recording. Part of the fun, however, is that there are no rules—much of modern music benefits from a lush mixing of different sonic and reverberant textures. So with a bit of experimentation, 'plate' drums, along with a 'small room' guitar and a 'chamber hall' synthesizer could be one of many satisfying room combinations.

Room Size. This control allows the physical volume of a simulated room to be changed. It's generally expressed either in cubic meters, or in terms of the distance in meters from the 'stage' (dry sound source) to the far wall. Whereas the room type control changes the types and angles of reflections, room size alters the time it takes for sounds to travel throughout the room, before and after they reflect. A well-designed reverb can truly make a room change in size, so that we are psychoacoustically tricked into hearing larger and smaller spaces.

Early Reflections. On some reverbs, there are two 'ER' controls: One for the *density* of the early reflections, and the other for their amplitude *level*. Again, early reflections are the first echoes our brain picks up, before the 'wash' of densely-packed reverberance. By changing the density and level of the ERs, their sound can change from distinctly audible echoes to very close, quickly reflecting sounds. In real life, it's difficult for us to perceive these early reflections from the ensuing reverb, so these are difficult sounds to imagine without having heard them.

Diffusion. Not found on all programmable reverbs, diffusion allows you to control how *diffuse* the reverberant reflections are. High diffusion levels will create very mixed and indistinct reverb sounds; low diffusion will allow the reflections to become more audible as distinct echoes.

Figure 8.20 The Ibanez SDR1000 is a fully programmable digital reverb. It can function as a stereo reverb or as a dual-channel device, with each channel capable of different reverb or delay effects.

Some preset reverbs allow their settings to be called up remotely via MIDI. The ART ProVerb is one such reverb. It has 99 preset programs, all of which can be called up either via a front panel switch or MIDI (we'll examine MIDI effects on page 109).

What if you want to create your own reverb effects, rather than using factory presets? The most recent incarnation of the original Lexicon 224, the Lexicon 480L, costs over $8000, but there are fully-programmable digital reverbs for well under $1000. These units don't do everything that the 480L does, still they do allow you to choose

and the first reflections. If offered, the range is typically from a few milliseconds up to a half second or longer. Most of the preset digital reverbs (those without adjustable parameters) have preset pre-delays built into their various programs, in order to enhance the realism of the programs.

Aside from adding to the realism of reverb programs, pre-delay can be used as a special effect. For example, the timing of the pre-delay can be set to match the beat of the song, so that the delayed reflections happen a quarter- or an eighth-note after the dry signal. The formula which correlates delay

Decay Times. In all programmable digital reverbs, there is at least one decay control, which allows you to adjust how much time passes from the first reflections until the processed signal decays to the RT_{60} level (page 50). Decay times range anywhere from about 10ms to 99 seconds, depending upon the unit. If you want a 'natural' decay, typical real-life rooms have from 10ms to three or four seconds of decay.

Many programmable reverbs allow you to establish *separate* low and high frequency decay times. When there is a means of adjusting the high frequency decay, there's often a *crossover* frequency adjustment: This allows you to choose at which frequency the low band ends and the high band begins (the choice is usually from about 2 to 8 kHz).

In most real-life settings, it's rare to hear reverberant frequencies much higher than 10 kHz, and frequencies above 6 kHz don't tend to last much longer than half a second or so. For this reason, when simulating a real setting, the high frequencies should decay appropriately (an equalizer can be used if there isn't a high-frequency decay control). There's no law, however, that says you can't create surreal, synthesized acoustic spaces —your decays can have any setting you want. When just low frequencies are set at a long decay, the space can sound long and narrow, like an oil pipe or sewer. This is particularly effective with kick drums and lower frequency percussive sounds. On the other hand, if only the high frequencies are given a long decay, the sound becomes ethereal, and makes instruments seem as if they're floating or suspended in air—this is great with electric guitar, and for certain vocal special effects. Do keep in mind that long decay settings can make the sound a bit jumbled—for this reason you may wish to have your decay decrease as the song's complexity increases.

Reverb EQ. With many reverbs you'll find some type of built-in EQ, either programmable or not. A built-in EQ is useful, since it allows you to tailor the EQ of the reverberated signal without tying up any outboard or mixer EQs. The options are vast, and—as with all of these parameter controls —use your own taste to find the right setting. For reasons related to natural high-frequency decay, cutting the higher frequencies will tend to make the reverberant setting sound darker, less reflective; boosting higher frequencies and cutting lower and mid-frequencies will help create a bright, very alive space.

Some reverbs, rather than offering a true EQ, have high-and lowpass filters. Still others offer a control known as high frequency *damping*—a cross between a lowpass filter and a high-frequency reflectivity control. Damping softens the high end while often simulating fewer reflections.

Special Effects. As part of the different room selections, most digital reverbs offer at least a few special effects settings. The three most common special effects include *gated*, *inverse*, and *infinite* reverb.

The gated reverb sound was first made popular by British producer Hugh Padgham, with artists Phil Collins and Peter Gabriel. The sound was originally created by taking a long decayed reverb sound of a drum, and *gating*, or quickly cutting off, the reverberant sound before it's had a chance to decay. It's a very distinctive sound, rather like the sound of a huge, exploding drum which disappears instantly. While Padgham and many others have created this sound using a separate reverb and gate (which we'll examine on page 57), many reverbs have this sound programmed internally, often with an adjustable gate time. While gated reverb is a great sound for drums and bass guitars, it can become a bit wearisome if overused.

The inverse sound is pretty wild: It's reverb in reverse! Basically, the sound starts with a quiet decayed signal, and builds up in volume and intensity until it suddenly stops. The effect isn't too unlike a train coming closer and closer, until it reaches you and suddenly disappears. Great for sound effects (alien landings and so forth), but of limited musical use.

Infinite reverb is a classic space age/new age music effect. Some reverb manufacturers have referred to it as the 'bottomless' room. Sounds which enter this mode reverberate indefinitely. With careful use of the front panel switch or footswitch (to 'open' and 'close' the door of the infinite room), you can build entire choirs by singing one note at a time; previously sung notes will just keep going forever, until you switch the effect off. Great for just about any instrument or voice, though the sound can become garbled and muddy if too many notes, or any repeated percussions, are played at once. The notes which enter this room should be harmonically complementary, unless you want a dissonant sound (*i.e.*: if you're in the key of C, notes C, E, and G will create major melodic results, C, Eb, G, and Bb will create minor-7th results, and so on).

Compressors And Other Dynamic Processors

Compressors, limiters, and gates are the best-known of a group of signal processors known as *dynamic processors*. Dynamic processors do what their name suggests: They control the amplitude levels—the dynamic range—of audio signals. Depending upon which device, and how it's set, a dynamic processor can:

- Prevent signals from overloading inputs or tape, or from destroying loudspeakers.
- Reduce or eliminate noise from an instrument or mike.
- Increase the apparent sustain of instruments which decay, such as bass guitars.
- Remove unwanted sibilance ('sss' and 'shhh' sounds) from vocal tracks.
- Increase the apparent volume of a complete signal.
- Be used with reverb to create popular special effects.

These processors can be placed into two broad camps, those which *reduce* dynamic range, including:

- *compressors, limiters, de-essers,* and *duckers*

and those which *increase* dynamic range, including: ʼ

- *expanders* and *gates.*

Some of the planet's better mixers include these units as built-ins to each channel, much the same way as they would include EQ; this will certainly be a growing trend, as mixers become more powerful and less expensive. In the meantime, most of us will be using outboard, rack-mountable dynamic processors. As we'll learn, some of these devices can perform many different dynamic functions, while others are built with one application in mind. (Some manufacturers offer foot pedal dynamic processors, such as compressors and noise gates; while this chapter will also apply to them, they're generally limited in the way of functions and controls.)

Let's begin with a look a compressors and limiters, which will serve as good models for understanding all of these dynamic processors.

Compressors And Limiters. Compressors reduce the overall dynamic range of the signal, by making loud passages quieter; that is, they compress. Since the total range of level between the loudest and quietest passages is reduced, a compressor's net effect is to make quiet passages appear louder—at least in relation to the loud passages. Compressors can be used to make the volume of a dynamically-uneven signal more consistent—such as that from a vocalist who may have trouble singing at consistent levels.

As an engineer, there are lots of signals you'll encounter, such as vocals, which have widely varying levels. When recording or mixing down these kind of signals, you'll have to adjust fader levels in anticipation of the signal changes, in order to prevent overload and maximize the signal-to-noise ratios. The problem is that most such adjustments—known as *gain riding*, since one 'rides' the gain levels of the faders—happen too late to prevent the onset of distortion. A compressor allows you to have 'automated' gain adjustments, since it can respond to and compress signals much more quickly than a set of ears and hands. A compressor allows you to preset a *threshold* level control: Signals below this threshold pass through the device unaffected, and signals above the threshold are processed by the device.

A limiter is a type of compressor with a specialized function: It can set a maximum level, or *ceiling*, for a signal's level. With a limiter, once a signal has reached a preset limiting threshold, the signal is limited, and no matter how loud the input gets, the output of the device stays the same. As with compressors, signals below the threshold level are unaffected.

Limiters are ideal in any application where it's bad news if a signal exceeds a maximum level. Because of this, they are frequently used to prevent signals from overloading tape decks or amplifiers.

When you listen to a radio station, you're

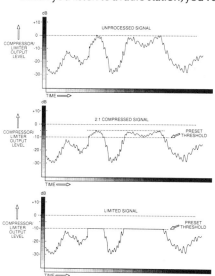

Figures 8.21a, 8.21b, 8.21c *Compressors reduce the level of signals which pass a threshold, while 'hard' limiters prevent those signals from exceeding the threshold.*

listening to compressors and limiters in action. Radio stations use compressors in order to sound 'louder': By making all the quiet passages seem louder, the apparent overall volume of the station is increased, so that it stands out on the radio band. Depending on how commercially-minded the station is, different amounts of compression are used; if you ever hear an announcer sounding particularly 'breathy,' or 'squashed,' with a volume level that sounds the same if he or she is whispering or shouting, you're hearing a lot of compression. Similarly, radio station use limiters to prevent *overmodulation*—operating at too high a broadcast level. Overmodulation is federally prohibited, since it can cause interference on an adjacent wavelength.

When you listen to most analog records, you're also hearing compressors and limiters at work. As we know from Chapter One, the dynamic range of human hearing is about 150 dB. Most live music covers a dynamic range of about 80 to 100 dB, from the quietest to the loudest passages. Classical music, in fact, generally has the widest range; rock music usually has a narrower range. But even 80 dB is more than an LP record can accommodate: Using the quietest vinyl, a record has a dynamic range of 60 to 70 dB—from the quietest audible passage to the loudest peaks before distortion. In order to 'squash' 80 to 100 dB worth of dynamic range into 60 or 70 dB, record mastering labs use compressors. In order to prevent any accidental, distorting peaks, they use limiters.

While there are separate devices available, for the most part compressors and limiters are found as one combined unit, called a *compressor/limiter*, or *comp/ limiter* for short. Such units, made by Furman, Symetrix, dbx, Fostex, Orban, Yamaha, and many others, are designed to perform either compression or limiting, and a few will perform both functions simultaneously in the same channel. Many of these are 2-channel devices, allowing you to perform compression in one channel and limiting in the other. Two-channel comp/limiters can operate in stereo, as well: By selecting the second channel to 'slave' from the first, the controls of channel 1 also control channel 2, and the two channels respond identically.

Most comp/limiters use *VCAs*—voltage controlled amplifiers—to adjust gain. VCAs respond to varying voltages, such as those from an input signal. With comp/limiters, when the input signal exceeds threshold the VCA begins to decrease gain. The *amount* of gain reduction is set by a *ratio* control.

Why a 'ratio' control, rather than an 'amount' control? The reason is because dynamic processors measure the amount of their effect as a ratio of the unaffected input level to the processed output level. Let's consider a compressor. If we set its ratio control to a 1:1 setting, for every decibel that the input level increases or decreases, the output level also changes by 1 dB. Consequently, if we sang through a mike into a compressor with a 1:1 ratio, we'd hear no change when comparing the input to the output of the device.

If we set the ratio control at 2:1, however, it takes 2 dB of input level change to cause a 1 dB output level change. If for example, our singing level increased by 6

dB, we'd only hear a 3 dB change. In other words, our mike level would be compressed at a 2:1 ratio.

Remember, compression works for both increases and decreases in level, so that if we sang 6 dB quieter, we'd hear the mike level decrease by only 3 dB (assuming the input was still above threshold). As you can imagine, a 2:1 compression ratio can help even out the mike levels of an inconsistent singer—all level changes would be reduced by 50%.

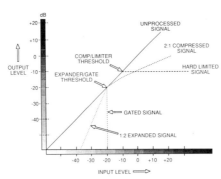

Figure 8.22 Signals which exceed a preset threshold of a compressor or limiter are processed. With expanders and gates, however, signals which drop below a threshold are processed, as indicated. Below that threshold, expanders will make quiet signals even quieter, and gates will virtually silence them.

Compressors usually operate with ratios of 1.5:1 to 10:1. At levels above 8:1 or so, the compressed signal can sound very 'squashed,' since it takes an input level change of 24 dB or greater to result in an audible output change of 3 dB. At those high settings, all signals above the threshold level tend to sound close to the same volume, whether they were originally quiet or loud. (Depending upon the desired effect, compressors can be set with high or low thresholds, as we'll see shortly.)

Limiters operate at compression ratios of 10:1 or greater. If your compressor offers a 10:1 or higher ratio, it can behave as a limiter, and is in fact a comp/limiter. Here's how this ratio setting turns a compressor into a limiter: At high ratios, there's so much compression that no matter how high the input signal becomes (once it has exceeded the threshold), there's no audible level increase at the output. For example, at a ratio of 20:1, it takes an increase of 60 dB to raise the output level by just 3 dB.

So, for example, let's say we wanted to limit a miked vocal. The first step is to have the vocalist sing alternately loud and very loud passages. We could then adjust the threshold control so that only the very loud passage would be affected by the limiter. Consequently, at levels below threshold the vocals would not be limited. Above the threshold, no matter how much louder the vocalist sang, there would be no discernible change—a very useful way to prevent input overloading.

Some limiters allow ratio settings of 40:1 or even ∞ :1. When you have settings this high, the device can function in what's known as an audio 'brick wall,' and output level changes are completely stopped.

In Figure 8.22 notice the points on the chart at which the processing engages. With the compressor, that point is slightly rounded, whereas with the others the point

is sharp. These processing points represent, respectively, *soft-knee* and *hard-knee* processing. Many compressors are soft-knee, where the introduction of processing is somewhat gradual and less audibly noticeable; dbx calls this 'Over Easy' compression. Given the nature of limiting—avoiding instantaneous overload and distortion— most limiters engage instantly, creating a 'hard-knee' on the graph.

Aside from ratio and threshold controls, most comp/limiters have *attack* and *release* controls: These are used respectively to adjust how quickly the compression or limiting takes place, and how soon it stops. We've already said that signals which exceed the threshold are processed. The attack control adjusts how much time passes once a signal has exceeded the threshold before the signal is processed (signals which are below the threshold setting are not processed). The release control determines the time it takes for the processing to stop once a signal has dropped below the threshold level. Remember that the threshold sets the *level* at which processing starts or stops, and the attack and release controls set the *time* it takes for the processing to start or stop once the threshold has been crossed.

Most comp/limiters have some type of metering, to show the amount of gain reduction (in dBs) that's occurring. At first, these meters take a bit of getting used to, since their displays 'increase' as the level reduces. For example, if your comp/limiter has an LED meter, the more compressed a signal above threshold becomes, the more LEDs that light up. This is different from a regular LED level meter, which would light up more LEDs as the signal became louder.

There are some musically useful effects which can be performed by compressing and limiting signals. Compressors, for example, are often used for getting smooth, sustained, bass sounds. By compressing bass notes, attacks are lower, but decays are sustained, since compressors make quiet passages relatively louder.

Here's how to get a sustained bass sound from a comp/limiter. This will also work with a synthesizer or sampler with a bass guitar patch or sample, or with any instrument that has an inherent quick attack and slow decay:

1. Connect the compressor to your mixer, either via a mixer send/receive (insert) jack or an aux send/return (see page 93 if you need more information).
2. Adjust the level of the bass, which is plugged into the mixer, so that the comp/limiter receives an input signal. Your comp/limiter may have an output level control of its own—make sure this is also turned up.
3. Press the comp/limiter's 'bypass' switch, and make sure you get a signal from your bass. If not, check your levels and connections carefully. When everything's okay, engage the compressor (turn off the bypass).
4. Set the attack to 'fast,' and the release to 'slow.' They can be readjusted later, but for now these settings are best, in order to have the compressor respond quickly and continue to respond.
5. Set the ratio control to approximately 6:1. You may wish to lower this to 3:1 or

less, but this is a good place to start, in order to hear the compressor at work.

6. Adjust the threshold control to its lowest level (usually fully counter-clockwise). This is also re-adjustable.

7. Now play a moderately loud note on your bass. An open string will work well, and let it sustain. Your gain reduction meter will light up, as the device compresses the signal, and lowers the note's attack. As the note lowers in input level, the compression will lessen.

8. You should hear the comp/limiter at work—try bypassing the device to compare the dry signal with the compressed signal. The note's attack should sound quieter, with less impact than the dry signal, but the apparent sustain of the note should be greatly increased.

9. Now try raising the threshold level slightly, and set the attack control somewhat slower. When the threshold is raised, the note will have to be louder to be compressed, and with a slower attack, the initial attack of the note will be less compressed, restoring some of the 'punch' and life of the note.

10. When you feel comfortable with these settings, and what effect they induce, try readjusting the ratio and release controls. Take careful note of how things sound different as you readjust the controls—you may find a setting which sounds great with your particular instrument!

It takes a lot of practice to feel comfortable using any dynamic processor, since their adjustments are much more subtle than those, let's say, of a digital delay or equalizer. Below is a chart of some various settings you might find useful with different instruments for different effects.

De-Essers And Duckers. Two variations on the theme of compression are *de-essing* and *ducking*. While there are dedicated devices, most comp/limiters can be configured to behave like de-essers and duckers. Let's find out more . . .

A common problem when using a microphone is excessive *sibilance*—'sss,' 'sshhh,' 'tshh,' and other such sounds. Try saying *sensuous slithering snakes solicit solace* and you'll hear sibilance. Now if you try saying the same sentence into a microphone, there's a good chance the sibilance will be overbearing, since many mikes are designed to offer enhanced frequency response at sibilant frequencies, in order to improve articulation in live performance settings. De-essers are designed to reduce the problem by compressing the appropriate frequencies—about 2000 to 6000 Hz—at which the sibilance occurs. Compression is more effective than equalization, by the way, since the greater the level of 'sss' sounds, the greater they're reduced. Using an equalizer alone would reduce the 'sss' sounds by a fixed amount.

Dedicated de-essers usually have an *amount* control, which adjusts the compression ratio, and a *tune* control, which selects the problem frequencies. When a comp/limiter is used as a de-esser, it's necessary for us to 'tell' it which frequencies we want compressed, since otherwise a comp/limiter compresses all frequencies evenly. In order for the comp/limiter to know which

Figures 8.23a, 8.23b, 8.23c, 8.23d Various dynamic controller settings, shown with a Symetrix 522 comp/limiter/expander/gate/ducker. From top to bottom we see: 1) A typical 'soft' compressor setting for sustaining bass or controlling a vocal; 2) A 'hard' limiter setting, to prevent overload; 3) A moderate expansion setting, for reducing noise or background sounds; 4) A 'hard' gate setting, for silencing a track instantly. Note that the threshold setting is dependent upon the level of the incoming signal, and that the meter is showing the amount of processing that's taking place.

frequencies we want compressed, we need to use an equalizer and a special input to the compressor, known as the *side chain* (also called *key* or *control loop*) input. Please see "The Side-Chain" on page 58 for a description of how this system works.

We've all heard radio advertisements where the announcer 'talks over' the background music. During pauses in such ads, we've heard the music get louder, only to become quieter once the announcer resumes. There are two ways to do this. The first is to have the announcer or engineer 'ride gain,' so that the fader levels of the music and announcer are manually adjusted. The other is to use a ducker, which can automatically reduce the gain of one signal—such as music—in relation to another signal—such as an announcer. Almost all current duckers are in fact compressors, with the side-chain input being used to 'duck' the compressor's input signal beneath the level of the side-chain input. This method is also described in "The Side-Chain."

Expanders And Gates. Earlier we described how compressors can reduce a signal's dynamic range. As an example, we mentioned how live music recordings of 80 dB or greater are compressed to fit within an LP record's dynamic range of 60 to 70 dB. Expanders are functionally the opposite of compressors. Whereas compressors reduce the difference in level between quiet and loud passages of music, expanders increase the level between quiet and loud passages. By playing back an LP record through an expander, for example, you can recover the lost dynamic range.

Expanders function with the same sort of controls as are found on compressors,

though the threshold control works in an opposite manner to compressors: With an expander, signals are processed when they drop *below* the preset threshold, and signals which are above the threshold are unprocessed. Consequently, it's common to set the threshold control quite high when using an expander.

Musically, expanders have a more specialized function than compressors. As we've described, they can be used to restore or further enhance an instrument's—or group of instruments'—dynamic range. In some settings, this can create a more 'alive' sound, though the trade-off is that quiet passages often can be made too quiet, and get 'lost' in noise. Expanders can also be used to reduce noise—such as tape hiss—

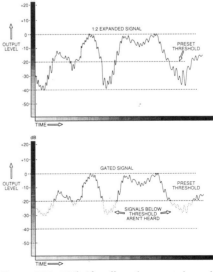

Figures 8.24a, 8.24b The effect of an expander and a gate on a signal such as that of Figure 8.21a.

since noise is usually low level, and expanders make low level signals even lower.

Typically, expanders use ratio settings of 1:3 or less. The ratio is also backwards, compared to compressors: A 1:3 ratio would mean that for every 1 dB of input gain, the output gain would increase by 3 dB. Similarly, for every 1 dB of input decrease, the output would decrease by 3 dB.

Gates are a type of expander, and they're more commonly used than the 'regular' expanders just described. Gates, also known as *noise gates*, have a simple-sounding task: They are either 'open' or 'shut,' depending upon the input's signal level. When input signal levels exceed the gate's threshold, the gate opens—signals pass through to the gate's output without any processing. When signal levels are below the gate's threshold, the gate 'shuts'—the signal doesn't pass, and we hear nothing from the output of the gate. In fact, gates are expanders with extremely high ratios of 1:10 or more. Many expanders can function as gates, much as compressors function as limiters.

Gates have all kinds of musically and sonically useful roles. In addition to singing, for instance, a mike can pick up all sorts of unappetizing sounds, such as lip smackings, breath noises, throat clearings between phrases, and so forth. With a gate, the threshold control can be set so that any singing passes through without being 'gated,' and so that all relatively quiet sounds are gated. If the controls are set properly, the result is a nice, clean vocal track, with singing during the vocal phrases, and silence during the pauses. Similarly, gates can help rectify crosstalk between musical phrases on a track, or any other low-level intrusive noises.

Just as with comp/limiters and expanders, gates often have attack and release controls, which determine how quickly the gate 'kicks in,' or closes, and how long it takes for it to open up. Some gates have just a threshold, attack, and release control, with a non-adjustable ratio. Multi-channel gates are popular: Some have as many as four

---

The Side-Chain

The side-chain—a component of almost all rack-mount dynamic processors—plays a very useful though often misunderstood role. To learn about its utility, let's look at a general model of how dynamic processors work . . .

In a typical dynamic processor, an input signal enters the device, is processed by the VCA (voltage controlled amplifier), and leaves as a processed output signal. The VCA is itself controlled by whatever signal is present at the device's side-chain. Normally the side-chain signal is the same as the input, so that the processing—compression, gating, whatever—occurs in response to changes in the input's level. The processing is then applied to the input signal. Figure 8.25a shows a block diagram of a normal processing arrangement, with a microphone being processed.

What if we were able to access that side-chain? If we could, we would be able to let signals *other* than the device's input level control the processing. In that way, the signal could be processed by something completely different. It so happens that most rack-mount dynamic processors do allow us to access the side-chain, with a side-chain—also called a *key* or *control loop*—input. Why is this useful to us?

Take a look at Figure 8.25b. What's pictured here is a typical ducking situation. We have a turntable as the input to the compressor, and a microphone connected to the side-chain input. Normally—without anything connected to the side-chain—the turntable would 'compress itself,' so that as its signal became louder or quieter, its level would be reduced or increased. In the situation pictured, however, as the level of the microphone increases above threshold, the turntable's signal is compressed and lowered. As the level of the mike decreases, the turntable's signal is raised. In other words, the mike is ducking the turntable—a DJ's dream, and a perfect example of how an external signal at the processor's side-chain can control the input signal.

De-essing is another popular use of a compressor's side-chain. Here's how it works: Take a mike signal (or a mike track from tape), and split it so that one signal goes to the compressor's input, and the other goes to an EQ (Figure 8.25c). At the EQ, boost the troublesome sibilant frequencies—usually between 2000 and 6000 Hz while cutting the non-sibilant frequencies. Then take the output of the EQ and run it into the compressor's side-chain. The re-

sult? The sibilant frequencies are controlling the VCA, and they'll reach the threshold level before the non-sibilant frequencies. In turn, the VCA will induce *frequency-dependent* compression, and compress the problem frequencies of the input signal before it compresses the regular frequencies. Lo and behold, a de-esser from a compressor.

When using the side-chain, keep in mind that it's the input to the side-chain which crosses the threshold and controls the VCA. Consequently, the levels of the regular input have no effect on the device's threshold.

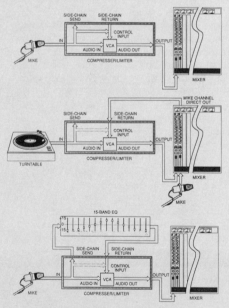

Figures 8.25a, 8.25b, 8.25c Normally, a dynamic controller's VCA is controlled by whatever signal is entering the device (top). With the side-chain, however, a comp/limiter can behave as a ducker (middle), or even as a de-esser (bottom). The side-chain send is useful for any frequency-dependent processing.

Side-chaining a gate can be a really effective practice. One technique is frequency-dependent gating. For example, let's say you were miking an acoustic drum kit, and everything sounded great except for a squeaky kick drum pedal, which was being picked up by the hi-hat mike. The problem could be reduced in this manner: Split the hi-hat mike's output, so that one signal went into a gate, and the other to a parametric EQ. At the EQ, *cut* the offend-

ing squeak's frequency—which might be 1500 Hz or so—then run the output of the EQ into the side-chain input of the gate. Consequently, if the threshold is set properly, the gate opens for all frequencies except the squeak: If the pedal is moved just on its own, it won't generate enough level through the EQ and side-chain input to open the gate. Of course, when the hi-hat is being played, the gate is open, but the squeak should be masked by the volume of the hi-hat.

Frequency-dependent gating is very common in top studios—so much so that some gates made by Drawmer and other companies include a built-in EQ, which can be sent to the side-chain with a switch. Note that when you use an EQ in the side-chain, you don't equalize the input signal, you simply determine which frequencies first cross the threshold of the VCA. Also note that some processors include a side-chain *send*, which splits the processor's main input signal, so that you can send a signal to an EQ or other device.

The other applications for the side-chain are too numerous to mention, and no doubt there are many applications waiting to be discovered. Use your imagination! Here's one last gate application which might encourage you to discover your own side-chain tricks: On Kate Bush's *Hounds Of Love* album [EMI ST-17171, 1985], there's a cut called "Waking The Witch," where Bush's voice is interrupted continuously and rhythmically while she's singing, as if someone were quickly switching off and on the mute button for her vocal track. It carries on for some time, so it soon becomes clear that no engineer could have the timing, speed, or endurance to be hitting a switch. How is that effect achieved?

One way to create a rhythmic on/off for a track would be to use an elaborate automated mixing system, though there's a simpler, less expensive way, by creating a *trigger* for the gate: Run the vocal track through a gate, and adjust the gate threshold so that the vocal is at too low a level to open the gate. Then take a percussive source of rhythm, such as a kick drum from a drum machine (it's not necessary that the source be heard). Plug the drum into the side-chain, and set the threshold so that the gate opens whenever the drum hits, and closes when the drum is silent. If a rapid attack and release are chosen, you'll hear the vocal cut off and on, as the drum triggers the gate open each time it hits.

independent gates. And some comp/limiters have built-in gates, such as the dbx 166 and the Symetrix 525. With these comp/limiter/gates, there's usually just a single threshold control for the gate, with preset ratio, attack, and release settings.

In the early 1980s, British producer Hugh Padgham popularized a very distinctive drum sound with Phil Collins and other artists. His technique is to take a highly reverberant drum sound, such as a snare, and gate it. By adjusting the gate's attack, the reverberant snare can be heard for half a second or so, until it suddenly disappears. When hit on the following beat, the snare sounds as if it's exploding out of silence.

This gated drum sound is so effective because it's performing a bit of a sonic trick on our ears: When we hear a lot of reverb, we're conditioned to hearing a long decay, perhaps two seconds or more, accompanying it. In addition, a lot of reverb can suggest a very 'big' sound, as if we're listening in an arena. So when we hear that snare drum suddenly cut off, the result is very dramatic—it's as if briefly, someone opened a soundproof door to a giant arena with a giant snare, and then suddenly slammed the door shut!

If you record live drums or own a drum machine with an individual output for the snare, it's very easy to create this effect: Simply run the snare channel's output into a reverb, then route the output of the reverb into the gate. By adjusting the threshold, attack, and release controls in various ways, you can create different gated reverb sounds, with varying decay rates and intensities.

As with other dynamic processors, many gates have a side-chain input—once again, please refer to "The Side-Chain."

Other Signal Processors

Equalizers, spatial effects (delays and reverbs), and dynamic processors are the most common and generally useful signal processors. There are many other processing devices on the market, however—some popular, some obscure. As digital processing continues to allow more features for less money, we can expect to see more of the following effects.

Pitch Transposers. Also known as a *Harmonizer*, for the first such device marketed by Eventide, a pitch transposer does as its name suggests: It can transpose the pitch of a note or group of notes. The degree of transposition is selectable on the front panel of the device, and some transposers allow you to store preset settings, for instant recall.

Pitch transposers are usually digital devices, capable of storing a sound as a group of binary numbers, manipulating that sound, and spitting it back out as the transposed signal. On most units, transposition can be as little as a musical quarter-tone or less, or as much as two octaves.

Performance artist Laurie Anderson has used pitch transposers extensively both on her violin and with her voice. A common effect of Anderson's is to pitch her voice down an octave or so, so that her voice sounds like a male voice. Aside from these types of special effects, pitch transposers can be useful for 'thickening' the sound of a voice or an instrument. The method is to mix the dry signal with a slightly off-pitch

signal: The combined signal sounds fuller than the original dry signal. In addition, with the help of a pitch transposers you can correct tape tracks that were recorded at wrong speeds, or even correct a slightly off-pitch note.

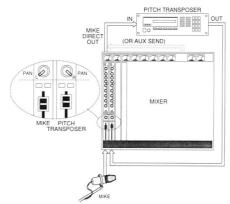

Figure 8.26 Thickening with a pitch transposer.

Exciters And Enhancers. In the late '70s, a mysterious device known as the Aphex Aural Exciter began to show up at some Los Angeles studios. It was for sale, but in order to use one for a commercial recording, it was necessary to sign a licensing agreement and pay royalties to Aphex. If that wasn't enough to generate talk, a lot of people felt that the Exciter could turn a good-sounding recording into a great-sounding recording. In fact, once some engineers heard their best recordings processed by an Exciter, they refused to work without one. Today, there are still some engineers who swear by their Exciters, recording the effect on each individual track as well as the complete mix. What is this *wunderbox?*

Essentially, any signal that's been processed by an Exciter sounds brighter, and perhaps more 'alive.' Typically, the Exciter is connected between the console and the 2-track during mixdown. By adjusting some controls on the front of the device, you can add the desired amount of effect. And what is the effect? In essence, when you 'excite' a signal, you are adding musically-melodic harmonics—the device is adding clean-sounding, third harmonics to whatever music is being excited. The bright-sounding result is different from an equalized signal, since the harmonics change with the music, and are not an across-the-board boost of certain frequencies.

An exciter isn't for everyone, however. Some people find them harsh sounding, particularly if used at a high setting. Other people find that at first the excited signal sounds great, only later to experience 'lis-

tener fatigue'—their ears simply get tired of hearing the bright, excited sound.

In 1985, a new type of signal enhancer appeared on the market by BBE, a division of Barcus Berry (a company which specializes in contact transducer/pickups for acoustic instruments). The BBE enhancer sounds at first a bit like an exciter, adding a dramatic amount of 'life' to the music. Unlike some exciters, however, few people report listening fatigue with the BBE. In fact, the BBE processor seems to make it *easier* for people to listen to music for extended periods of time, while making the signal sound bright and alive.

The BBE system does not involve harmonics. Instead, it works by performing *phase correction*. Back on page 3, we learned that when two identical sound waves shift slightly out-of-phase with each other, there's some phase cancellation, and some frequencies are lost. The BBE works on the principal that most audio signals contain slightly out-of-phase signals, and seeks to correct those phase relationships so that the sound is restored to its original in-phase sound. A BBE processor also contains a low frequency enhancement control, which helps to add more definition and punch to the bass.

Many engineers greet these enhancers with skepticism, partly because it's a bit of an offense that some 'black box' can improve upon the sound of their mix; others just dislike their sound. Nonetheless, other engineers praise enhancers as important studio tools. From this perspective, the process of phase correction—rather than harmonic addition—may be the most useful tool. But these are just opinions: As with any processor, the ultimate test must be your own ears and judicious application.

Vocoders. One of the most distinctive effects is that of a *vocoder*, which was originally developed in World War II to encode messages. If you've heard the sound of musical instruments 'talking,' or of voices sounding like instruments, likely you've heard a vocoder. The concept is fairly straightforward: A mike is plugged into a device which contains analyzers. These analyzers divide the vocal into various frequency bands. Each band's volume and harmonics can be controlled by an external signal, such as a keyboard or guitar. In this way, whenever the external signal is played, the corresponding vocal bands take on that signal's character,

Figure 8.27 The Roland SVC-350 vocoder has 11 bands of processing.

and cause the vocals to sound as if they are articulating the instrument. The effect is similar to placing a small headphone element or speaker in your mouth and moving your lips to articulate the sound coming from the speaker.

Laurie Anderson, Stevie Wonder, and Black Uhuru are some of the artists who have popularized vocoders made by Korg, Sennheiser, and Roland.

Noise Reduction

For many studios, *noise reduction* is the most important form of signal processing. There are some professional studios, such as those with digital tape recorders or recording with professional machines at 30 ips, who have no need for noise reduction. For most of us, however, noise reduction is a fact of life.

There are two main categories of noise reduction. The simplest, and least common category, is known as *single-ended* noise reduction. Symetrix, Rocktron, and other companies offer these as outboard devices, designed to reduce noise from any source, such as a tape recorder, mixer, or whatever. Unlike a gate, which shuts off a signal's flow to eliminate noise, these single-ended processors are more like frequency-sensitive expanders—reducing the volume of low-level high frequency noise, while leaving the rest of the signal unprocessed. Unfortunately, they also reduce some of the high frequency information to varying degrees.

When most people think of noise reduction, they have in mind the most common category: *tape* (also known as *encode/decode*, *two-stage*, or *compander*) noise reduction, such as dbx or Dolby C. For the balance of this section, when we speak of noise reduction, we're talking about this category.

Virtually all gear in any studio produces some level of noise. In analog (non-digital) studios, tape hiss is the most problematic noise source, assuming everything else is working okay and that there are no external noises being induced into the system. As we learned back on page 5, when tape is unrecorded, its oxide particles are at random. If we just listen to blank tape, without noise reduction, we hear a hiss: That's the sound of random particles at rest, and what we're hearing is a rather broad and even range of frequencies, similar to *white noise* (which is the sound of all frequencies at the same level). After we make a recording, we can still hear some unoriented particles, and that's the sound of *residual*, or 'left over,' tape hiss.

The amount of tape hiss is dependent upon many things: The type of tape used, the quality of the recorder's electronics, and so forth. All other things equal, however, tape hiss increases as tape speed and track width is reduced. For example, a 1/4" 8-track tape recorder operating at 7½ ips will suffer much more tape hiss than a 1" 8-track operating at 30 ips. Most 4-track cassette recorder/mixers are unusable without noise reduction.

Referring back to the definitions of signal-to-noise on page 21, few people would want to use a recorder that had a S/N ratio much worse than 50 dB, without noise reduction. Tape recorders operating at 30 ips—including 1/2" 8-track, 1" 16-track, and 2" 16- or 24-track—can sound quite quiet without noise reduction, offering a S/N ratio of 60 to 70 dB. Below these thresholds, however, noise reduction is important if not essential. Noise reduction is either built-in,

as with all ministudios and many open-reel machines, or available as an outboard processor, located between the mixing console and the tape recorder.

The most common noise reduction systems are made by dbx (Type I and II) and Dolby (A, B, and C). All of these systems share a few things in common. For one, they require that the recording be *encoded* with noise reduction during the recording; this encoded signal is later *decoded* by the noise reduction system during playback. Unlike single-ended noise reduction, which can be applied to any source being played back, this encode/decode process is a necessary part of all systems made by dbx and Dolby—encoded signals played back without decoding sound overly bright (as with Dolby) or virtually unlistenable (as with dbx).

As part of the encode/decode process, both systems use compression during recording and expansion during playback; that's why they're called 'companders.' Remember, compression reduces dynamic range, and expansion increases dynamic range.

Basic Theory. Turn on a water faucet, and listen to the flow of the water. If there's no other loud sound in the room, the water sound should be very noticeable—in much the same way as tape hiss is noticeable in the absence of any music.

With the water still running, play your stereo quite loud. Even though the water is still running, the volume of the stereo should *mask* the sound of the water—so that all you hear is the music. At this point, you have a high signal (music) to noise (water) ratio. Finally, adjust the volume of the stereo up and down, so that you are able to occasionally discern the sound of the running water.

This model is a perfect example of the effect of noise during a recording. When the music is loud, the tape hiss is masked; when the music drops in level, the tape hiss becomes audible. If this suggests to you that one is more likely to hear tape hiss with dynamically varying music (such as chamber music) than with consistently loud music (such as 'heavy metal'), then you understand the nature of noise and masking. For now, tuck this bit of information away, and let's look at companding.

Tape noise is a constant. Without noise reduction, its level stays the same, no matter how loud or quiet the music. Noise reduction's purpose is to reduce our perception of that constant, and the basic idea is as follows: The encoding process *compresses* a signal before it's recorded on tape, reducing its dynamic range. Remember that compression makes loud musical passages quieter, and quiet passages louder.

That's the encoding process. We need to decode, and here's why: A compressed signal has a reduced dynamic range, causing everything to sound much less lifelike. If we compress a symphony orchestra at a 2:1 ratio, its dynamic range is reduced by 50%. Listening to an encoded tape without decoding is not a musical treat. The problem is solved, however, by *expanding* the signal during the decoding process.

Expanding during decoding does more than just restore the dynamic range: It's *the key* to reducing the noise. Take a look at

Figure 8.28: We start with the original, unencoded music, with a dynamic range of about 90 dB in this case. Next, the music is encoded by compression, and then recorded onto tape. For our example, the compression ratio is 2:1. As we can see in our example, the tape hiss is sitting at a level of –45 dB, and the compressed music is recorded at levels from –40 to +5 dB.

When the tape is decoded during playback by expansion, everything is expanded at a 1:2 ratio, including the tape hiss. The result is that loud music passages are made twice as loud, and quiet passages are made twice as quiet. The final step shows what we hear: The music is restored to its original 90 dB dynamic range, and the tape hiss is expanded downward from –45 dB to a level of –90 dB—which is barely audible!

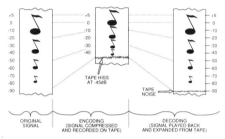

Figure 8.28 Compression and expansion: The basic principle of 'compansion' noise reduction.

Bear in mind that with any encode/decode tape noise reduction system, only tape hiss and other noises caused by the recording process are reduced. Any noise which is recorded with the original signal—such as a buzz from a guitar amp, or hiss from the mixer—will remain the same and not be reduced!

That's the theory. In practice, there are a few different approaches . . .

dbx. There are two types of dbx noise reduction. Type I is a system designed for broadcast use. It operates at +4 dBm levels and at a reduced bandwidth—from 40 Hz to about 12 kHz only. In the world of multi-track recording, the only system you should expect to encounter is dbx Type II, designed to operate at either +4 dBm or –10 dBV levels, and across the full frequency band.

For the most part, dbx operates as the compander system pictured in Figure 8.28. There is one major difference, however. During the encode stage, dbx boosts the high frequencies with a simple equalizer circuit: This boost is known as *pre-emphasis*. During decoding, those frequencies are returned to normal with another EQ circuit, in a process known as *de-emphasis*. By lowering all the high frequencies during playback, the benefit is a further decrease in noise, since tape hiss is largely high frequency information. All in all, dbx can reduce tape hiss by a lot—as much as 30dB.

Dolby. There are three common types of Dolby noise reduction: Dolby A, B, and C (Dolby SR is a less common type, which we'll look at in a moment). Dolby A is the most effective, reducing noise by 15 to 25 dB. Dolby C follows, with an average 20 dB reduction, followed by Dolby B, which reduces noise by about 10 dB.

Like dbx, and as shown in Figure 8.28, all three Dolbys are companding systems. Here's one major difference between dbx and Dolby, however: The Dolby systems switch off when the levels are consistently loud enough to mask the residual tape hiss. This contrasts with dbx, which reduces the amount of noise reduction, but doesn't switch off, and represents a philosophical difference. The Dolby people feel that it's not necessary to apply processing 100% of the time, but only when it's necessary. Consequently, Dolby circuits have level detectors which disengage the encoding or decoding when the overall signal levels are loud enough.

Another difference between dbx and Dolby is that dbx applies the same companding to the entire frequency band, to reduce noise at all frequencies; Dolby systems don't offer the same across-the-band reduction. For example, Dolby B only works from 1000 Hz and up; below 1000 Hz there's no Dolby B processing. This is another philosophical difference: The Dolby people feel that since tape hiss primarily happens at higher frequencies, that's where the processing should take place, whereas the dbx people feel that noise at any frequency is of consequence. Dolby does agree, to some degree, with dbx on this issue. For example, Dolby C operates on two independent bands, from 400 Hz to 1000 Hz, and from 1000 Hz on up. And Dolby A, the most expensive and effective system, operates on four different bands: from 80 Hz on down; from 80 to 3000 Hz; from 3000 to 9000 Hz; and from 9000 Hz on up.

Other Systems. The most powerful noise reduction system of all is a new type of Dolby, which operates on much more complicated and elaborate principles than the ones described above. Known as Dolby SR, for *spectral recording*, it's a multi-band system that is capable of providing performance that rivals the world's most expensive digital tape recorders. Dolby is guarding the process very carefully, however, and as good as it is, inexpensive digital recording may beat SR into the home studio: SR costs over $1,000 per channel.

In Europe, noise reduction systems made by ANT/Telefunken, known as Telcom, are quite popular. One system resembles Dolby A, and another aims to compete with dbx and Dolby SR. Just like Dolby A and SR, however, Telcom is not commonly found in the home studio.

Growing in popularity is something known as Dolby HX Pro. This is *not* a noise reduction system, *per se*. Rather, it's a built-in circuit—developed by Bang & Olufson and Dolby—which improves the headroom of recording circuits, so that there's less tape saturation (covered on page 20). The result is that higher levels can be recorded with less loss of high frequencies. HX Pro is often found in conjunction with Dolby C or other noise reduction systems.

Which System Is Best? Many professionals would agree that Dolby SR is the best noise reduction made. For most people, however, its cost is prohibitive.

In home recording, there are three common noise reduction systems: dbx Type II, Dolby C, and Dolby B. Dolby B is the least effective of these three, and is the only noise reduction for a few of the least expensive ministudios. For the rest of the market, the debate of dbx vs. Dolby C is hotly contested. Tascam, Yamaha, and others would have you believe that dbx is best; Fostex, AMR,

Audio-Technica, and others advocate Dolby C. These opposing camps exist largely thanks to effective marketing by both dbx and Dolby, though there are true believers on both sides of the fence.

Here are the facts: dbx gives you more headroom than Dolby C, so that you can record 'into the red' on your meters, with less fear of tape saturation. As well, dbx does reduce more noise than Dolby C. In fact, if you just listen at a high level to blank tape with dbx engaged, you'll hear practically no noise; with Dolby C you'll still hear a tiny bit of hiss—though a *lot* less than with Dolby B. But most of us spend little time listening to blank tape—how do dbx and Dolby C sound with music?

Some people claim Dolby C sounds best because it doesn't process all frequencies at once: It has two separate bands which turn on separately when levels get high enough. Since dbx works all the time on all frequencies at once, some feel you can hear it working from time to time. For example, with dbx, when just low notes are played back, it's possible occasionally to hear the hiss expanding upward—this is what people refer to when they claim that dbx 'pumps.'

There are two other categories where Dolby C may be preferable to dbx. When syncing drum machines and other devices to tape via a sync code (as we'll examine on page 112), in most cases it's necessary to record the code without dbx, though it's okay to record it with Dolby C. The reason is that the processing of the dbx circuit can distort the code. Tascam and other manufacturers have conquered this problem on some ministudios by installing a 'dbx off' switch for one of the tracks, or by offering a 'sync input' and 'sync output'—which is an input and output to one track (usually track 4 on 4-tracks) which bypasses the dbx circuit.

Finally, another quirk of dbx is related to headbump: You may recall, back in Figure 5.4, we learned that the design of tape heads results in a slight increase of frequencies around the 120 Hz range. A noise reduction system can worsen this headbump in the following way: One potential problem with *all* companding noise reduction systems is that any frequency deviations—increases or decreases in levels from flat response—can become exaggerated. When tracks are bounced, or ping-ponged together, a companding noise reduction system can further exaggerate deviant frequencies. Since dbx works on all frequencies, including headbump frequencies, if tracks are bounced together without switching off the dbx, the expansion process can cause the headbump to audibly double. Musically, this can make

a bass guitar sound 'boomy' and undefined. Dolby C doesn't work at frequencies below 400 Hz, so bouncing with Dolby C engaged does not worsen headbump problems.

So far, it may sound as if Dolby C is the clear winner over dbx: This is *not* necessarily the case! Some users enjoy the extra degree of true noise reduction that dbx offers over Dolby C. And Tascam, Yamaha, and other manufacturers who incorporate dbx in their gear, have effectively addressed the problems we've described by including 'dbx defeat' switches on ministudios. These defeat switches can work on a single track —for sync code—or they can work on all tracks—for bouncing. If you're shopping for a recorder/mixer with dbx, make sure you find one with these defeat options. If you do, the problems we've described will be alleviated, and you can count on a noise- and trouble-free recording.

If you own an independent open-reel machine without noise reduction, such as any of the Tascam or Otari machines, your outboard noise reduction choices are dbx, Dolby A, Dolby B, or Dolby SR. Dolby no longer licenses the manufacture of outboard Dolby C processors.

In the last analysis, your ears must once again make the decision—whatever your choice, however, any quality system will help you make clean, quiet tape recordings.

One final note about noise reduction, which addresses a problem that many of us have encountered. The old adage about Dolby B is that "It should be switched off—it reduces high frequencies!" Certainly many of us have defeated the Dolby B switch when playing back tapes, to cure a muffled sound. Dolby B does not reduce high frequencies, however, unless it is improperly calibrated. And the fact is, very few cassette decks, multi-track or not, are properly calibrated by the time they reach your living room from overseas. The solution: Have a technician properly align and calibrate your tape machine! This applies with any tape deck, and with any noise reduction system. Dolby C and dbx are more tolerant of miscalibration than Dolby B, but nonetheless, calibration will greatly improve your tape deck's performance.

* * * *

With equalizers, delays, reverbs, comp/limiters, gates, noise reduction, and more, there's a lot of signal processing gear from which to choose. Even the best studios are not completely equipped with every type of signal processor on the market, and one of your tasks in setting up a studio will be to decide what processing will serve you best.

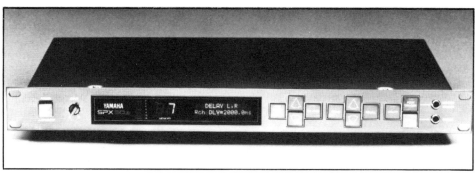

Figure 8.29 Yamaha's SPX90-II offers compression, reverb, EQ, and more in one box.

Fortunately, as we noted earlier, a growing trend is the incorporation of many effects into one box. The Yamaha SPX90-II is a prime example, offering reverb, delay, pitch transposition, compression, and more, in one relatively affordable package. In a similar manner, we can expect to see effects other than just EQ incorporated into more mixing consoles.

All of this portends good news for both personal and professional recording studios, offering us greater creative options. Though signal processing can do little to improve a poor performance, it can make a great performance sound even better. ☐

CHAPTER 9: MICROPHONES

In the preceding chapter we learned how signal processing for the engineer is analogous to lighting for the photographer, since both allow moods and atmosphere to be created and expressed. If that holds true, then microphones are our lenses, and determine how we audibly 'view' our acoustic subjects. And just as different photographers will approach the same subject with different lenses, veteran engineers are more opinionated about microphones and miking techniques than perhaps any other topic.

With the advent of affordable digital drum machines, and with sampling keyboards capable of remarkable piano, string, and other lifelike sounds, the role of microphones in the average home and professional studio has diminished greatly. Whereas an arsenal of six to 15 or more mikes may be necessary to record acoustic drum kits and pianos, many home studios manage fine with one or two quality mikes, for vocal or guitar tracks—or for recording samples!

While the overall role of mikes may be diminished, however, perfectly recorded digital drum sounds and other high quality samples challenge us to make mike recordings of equal quality. For those of us with just one or two mikes, our choices and techniques are as important as ever.

If you find yourself wanting to learn more about mikes and miking techniques than this book can allow space for, *The Microphone Handbook*, by John Eargle, is highly recommended. The world of microphones encompasses many phases of science, art, and even some witchcraft, and deserves a book such as Eargle's.

Before we get into the details, here are a couple of things to keep in mind: Microphones can be *high* or *low impedance* ('Z'), and can be *balanced* or *unbalanced*. As we learned back on pages 22 and 23, low-Z (600 ohms or less) balanced mikes are preferable to high-Z (2000 ohms or higher) unbalanced mikes, since they are less susceptible to noise and can have cable runs of greater than 20 feet without high frequency losses.

If you already own a high-Z unbalanced mike, or low-Z balanced mike, the following information will apply to you. Remember though, even if your mixer or ministudio only has 1/4" unbalanced mike inputs—as do most ministudios—low-Z balanced mikes can be used with a transformer, and will offer better performance.

Microphone Types

In Chapter Two we learned how a microphone is a transducer, capable of turning sound energy into electrical energy. While there are many mikes on the market, almost all fall into one of three categories: *dynamic, condenser,* and *ribbon*.

Dynamic, or Moving Coil Mikes. Referring back to Figure 2.2, we can see a microphone with a wire coil attached to its diaphragm. As sound strikes the diaphragm, it moves—causing the coil to move within a fixed magnet and in turn generating electrical signals. This is a description of a dynamic, or *moving coil*, microphone.

Figure 9.1 The SM-57 is very similar to the '58,' but lacks the built-in pop filter—it's a popular choice for drums.

Dynamic mikes are very common in live performance, since they're traditionally inexpensive compared to condenser and ribbon mikes, and their design makes them rather indestructible; physical trauma can lessen their quality, but they'll usually continue to make sound.

Another benefit of a typical dynamic mike is its ability to resist overloading. That is, its diaphragm is resistant to distortion, since it's relatively stiff—even the loudest guitar amplifier or kick drum can be picked up without distortion from most dynamic mikes.

All this ruggedness and resistance to distortion has a price: Many dynamic mikes have a relatively uneven frequency response when new, and much worse after abuse. Many also have a poor *transient response*. A *transient* is a relatively high level signal with a sharp attack and decay, such as the instantaneous attack of a guitar string or a stick on a snare drum. In order to mike these kind of transients accurately—and to keep them sounding bright and punchy—a diaphragm has to be able to move quickly. The problem with many dynamic mikes is that their diaphragms are too slow to do this, since the attached coil adds a relatively large amount of mass.

There are exceptions to the rule, however: The Beyer M201, for example, is a dynamic mike which has been designed to offer superior transient and high-end frequency response. And there may be many circumstances which don't require great transient or high frequency response, such as miking a guitar amp. Similarly, there are some miking situations which simply demand ruggedness or resistance to distortion, such as miking a kick drum.

Condenser Mikes. Condenser microphones don't use a moving coil and magnet, as we described for dynamic mikes. Rather, they use a *capacitor* to transduce electricity from sound.

Here's how they work: A capacitor is an electronic device with a voltage potential between electrically-charged 'plates' in close proximity, one positive in charge, the

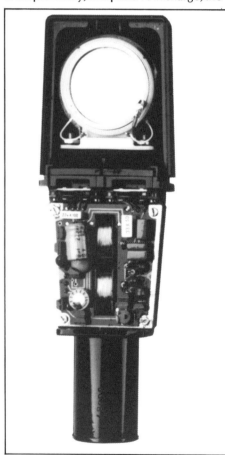

Figure 9.2 A cutaway view of an AKG C414 condenser microphone. Like many finer condenser mikes, the C414 has a large diaphragm, and requires 48 volts of external phantom power. Beneath the diaphragm we see the mike's preamp. Most mikes, incidentally, can be repaired if damaged by a sudden blast of air, such as from a kick drum: When the diaphragm is replaced, they're almost as good as new.

other negative. Due to the properties of *capacitance*, when two plates are near enough to each other, they can pass voltage between them; the closer the plates get to each other, the greater the voltage. With a condenser mike, the diaphragm is actually one of the plates, and the other is fixed. As sounds strike the diaphragm, they cause it to move to and fro—and as the distance varies between the two plates, so does the voltage. It's different from the moving coil scheme, but the end results are rather similar.

A condenser mike requires some form of power supply, to provide voltage to the plates, and to power the mike's *preamp*— the output levels from the electrodes are so low that a small amplifier is needed before the signal is sent down the cable to the mixer. The traditional power supply is an external box inserted between a mike and the mixer, referred to as a *phantom power* supply. Some mixers, however, have built-in phantom power. The actual power is 12 to 48 volts, sent up through balanced mike cables. It's called 'phantom' since the voltage is only used by condenser mikes —dynamic and ribbon mikes in good working order functionally ignore the power as if it weren't there. (Some engineers claim that they can hear the effect of phantom power on ribbon mikes in particular; more than likely the mike's balancing transformer is defective, and is allowing voltage to affect the sound.) Phantom power must be sent only through balanced cabling to balanced mikes, by the way, to avoid damage to the mike or power supply.

Some condensers, especially *electret* condenser mikes, can use an internal power supply such as a 9 volt or 1.5 volt penlight battery. An electret mike is very similar to a true condenser, except that the diaphragm and fixed electrode are permanently charged, so that only the preamp needs power. Many of the more affordable condenser mikes are in fact electret mikes. In practice, if an electret's preamp is receiving 1.5 volts from an internal battery—as com-

Figure 9.3 The Shure SM-81 condenser microphone has an adjustable high-pass filter for reducing excessive bass and rumble. It performs well with drums (snare and overhead) as well as acoustic instruments.

pared to 48 external volts for many true condensers—its preamp doesn't have as much headroom, and can distort more easily. Otherwise, electrets sound very similar to full-fledged condensers, and for the rest of this book, we'll treat them as such. And how do condensers sound?

If you want a crisp, bright-sounding mike with excellent transient and high frequency response, chances are you want a condenser mike. Condenser mikes are often the engineer's choice for acoustic guitars, pianos, overhead or snare drum microphones, and other such settings. They're also the mike of choice for most vocalists, since better condensers—such as the Neumann U-87—are extremely smooth-sounding across the entire vocal range.

Figure 9.4 Two legendary Neumann condenser mircophones: the U-89 (left), and the U-87. Like the C414, these require external phantom power, and can be switched between different pickup patterns (see Figure 9.6).

If they're so wonderful, why doesn't everyone use condensers exclusively? There are several reasons. One is that, by and large, condenser mikes are more fragile than dynamic mikes—their diaphragms are so light that they can be easily damaged. Rock star tricks of swinging and dropping mikes will trash most condensers (the Shure SM-81, pictured in Figure 9.3, is a relatively hardy exception to this rule). And, as we mentioned, condensers can overload more easily and are not usually recommended in very high volume settings, such as inside a kick drum or in front of a guitar amplifier. Finally, good condenser mikes aren't cheap —the U-87 pictured in Figure 9.4, costs over $1,000. Some older Neumann condensers, particularly those with tube rather than transistor electronics, can cost much more.

There is good news for the home studio, however: Relatively high-quality and low-cost condensers and electrets from Toa, Sony, Shure, Electro-Voice, Audio-Technica, and others, have brought the condenser sound to the home studio. Consequently, a matched pair of high quality, low cost condensers is the ideal mike choice for many of us who own drum machines, and use mikes simply for vocal and guitar tracks, or to record samples.

Ribbon Mikes. A third type of mike, the ribbon mike, is actually a type of dynamic mike, though it's usually thought of as being

in its own category. Rather than using a moving coil, however, a ribbon mike uses a thin, lightweight, metal ribbon as a diaphragm. This ribbon is surrounded by a fixed magnet. Then—as with a moving coil mike—when sound waves strike the ribbon, electro-magnetic variations are induced.

Figure 9.5 The Beyer M-160 ribbon microphone is legendary among oboe and violin players for its sensitivity.

Ribbon mikes predate condensers, and have been rare birds since the 1960s. The primary drawback of the ribbon design is that the diaphragms themselves are very fragile, and a direct blast of air from a singer or kick drum is enough to put most ribbons completely out of commission. The flip side of the coin, though, is that a quality ribbon mike ribbon is extremely sensitive, with excellent transient response capable of picking up very subtle nuances in sound.

Thanks primarily to the efforts of the German company BeyerDynamic, the ribbon mike is enjoying a resurgence of popularity. Fostex makes a variation of ribbon mikes known as *regulated phase* mikes. These mikes use a round diaphragm which has a coil 'printed' on the mike. This diaphragm is in turn suspended between two magnets—which have enough perforations in them to allow soundwaves to pass unimpeded. This system has the advantage of excellent transient response along with the durability of a dynamic mike.

Microphone Pickup Patterns

Also known as *directionality*, or *polar response*, a microphone's *pickup pattern* describes from which directions it's sensitive to sound. These patterns reflect how different mikes respond to sounds which are *on-axis* (directly in front of the diaphragm), and those sounds which are *off-axis* (not in front). Some mikes, as we'll learn, are equally sensitive to sounds from any direction—on- or off-axis—others are sensitive only to sounds at which they're aimed. In order to use a mike effectively, it's essential to choose the right pattern for the right job.

Dynamic moving coil, condenser, and ribbon mikes are made in all polar patterns. Some mikes even have switchable pickup patterns, such as the AKG 414 (Figure 9.6). Others have interchangeable *capsules* or *elements*—the end of the mike with the diaphragm—to offer different patterns.

Figure 9.6 AKG's C414 offers a choice of omni, cardioid, hypercardioid, or bidirectional pickup patterns.

Omnidirectional. As the name suggests, an *omnidirectional* mike is sensitive to sounds coming from all directions—in front, behind, to the side, wherever. Returning to our lens analogy, an omnidirectional is to the recordist as a 'fish eye' or super-wide angle lens is to the photographer. An omnidirectional mike is the most straightforward in design, and can theoretically offer the best frequency response of any pattern.

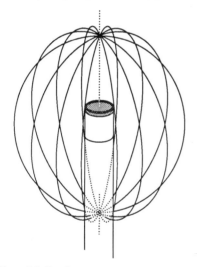

Figure 9.7 Omni response.

'Omni' mikes have limited utility in live work, since they're most susceptible to feedback. In recording, an omni is fine when you have a single source to mike, or don't have to worry about picking up unwanted sounds throughout the room. Let's say, for example, you were making a monaural recording of a piano in a good-sounding room, and didn't have to worry about any external noise. To pick up both the piano and the natural reverberance of the piano in the room, an omni mike would make an excellent choice. Similarly, if you had a single mike and were recording a dialogue between two people, an omni mike could be placed equidistant between them, and would pick up both rather well.

The problem for most home studios is that omnis pick up everything *too* well: If you're recording an acoustic guitar or vocal in the same room as your tape recorder, it's usually desirable to have a mike that's most sensitive to what you wish to record—one that will reject off-axis sounds, such as the recorder's transport. Similarly, you may have a problem with some external sounds. Many a home studio has an omni or two gathering dust—the result of one too many tracks with the neighbor's dog providing background vocals.

Cardioid. Also known as a *unidirectional*, a *cardioid* mike is designed to pick up sounds which are mostly in front of the diaphragm. It rejects sounds emanating from behind the mike, and is similar to the visual range of a 'normal' lens. The name 'cardioid' comes from the shape of the pickup pattern: It looks like a heart, as we can see in Figure 9.8.

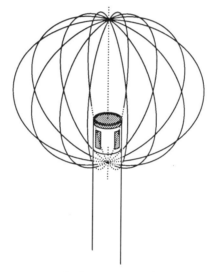

Figure 9.8 Cardioid response; note the ports.

Cardioid mikes are made directionally sensitive thanks to *ports*. Off-axis sounds (which emanate from behind the diaphragm) enter these special acoustic slots and eventually reach the back of the diaphragm; they also strike the front of the diaphragm. The ports are designed so that off-axis sounds phase cancel themselves inside the mike, by causing opposite but equal pressure on the front and rear of the diaphragm. If you've ever cupped your hand over a cardioid mike to try and stop feedback, you've likely found that the feedback only gets worse. The reason? By covering these ports, you temporarily turned your cardioid mike into an omni.

A cardioid mike's off-axis rejection is ideal for most personal recording scenarios: If your tape recorder is whirring quietly away—though whirring nonetheless—it's a handy thing to be able to point a mike away from it, and record your voice or whatever with minimal background noise.

Similarly, any time more than one microphone is used in the same room—such as recording a sax and piano at the same time on two separate tracks—two cardioid mikes will offer reasonably good separation between the sources. If you were using two omnidirectional mikes in the same setting, the sax's mike likely would pick up lots of piano—and the piano's mike would pick up lots of sax. The end result would be sax and

piano tracks that were hardly distinct from each other. (The problem could be lessened by using goboes, the acoustic isolators we discussed on page 14.)

The trade-off for this isolation help is that cardioid mikes generally have more uneven frequency responses than similarly-priced omnidirectional mikes. Nevertheless, cardioids are perhaps the most generally useful pattern for most studios.

Hypercardioid. A variation of cardioid is the *hypercarioid*, or *super cardioid* pattern—which is similar to the cardioid pattern though even 'tighter,' with a very strong off-axis rejection. It also uses ports to create directionality. A hypercardioid mike is analogous to a short focal length telephoto lens, perhaps a 135 mm for those shutterbugs among us.

Hypercardioid mikes, such as the Sennheiser 441, are very immune to feedback, and are a good choice where isolation is critical—such as a live recording session with many acoustic instrumentalists. To an even greater degree than cardioid mikes, though, hypercardioid mikes trade a gain in off-axis rejection for even frequency response. Unless there's a real need to use a hypercardioid mike, most home recordists are usually better off using a cardioid.

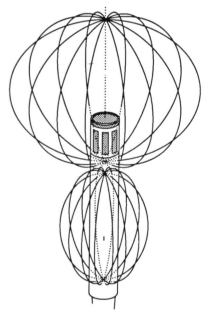

Figure 9.9 Hypercardioid response.

'Shot Gun.' At any major news conference, amidst the artillery of telephoto lenses, one's sure to see a number of *shotgun* mikes. Take a look at Figure 9.10 and the name will explain itself: They're the long, thin mikes designed to isolate and pick up a distant, focused subject—which is almost exactly the same purpose as the long telephoto lenses with which they're associated. A large number of ports on the side of the 'barrel' create the shot gun's ultra-cardioid behavior.

Shot guns—infrequently known as *ultra-directionals*—are definitely special-purpose mikes, since they sound lousy for general-purpose work. Aside from news conferences and other journalistic endeavors, shot guns are useful for isolating orchestral soloists, recording environmental sounds (birds, frogs, and other critters), or in theatre and film applications, such as miking singers on a stage.

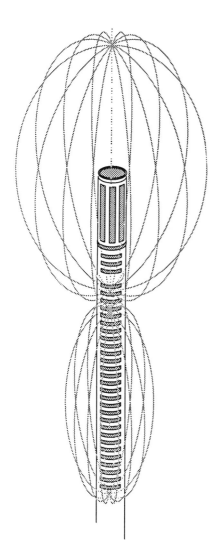

Figure 9.10 A shotgun mike's pickup pattern is ideal for many radio and film applications.

Bidirectional. As Figure 9.11 graphically explains, another name for a *bidirectional* mike is a *figure-8* mike. This figure-8 response pattern tells us that one of these mikes is most sensitive to sounds emanating from either side of the mike, though not in front or behind the actual mike. Unfortunately, our lens analogy fails us with bidirectional mikes—perhaps a lizard's ability to see in two opposite directions at once may work instead.

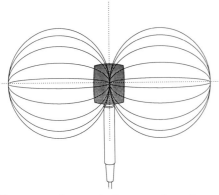

Figure 9.11 Bidirectional mikes respond equally well to sounds from opposite directions.

This pattern can be achieved in one of two ways. The first is to take a ribbon, mount it between a magnet, and then allow sounds to strike either side of the ribbon. The other is to mount opposingly two dynamic or condenser cardioid-pattern diaphragms

inside one mike. The ribbon, or dual-cardioid element, is turned sideways within the mike, so that the mike actually has two 'faces.' Bear in mind, however, that one of these faces is the 'in-phase' face, and will produce a positive voltage when it receives pressure. When miking just one primary source, this face should be used—it's usually identified with a pattern marking (an "8"), a special color, or the mike's model number.

The applications for bidirectional mikes are quite specialized. One application is to place the mike between two singers, saxophonists, or other instrumentalists, who want to face each other during the recording. Another place for one of these mikes is in between two drums, such as two toms on a drum kit; in that way, only one mike is needed to do the job of two. Some engineers like to use a bidirectional with a single vocalist, so that the primary face records directly, and the other face records the ambient sound of the room.

Other Specialized Mikes

Aside from the basic cardioid, omni, and other pattern variations dynamic, condenser, or ribbon mikes, there are several specialized mikes which you may encounter. Here's a brief rundown:

Boundary Mikes, or PZMs. Boundary mikes are quite remarkable devices. They don't look like mikes: Rather, most look like a flat metal plate with an attached wire.

Figure 9.13 A Crown PZM mike (see Figure 9.16).

Lavalier Mikes. On any television news show you can see lavalier mikes: They're the small 'tie-clip' mikes attached to the newscasters. While the film and broadcast applications for lavaliers are obvious, there are also some applications in the personal studio. For example—while most 'lavs' are omni condensers subject to overload at relatively low levels—Countryman, Shure, and others offer cardioid or even hypercardioid lavs capable of withstanding fantastically high sound pressure levels without distortion or damage. A set of the Countryman Isomax II or similar mikes are excellent for drums, piano, or even vocals; with adapters they can fit inside the bell of a sax or the sound hole of a guitar.

The chief advantage of these lavs is their size, though some are very credible performers in their own rights. The Countryman mikes have an added advantage: When placed, with the diaphragm face down with sticky foam on a flat surface, they behave like a boundary mike (see Figure 9.16).

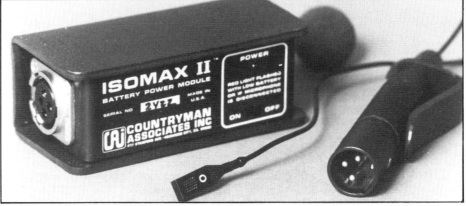

Figure 9.12 A Countryman Isomax II omni lavalier, with battery power supply.

For the most part, if the room sounds good, you can throw a boundary mike in front of just about anything—a piano, a guitar amp, a jazz combo, or even a symphony orchestra—and get a reasonably good-sounding recording. The word 'throw' is almost literal—a boundary mike can be placed directly on the floor, it can be attached to a wall or stand, or it can be mounted on a wall.

First popularized by Crown as *PZMs—pressure zone microphones*—boundary mikes are typically omnidirectional condenser mikes. Crown, Shure, Beyer, Radio Shack (Tandy), and others offer these as flat-sounding recording mikes designed for versatile placement. In order to understand how they work, and for an explanation of the name 'boundary,' please see the section "Phase And The Single Microphone," ahead on page 67.

These mikes are very sensitive—one omni boundary mike placed on a wall can record whispers in a large room. And specialized mounting plates are available which will yield cardioid response patterns.

There are a number of home recordists who feel that a pair of these mikes are extremely versatile, and can replace conventional mikes.

Contact mikes. Also known as just *transducers*, *contact mikes* are quite popular with many musicians. They're not true mikes in the sense that they don't transduce changes in air pressure to changes in voltage. Rather, they transduce physical vibrations into electricity through direct contact with guitars, drums, woodwinds, and other instruments. Though most transducers are intended to be used with a manufacturer's preamp, many will work directly in mike or instrument-level inputs.

One clever transducer system is the C-Ducer, by C-Tape Developments. C-ducers (which look like flat, padded tape) come in various lengths, and can be used in many different applications, such as guitar, piano, drums, or almost any acoustic instrument.

Contact mikes offer the advantage of high isolation: It's possible to record with one while the monitor speakers are turned up, with minimal fear of feedback, or to record several instruments at once without 'leakage.' This makes them ideal for live performance recording. Although contact mikes sound very different from mikes—causing the instruments to sound more 'electric' than acoustic—a popular technique is to mix the sound of the contact mike with that of a conventional mike. By experimenting with the relative levels, it's possible to get a really full and balanced acoustic guitar sound in this way.

Stereo Mikes. A single stereo mike can be very effective as a drum overhead mike, or for recording orchestral or chamber music.

Most stereo mikes are known as *M-S*, or *mid-side* mikes. The M-S design actually uses two microphone designs within one housing: a cardioid mike, and a bidirectional mike. The cardioid element is situated on the 'top' of the mike, and receives sound directly from whatever's being miked. Underneath the cardioid element is the bidirectional element, receiving sound from two opposite sides of the mike. In this way, the bidirectional element is most sensitive to ambient, reflected sounds.

The output of the M-S mike is then sent to an *M-S decoder*, which can adjust the balance between the direct and ambient sounds. The more of the bidirectional, ambient signal, the 'wider' the stereo image. Conversely, the more of the cardioid, direct signal, the more 'mono' the sound becomes. The decoder has a left and a right output, which can be fed to two normal mike inputs. Some manufacturers, such as Sony, offer stereo mikes with built-in decoders, though most are 'outboard.'

M-S stereo mikes are offered by AKG, Neumann, Fostex, Sony, and others. Most use condenser elements, though the Fostex uses the regulated phase design.

There are also stereo recording techniques which can be performed using two specially-placed microphones. Please refer to Figures 9.18a and b for stereo miking techniques.

Binaural Mikes. One of the more remarkable mike techniques is known as *binaural* recording. It's actually a variation of stereo miking, though there's one major difference: Binaural recording uses a dummy human head, with microphones placed inside the 'ears.'

The concept is to place the dummy head as you would actually wish to hear something. If you want to record a live symphonic orchestra, no problem—just stick the head in 10th row center, and record its two outputs on two separate channels! The most astounding result of binaural recording is what happens when you listen to the playback on headphones—the recording is phenomenally life-like, as if you were sitting exactly where the head was.

Microphone Accessories

Pop Filters And Wind Screens. Diaphragms work thanks to moving air, but sometimes that air can present a problem. We all know that humans have a tough time with the tongue-twister *Peter Piper picked a peck of pickled peppers*, but we just have to say it—a mike has to reproduce it!

The problem with "p's" is that they create high velocities of air. Once again, as part of the price of knowledge, we're called

upon to dangle a piece of paper in front of our mouths: This time, hold it by the top with two fingers. Say something normally, and then try "Peter Piper." You should see and feel a noticeable increase in the paper's movement. That's exactly the same thing your mike's diaphragm has to deal with every time you sing or say a "p," and to a lesser extent, a "b."

Specially-designed foam or mesh diaphragm covers known as *pop filters* help reduce these extra air blasts. A few years back, a rather odd pop filter began to show up in studios: a piece of a woman's pantyhose, strung across a bent wire coat hanger, and placed in front of the mike's diaphragm. Not very elegant, but certainly effective, since the air blast is lessened long before it reaches the diaphragm. Several companies

Figure 9.14 The Popper Stopper: An improvement on pantyhose.

have since packaged the concept.

Wind screens are designed with the same goal in mind as pop filters—stopping excessive air blasts—but they are much denser, and by necessity cover not just the diaphragm, but whatever ports may be on the mike. They're necessary equipment for almost any outdoor recording. Large windscreens designed for shot gun mikes are known as *zeppelins*, since they resemble the famous dirigible.

Both pop filters, and to a greater degree wind screens, reduce a mike's high-frequency performance and slightly reduce its overall sensitivity.

Mounting Devices. Rubber or nylon *mike clips*—rather than plastic—are preferable since they're less prone to breaking.

Booms allow you to get the mike in hard-to-reach places, such as over a drum set, or inside a piano lid. A boom is a nice luxury for just about any miking setup, especially an acoustic guitar or a vocalist. Some booms have large counterweights, which are necessary for heavier mikes such as a large Neumann condenser or an Electro-Voice PL-20, or may be necessary if you need to extend the boom all the way.

A *gooseneck* is a flexible metal tube, and is great for any weird but necessary mike-placement contortions—such as a tight mike placement between drum kit's hi-hat and snare. Make sure that the gooseneck you choose is able to support the weight of whichever mike you plan to use.

A tripod style *stand*—the most stable in most situations—has three foldable feet, and is great for easy transport. A heavy circular base is less stable with a long boom, and is

Direct Boxes

Almost all synthesizers and other electronic keyboards can produce line level signals, and can be plugged directly into most mixers. (Levels are discussed on page 19.) But what about other instruments, which produce much lower levels?

Many mixers, and all ministudios, allow you to plug in instruments directly so that, for example, you can record a bass guitar without having to mike its amplifier.

What if your mixer doesn't accept anything but mike and true line levels? It's still possible to record an instrument directly by using a *direct box*, also known as a *D.I.* (for 'direct injection,' or 'direct input'). A direct box takes an instrument's output (instrument *or* line level) and reduces it to a microphone level—and also balances the signal. The output of the direct box can then be fed directly into a mike input. Most direct boxes are single channel, though 4-channel versions are available.

The average direct box has a 1/4" input jack and a 3-pin XLR output. Some also have a 1/4" *foldback* or 'output' jack, which is an unaltered output of whatever's plugged into the input jack. By connecting the output of this foldback jack to an amplifier, you can record an instrument directly while still hearing it through your instrument amp.

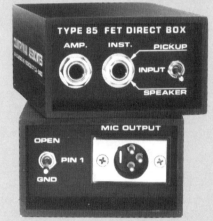

Figure 9.15 Countryman direct boxes.

In order to create a balanced signal, direct boxes have balancing circuits (see page 23). And just like balanced mike inputs, direct boxes can be transformer balanced—known as *passive* boxes—or active balanced. Most engineers prefer the sound of active circuits, though a transformer-balanced direct box has two advantages. The first is that since the transformer actually isolates the signal, it can prevent a nasty electrical shock with potentially faulty gear. The other advantage is that passive DIs can run without batteries or external power. Just like condenser mikes, most active DIs are designed to run off an internal battery or phantom power.

Electric guitars and some other instruments get much of their distinctive sound from their amplifiers and speakers. Consequently, they often sound better if miked than through a direct box or regular input. For basses and even synthesizers, however, one useful tip is to mix a direct *and* miked signal together onto one track.

harder to transport, but it does have two advantages: It's better equipped to right itself if knocked, and it takes up less floor space than the tripod style.

Shock Mounts. Mikes not only pick up sounds in the air—they're also useful for picking up feet tapping, trucks rumbling, and other vibrational intrusions. Without complete isolation, some of these low frequency noises can be physically transmitted up stands and through clips to the mike itself. A *shock mount* is the solution. It's usually a 'cage' of intertwined elastic bands or 'air suspension' rubber which replaces the clip, and the mike sits suspended in it—away from direct, hard contact with the boom and stand.

Parabolic Reflector. This is a very specialized accessory, designed to capture very distant sounds with greater sensitivity and fidelity than a shot gun mike. The idea is that the bowl-like parabola is pointed towards the source, and a mike (usually cardioid) is placed *facing* the center of the parabola. In this way, the mike's at the 'sweet spot,' and will pick up whatever's reflected towards it. There's almost no need for one of these in the studio, though they are growing in popularity: More people are using samplers to record exotic sounds, and a parabolic reflector is a useful tool.

Cable. Your cables are the vital link between your mike and mixer—don't skimp on them, or maltreat them! See page 77 for more about cables and connectors.

Microphone Techniques

If you've read interviews with big-time engineers or producers, undoubtedly you've read of special miking techniques for guitars, pianos, drums, and other sources. While there's quite of a bit of science and theory related to using mikes, for many it remains an art, where the requisite for good miking is not a theory but *how it sounds*.

There are several reasons for this. One is that most engineers have learned special tricks or mike choices from their mentors, and carry on the 'flame.' Another is that there are so many variations for choice and technique that it becomes difficult to know which is ideally best under any given circumstance. But most of all, mike technique *is* an indefinite science—while there are theories and ideal mike choices, the fact is that some of the most unlikely techniques can sound great. Your recordings will be judged by how they sound, and not by whether or not you followed the rules.

Having said that, we're going to look at some of the most common theories and techniques. Pick and choose from what works for you, but most of all, use your ears!

Phase And The Single Microphone. Let's take a look at Figure 9.16: This shows a single microphone *distant miking* a vocalist from 10 feet or so. As the figure shows, both direct and reflected soundwaves are arriving at the mike—but notice that they're out of phase with each other. This is because the reflected waves are delayed. If we could listen to what we're seeing, we'd hear some phase cancellation, causing a slight change in the overall frequency response.

This is a good opportunity to see how PZM and other boundary mikes work. When a *conventional* mike is placed on the floor, it receives the direct and reflected

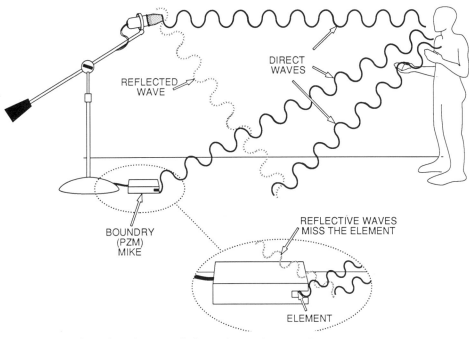

Figure 9.16 Boundary mikes suffer minimally from reflective phase cancellation.

sounds at essentially the same time, and almost perfectly in phase. The result is minimal phase cancellation, and an increase in sensitivity by almost 6 dB, since in-phase waves add in amplitude (as we learned on page 3).

Boundary mikes work on this principal: When placed on a large reflective surface, such as a floor, wall, or desk top, they enjoy increased sensitivity and phase performance. This surface acts as the boundary for reflected soundwaves. PZM and some other mikes have an added benefit: They carry their 'boundary' with them—a large plate—which can be placed on a stand or suspended from a ceiling.

But boundary mikes aren't everyone's choice in every situation, and even fewer people like to place their best conventional mikes on the floor. Consequently, phase cancellation must be dealt with. The obvious, and usually effective solution is to *close mike*—to place the mike right next to the vocalist or other source—so that the mike primarily receives direct sounds. Another solution is to use carpeting or another absorbant treatment on reflective surfaces.

In practice, however, many engineers will distant mike with a conventional microphone, and not worry too much about cancellations. There are some who feel the question of single mike phasing is overrated, since our own ears receive both direct and reflected sound waves in real life.

Phase And The Multiple Mike Setup. The questions of phase we've just been considering *do* become important when using more than one mike. The reason is that when two mikes are recording the same source, phase differences between the two can cause audible problems. This is because not only are audible delays being recorded (as with the single mike), but the phase irregularities are worsened when the outputs of the mikes are added electronically.

A common example of this problem is heard when miking a drum kit with two overhead mikes. Often a strange 'swishing' noise can be heard as the cymbals move—and this problem intensifies if you listen in mono (which causes the two mikes to add together 100%).

Nevertheless, there are many circumstances when two or more microphones are desirable, such as with a piano, guitar, or even orchestra. To the rescue are three solutions:

- Use a stereo mike, as described on page 66. Since the elements are placed very closely, phase cancellations are minimized.
- Use two mikes in a stereo miking technique. This approach places the diaphragms of two mikes very close to each other, minimizing phase problems.
- Use the *3:1 rule*.

The 3:1 rule states that two mikes should be placed apart from each other at least three times their distance from the source. In other words, if two mikes are placed 30 cm (about 1 foot) from a source, such as a drum kit, they should be at least 90 cm (3 feet) from each other. In this way, the soundwaves they receive are different enough to minimize phase cancellation.

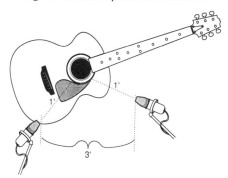

Figure 9.17 The 3:1 rule.

In the real world, this is yet another rule that has fallen by the wayside on many a hit record. When possible, however, the 3:1 rule will help increase the fidelity of your recordings.

With multiple mike setups it's also important to be sure that all of your balanced mikes are *wired* in-phase with each other. The problem is as follows: Most mikes and mixer mike inputs are wired so that pin 2 of the 3-pin XLR connector is the hot, or in-phase, conductor. Some mike inputs however, particularly on some older British consoles, are wired with pin 3 hot. If you should mix and match any mikes or mike cables that are wired differently from each other, you may run into some serious phase cancellation problems.

For example, let's say you were miking an acoustic guitar with two mikes, one wired pin 2 hot, the other pin 3 hot. If the two mikes were recorded on separate channels and played back in stereo, phase cancellations may not be obvious. But if the two channels were summed together in mono during playback, much of the guitar's signal may disappear completely, since out-of-phase signals added together cancel!

If you have any doubts as to whether or not your mikes are all wired in phase with each other, perform this test: Connect one mike to your mixer, and pan it center. Take the grill cloth off both speakers, and while looking at the low-frequency drivers (the woofers), gently tap the mike with your finger. You'll need to turn the level up high enough to see the speakers move when you tap the mike. (If you start to get feedback, use an EQ to cut the high frequencies, or slightly lower the volume; if feedback remains a problem, you may have to record this trick without speakers, and then play it back through the speakers.) When a mike is wired in-phase, you should see the woofers move *outwards*—this is telling us that positive air pressure is indeed resulting in positive voltage. If the mike is out of phase, the woofers will move *inward* with each tap, and you'll want to rewire that mike.

By the way, if one woofer moves outward, and the other inward, your *speakers* are miswired: Be sure that the positive terminals of both the amp and speakers are connected.

Once you've found your first in-phase mike—and confirmed that your speakers are wired properly—you can check the other mikes in the same manner, or you can check them this way:

- Hold the in-phase mike and the mike yet to be tested in front of your mouth, with the diaphragms as close as possible.
- Put the two mikes in separate mixer channels, and pan both to center.
- While talking, bring up the level of the 'good' mike. Then bring up the level of the new mike (you can also use a channel on-off switch).
- If the mikes are out of phase with each other, you'll hear a 'swishing' sound in the high frequencies, and very 'thin'-sounding bass response. If the new mike is wired in phase with the original mike, the sound will merely get louder.

If you find yourself with mike wiring problems, you'll want to correct them instantly.

Close-Miking Vs. Distant Miking. Most musicians have used mikes in live sound reinforcement, where the concept is to place the mikes as close as possible to the source—vocals, drums, guitar amps, and so on—in order to minimize the chance of feedback. In recording, we're much more fortunate, since we use headphones rather than speakers around live mikes, and the only times we have to worry about mike feedback is if we accidentally place a 'live' mike near a loud headphone or forget to bring down the mikes when we turn on the speakers. Consequently, we're free to experiment with both close miking and distant miking.

Close miking, typically within 0.5 meters (less than 2 feet), tends to pick up many of the instrument's or vocalist's more 'intimate' sounds: hammers hitting strings, fingers moving across fretboards, breath and lip noises, and so forth. Regardless of whether you're using an omnidirectional, cardioid, or other pattern, close miking will mean that you record more direct sounds and fewer reflected sounds.

Distant miking, from 1 meter (3 feet) to 10 meters (35 feet) or more, will sound very different. First of all, you'll be recording much more of the room's sound, including reflections and general reverberance (see page 49). Secondly, the 'intimate' sound of the recording will be diminished—the track will end up sounding much more 'airy' and spacious, and have fewer lip smacks and other such sounds. This spacious quality will increase with the reverberance of the room, and the distance of the mike.

A mike's gain is directly related to how close or far it is from the source being miked. But the relationship is not linear: That is, a piano miked from 1 meter is much louder than a piano miked from 2 meters, not just twice as loud.

These descriptions alone don't tell the whole story. There's also a phenomenon known as the *proximity effect*. If you've worked with a handheld mike, you've likely noticed this effect: the closer you hold the mike to your mouth, the 'boomier' or bassier the response of the mike. The proximity effect is most pronounced when the mike is just next to your lips, or whenever the mike is close to an instrument. For example, by moving a mike closer to a guitar's sound hole, not only does the gain increase, but so does the bass response.

A number of mikes—including the Sennheiser MD-421, the Shure SM-81, and Toa K-1—have built-in EQ switches that will roll-off the accentuated bass. Other microphones, most notably the Variable-D series by Electro-Voice, have acoustically-tuned *ports* on the side of the mike which cancel the proximity effect. These ports are similar to off-axis cancelling ports (which we discussed on page 64), but they're tuned to be most sensitive to on-axis lower frequencies.

No matter what polar pattern mike you're using, omnidirectional, cardioid, whatever, bear in mind that most mikes have terrible off-axis frequency response: In other words, point the mike's diaphragm at what you're recording!

Some engineers will use both close and distant miking for one source. A common example is with guitar amplifiers: One mike, up close near the speaker, will capture the 'punch' of the guitar. This signal is then mixed with a mike placed farther away; the result is richer and punchier than either miking technique alone could achieve.

Microphone Choice And Placement. With all the variations available, how does one know which is the best mike for the job? There's no cut-and-dried answer to this question, though there are several points to keep in mind.

One important consideration for many home recordists is external noise: How much unwanted background noise is there when you want to use a mike? If you're unable to soundproof (see page 13) but still have noise problems, you'll likely need to mike closely, and you'll almost certainly need a cardioid or hypercardioid mike. If background noise isn't a worry, then the worlds of distant miking and omnidirectional mikes are open to you.

Another consideration is *leakage*. If you need to record two different sources onto two different tracks simultaneously—such as a piano and a vocal—you'll want to make sure that the two sources are as isolated from each other as possible. To do this, you may need to use goboes, and you may need to use cardioid or hypercardioid mikes, to further lessen the possibility of leakage.

In general, omnidirectional mikes have flatter, more accurate frequency response than any of the other polar patterns, though many good quality cardioid mikes have sufficiently good frequency response. The source, however, will dictate the ideal size of the mike's diaphragm. Most mikes have medium- to small-sized diaphragms. A few mikes, such as the Electro-Voice PL20, Neumann U87, and Tascam PE250, have relatively larger diaphragms. Larger diaphragms are best suited for low frequency sources: A large diaphragm dynamic, for example, is

Figures 9.18a, 9.18b Stereo miking techniques can be performed with any pair of cardioid microphones. XY miking (left) offers accurate stereo imaging with virtually no phase problems. AB, or coincident pair miking (right) offers a slightly 'wider'-sounding stereo image.

the ideal choice for a kick drum.

On the other hand, smaller diaphragms are the choice for higher frequency sources. In particular, a small diaphragm condenser mike, such as the Shure SM81, makes a great overhead or acoustic guitar mike.

Mike placement is a very tricky subject—and that's what makes it so much much fun! There is no 100% correct formula for placing the mikes—a mike placed 1 meter from one vocalist may need to be placed 0.5 meter away from another vocalist.

Earlier we described stereo mikes. With pianos, choirs, and other acoustic ensembles you can use a technique known as *XY stereo recording*: This allows stereo miking with two cardioid or bidirectional mikes. The idea is to place two mikes so that their diaphragms are as close together as possible, but facing towards the source at 90 degree angles to each other (see Figure 9.18). The outputs of the two mikes can then be recorded on two separate tracks.

If you keep in mind the 3:1 rule we just described, you may wish to try *coincident pair*, or *AB*, stereo recording. With this technique, two mikes are placed apart from each other, such as over a drum kit, and are recorded on separate tracks. This gives a 'wider' stereo image than XY stereo, though it's more prone to phase problems.

* * * *

In the world of recording, where rules and formulae can sometimes seem overbearing, the opportunity to place, experiment, and record with mikes can be a wonderfully creative experience. And as synthesizers and MIDI-mania further dominate the home recording scene, it's still really satisfying to record something that actually makes the air move! ☐

CHAPTER 10: MONITOR SYSTEMS

On the surface, it may seem that a monitor system is simply a set of loudspeakers and a power amplifier, or a pair of headphones. And if all you want from your monitor system is to hear more or less what you've recorded, a home stereo and any old pair of headphones will do the trick.

A proper monitor system, however, is much more than just a playback system. Monitor systems are all about trust and understanding. You need to be able to trust that what you're hearing through the monitors is actually what you recorded—with all its sonic nuances and colors—in order to understand how your music will sound in environments other than your studio.

This last point is important: If you only intend to record and playback your music through your *own* monitor speakers—and never want to press an album or even distribute a tape to friends—most any system might work. For example, let's say your speakers have excessive high frequency response, and cause your music to sound overly bright. (Many home stereo speakers are designed to 'enhance' the music with thunderous bass and shimmering highs.) To compensate, your natural tendency will be to cut the high frequencies when you record and play back tracks as well as mixdown. By doing so you can wind up with a product that sounds good in your studio. If you then take your mixdown master tape to another studio, however, the same greatsounding tape will sound muffled and dull when played back over a speaker system that doesn't overaccentuate the high end.

For this sort of reason, the ideal monitor speaker has a fairly simple but difficult mandate: to disperse soundwaves—through the air and to your ears—which are exactly the same as the audio signals it receives. In other words, a monitor speaker should present, as much as possible, an *accurate* sonic picture of what we record.

As we mentioned, a basic monitor system consists of three components:

- A pair of monitor speakers.
- A monitor amplifier.
- A pair of headphones, for work with microphones.

Let's take a closer look at these individual components.

Quality monitors needn't cost a fortune. Even a small, inexpensive pair of quality pro monitors, or accurate home speakers—such as those by B&W, KEF, and ADS—are preferable to a humongous pair of departmentstore specials; the latter set may give a lot more 'boom and sizzle'—but that's not what we're after, right?

Figure 10.1 Open-field monitors by Westlake, mounted in soffets.

There are three things which can contribute to a loudspeaker's accuracy:

- First of all, accurate performance from the speaker itself. Ideally, an accurate speaker offers flat and even frequency response across the audio range. In reality, however, the super-flat frequency response of most electronic equipment is unattainable by speakers.
- Secondly, good acoustics in the listening room. If the room is overly reflective, for example, the high frequencies may sound accentuated. If the room has parallel walls, standing waves may build, causing cancellation of some frequencies and accentuation of others. Speaker placement is also an important consideration, since the room's sound can change with just a minor placement change.
- Finally, correction may be employed. This

can be special room treatment, or it can be an electronic fix such as monitor equalization. Whatever's done, the goal is to help the listener get as accurate a sound as possible from the speakers within your listening environment.

The performance of speakers is measured in *anechoic chambers*. These little rooms have no natural reflections, and are the only environment where you can measure the accuracy of speakers (and microphones as well) without environmental effects. But even in these unnatural surroundings, few speakers are able to achieve response better than 50 Hz to 20 kHz, ±6 dB—this contrasts with typical mixer response of 20 Hz to 20 kHz, ±3 dB. When placed in a room, this kind of frequency response can vary further.

The major components of a loudspeaker include:

- The *drivers*.
- A *crossover network* (where applicable).
- The *cabinet*.

Drivers. Lowest and highest frequencies are handled by drivers known respectively (and affectionately) as *woofers* and *tweeters*.

Woofers are almost always a relatively large cone-style driver. They are usually built to handle frequencies less than 1000 Hz, and as low as 50 to 20 Hz.

Tweeters—which typically operate from about 20 kHz on down to 2500 Hz or as low as 1000 Hz—are one of three different designs. There are cone tweeters, which rather resemble miniature woofers, and are usually the poorest performers. There are also *horn-loaded* tweeters—which consists of a high-frequency driver mounted behind a flared horn. A horn-loaded tweeter is a

Figure 10.2 JBL's Control 1 2-way monitors are designed for near-field monitoring.

good choice for larger speakers positioned more than two meters (six feet) away from the listener. Finally, there are *dome* tweeters, which consist of a small dome. This design is well-known for its ability to evenly *radiate* or disperse, high frequencies.

Some speakers offer *midrange* drivers, in either cone, horn, or dome designs. They bridge the gap between woofers and tweeters, typically covering a range from 800 to 3000 Hz.

Another driver design you may encounter is known as a *coaxial* driver. A 'coax' driver is a cone woofer with a horn tweeter mounted squarely in its middle. At first glance, it may look like just a woofer, but it's not! The coax driver has some distinct advantages, which we'll cover below.

Some speaker designs use a *passive* woofer, also known as a *passive radiator*. This is a cone which has no electrical con-

Figure 10.3 The Fostex RM865 time-aligned monitor has a 2-way coaxial driver for highs and mids, and a separate woofer for the lows. The controls on the lower right adjust the high-frequency response, and contour the bass response for placement near a wall.

nections. Rather, it vibrates in sympathy with whatever the woofer is doing, and enhances the lower frequencies.

Finally, there are two drivers designed to cover the extremes of the frequency ranges. The *super-tweeter* is usually a dome operating from 14 or 15 kHz on up. A *subwoofer* is designed for the lowest of frequencies—some of which may even be inaudible. Typical subwoofer response is from 80 Hz or 50 Hz on down, to perhaps as low as 30 to 15 Hz. Subwoofers are often mounted in their own cabinets. Some monitor systems consist of a single subwoofer cabinet and two *satellite* speakers. The satellites—placed like normal left and right speakers—cover the high-, mid- and lower-mid-frequencies, while the monaural subwoofer tackles the lowest frequencies. Very low frequencies are relatively non-directional to our ears; hence, a subwoofer can deliver a mono sum of the lowest left and right frequencies, and can be placed just about anywhere in the listening room.

Figure 10.4 Toa RSM-21 full-range monitors are designed as an 'alternate' monitor reference for mixdown.

Crossovers. Some smaller speakers, such as the Auratone 5Cs, use a single *full-range* driver. Neither a true woofer or tweeter, the full-range speaker has the task of being a 'jack of all frequencies,' though a master of none. Consequently, most monitor speakers have a *passive crossover network*, which splits up the incoming audio signal from the amplifier into different frequency bands. In that way, each band is sent to a driver optimized for the job at hand. A 2-way speaker divides the audio into two bands, with lower frequencies sent to a woofer, and higher frequencies sent to a tweeter. The frequency at which the signal is split is known as the *crossover frequency*. A common 2-way crossover frequency is about 1 kHz.

Note that the number of frequency bands doesn't necessarily tell you how many drivers a speaker has, or what type of drivers. For example, a typical 3-way speaker has one woofer, one midrange driver, and one tweeter. But it could also have one woofer, one tweeter, and one super-tweeter. Or it could have two woofers, two midrange drivers, and one tweeter—and still be called a 3-way monitor.

Some speakers can be *'bi-amped'* or *'tri-amped.'* These systems use an *active*, or *electronic*, crossover, placed between the mixer and the amplifier. Just like a passive crossover, an active crossover splits the audio signal at a crossover point; the difference is that an active crossover's outputs go to two or more power amps, rather than directly to drivers. An actively-crossed system has two advantages. The first is that the levels of the different drivers can be controlled independently by output level controls on the crossover. This added degree of control can enhance the overall performance of the speakers.

The second advantage is in terms of efficiency: Passive crossovers waste a lot of an amplifier's power. As much as 30% or more of an amp's power can be spent as heat at the crossover, rather than going to the drivers. This loss of efficiency means the amp has to work harder, with more distortion, to deliver the required volume. An active crossover network allows the amp to deliver 100% of its power to the drivers. (In fact, drivers are also inefficient—typically wasting up to 90% of the amplifier power they receive—but that's another story.)

There are also combined actively- and passively-crossed systems, with an active crossover separating the lows from the audio signal, and a passive crossover then separating the mids from the highs.

A common control is a high-frequency *attenuator*. This is a passive electronic control which reduces the level of the high and sometimes mid-frequency drivers. And a few speakers offer *active electronics*—which is actually an equalizer circuit between the amplifier and the monitors (this isn't the same as an active crossover).

Speaker Cabinets. As a generalization, the greater the cabinet's physical internal volume, the lower its frequency response. To get that internal volume, it's preferable to make the cabinet deeper rather than wider. The reason is that a wide *soundboard* (the front of the cabinet) can add more *diffraction* of sound. Diffraction, for the most part, happens when high frequencies radiate from the tweeter and strike the soundboard. This can cause the imaging—the localization of sounds—to 'smear,' making it difficult to place sounds in the left-to-right panorama between two monitors.

There are several cabinet design variations, though most monitor speakers have either *acoustic suspension* or *ported* cabinets. Acoustic suspension monitors are completely sealed. Ported cabinets have a hole, or port, which is 'tuned' to maximize bass response. While a ported cabinet has to be slightly larger than an acoustic suspension cabinet to get the same bass response, it is more efficient, and requires less amplifier power to deliver the same average SPL (sound pressure level).

Growing in popularity are *magnetically-shielded* speaker cabinets. Here's the story: Speaker drivers use magnets and coils, as we learned way back on page 5. These magnets can cause two problems. One is that they can partially erase magnetic tapes. The other is that they can distort the picture of any CRT (cathode-ray tube) in close proximity. That means that magnetic tapes, along with video, computer, and television monitors, have to be kept at least an arm's length from

Figure 10.5 JBL 4412 monitors, used for near-field or open-field monitoring. Note the mirror-imaging of the speakers.

any speaker cabinets. Unless, that is, the cabinets are shielded—in which case, no worries!

You may also run across *mirror-image* cabinets. As the name suggests, the location of the drivers in the left- and right-hand cabinets is symmetrical, as we can see in Figure 10.5. The advantage to this design is an audible matching of 'location,' so that high frequencies which may emanate from the top-right of the right-hand cabinet will be matched by high frequencies from the top-left of the left-hand cabinet.

Most *speaker grill cloths* are designed to be 'acoustically-transparent,' though in truth they do cut down slightly on the high frequencies.

Basic Speaker Specs

Loudspeakers are the recording studio's weakest link, as the average speaker's frequency response reveals. Not surprising, perhaps, since they have the tough job of transducing electrical signals back to moving air.

The following specs are some of the more common ones you may come across. As we've suggested with almost every other bit of gear mentioned, remember that the ultimate speaker test is how it sounds, and not how it looks on paper.

Frequency Response. If you own smaller speakers—the most common choice for the smaller studio—you can consider yourself lucky if they deliver relatively flat response as low 60 Hz before dropping off 3 dB or more. Speaker systems also have difficulty maintaining flat performance through the crossover frequencies. This much said, smaller speakers might offer a typical spec of 60 Hz to 20 kHz, ±6 dB; larger and more costly speakers would offer more along the lines of 45 Hz to 20 kHz, ±3 dB.

Power Handling. As discussed on page 73, it's better for a speaker to be slightly overpowered than greatly underpowered. Still, you'll want to be sure that your speakers can support as high a continuous amount of power as you may need.

If you end up 'bi-amping' or 'tri-amping' your speakers with an active crossover and separate amps, keep in mind that the higher frequency drivers will require much less power than the lower frequencies. For example, a common bi-amping arrangement is a 200 w/ch amp for the lows, and a 50 w/channel amp for highs.

Impedance. All speakers have an average *impedance* rating. While actual imped-ance ratings can swing wildly depending upon the frequency of the information going through the speaker, almost all monitor speakers are nominally rated at either 8 or 4 Ω (ohms).

Efficiency, or Sensitivity. Different speakers, even with identically-sized drivers and the same impedance ratings, have different *efficiencies*. If speaker 'A' is more efficient than speaker 'B,' the former will sound louder than the latter, given the same music at the same amplifier power.

Efficiency is usually expressed as a speaker's *sensitivity* to a given amount of power at a given frequency or range of frequencies. Typically, a speaker is fed 1 watt of *pink noise*, which is a combination of all audible frequencies, 'weighted' to sound flat to our ears (more on page 74). The amplitude of the pink noise is then measured at a distance of 1 meter from the speaker with an SPL (sound pressure level) meter. This resulting measurement is expressed in dBA, or just dB. A typical spec for a fairly 'average' monitor is something like "89 dB @ 1w/1m."

A downward change of 3 dB represents a doubling of amplifier power when talking about speaker sensitivity. Thus, a speaker rated at 86 dB will take twice as much amplifier power to deliver the same volumes as a speaker with an 89 dB sensitivity. Similarly, a speaker with a 92 dB sensitivity rating is *twice* as efficient as an 89 dB speaker. As you can imagine, variations in efficiency play a large role in determining how much amplifier power you need. While speakers below an 85 dB rating are considered very inefficient, there are few accurate monitoring speakers with a sensitivity greater than 95 dB or so.

Dispersion, or Radiation. These terms describe how evenly a speaker's frequency response is dispersed, or radiated, to different off-axis (off-center) listening positions. Sometimes this spec is listed in degrees. For example, a common horn tweeter dispersion is 90 degrees horizontal by 60 degrees vertical. In order to hear the tweeter properly, an engineer should be positioned within that dispersion pattern.

Monitor Amplifiers

While there's a lot to be said about power amplifiers in general, for our purposes we can keep it rather simple. After all, a studio power amp's job is to drive monitor speakers—not to survive the physical tortures of the road. Consequently, a home stereo receiver or integrated amplifier may work fine for you, especially if you don't plan to run it at high levels 24 hours a day. Or you may prefer to use a professional power amplifier, should you plan to take your studio on the road, run your monitor system hard many hours a day, or just desire something that's optimized for the job.

(If you do use a home stereo receiver, incidentally, make sure it has a defeatable 'loudness' or 'contour' control. This feature emphasizes low and high frequencies at lower volumes, and can throw off the overall accuracy of your monitor system.)

There is no perfect monitor amplifier—every different setting has different demands. The first question most people think of when it comes to choosing a monitor amp is "What's the wattage?" As many musicians know, a power amplifier's nominal output is measured in *watts, RMS*. As we learned back on page 18, a watt is an expression of how much work a device can perform. The 'RMS' stands for *root-mean-square*, and represents a standardized way of measuring continuous—rather than peak—watts. Since most amps are dual-channel devices for stereo applications, amps are usually rated in *watts per channel*, or *w/ch*. There are four other important specs to take into account when evaluating a power amp's output:

• One is the load impedance rating. For example, you might see a spec such as "100 w/ch @ 8 Ω, 140 w/ch @ 4 Ω." As we noted back on page 22, with resistance, when impedance drops, more work can be performed. Your speaker's impedance rating will determine your power amp's maximum output power. Beware

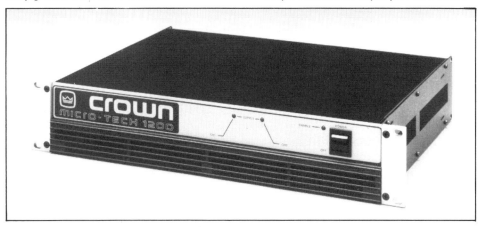

Figure 10.6 The Crown Micro-Tech 1200 power amp is capable of delivering over 600 watts per channel during peaks.

of using 4 Ω speakers with some cheaper home stereo amps that may be rated for 8 Ω speaker only—the amp may work hard enough to self-destruct! Similarly, few amps are designed to operate with speakers less than four ohms.

- The distortion rating is another factor related to an amp's output (we learned about clipping, total harmonic distortion, and other types on page 20). An amplifier that's rated at "50 w/ch @ 0.05% THD" may actually put out more real power than another amp rated at "80 w/ch @ 1.0% THD." Remember that THD approaching levels of 1% or greater is audible.
- The difference between an amp's rated output and it's actual maximum output without clipping distortion during brief musical peaks is known as its *headroom*. Only a few companies actually list headroom, but it's a very useful spec. You may recall from page 71 that an increase of 3 dB is a doubling of output power. If an amp rated at 50 watts has a 3 dB of headroom, it's actually capable of a peak power of 100 watts.
- Output power should be rated at *full bandwidth*, from at least 20 Hz to 20 kHz.

Headphone Amps. Most mixing consoles and all recorder/mixers have built-in headphone amplifiers. If you are working with another musician, your mixer's headphone output may be strong enough to run a couple pair of headphones. If it doesn't have two outputs, a *splitter box* should help you out. Or your power amplifier may provide another headphone output.
output.

If you're still out of luck, or need to power additional headphones, you may need a *headphone amplifier*, such as the Rane HC 6 shown in Figure 10.7. With the HC 6, up to six headphones can be driven in stereo, each with its own volume control. The HC 6 also has six individual monaural inputs, so that each headphone can receive its own signal. This is really useful when different musicians want to hear different things. Since headphones can have wildly different impedance ratings, headphone amps are sometimes rated at how loud (in decibels) they can drive a pair of headphones at a given distortion, rather than watts.

Headphones
Headphones are actually small speakers, encased in comfy partial 'cabinets'; the other parts of the 'cabinets' are your ears. Anyone in the same room as a live, or 'open,' mike must wear headphones if they

want to hear what's going on through the system. There are two reasons for this:

- If you're recording a mike track, chances are you'll want to hear the track you're about to record. With regular monitor speakers, the mike would feedback. Headphones minimize the chance of feedback, since their output is very quiet, and isolated.
- During a mike overdub, headphones isolate previously recorded tracks (that are being monitored) from the live mike. Without this isolation, earlier tracks would be rerecorded (albeit at a lower level) on the mike's track—destroying the engineer's ability to control the levels of tracks when it comes to mixdown.

Aside from these 'must' cases, 'phones are great for maintaining good relations with your neighbors when it's 3:00 am and you have a creative urge, and are also useful for providing a secondary reference to your speakers.

Headphones come in four main styles: *closed-ear*, *semi-closed* (or *ported*), *open-ear*, and *in-the-ear*.

Closed-ear headphones, such as Beyer DT100s, offer the greatest amount of isolation, though the trade-off is the unpleasant 'sea shell' effect—your ears feel cupped and cut off from any ambient sounds. The AKG K240Ms are very high quality semi-closed headphones, and can be used at relatively high levels near open mikes. This semi-closed design cups the ears as does a closed-ear design, but ports alleviate the sea shell effect.

Open-ear 'phones such as the Sennheiser HD411s are very comfortable and extremely lightweight, though they do provide the least amount of isolation, and must be used quietly near an open mike. Finally, the in-the-ear style of headphones—such as Toa PH1s—have become popular, since they're lightweight and relatively cheap. Their greatest trade-offs are a lack of isolation and inaccurate frequency response.

For a variety of reasons, headphones don't make ideal monitors. Just like many home stereo speakers, many are designed with that extra 'something,' and are inaccurate. The AKG K240Ms, the Sennheiser HD422s, and a few others are notable exceptions, are designed to offer very flat frequency response.

And there's one other problem with headphones: Even the most comfortable pair can deliver a stiff case of 'headphonitis.' This nasty affliction—common with many who spend hours wearing 'phones—is characterized by an aching head, fatigued and

hot ears, a mad-scientist coiffure, and a 'sea-shell syndrome' that won't go away. The remedy? Use a pair of quality monitor speakers whenever possible.

Figure 10.8 AKG K141 open-ear headphones.

Monitor System Options
When evaluating your own monitor needs, first consider *how* and *where* you'll be using your system. Are you living in a flat with thin walls? You may have to use headphones a lot of the time, and should get the best pair you can afford. Are you working alone, and without mikes in a place where you won't disturb others or be disturbed? You may be able to use speakers almost all the time. How much room do you have to place the speakers, and how are the acoustics of your room?

Open-Field. The traditional approach to monitors in most professional studios has been 'big' and 'far away,' with professionally-designed room acoustics. Figure 10.1 shows us a typical such system, with 'icebox'-size speakers mounted in *soffets*—acoustically-designed mounting cavities. Using big and far-off speakers is known as *open-field* monitoring, and while it can deliver excellent bass response and imaging, it's important to make sure the room is properly designed. The reason is that when you monitor from a distance with big speakers, much of what you hear is the sound of the room: reflections, resonant frequencies, and the like.

Near-Field. A few years back some engineers realized that while enormous speakers are impressive, they don't always make the best monitoring reference. The simple rationale is that few consumers—those who listen to the finished product—have huge speakers and acoustically ideal rooms. Mixing on large monitors doesn't tell you what things might sound like on a smaller home system. In response to this, a new approach—called *near-field* monitoring—was developed. The idea is to use smaller speakers, and to locate them close in front of the engineer. Just as with larger speakers, the two speakers and the engineer's head should form an equilateral triangle (Figure 10.9.).

For the personal studio, near-field monitoring is an ideal way to go. Less amplifier power is needed, since the speakers are closer, and ideal room acoustics aren't as important—since most sound is heard

Figure 10.7 The Rane HC6 headphone amp can provide six mono signals or one stereo signal to six headphones.

directly, and not reflected.

In professional studios with large open-field monitors, the most popular near-field reference monitors are the Yamaha NS-10 speakers. Many engineers find they have an exaggerated high frequency response, however, and it's quite common to find the NS-10s with tissue paper taped over the tweeters! (Yamaha has since addressed the problem with the NS-10Ms, which have a reduced high-end response.) Aside from the NS-10s, there are a good many other speakers which work well in a near-field application.

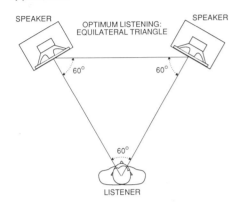

Figure 10.9 Optimum listening.

Phase Coherence. Figure 10.10 shows us a 2-way UREI 809 monitor. Note the coaxial driver, with a high-frequency horn centered in the woofer. This approach—also favored by Tannoy, Fostex, PAS, Altec-Lansing, and Cetec-Gauss—results in a *single-point*

Figure 10.10 The Urei 809 time-aligned, single point source, coaxial monitor.

source, *phase-coherent* monitor. Here's what all of that means: A typical 3-way monitor has sound emanating from three separate drivers. As instruments and vocals change pitch, they pass through crossover points and come out of different drivers. Some feel it's possible to hear instruments shift from one driver to another. Even though it's slight, the movement of a sound from a mid-range driver to a tweeter can disturb your sense of imaging. This problem is most prevalent in the mid- and high-range frequencies, since, as we know, our ears have more trouble localizing lower frequencies. By mounting the tweeter and woofer together, a coaxial driver provides a single-point source from which the music emanates.

Similarly, with conventional monitors, the tweeters and mid-range drivers are mounted ahead of the woofers, so that sounds from the higher drivers reaches our

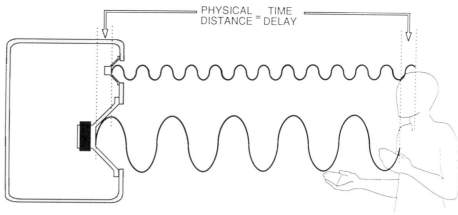

NORMAL 2-WAY SPEAKER

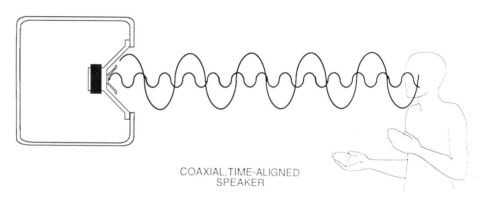

COAXIAL, TIME-ALIGNED SPEAKER

Figure 10.11 Time alignment yields phase coherence.

ears first (see Figure 10.11). Coaxial drivers are usually designed so that sounds from both the woofer and the horn arrive at our ears at the same time, in phase. Similarly, some non-coaxial speakers—such as the B & W 802s—have their drivers staggered, so that sounds still arrive in phase. Hence the term 'phase coherent,' or *time-aligned*. Just as with single-point source designs, some people notice a difference, and others don't.

All these specifications and buzzwords only tell part of the story when it comes to choosing speakers. Ultimately, as with so much other gear, you'll still have trust your best friends in the audio world: your ears.

How Much Power? The question of power handling, and matching your amp to your speaker, is a bit trickier than it sounds. If your monitor speakers are rated for a maximum power of 70 watts each, it seems reasonable that your monitor amp can't be rated any higher than 70 watts per channel. The truth is, however, it ain't necessarily so! When choosing a power amp, here's something that may contradict everything you know about matching power amps and speakers: It's better to *overpower* a speaker by a small amount than to *underpower* it by a large amount.

If that seems like a misprint, consider this: Speakers have a very difficult time trying to reproduce distorted, clipped signals, and their voice coils can suffer a 'meltdown' if asked to do so for a long time. Quality speakers are, however, very tolerant

Figure 10.12 The Sandbox, a studio in Fairfield County, Connecticut. Note the Tannoy NFM-8 near-field monitors on top of the Neve Series V mixer. Mounted in soffets are JBL 4435 Bi-Radial monitors. A Yamaha KX88 MIDI controller is in the foreground, and two Otari MTR-90-II 24-tracks are at left. To the right of the console we see two Otari remote controllers mounted on top of an autolocator, and a Studer A820 2-track.

of brief but relatively undistorted high-power transients. Consequently, a speaker rated at 70 watts is much more likely to be destroyed by a constant supply of 30 highly-distorted watts than by quick peaks of 100 or even 150 clean watts.

The lesson? Make sure your amp has enough power or headroom to deliver your music loudly enough with minimal distortion. In most home studios applications, 30 to 70 watts per channel should be adequate for lower to moderate listening levels; consider 70 to 200 watts per channel if you listen loudly or have a large room to fill. With this in mind, you can then choose a speaker with an appropriate rating. (The speaker's efficiency plays a large role in determining how much power you actually need—be sure to see "Basic Speaker Specs" on page 71.)

The quality and choice of cabling between your mixer, power amp, and speakers is also very critical. Please see page 78 for details.

Alternate Monitors. Just as many professional studios may use a pair of near-field monitors as an alternate reference, it's also quite common to have a pair of very small, mediocre-sounding speakers. After all, many consumers may be listening to your music through some pretty trashy stuff—the least you can do is make sure your music still sounds as good as possible! The common choices are full-range Auratone 5Cs or TOA RSM-21s, though some engineers think these sound too good, and prefer to use almost any 'lousy' speaker! In this way they can ensure that the mix, once it sounds great on a professional monitor, will 'transfer' well to cheaper systems and still sound balanced.

If you choose to add alternate monitors to your main speakers, you'll need to be able to switch between the two systems. Some power amps—and almost all home stereo receivers—give you this option. Professionally-oriented mixers offer alternate speaker switching, though be aware that this is designed to switch the mixer's output to a second amplifier. Otherwise you may need a speaker switcher; be sure they're rated to handle the full output power of your amp.

Whatever system you have, alternate references are critical. Some producers, once they've finished a mix, take a cassette out to their cars for the final stamp of approval. Basically, anything goes: 'boom boxes,' your friend's stereo, whatever—they're all legitimate tests for your mix!

You may have noticed that up to this point we've been discussing *control room* monitors. What if you have a studio, or live room, separate from the control room? If you're working with at least one other person in such an arrangement, the easiest option is to offer just headphones, rather than speaker monitoring, in the studio room. Otherwise, while some studios have the same speakers in both the control and studio rooms, that's rarely necessary: You may get by just fine with an inexpensive amplifier and pair of P.A. speakers.

Speaker Placement And Analysis. If you've opted for a near-field approach, your speakers should placed at the same sort of distances and angles as shown in Figure 10.9. If you're using larger monitors at a distance, the angles should remain roughly the same.

Keep your monitors at least 0.5 meters

(1½') away from any walls or corners. The reason is that a wall can act like a kind of 'passive radiator' and increase the apparent bass response of the speaker (monitors by Fostex have a switch designed to compensate for such placement). In fact, placing a speaker in a corner where two walls meet can increase the overall bass response by as much as 6 dB, and a meeting of two walls and a floor can add 9 dB of low end! Even if your speakers are deficient in the low end, this kind of enhancement will only detract from their overall accuracy.

Most speakers are built so that the tweeters of the left-and right-hand speakers can be on the 'inside,' or the 'outside.' While acousticians sling diatribes at each other over which way is best, here's a simple guide: If the speakers must be placed close together (closer to each other than they are to you), tweeters 'out' is best, to compensate for the apparent loss of stereo panorama. If, on the other hand, the speakers are far apart (further away from each other than they are to you), placing the tweeters 'in' will reduce the exaggerated panorama.

Once your system is in place, you may want to check it out with a *spectrum analyzer*, which can tell you how accurately your system is performing in your studio. The overall concept goes like this: *White noise*, somewhat like the sound you hear when waves crash on a beach, is noise with equal energy amounts at all frequencies. *Pink noise*, on the other hand, is noise which has been 'weighted' to sound flat to the average human ear at all frequencies. (You may recall from page 3 that our ears are more sensitive to high frequencies than low frequencies at most levels; pink noise is white noise corrected for these discrepancies.) If you take the output of a *pink noise generator* and run it through your mixer, power amp, and ultimately your speakers, the resulting sound will be relatively flat at all frequencies if your system is relatively accurate. And how do we tell if that sound is flat?

The spectrum analyzer uses a calibrated microphone, and has an LED display—usually divided into 30 or 31 one-third octave bands. By adjusting the sensitivity of the analyzer, and by placing the mike in the engineer's position, you can see instantly which frequencies are being over- or de-emphasized by your monitor system.

The finest systems and rooms can deliver performance in the range of 20 Hz to 20 kHz, ±3 dB, without any correction of the monitor system beyond active crossover level adjustments. With the typical personal studio and system, however, there may be 'peaks' and 'valleys' of 6 dB or more, which can be corrected. For example, let's say the analyzer registers a peak of 5 dB at 2500 Hz when the mike's in the engineer's position, but placing the mike next to the speaker shows a rise of just 1 dB at 2500 Hz. That tells us that the room is adding the extra frequencies. The first remedy might be some sort of acoustic treatment, such as Sonex on the walls, to break up the higher frequency reflections. Or perhaps the monitor has a high frequency attenuator which could help the problem. As a last—though commonly-employed resort—*room equalizers* can be pressed into action.

A room equalizer is ideally two channels of one-third octave, passive EQ (see page 43). One-third octave provides the necessary amount of resolution; passive rather than active EQs will cause the least amount of signal distortion, and don't introduce any additional noise. While one-third octave EQs are affordable, passive EQs are ultra-pricey, so most people settle for active EQs.

By placing a room EQ between the mixer's L/R monitor output and the power amplifier, the frequency response of the monitor system can be tailored to suit the room. While feeding the system pink noise at an average listening level, and watching the analyzer, the EQ can be adjusted to the flattest possible response.

This process of speaker correction, by the way, is used all the time at large concerts.

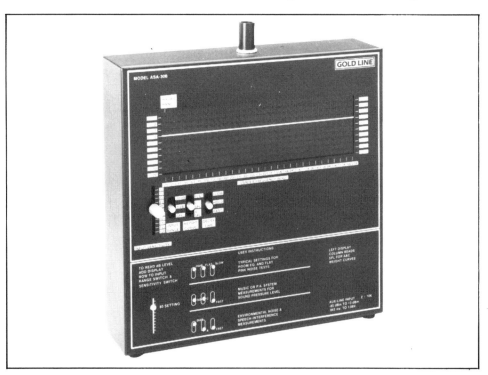

Figure 10.13 The Goldline ASA-30B hand-held spectrum analyzer has 30 bands of LED display—offering one-third octave analysis—and an internal, calibrated microphone.

Sound reinforcement companies correct their systems' response from hall to hall. This not only improves the overall sound, but also minimizes feedback, which is most prone to occur at overly 'hot' frequencies.

Professional analyzers are expensive, even to rent—and even then, analysis and EQ correction may not be worthwhile. After all, if you're near-field monitoring with a quality pair of monitors, you'll listen mostly to the speaker and not the room. In this case, no EQ may be the best solution overall, since your monitor system will sound much like near-field monitor systems in other studios.

* * * *

A well-appointed and accurate monitor system is at best a tool to help you the creative process. And while it *will* tell you when your music is sounding good, it won't *create* a good recording—that's up to you alone.

Starting on page 86, we'll examine some recording and mixing techniques which will help you get the best sound possible from your recording and through your monitors. Before we get there, however, there's one last important category of equipment we need to consider: your studio's cables and connectors. □

CHAPTER 11: HOOKING IT UP -- INTERCONNECTION

For many people setting up their first studio, the components which connect tape recorders, mixers, effects, and other equipment are almost afterthoughts. But while a few haphazardly-patched cables might let you make sound with your equipment, the overall quality of that sound is dependent upon a interconnection system that needs to be well thought out, and well made.

In the coming pages, we'll consider:

- Connectors and cabling.
- Patch bays.
- How to hook up the equipment in your studio.

As we discuss these, a couple terms we'll be seeing a lot of are *unbalanced* and *balanced*. Balanced systems are designed to reduce the chance of externally-induced noise, such as RFI (radio frequency interference). Many components intended for personal recording, on the other hand, are unbalanced. Since we'll be discussing these two systems quite a bit in this chapter—as well as terms such as 'hot,' 'cold,' 'ground,' and 'shield'—you may wish to go back and scan "Unbalanced Vs. Balanced," starting on page 23.

Finally, we'll encounter once again the terms 'low-Z' (low impedance) and 'high-Z' (high impedance). As a quick review, 3-conductor cables carry low-Z output signals into low- or high-Z inputs. With 2-conductor systems, most cables are carrying low-or high-Z output signals into high-Z inputs. Low-Z signals can cover a long distance without losing any frequency response—up to several hundred meters or farther. High-Z signals, on the other hand, are usually limited to less than 10 meters (33 feet), before suffering unwelcome losses to high-end response. If you have any questions about impedance, please refer back to page 22.

Connectors

There are four common types of audio connectors in the recording studio. These are:

- *RCA*, or *phono*, connectors.
- *1/4"*, or *phone*, connectors.
- *3-pin*, also known as *XLR* or *Cannon*, connectors.
- *TT*, or *bantam*, connectors.

All of these connectors come in two genders: *Female jacks*, and *male plugs*. With XLRs, males are output connectors, and females are input connectors, either on equipment or cables. With RCA, 1/4", and TT connectors, female jacks are usually mounted on equipment, and can be inputs or outputs; male plugs are used on either end of cables. It's a common mistake, by the way, for people to interchange the words 'jacks' and 'plugs.' In this book, a jack is always female and a plug is always male.

RCA Connectors. Made by many manufacturers (though no longer by RCA), these connectors are common with home hi-fi as well as personal recording gear. RCAs are 2-conductor, unbalanced jacks and plugs (see Figure 11.1). The male RCA plug has a *post*, or *tip*, which carries the positive signal, while the *sleeve* or *collar* conducts the signal ground.

While RCAs are small and inexpensive, they make pretty flimsy connectors, and are prone to break if frequently unplugged and reconnected.

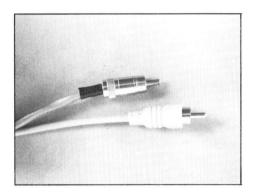

Figure 11.1 RCA plugs, molded plug and Switchcraft-style connector.

1/4" Connectors. Common on the ends of just about any guitar cable ever made, 1/4" (diameter) connectors are sturdy, are quite compact, and are cheap. They're also known as 'phone' connectors, since they were popularized as telephone switchboard connectors.

There are two types of 1/4" connectors. The garden-variety, unbalanced 2-conductor is what you see on guitar, keyboard, and other instrument cables. The male plug has a *tip*, which conducts the hot signal. The *sleeve* conducts the signal ground, and is connected to the outside case of the plug (Figure 11.2).

Aside from instrument cables, 2-conductor 1/4" connectors are found with unbalanced line-level cables, and occasionally as speaker cable connectors.

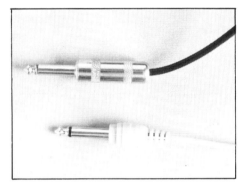

Figure 11.2 2-conductor 1/4" 'phone' connectors.

The 3-conductor version of this plug is known as a *TRS* plug—since its conductors are called the *tip*, the *ring*, and the *sleeve*.

TRS connectors are handy little varmints, with several different roles in the modern studio. The most common is as a stereo headphone plug. In this case, the tip is the left positive signal, the ring is the right positive, and the sleeve acts as a common ground for both the left and the right.

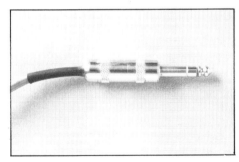

Figure 11.3 3-conductor 1/4" TRS connector.

Another common role for a TRS plug is as an *insert* plug, for the access send/receive jack on many mixers. As we learned on page 33, many mixer inputs and outputs have access jacks, where an effect can be inserted electronically in line after the fader. An insert cable is pictured in Figure 11.4. Some mixers use two RCA jacks, and others use two 1/4" jacks as separate send and receive jacks. When there's just a single insert jack, it's in fact a 3-conductor TRS jack. In this case, unfortunately, there isn't a standard wiring, and it's necessary to check with your owner's manual before connecting an insert plug. Depending upon the mixer, the tip can be wired as either the *send* or *receive* to or from the effect. The ring can either be the receive or the send, and the sleeve is a common ground for both the audio signals.

locking tab, which must be depressed to release the connector (Figure 11.5).

Virtually all balanced mikes are wired to mixers with XLR connectors. Most mixers and a growing number of ministudios have XLR mike inputs. Many professionally-oriented mixers also have XLR line inputs

8-track recorder, has unbalanced 3-pin XLR outputs. These are usually wired as:

Pin 1:   Signal Ground
Pin 2:   Positive
Pin 3:   Not connected

TT, or Bantam, Connectors. Most commonly used in professional studio patch bays, some people call these "Tiny Telephone" connectors, since they resemble miniature versions of 1/4" 2- and 3-conductor connectors. And functionally, they are the same as their larger cousins, right on down to the wiring of the tip, ring and sleeve connectors.

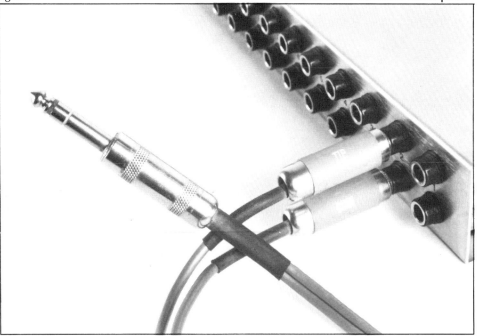

Figure 11.4 A typical TRS insert cable, shown with patch bay connections. In this case the tip connector (top) carries the 'send' signal, and the ring carries the 'receive,' or 'return' signal.

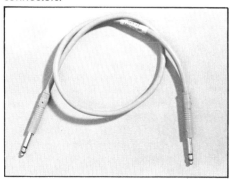

Figure 11.6 A 3-conductor TT cable—commonly used with professional patch bays.

Finally, 1/4" TRS connectors are used as balanced audio conductors. In this case, the wiring is as follows:

Tip: Positive
Ring: Negative
Sleeve: Signal Ground

Most manufacturers who use TRS jacks on their gear, such as Rane and Symetrix, wire them so that they can be used with either 1/4" TRS plugs or 'regular' 1/4", 2-conductor plugs. If a TRS plug is inserted, the output is balanced, and unbalanced if a 2-conductor plug is inserted into the jack. Take care with other gear, however—some older TRS jacks will short out if used with an unbalanced plug, so check those owner's manuals!

If a TRS plug is used in an *unbalanced* situation, by the way, it should be wired in this manner:

Tip: Positive
Ring: Signal Ground
Sleeve: Signal Ground (tie to ring)

3-Pin XLR Connectors. The 3-pin XLR design makes a positive connection, with a

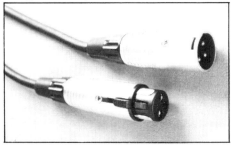

Figure 11.5 3-pin XLR connectors.

and outputs, rather than (or in addition to) 1/4" or RCA line connectors.

If you look on the external or internal moldings of an XLR connector, you'll see that the pins are numbered. While there's only one *official* wiring standard for these pins—as agreed to by the International Electrotechnical Commission (IEC)—for years there have been two *de facto* standards. These wirings are:

IEC Official Standard	Alternate Wiring
Pin 1: Signal Ground	Pin 1: Signal Ground
Pin 2: Positive	Pin 2: Negative
Pin 3: Negative	Pin 3: Positive

Fortunately, most new equipment is built to the IEC standard. There are, however, mixers and other gear still in circulation with the alternate wiring. Mixing and matching the two wirings is bound to lead to trouble: For example, if two mikes on a piano are wired with opposite polarity—one with pin 2 positive, the other with pin 3 positive—and are combined at a mixer, the likely result is lots of phase cancellation. (The phase reverse switch on some mixer inputs will correct this problem.)

Consequently, make sure that any 3-pin XLR connections are wired consistently. The best way to do this is to confirm the wiring of the XLR inputs and outputs of your mixer. Again, most modern mixers should be wired pin 2 positive. Then check the specs for your various mikes and other possible which uses 3-pin connectors. If you can't confirm those specs, follow the test we described on page 68, which will help you determine whether or not your wiring is in phase with your mixer.

Some gear, such as the Otari MkIII-8

The greatest advantage of TT connectors is their size: Equipment panels and patch bays can hold over twice as many TT jacks as 1/4" jacks. Wonderful, but with a price: TT jacks and plugs are expensive, sometimes five to 10 ten times the cost of equivalent 1/4" components!

Other Connectors. The *mini* plug is an 1/8" diameter plug that's found on various ministudios, synthesizers, and other gear. These days they're most commonly used as 'tape sync' input or output connectors (see page 112). The 3-conductor mutation of the mini plug is found on the end of most Walkman-type headphone cables. Yup, they sure are small—but the female jacks, in particular, sure are flimsy! Avoid them, if you can.

Some stereo mikes have two 3-pin XLRs for the left and right channels, others use a 5-pin XLR connector for balanced operation. Consult the owner's manual for how these pins are wired for specific mikes.

If you're using MIDI equipment, the 5-pin *DIN* (Deutsche Industry Norm) connector is the standard interconnect for data transfer—this is not an audio connector, however.

For all the connectors we've mentioned, there are a myriad of adaptors to help you interface any cable with any other gear to your heart's content. Common in the engineer's arsenal are female RCA-to-male 1/4", female 1/4"-to-XLR male or female, and other adaptors. While they're great for occasional quick patches, try and avoid them for any sort of permanent or roughly-handled application. It's much better to get the right cable and connectors (or build the right one—see page 78) than to add unnecessary connections to your system. These adaptors, after all, won't stand up to abuse, and they are extra contacts to worry about, either for possible noise or for accidental disconnection.

Finally, there are a couple other connectors you may run into, mostly as speaker connectors. One is the very hip *banana* plug and jack. This connector is unique in that you can stack them in multiples, since each banana plug also has a jack on its end. This versatility has made banana plugs popular with modular synthesizer users, who can route module outputs to several different destinations, without using 'Y'-cords or patch bays. The other popular speaker connector is known as a *spade* connector, which clamps to the end of speaker wires

Conductor Care And Feeding

You may not realize it, but the conductors in your studio need regular maintenance! This includes plugs, jacks, and even faders and rotary pots such as volume controls—in short, anything that passes signals other than a straight wire may need some attention from time to time.

The ability of plugs and jacks to conduct electricity can diminish, thanks to several causes including:

- Sea air (corrosion).
- Smoke (a big offender—it 'coats' the plugs and jacks).
- Time (oxidation).
- Finger contact (tarnishing).

When connectors become tarnished, oxydized, or corroded, their conductivity is reduced. In a worst case, you could find courself inserting a plug and hearing no sound at all. With less severe problems, the signal may be intermittent; in a mild case, 'grittiness' or slight distortion may be obscuring your music.

A related problem can occur in jacks and in any sliding fader or rotary pot: Dust—along with smoke, tarnishing, and so forth—can greatly reduce the quality of your sound. A typical symptom of this problem is a 'crunching,' 'crackling' sound as the pot is moved.

Better Life Through Chemistry. The problems we've described can all be eliminated through regular cleaning. For example, if you're using brass plugs, old-fashioned brass cleaner is the right stuff to keep them squeaky-clean. And pure isopropyl alcohol on the end of a cotton swab can clean jacks quite nicely.

But it so happens that the best stuff of all is a dangerous-smelling compound known as Cramolin, by Caig Laboratories. Available as a paste, spray, or liquid, Cramolin acts as a conductivity enhancer as well as a cleaner. By legend, it's used on the giant generators at Hoover Dam, to reduce arcing and increase the conductivity between the commutators. In the studio, small amount of Cramolin can be applied to every plug and jack—as well as sprayed inside faders and pots. This procedure will not only prevent problems, it will actually improve the overall sound of your studio. Cramolin comes in both cleaner and preservative formulations, and as Caig Labs tell us, "The less you use the better it works."

and facilitates attachment to amplifier output and speaker input posts.

Cabling

Joining the connectors to each other is cabling. Even though cables may look alike from the outside, what's inside isn't always the same.

Shielded Cable. For interconnecting gear, connecting mikes, wiring patch bays—virtually any application *other* than amplifier-to-speaker connections—cabling should be shielded. Shielded cabling consists of one to three internal wire conductors, surrounded by a *shield*, which is on turn surrounded by a flexible insulator (see Figure 11.7).

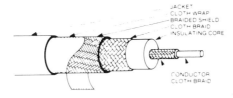

Figure 11.7 Single-conductor cable cross-section.

The shield is critical for any low-level (*i.e.*: other than speaker level) application, and here's why: Several meters of any wire can make a pretty good antenna, sensitive to radio stations, CB radios, microwave signals, cellular telephone signals, and lots of other sources of RFI (radio frequency interference). The shielding is either a metal foil or braid, and protects those helpless internal wires from the invisible hazards of the real world. The insulation protects the whole package from being stepped on, or other such direct hazards, and also reduces handling noise.

Many cables use the shield to conduct the signal ground, rather than an internal conductor. In this way an unbalanced 2-conductor cable can be made with just one internal wire, and a 3-conductor balanced cable (such as a mike cable) can be built with just two internal wires. Using the shield as a

conductor is not always desirable, though, as we'll see shortly.

If you are interconnecting MIDI equipment, the cabling should be shielded, though MIDI cables transfer data and not audio information.

Speaker Cable. Speaker cable is the simplest type of cable, and is different from other audio cabling. It has two conductors, one positive, the other negative, surrounded by insulation. Since the signals travelling through speaker cables are relatively high levels, and won't be reamplified before hitting the speakers, there's no need for shielding.

In fact, shielded cable should definitely *not* be used as speaker cabling: Having one strong current travelling through the shield while surrounding the internal wire's current can result in strange and audible inductance problems.

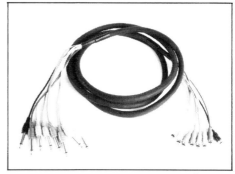

Figure 11.8 An 8-channel 'multi-track' snake by Hosa.

Multi-Pair Snakes. So far, we've been talking about audio cables designed to carry just one channel of audio. It's often easier to use a single large cable capable of carrying multiple channels of audio between two pieces of gear such as a tape recorder and a mixer, rather than lots of individual cables.

Usually designed to carry four to 32 channels, this type of a cable is known as—and rather resembles—a *snake*. Since each channel has at least a pair of shielded internal conductors—a positive and signal ground, and a negative if balanced—they're also known as *multi-pair snakes*. An 8-pair

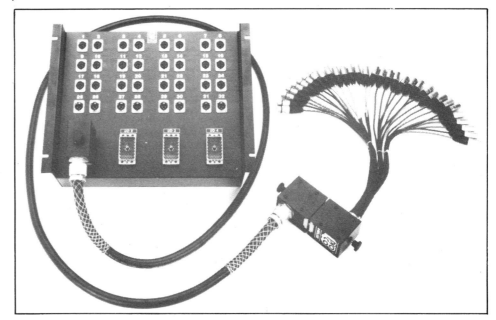

Figure 11.9 A 32-channel mike snake by ProCo.

snake, for example, is designed to carry eight individual channels of audio information. There are unshielded speaker multi-pair snakes, but they're not common.

An obvious snake application is to carry mike signals from a studio to a control room—a single snake can take the place of up to 32 mike cables. The mixer end of a mike snake has individual XLR mike outputs, and the studio end usually has a *floor box* or *wall-mounted box* with female XLR inputs.

For other gear, snakes can be ordered with whatever connectors you need. For example, let's say we were connecting the eight group outputs from a Soundcraft 600 mixer to a Fostex Model 80 8-track tape recorder. The mixer end of the 8-pair snake would need eight male 1/4" plugs, and the recorder end would have eight male RCA plugs.

If we wanted to get really efficient with the same set-up, we could use a 16-pair snake. With this, we could connect not only the audio signals going *to* the recorder, but also send the outputs of recorder *back* to the mixer. What would otherwise take up to 16 individual cables can be accomplished with one single snake!

But we're jumping a bit ahead of ourselves. Before we get to some hard-core equipment interconnections, let's learn about a really useful and often misunderstood accessory: the patch bay.

The Patch Bay

Remember the old-time telephone switchboards? Not first-hand, perhaps—but likely you've seen movies of pre-1950s telephone operators sitting at giant panels of jacks, armed with dozens of patch cords, and capable of routing any caller to any destination on the switchboard. A *patch bay* is the recording engineer's switchboard.

Now if all you're using is a small ministudio, perhaps one synthesizer, one mike, and just one effect, then a patch bay isn't going to do you much good. After all, with such a simple setup most everything can stay connected all the time, or is simple enough to connect when needed. But if your set-up is a bit more elaborate, even just a ministudio and two or three effects, a patch bay can do you a world of good. Let's find out why.

Each component in your studio has input and output connectors, typically on its back panel. Some components may be normally connected to each other, such as the group outputs of your mixer to the tape recorder inputs, or an auxiliary send output to one of your effects. In these cases, a snake or individual cable directly connecting the components could do the trick.

But what if the tasks at hand require that you rewire those 'normalled' connections from time to time? For example, what if your ministudio or mixer has just one auxiliary effects send, and you wish to use it to feed different effects at different times—without having to disconnect and reconnect effects all the time? Or another example: Let's say you're overdubbing, with your tape recorder's outputs feeding the mixer's tape monitor inputs (as we learned in Chapter Seven). When the overdubbing's through and it's time to mixdown, some mixers are designed so that you have to *replug* the tape recorder's outputs to the mixer's line inputs, rather than just hitting a 'tape input' switch on the channel inputs. To do this without a patch bay, you have to reach behind your mixer, find the output cables from the tape recorder, unplug them from the tape monitor inputs, and then plug them into the mixer's line inputs. Amidst the tangle of other cables in the back of your mixer, this is an arduous job.

A patch bay, however, allows you to bring the connectors on the back of your gear to one central and organized location. You can bring as many of those connectors to the patch bay as you like. Of course things that rarely need repatching—such as the monitor output that feeds your control room amp—need not show up at your patch bay. The more *sources* (equipment

Basic Soldering Tips

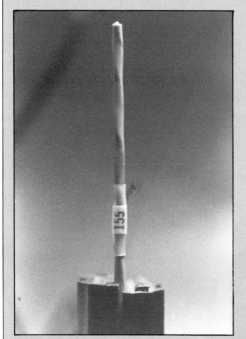

Figure 11.10

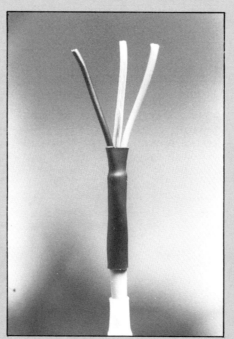

Figure 11.11

Figure 11.12

It's not difficult to solder your own cables—but it takes practice. You'll need a soldering iron rated from 25 to 60 watts, some 60/40 rosin-core solder, wire cutters and strippers, needle-nose pliers, and a proper surface to work on. Here are the basics of preparing and wiring a multi-pair snake to a rear-panel-wired patch bay (without 1/4" or RCA connectors)—the same techniques apply to a number of different soldering applications. Gently strip back the outer insulation of the snake, and isolate each channel (Figure 11.10). They're likely color-coded, or you can number them. Next, strip the wire back to the internal three conductors (use just two conductors, for hot and ground, if it's unbalanced). These can be 'shrink wrapped,' with special tubing that can be cut and shrunk with a heat gun (Figure 11.11). Strip each conductor about 1/16", and 'tin' them. To do this, place the tip of the iron on the wire, and let the solder run onto the hot wire, instead of the tip of the iron—this avoids a possibly fragile 'cold solder.' Finally, the 'dressed' wires are soldered to the bay (Figure 11.13). Note how wires are held between the thumb and the ring finger, and the solder is held between the index and middle fingers. For a clean joint, heat the posts to melt the solder, with the wire near the iron's tip on the hot post. These same techniques apply when soldering 1/4" and other plugs for cables.

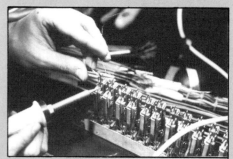

Figure 11.13

outputs) and *destinations* (equipment inputs) that you bring to the patch bay, however, the more flexible you are.

Figure 11.14 Telephone operators of yore were able to route any caller to any destination on the switchboard, simply by using a patch cable—a system we can apply.

All patch bays have two panels. The front panel is like a switchboard, with input and output jacks designed to accommodate *patch cords*. The front panel jacks can be RCA, 1/4" (balanced or unbalanced), or T.T. (balanced or unbalanced). While outboard 1/4" and RCA front panel jacks are most common in personal studios, professional studios usually have T.T. patch bays, either outboard or built into the mixer. Front panel jacks are often referred to as *patch points*.

In order to have access to a device through the patch points—whether it's your mixer, tape recorder, reverbs, or whatever—that device's inputs and/or outputs must be connected to the patch bay's rear panel connectors. These rear connectors feed directly to corresponding front panel jacks, allowing you to patch in or out of a device through the front panel (see Figure 11.18).

Symetrix, Furman, and others offer patch bays with convenient pre-wired rear panel jacks, usually RCA or 1/4". For flexibility's sake, some bays' rear panels are mixed-and-matched, partially loaded with RCA jacks and partially loaded with 1/4" jacks. Most T.T. bays, on the other hand, have rear panel connectors to which cables need to be attached, either through soldering, 'punching,' or some other method.

Quality Cabling

Quality cables are often worth extra money, not only for durability but also for sonic performance. 'El cheapo' cables typically have connectors which are molded to the cable, rather than soldered. The big problem with molded ends is that cable problems can't be diagnosed or repaired without cutting off the connectors. While there are some quality cables with molded ends, many are bargain-basement designs using poor quality conductors, and are often victims of RFI, due to poor or incomplete shielding.

The good stuff, on the other hand—cables made by ProCo, Whirlwind, Belden, Connectronics, and others—can be

Figure 11.16 Monster Cable's 8-channel Prolink snake. As we can see, each channel has two conductors, hence it's an '8-pair' snake.

Many professional studios have just about every conceivable input and output 'up' on the patch bay—including microphone outputs. Here are some other connections you may find useful on your bay:

- Mixer buss outputs, line inputs, and 'tape' inputs (if applicable).
- Multi-track and 2-track tape recorder inputs and outputs.
- Mixer auxiliary send outputs and auxiliary inputs (effects returns).
- Effects inputs and outputs, including *sidechain* inputs (see page 58).
- Channel or buss output insert sends and receives.
- Synthesizer, drum machine, and other electronic instrument outputs.

trusted to perform well and quietly. These cables are typically outfitted with dependable and readily-serviceable connectors from Neutrik, Switchcraft, and others. These connectors have heavy-duty *strain reliefs*, which will help protect the soldered electrical connections from being torn asunder. In addition, they exhibit lower *capacitance* than the bargain basement variety, which means they can run longer lengths with less high frequency loss.

Top-grade cabling—such as offered by Monster Cable, Canare, and Mogami—is favoured by many engineers as being sonically superior. These use 'oxygen-free' copper conductors throughout, and gold-plated contacts on the connectors for maximum conductivity and tarnish-resistance. While these *will* offer superior high-frequency performance over long distances, some golden-eared individuals claim big sonic advantages even in short runs. These cables are often quite expensive, however, when compared to lesser-grade quality cables. Use your own ears to see if you hear a difference worth the price.

When it comes to *speaker* cable—the stuff which connects amplifiers to speakers—top-grade cable *is* audibly superior and worth the price. Monster Cable, Kimber, and others use large-guage, highly-conductive wiring. The audible results are much more 'definition' in bass response, better highs (especially over long distances), and greater amplifier efficiency—which results in lower distortion.

conventional bay, if you want to connect one device's output to another device's input, you take a patch cable and connect the two via the patch panel.

Many bays have *normalled* front panel jacks. With a normalled patch bay, it's possible to have one device's outputs feeding another device's inputs *without* a patch cable. This is very handy for all the connections which are 'normally' connected to each other, such as mixer buss outputs to tape recorder inputs, or auxiliary effects sends to various effects. How do normalled bays work?

A normalled patch bay has front panel jacks which are wired so that the top and bottom row jacks are electronically connected. In this way, a top-row source will normally feed whatever bottom-row destination is directly below it—without a patch cable.

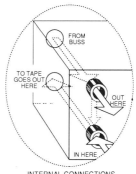

Figure 11.17 A close-up view of a normalled patch bay. Please refer back to page 39 to see a typical normalled application.

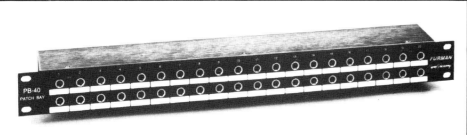

Figure 11.15 This Furman PB-40 patch bay has 40 ¼" front-panel patch points. Its top jacks are normalled to the bottom jacks—the normal can be disconnected internally. The PB-40 comes with a choice of 1/4", TRS, or RCA jacks.

While larger bays—particularly T.T.-style—can have dozens of rows and hundreds of patch points, most bays have two rows of 16 to 24 patch points. Depending upon how many connections you want access to, anywhere from one to six or more patch bays may be necessary.

'Normalling.' In almost all patch bays, equipment sources (outputs) are connected to the bay's *top* row, and equipment destinations (inputs) are connected to the bay's *bottom* row. (To remember this, think of outputs flowing *down* into inputs, as a waterfall flows down into a river.) With a

Normalled front panel jacks are also wired in such a way that the normal is *broken* when a patch cord is inserted into destination's patch point. That is, the patch cord's plug breaks a switch in the jack, causing the top-row source to no longer feed the bottom-row destination (see Figure 11.17). This way, you can plug a different device's output into that input. What happens if you plug a patch cable *just* into the top-row output? Nothing—the normal isn't broken, and the output still feeds its corresponding input. This allows you to split outputs, which can be very convenient.

For example, let's say *all* your auxiliary effects sends are normalled to various effects' inputs. What if you want to keep all of those effects in the mix, but need to add one *more* effect? Here's a solution: Plug a patch cable into one of the aux send outputs. You can then feed that send's signal to the extra effect's input. Since the original normal isn't broken, that same aux send is now feeding two effects' inputs.

In the typical studio, as we mentioned, many devices are normally connected to each other; it's only from time to time that you want to break that connection. Here are some of the most commonly normalled connections:

- Mixer buss outputs to tape recorder inputs.
- Tape recorder outputs to the mixer's 'tape' or 'line' inputs.
- Auxiliary effects (post-fader) sends to effects inputs.
- Insert sends (outputs) to insert receives (inputs)—see Figure 11.4.
- Mixer left/right outputs to 2-track mixdown deck inputs.

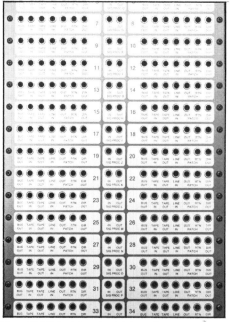

Figure 11.18 The integral patch bay of a Soundworkshop 34B mixing console. It's a true in-line console, so each channel has 'line' and 'tape' inputs and outputs, as well as 'bus' outputs.

Traditionally, normalled bays have been 1/4"- or T.T.-style. At least one manufacturer, Fostex, offers a normalled RCA bay, with tiny switches in the RCA jacks that are broken when an RCA plug is inserted.

Normalled bays, or portions of normalled bays, can be un-normalled for those applications where you definitely *would not* want the top-to-bottom row connection to be normalled. For example, let's say you can only afford one patch bay. With a limited number of available patch points, you may

have to wire a device so that it's inputs are directly beneath its own outputs. If the connections are normalled, this would result in a nasty feedback loop, with the outputs constantly refeeding the inputs. By following the manufacturer's instructions (usually cutting a circuit or disconnecting a jumper on a circuit board) the normalling for the appropriate connections can be disabled semi-permanently.

Electronic Patch Bays. For years the broadcast industry has used 'switchers' to route outputs of certain devices to inputs of others. These switchers use electronic matrices, with equipment sources along one axis and destinations along another. They're rather like a glorified patch bay with electronically-engaged connections instead of patch cables.

In time, this type of electronic patch bay is sure to be a common fixture in many studios. The Akai Digital Patchbay is one example of what's in store. Its 'brain' is in fact a self-contained computer, which displays and stores different matrix 'setups.' By adding 'patch modules,' the brain can control an entire studio's ins and outs, including video. It can even be controlled via MIDI.

Hooking Up Your System

Whether or not you use a patch bay, one important guideline for interconnecting your gear is to try and keep cable runs as short as possible. For example, if a 1 meter (3') cable will work fine, don't use a 3 meter cable for the same job.

There are several reasons for this. As we pointed out earlier, many mixers have high-impedance output signals, which will lose high frequency performance in runs greater than 7 meters (20 feet). And as we've also

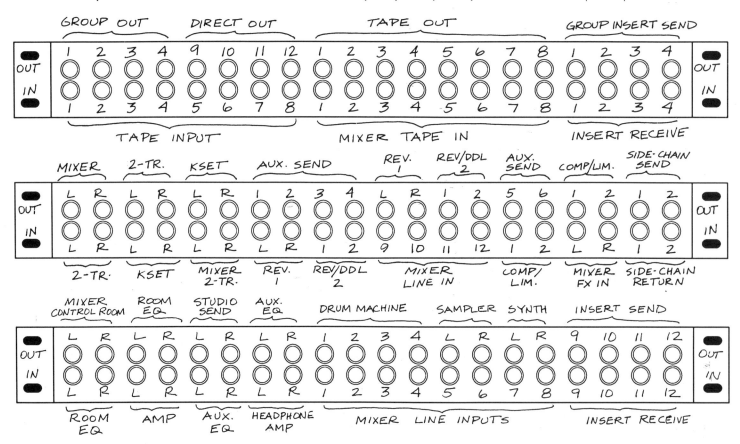

Figure 11.19a, 11.19b, 11.19c When you put together your own patch bay network, you get to customize the routings. Here's a good example of a typical, normalled, patch bay system, with outputs on top and inputs on the bottom rows—if any device's outputs were located above its inputs, those points would be 'un-normalled.' This system has been designed for a 12x4x2 mixer with an 8-track tape recorder. Most people find studio life much more pleasant with a well-planned patch system.

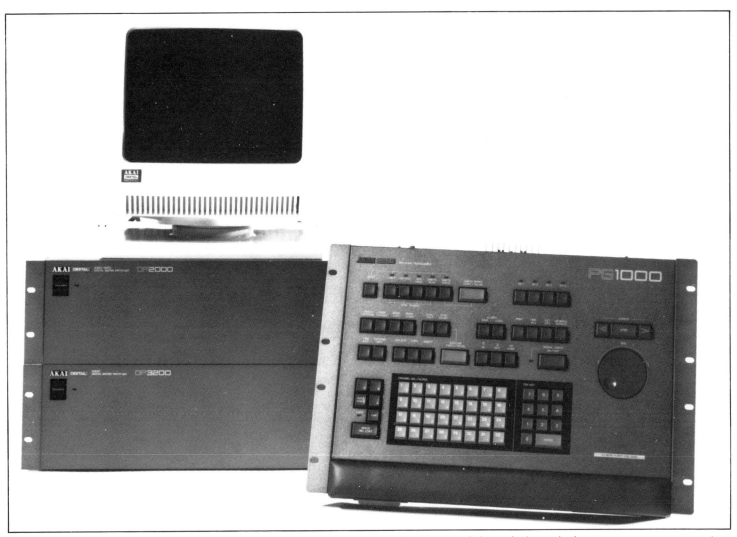

Figure 11.20 Akai's Digital Patchbay system can store and recall various audio and video patch bay routings with the touch of a switch. The system can sync to an external source, such as MIDI or SMPTE, to allow for automated patch changes during a mix.

mentioned, cables are susceptible to radio frequency interference; the longer, the more susceptible.

You'll want to make sure that cable wiring standards are the same between your different devices. If they're not, you'll need to have your cables wired to solve any potential problems.

When planning an interconnection system, make a diagram of all your gear and make a list of all the cables you'll need to hook it up. If you're going to use a patch bay system, be sure to calculate which cables you need to incorporate the patch bay, which gear will go to the patch bay, and which gear will interconnect without a patch bay.

Remember that *speaker polarity* is critical—be sure to connect the positive output of each amp channel to the positive speaker terminal, and not the negative.

When you actually run the cables or snakes, be sure to keep them organized. A piece of Velcro cut in half and sewn (as you can do yourself or buy from Ultimate Support), can make a great cable tie. Otherwise, electronic stores sell both permanent and reusable plastic cable ties.

When tying cables together, try to organize them for easy future reference. One idea is to take colored plastic tape, and put a strip at each cable's end; if you keep a legend, cables can be quickly identified. Also available are books of adhesive number strips, to number each end of each cable—anyone who's tried to troubleshoot a

Medusa's head of cables will appreciate a number book's value. Finally, when bundling cables, be sure to keep AC, speaker, and audio cables separate from each other (we'll learn why in a moment).

Avoiding RFI, Hum, And Other Party Crashers

Even the best laid-out system may find itself entertaining radio frequency interference (RFI), hums and buzzes, and other unwelcome guests—and they can strike anytime. Just imagine having recorded the best accordion polka solo on the planet, only to play it back and hear the local Top 40 radio station faintly recorded in the background.

But RFI, hum, and similar noises are in our systems by invitation, so to speak—since certain interconnection practices can leave sonic doors wide open for them! If we understand their causes, we're often able to eliminate them.

There are three major problems which can contribute to externally-induced noise:

● Poor shielding of cable and equipment.
● Improper placement of gear and cabling.
● *Ground loops*, which occur when gear is grounded to more than one location.

Shielding And RFI. As we know, all audio cabling (other than speaker cabling) should be metallically shielded, so that the inner conductors are 'protected' from RFI. RFI is everywhere, unfortunately—in the form of

AM, FM, Short Wave, CB, TV, and other radio transmissions. Consequently, anything that carries an audio signal should be shielded, including equipment itself. Most gear is designed so that its case behaves like a shield; with cases and cabling well shielded, audio signals should theoretically be immune to RFI.

In real life, unfortunately, there can be 'holes' in your system. Cheap cables may have places that aren't shielded, such as inside plastic connector housings. Or the shielding choice may be inferior, such as a conductive plastic rather than true metal shield. Unnecessarily long cable runs increase the cable's effectiveness as an antenna—and we all known what that means.

There may be some pretty powerful RFI lurking around your neighborhood—so powerful that even quality shielding can let you down. For example, anyone setting up a studio near a radio station's transmitter and antenna can expect a potential RFI nightmare. Or if your next door neighbor's a 'ham' radio or part-time espionage buff—as an arsenal of wild-looking antennae may suggest—you can expect to hear from our friend RFI.

In these kinds of worst-case scenarios, sometimes the only resort is to build a *Faraday cage*. Named after the famous 19th Century scientist Michael Faraday, the scheme is as follows: When shielding of cabling and equipment fails, as do all other RFI-rejection methods (which we'll discuss in a moment), you may have to build a shielded room. Typically, as done in many radio stations or electronic labs, copper mesh is laid into the floor and affixed throughout each wall, door, and the ceiling. Once the door is closed, every square centimeter of the room's dimensions must be shielded, or the whole effort's down the drain. If done properly, and with the right materials, complete immunity to RFI can be yours (for just a minor fortune).

Life in a Faraday cage isn't too feasible for most of us. But it does give you an idea of the kind of problem we're fighting. Balancing is one way many manufacturers have chosen to fight RFI. As we learned on page 23, balanced audio signals cancel out most RFI and other sonic junk they collect in their cable runs. To be most effective, however, your entire studio has to be balanced.

Equipment Placement And EMI. Your gear's placement can directly affect how much hum and buzz you hear. For example, if airborne RFI is a problem, some people find that placing gear further away from windows can help—particularly if they live in iron- or steel-reinforced buildings. Depending upon the circumstances, such reinforcements can act either as antennae or shielding. If you live in such a building, try moving gear around, and see if noise diminishes.

One common source of buzzing and humming sounds is known as *EMI* (Electro-Magnetic Interference), sometimes called *AC hum*. AC power operates at a frequency of 60 Hz in North America, and 50 Hz in most other places. When you hear buzzing, you're either hearing 60 or 50 Hz, or you're hearing harmonic multiples of it, such as 120, 240, or even 480 (in North America). Ground loops can cause these sounds, as we'll learn in a moment. One common culprit, however, can be your equipment.

For example, power amplifiers — and power supplies — have internal *power transformers*. These transformers convert the incoming 120 or 220 volts down to 12, 18, 24, or some other internal circuitry voltage. (Designers prefer to have their gear operate internally at lower voltages, since better-performing, lower-cost components—such as transistors—can be used.) Unfortunately, transformers emit EMI. If you've ever place a low-level device, such as a mixer or effects foot-pedal, next to a power amp and heard an increase in buzz, you've heard EMI.

So one moral from this lesson is to keep amps and power supplies as isolated as possible from other gear. Professional studios often locate amps and power supplies in a completely different rack from signal processing gear. If you don't have the room to do this, place them at the bottom of the rack, and try to leave as much space as possible between them and other components. But the lesson doesn't stop here.

The 'mains' AC power cords to all your gear can also emit EMI. Bundling audio, speaker, and mains cords together is a common cause of buzz, since the EMI radiating from the mains cords can be heard when the audio cables reach their destinations. Shielding will help, but usually not enough. The solution? When you're laying your cable paths, keep mains, audio, and speaker cables separate as much as possible. If they have to cross paths, try to have them

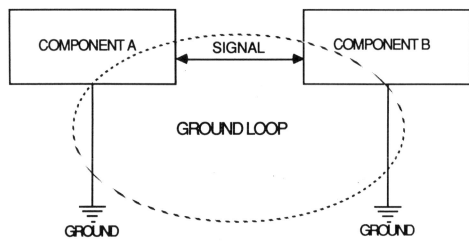

Figure 11.21 If you have buzzing and hum in your system, chances are it's hooked up in such a way as to induce a ground loop. Simply, whenever two or more connected pieces of gear are grounded to two or more different ground points, a ground loop may exist—and the dreaded ground loop is something to keep at bay. The best solution is to ground everything to a central point (Figure 11.22).

cross at a 90 degree angle to each other—this will help minimize noise.

Fluorescent light fixtures, as well as light dimmers (known as *rheostats*) also emit large amounts of EMI. The problem with fluorescent lights is their *ballasts*, the 'power supplies' for the tubes. These ballasts turn the fluorescent lights on and off 50 or 60 times a second, and our equipment and cables can pick this up. One solution is to relocate the ballasts out of the room and on a different power circuit than your audio gear. A better solution is to stick with good old-fashioned incandescent lighting—it won't cause problems, and won't cause headaches or other such fluorescent side-effects. If you want to use light dimmers, by all means try an inexpensive rheostat, but be aware that they often induce AC hum. Professional studios spring for big-time dimmers known as *Varivacs*, and these may be your expensive alternative if dimmed lights are indispensable to your creative process!

Ground Loops. If your studio is a victim of hum, buzz, or other sonic rubbish, more likely than any other cause, it's suffering from a phenomenon known as *ground looping*. There are three quick steps to eliminating ground loops, which we'll cover in a moment. Feel free to jump ahead to them, though we're going to take a few moments to understand the nature of the problem.

Here's an overview of the problem: When one or more pieces of gear are grounded to a *common* point, everything's fine. Should any component be grounded to *more* than one ground point, however, a ground loop exists. When there's a ground loop, the system is prey to AC hum, RFI, and other noise. Let's explore this a bit further.

Most modern equipment is designed to be AC-, or *chassis grounded*. Anytime you see the telltale 3-prong AC plug, that device has a grounded case, or chassis. The purpose of this ground is for your safety: Internal wires can become loose and touch the chassis, for example, or a drink could spill on the device, causing its chassis to become 'live.'

When you touch a live chassis, your body can become a path to ground, and whatever electricity is flowing to ground is going to flow through you! If a chassis that's already grounded through the AC cord become live, the result should be a relatively dramatic yet safe short-circuit—causing a

blown fuse or circuit breaker, and possibly some brief pyrotechnics—but sparing you electrocution. That's why we have AC grounded gear.

Audio gear also has internal *signal grounds*. Any incoming, outgoing, or internal signals need to flow to this signal ground, in order to complete an audio circuit. Many components' signal ground is the same as the chassis ground—and this is unfortunate, as we'll see.

Imagine a mixer and an outboard effect, such as digital reverb. If each has a 3-prong AC plug and we plug both of them into the same grounded AC circuit, they're grounded to a common point. So far no problems. If we take an audio cable and connect the two, however, there's a good chance that we'll be creating a second AC ground connection between the two through the signal grounds, as we can see in Figure 11.21. Whoops—the dreaded ground loop!

The simple solution for most studios is known as *star grounding*. The idea is to ground everything to one central point and eliminate all other possible grounds. If you have hum and buzz problems, this scheme will likely put an end to them. Here's how it's done:

1. Choose one component to be the 'central' device to which all other gear is grounded. Most studios use the mixer, since everything is directly or at least indirectly connected to the mixer. Whatever you use, make sure that it is well grounded to AC. If it only has a 2-prong ungrounded AC plug, either choose another device, or ground it in this way: Attach a heavy wire from a metal point on its chassis to a metal plumbing pipe or to the central metal screw that's found on most grounded AC outlets. Be sure that you are connecting the wire to metal and not paint or rust.
2. 'Lift' (disconnect) the AC grounds on all other gear that has 3-prong plugs. An easy way to do this is with *ground lifters*, the 3-prong-to-2-prong AC adaptors available at hardware stores. Any ungrounded gear, with just 2-prong AC plugs, can be connected to AC power as usual.
3. Then connect all audio cables so that

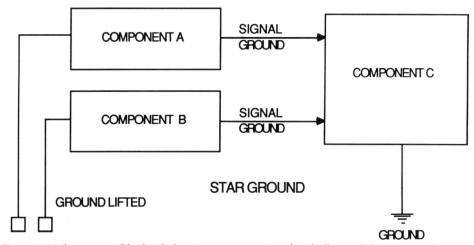

COMPONENT A — SIGNAL GROUND →

COMPONENT B — SIGNAL GROUND →

COMPONENT C

STAR GROUND

GROUND LIFTED

GROUND

Figure 11.22 Whenever possible, the ideal way to connect gear is so that it's all grounded at one central point. It's remarkable how many sonic ailments can be solved by created a 'star ground' network, as shown above. Be sure, however, that all gear that should be grounded is in fact grounded—otherwise, in some circumstances, you may run the risk of electrical shock. You may wish to consult an electrician for safety's sake.

each device is connected—either directly, or through other gear, or through a patch bay—to the central component.

And that's it. If only the central component is grounded, all possible ground loops should be eliminated. Two very important points that you must bear in mind, however:

- Depending upon the manufacturer and possibly the cabling, some gear will be AC chassis grounded to the central component through the signal grounds, and some gear won't be. This is important for this reason:
- Any device that's *not* ultimately grounded to the central component is potentially dangerous, since you are now the potential path to ground should its chassis become live. Be sure that all your gear is in good working order, with solid AC cord connections. If in any doubt, be sure to check with a qualified electrician. Some 'safety insurance,' as is practiced in many radio stations, is to connect each device's chassis to the centrally-grounded component with copper cable or strapping. In turn, these stations will ground that central component to a copper stake buried deep in the ground. This way, each component can be lifted from its local ground *and* still be grounded.

Why should connecting two grounded devices present a problem? Why does being grounded to more than one point induce noise?

The reason is that not all grounds are the same. A ground can be a true ground to earth, or it can be a *virtual* ground, such as an device's internal ground. When two such

grounds are connected—as they are in the ground loop example we just gave—there's typically a *voltage potential* between the two. The reason is that an AC ground is usually 'more' of a true ground than a virtual ground. As voltage (usually very low) flows between the two, we get to hear the current cycle at 50 or 60 times a second. When we hear that, we hear a buzz. These voltage potential differences can exist between any two grounds, even true earth grounds, since soil and other factors can play a role.

That explains the buzz—but why are ground loops also susceptible to RFI? Since they're a complete circuit, they can behave like a crude antenna, in the same way as signal cabling.

By now you may be wondering about all the components in your own system—how many 3-prong AC plugs you have, and about all the interconnect cables which are secretly creating scores of ground loops. The problem is promoted by two factors:

- As we mentioned, some manufacturers tie together their signal and AC grounds. This means that an AC ground path is established with every audio connection—and we know what that means!
- Balanced, 3-conductor systems don't need a signal ground to interconnect. That's because their positive and negative conductors are enough to complete the system. The signal ground is just a redundant connector. Unfortunately, many balanced cables use the shield as the signal ground conductor. If 3-pin XLR connectors are used, this shield is usually tied to the device's AC ground, and there's the trouble. Even those manufacturers who keep the signal and AC grounds

separate have their efforts thwarted by cables which tie the two together.

Now we know why cable interconnections are able to create ground loops. Meanwhile, the people at Rane Corporation, makers of a diverse line of audio gear, have proposed some design standards which could eliminate ground loop problems. Their designs call for:

- Separate audio and AC chassis grounds on all gear.
- The use of 2-conductor wire in all unbalanced situations; this way the signal ground and shield (AC chassis ground) are kept separate from each other.
- Eliminating signal ground connections in between balanced devices. Since balanced lines already use two conductors (positive and negative), the signal ground isn't necessary and only acts as a potential noise source.

In Rane's ideal world, any devices could be AC grounded and be connected together with minimal fear of ground loops. While they also rally the battle cry of "Pin 2 positive!" for 3-pin XLR connectors, the good news is that more and more designers are becoming savvy to the problems of audio equipment interconnection, and are taking steps to eliminate problems. In the mean time, the best we can do is keep our cables shielded, our gear properly placed, and our grounds from looping.

* * * *

As we've seen, there are quite a few things to consider when hooking up your studio—far more than just getting some cables and plugging them in. Nevertheless, things are not as complicated as they may seem. There is some real rhyme and reason to avoiding external noise, and planning your own patchbay and cabling system can actually be a lot of fun.

The world of interconnection is changing. We're sure to see more programmable patch bays, and better communication between manufacturers will help sort out wiring standards. On top of this, there may be a time when ground loops and odd standards are a thing of the past: A new type of audio connector, the *digital audio buss*, has found its way into some gear. As we'll learn more about starting on page 128, this connection system can pass two channels of digital information through a noise-free and RFI-immune fiber-optic cable. It's certain that before long, connecting studio components will be an easier process.

□

Part III:
The Session

A theoretical understanding can help immensely, but there's no substitute for experience. In the following eight lessons, we'll run through—step by step—the various stages of a typical recording session, from the perspective of a musician/engineer.

The concepts remain very similar if you're working with other musicians. If you do find yourself in that situation, you'll learn first-hand how an engineer must possess the gifts of diplomacy, patience, and encouragement. As engineer, your job will not only require you to record the music as well as possible, but also to keep the session fun and worthwhile for everyone involved. If you are working on your own, however, in your own studio, you'll enjoy the luxury of being able to take your time, to actually transfer what you hear in your head to tape.

As with other chapters in this book, all major terms or concepts are referenced to the pages where they are explained in depth; be sure to refer back (or ahead) to those pages if you have any questions.

Lesson One: Getting Ready

It's time to put our theory into practice. The session is about to begin, but before jumping in with both elbows, there's a bit of preparation that must be done to guarantee a high-fidelity result.

Routine Maintenance

Your tape recorder's optimum performance and the well-being of your tapes can be remarkably enhanced by attending to two easy practices: tape head demagnetizing and cleaning.

Demagnetization. Tape's magnetic particles slowly magnetize many components in the tape path. Unless you *demagnetize* those parts on a regular basis, your performance can suffer. Most noticeably, high frequency response will begin to lessen, though in worst-case scenarios entire tracks —including sync code tracks—can suffer terribly. Most professional studios will demagnetize every few hours of use; no more than 10 hours of using any recorder should pass without demagnetizing.

Demagnetization consists of subjecting all metallic parts that are in the path of the tape to an alternating magnetic field. First, make sure that all tapes, computer disks, digital watches, and any other magnetically-sensitive devices are at least 10 feet away from where you're working with the tape head demagnetizer, and also be certain that your recorder is turned off. Failure to do so can result in damage to both meters and input electronics!

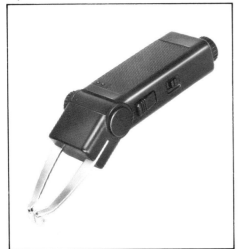

Figure 12.1 Tascam demagnetizer.

Then plug in and turn on the demagnetizer while it is at least five feet away from the recorder to be demagnetized; some units have an on/off switch, while others come on as soon as they're plugged in. Slowly bring the demagnetizer towards the recorder, taking special care to move very slowly in the last foot. Bring the demagnetizer as close as possible to the tape path without scratching any parts—it helps to have a plastic-coated tip, as most good demagnetizers do.

As the demagnetizer passes over metal parts within the tape path, it should be moved up and down very slowly, to alternate the polarity of the magnetic field. The goal is to randomize the magnetic charges in a given area, so that they end up neutralizing each other and add up to zero. Move the demagnetizer gradually from the left side of the tape path to the right, while undulating the tip of the demagnetizer up and down. When you've reached the end of the path, carefully begin to withdraw the demagnetizer from the tape recorder area, still moving it up and down to vary the magnetic field. When you're about an arm's length away, three to five feet, you can let go of the switch, or unplug/turn off the demagnetizer. It's important to remember these three points when demagnetizing:

- Do everything very slowly.
- Don't turn off or on the power while in close proximity to the tape path.
- Remember to move the demagnetizer up and down.

Tape Path Cleaning. Magnetic tape can leave a lot of residue in its path, since after all, its coating is essentially *rust*. The residue can cause dropouts during recording and playback, and can permanently mess up a tape's performance. In cassette recorders, a dirty tape path is a prime culprit for the machine's 'eating' of tapes. In general, you should clean your recorder every couple hours of use.

Cleaning is quite straightforward. First you'll need a good commercial cleaning solution such as those offered by Akai, Teac, Nortronics, and others, or simply ask your pharmacist for 99% isopropyl alcohol. If 99% is unavailable, 91% will work very well. But *don't* use standard rubbing alcohol, because even though it is 70% alcohol, the rest is water and spirits, which can result in rusty heads! The commercial solvents are slightly better in cleaning ability, but are complex chemicals that may be less than healthy to breathe and handle, whereas alcohol is relatively simple and harmless.

To do the scrubbing, cotton swabs such as Q-Tips can be used, although video head cleaning swabs, which are more expensive but made of non-shedding foam, are preferable.

Dip the cleaning swab in the cleaning solution, and use firm but not excessive pressure to scrub heads, guides, and pinch rollers. Be sure to change the swap frequently, since a dirty swab can damage heads. For cleaning the capstans, it helps to engage 'play,' if possible. Depending upon the machine, you may have to hold a tape

tension arm or press a tab in the cassette well to do this, but a spinning capstan is easy to clean—be sure to avoid catching the swab between the capstan and the pinch roller, however. The pinch roller is also easiest to clean when it's spinning.

Figure 12.2 Clean that tape path!

It's not necessary to get a special solution to clean rubber parts, by the way, although these are specially formulated to keep these parts soft, and could possibly extend the lifetime of these parts. Generally speaking, alcohol works fine for both metal and rubber, and is inexpensive and non-hazardous.

No matter how great you become at recording, failure to clean heads and properly demagnetize will sabotage the best of sessions. Take time to learn these simple procedures, and to apply them before every recording session!

Tuning Up!

It is remarkable how often the process of recording begins without the instruments playing in tune. This can have dire consequences, from driving people with perfect pitch crazy to being unable to add overdubs from instruments with fixed tuning, such as an acoustic piano. So make sure before commencing that a quartz-referenced tuner is used to reference all instruments to 'concert pitch.'

One further caution: Some synthesizers are calibrated to 442 Hz as concert pitch instead of the U.S. convention of *A-440*. This can usually be found on a "page" of master functions that is part of the instruction set of most synths. Because most of these functions reset every time the unit is turned off, check the master tuning every time the synthesizer is turned on, and set it to the appropriate reference (*A-440* in the U.S. and Canada).

Handling Tape

This is one of these topics that seems so trivial, yet a recording can be improved greatly by spending just a minute getting the tape into the best condition before recording. After all, the tape is the medium on which the performance will be stored—it deserves a little special handling.

Tensioning Cassettes. Most cassette

tapes are trouble-free, needing only to be opened and popped into a recorder to begin working. However, if tape is not wrapped securely around the two inside reels and is hanging loosely, it is possible for it to become looped around the guides and rollers within the cassette's tape path. Before recording, take a look at the cassette; if tape is loose, use a pencil eraser and gently turn one side or the other in a direction to take up the slack. It is also a good idea to wind a cassette all the way to one end and then all the way back again before recording. This eliminates any tension that might have developed from the cassette sitting on a shelf or being subjected to different temperatures while in transit or storage. The long-term storage potential of the tape is also improved.

Threading a Reel. Threading tape onto a reel can seem quite tricky, but there's an easy way to make it go on right. Even though reels have a slot in the hub (center of the reel) to slip the tape into, this has the unfortunate tendency to put a crimp into the tape, resulting eventually in destruction of the end of the reel of tape.

Instead try the 'Thumb Trick:' Thread the tape through the guides and across the heads, following the instructions for your recorder (there are numerous variations). If your recorder has a flip-up head shield (open-reel models) make sure it's down; otherwise the tape won't contact the record head! Lay the tape over the take-up reel, then insert your thumb through one of the openings in the side of the reel, pressing down on the last half-inch of the tape.

Now turn the reel one complete variation while holding the end of the tape. This has the effect of spooling one complete winding of tape over the end. Go a little past where you're holding the tape, and then withdraw your thumb while turning the reel a little further. The tape should wind on itself with sufficient tension to hold it onto the reel, and the tape end won't become mutilated. Note: It's important that the tape lay flat on the reel, without a bump or fold, which could create a lump and cause the tape to pack unevenly as it is taken up. It's better to try it over again instead.

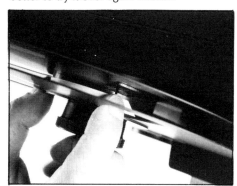

Figure 12.3 Threading a reel.

Set the Counter

When the tape is properly loaded and conditioned for recording, one more step remains: setting the tape counter. It's always beneficial to leave some unused tape at the beginning of a recording, especially on an open reel recorder. Otherwise, every time you rewind back to the beginning you'll need to re-thread the recorder and find the

beginning over again! The ends of a reel of tape also take a lot of abuse, so your valuable work is better protected by starting a minute or so into a tape. The same is true to a lesser extent of cassettes; the ends of the tape take the most wear and are easiest to stretch, even though a leader is fitted to both ends. It doesn't hurt to begin your recording 30 seconds or so into a tape. When you've reached the starting point, reset the zero point of your tape counter.

Rewind Before Recording. It's possible that if a reel of tape has been sitting on the shelf for a while before it's bought or put into use, it may have slowly tightened itself around the center of the reel. It's a good practice to take the new tape and place it on the right hand side of the recorder (normally the take-up side), thread it backwards, and then rewind it completely onto the left-hand side of the recorder. This relieves any tension that may have built up during storage, and has the further advantage that when the session is finished, the tape can be advanced onto the take-up reel and stored 'tails out'—that is, with the end of the tape as the outside windings.

Storage tension increases the transfer of magnetic energy between the successive winds of the tape, called *print-through*; this is the source of faint echoes of other sections of music or dialog during quiet passages, and is nearly impossible to eliminate.

Tails-out storage also minimizes the effect of print-through: Faint print-through echoes will tend to be masked by the music, instead of being heard *before* music starts.

Pre-think Tracks

Thinking ahead will save hours of frustration and agony later on. Even producers and artists with 48 tracks available try to plot the course of a session so that tracks are 'open' when they're needed. In the realm of 4-, 8-, and 16-track recording, this forethought is critical; otherwise the tracks won't be there later on, when it's time to spice up a performance with overdubs.

The Track Sheet. The track sheet is a chart that designates what signal is recorded on each track. A track sheet also may contain information such as the date of the recording, any special notes about recording techniques (microphones used, special equalization or other signal processing) and perhaps information about who the musicians are, if applicable. Its greatest value is as a planning tool, since filling it out forces you to think about the logical progression in which your recording session should proceed. A number of factors can influence how tracks should be laid out.

Bouncing. *Bouncing* tracks, also known as *ping-ponging*, is the process of pre-mixing recorded tracks onto an available unrecorded track, thus making tracks available so that further overdubs can be performed. When tracks are allocated on the track sheet, bouncing must be taken into consideration so that an open track is left over when it's time to combine. Some tape recorders don't do a very good job when bouncing to an adjacent track, one that is right next to a recorded track.

For instance, with some older 8-track recorders, it may not be possible to combine tracks 1 through 6 onto track 7, because 7 is right next to 6. There can be leakage between the two tracks (called *crosstalk*), which causes phase cancellation or even feedback. The problem can be exacerbated by boosting treble, but can usually be prevented by not recording the bounce at too high a signal level. At any rate, if you have a recorder that doesn't take well to adjacent track bounces, your track sheet should reflect this by leaving a blank guard track between the tracks that are being bounced and the track or tracks that are being recorded onto.

Remember to leave room for bounces. If you fill up all tracks of a multi-track machine, the only way to add more tracks to it is to mix all tracks together onto a second tape machine, and then re-record that mix back onto the multi-track. By doing this an extra

Rentahhl Studios San Francisco, California		CLIENT/PROJECT: S.B.H. / TRAVELS NAME THAT TUNE: WORLDS AWAY			DATE: 2/3 DEC 86 TAPE: 456 DOLBY C								
TRACK	TAPE/MIDI	INTRO	V1	V2	C1	V3	C2	BREAK	C3	OUTRO
BASS w/EQ	1 / #	?: →	START								
ACOUSTIC GUITAR L	# / 2		CHORUS – 1.5 ms					PERC		
ACOUSTIC GUITAR R	#/3		REV. HALL – 0.9 sec					PERC		
ELECTRIC GUITAR	#/4	DRY SOLO SM57 →						SOLO ↗		
VOX	5	RE-AMP →	REV. 29					MUTE		
BACKGROUND VOCALS L	#/6	K-1 → PICKUP						MUTE		FLANGE
BACKGROUND VOCALS R	#/7	K-1 → PICKUP						MUTE		FLANGE
ESQ-1 4-7 // 2-6	# / 1		BRASS / ORGAN SPLIT					CLAV. PATCH		
ESQ-1 1-2-1-3 // 2-7	# / 2	STRINGS						OCTAVE CLAV.		
PIANO MODULE	# / 3	+1 RANGE	REV. 67							
DRVM L/R	#/4		DRUM KIT # 7 NO GATE					KIT #12		
DETAILS	# / #	TAPE # 37 // SEQUENCE FILE : WOMBAT MUSINGS (JOURNEY OF CLIFF) TEMPO: 122 bpm (+ tempo map) / Key: D (Guitar Eb = D)								
CODE REFERENCES	SMPTE	TRACK 8 29.97 START 01:00:00:00								
	MTC	DIRECT TIME LOCK NO OFFSET								

Figure 12.4 The track sheet: a planning tool (and creative outlet).

generation of recording is added, resulting in far worse signal-to-noise and fidelity.

Stereo Recording. Another consideration is stereo. If five microphones have been used to record a drum set, or five tracks were employed to record a drum machine using independent outs, it's desirable to maintain some kind of stereo picture of the drum kit even when pre-mixing or bouncing tracks together. If you plan to pre-mix in stereo, make sure to leave two open tracks for this purpose, as well as a guard track if you encounter problems bouncing.

Outside Tracks Vs. Inside Tracks. Another factor to think about when laying out the track sheet is what to put on the *outside* versus the *inside* tracks. The outside tracks are nearest to the edge of the tape, such as tracks 1 and 4 on a 4-track recorder. Unfortunately, the contact between the tape heads and the tape is poorer at the edges, regardless of the caliber of machine. It is therefore preferable to put something solid on the outside tracks, a signal that won't be noticeably disturbed by minor variance in the contact of tape to tape head. Ethereal, sustaining synthesizer tracks may not sound so great on the outside, whereas bass or a fat organ part won't be affected. Consider this when planning which instrument to assign to each track.

Syncing With MIDI Or Drum Machine. Working with MIDI and synchronization—as we'll learn about on pages 106 and 110—is the ideal way to go, since it is still more expensive to get a recorder with more tracks than it is to increase the number of tracks by 'syncing' your drum machine and sequenced instruments to tape. These synced instruments are known as *virtual tracks*, and can play along with the tape recorder without being recorded.

However, this puts special demands on the allocation of tape recorder tracks. Most important, a sync tone that allows a MIDI-driven device to synchronize to a tape recording, must be recorded or *striped*. This is usually done on an outside track. When you stripe code, remember to stripe enough to last the entire song. SMPTE time code should be striped for the entire length of the tape.

If you're a newcomer to multi-track recording, you may wish to start off recording your drum machine and MIDI parts directly to tape. This way, once you're comfortable with the process of multi-track recording, you can move on to tape sync and other advanced techniques.

Getting Levels

The tape is threaded, and the track sheet has been laid out. Now it's almost time to get signals down on tape. But before pressing the 'record' button, there are a couple last steps to go through to assure a clean recording.

There's one easy trick that will most often give you the best performance from the inputs on your mixer. Every audio input has a gain range that it operates most efficiently in, yielding the best signal-to-noise ratio. What you're trying to achieve when setting levels is to give each signal the proper amount of preamplification to get it up (or down) to the right level to record. If you provide too much gain at the preamplifier, you'll need to cut it down later, but in so

doing noise will have been added to the input. If too little gain is applied, more pre-amplification will need to be added at a later stage; this too increases noise. It's not unlike shifting gears in a car to keep the engine from revving too fast or slow.

Most devices these days have a switch or rotary control for 'gain' (also called 'trim'), which controls the first stage of preamplification, and a second control, usually a straight line fader, which is the individual channel control (it also determines the second preamp gain setting). When setting levels, take the second control and set it to seven (that is, seven out of ten; if your controls aren't marked this way, set it three-quarters of the way to full gain). Now use the first gain control to achieve the ideal reading on the meters. Finally, if small adjustments are needed, you can move the channel fader (second control) to fine tune the setting and compensate for minor changes in volume. You'll find that this yields far better results than just using the channel fader for all gain changes!

As you adjust the first input gain control, be sure to watch your mixer's *input overload LEDs*, which will flash when the incoming signal is too hot. If your mixer lacks these, it should display input levels on one of the meters. Using the mixer's *solo system* (again, if it has one) will let you hear how individual channels sound while you adjust gain.

Remember that any differences in the levels of tracks will be balanced as part of the mixdown, so record individual tracks as 'hot' as possible without distorting them. You can always reduce the level of a track in a mix without adding noise, but boosting a weakly recorded track also amplifies whatever noise is present as well.

Levels And Microphones. Getting a level on a microphone input consists of finding the right amount of gain so that the signal will be recorded on tape with as little noise as possible, yet the input to the mixer won't be overloaded and distort. One thing that is unlikely to produce an accurate level is for someone to say "Testing" into the microphone. It is far more useful to run through a small section of the tune to be recorded.

Other Sources. With most line or instrument sources it is usually possible to anticipate what the maximum volume will be during a recording. Ask the instrumentalist to run through a peak section or play it yourself, using performance volume. It is also possible to get levels set up while the musicians are working out or practicing one section of a piece. Of course if you're using a sequencer, just start the sequencer for a quick run-through without recording. MIDI allows you to exactly control what volume and patch each instrument is playing, so it's easy to get the right level.

Routing (Track Assignments)

Track assignment, or *routing* is the process of getting signals from mixer inputs onto the desired tape tracks. Each time you record a new track, you need to assign the appropriate input(s) to that track.

If you own a recorder/mixer, this is done using the *direct assign* switches and/or the *busses*. If you have an independent mixer, you assign inputs to tape tracks by using the *direct outputs* and/or the *group buss*

outputs.

When working with four or eight tracks, it's often advantageous to mix inputs together to stretch the limitation on the number of available tracks. To do this you need to assign several inputs to the same track, by using a buss. This is done differently depending on the machine, but there are only a few variations.

Recording In Stereo

You may want to record certain sources in stereo, using two tracks at once. Drum machines and samplers with multiple outputs will generally sound much better in stereo, because the full panorama can be preserved. This way if a tom roll moves from left to right, the final recording will reflect this.

To record in stereo you need to make use of the odd/even panning feature. Assign all the inputs that are part of the stereo image to the same pair of tracks (for instance, three and four, or seven and eight). Use the 'pan' controls to determine where along the left-right perspective you want a given instrument to end up. If you're using independent outputs from a drum machine, or separate microphones for each drum, it's a good idea to try and keep the kick, bass, or any instrument with a preponderance of low frequencies in the center of a stereo mix, because these elements are so heavy that they throw an entire mix off balance if panned too far to either side.

If a drum machine or keyboard has stereo outputs, it may be simpler to use these outputs for stereo recording. Unless there's a compelling need to separately process each drum—which is only possible on drum machines and samplers with individual outputs—it is far less hassle to grab the stereo mix already provided by the unit. To record this in stereo, simply assign the left and right outputs to different tracks. It will make it easier to mix down if these tracks are

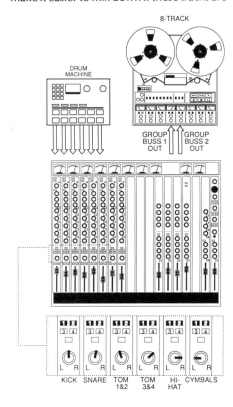

Figure 12.5 Recording to the multi-track in stereo.

right next to each other, but it's not strictly necessary.

For example, take the left output of the keyboard into input one, and the right into input two. Now assign input one to track three, and input two to track four. Recording individual instruments in stereo is most useful when you've got eight or more tracks to work with.

Here's a great way to maintain a professional sound while recording complex arrangements when working with four tracks: Record the entire rhythm track—including guitars and keyboards—in stereo. This avoids an extra generation of recording by making it unnecessary to 'bounce' tracks down (see page 92), and keeps the sparkle in the sound. To do this, assign all inputs to the same pair of outputs, and use the 'pan' control to place the instruments across a left-right perspective. This gives you the ability to record stereo instruments in stereo, as long as there are enough inputs available.

A *submixer*, as described on page 34, can come in handy at this point. A stereo P.A. mixer works just fine for this purpose. Pan the inputs of the submixer's inputs to its mono or stereo outputs. These can then be plugged into one (mono) or two (stereo) inputs on the mixer or ministudio, thus expanding the number of available inputs.

One shortcoming of many 4-track recorder/mixers is that the tape monitor section of the mixer is only monaural. That may make it impossible to preview the stereo premix. This can be very hard to overcome, but if the recorder has a way to listen to the outputs of the mixer section rather than monitoring the tape channels as usual, you can switch to this monitor mode to set up the stereo premix. Then change back to the tape monitor so that you'll hear the tracks already recorded when adding overdubs.

As you record, make the kick, snare, and bass guitar somewhat exaggerated, by boosting their level in the mix and making them stand out. You'll find that as you layer on additional tracks, these instruments will tend to disappear into the background. Of course when you record in stereo like this, you're giving up the ability to balance these instruments later—just as with bouncing.

Recording Several Tracks Live

Even though there's been a shift in recent years away from live recording, it has advantages. A live recording, with several musicians playing at once, often maintains a level of spontaneity that's hard to capture when laying down tracks one at a time. Very basic ministudios with only two inputs are made for use by one or two individuals, but units with four or more inputs are appropriate for use with a band.

Here the process is not much different than stereo recording, except that you assign inputs to as many tracks as necessary. Keep in mind once again that you may want to bounce tracks, that is, transfer a number of recorded tracks to an unused track so that you can continue layer more parts on a composition. In that case remember to preserve one or more blank tracks! When you're recording in stereo, assignment is to a pair of tracks; when recording live, usually all available tracks will get used.

Refer to your track sheet, and group the appropriate inputs to the chosen tracks. Try and keep critical elements, such as the lead vocal, isolated on a single track, because these are the things you'll need the most control over when it comes time to mix.

Monitoring Considerations

As we learned on page 27, the tape machine allows you to choose what you monitor (input, sync, or repro mode). In the case of a recorder/mixer ministudio there's very little work involved in setting up: The channel or channels that are selected for record will monitor whatever signal is being sent to the recorder inputs, because they automatically switch to input mode. Keep in mind that even if you put three different signals on the same tape track, you'll monitor all three signals from one tape channel, because they're being mixed into the recorder input.

Most current open-reel recorders automatically switch the monitor mode depending on whether they're in record or not, but if you are using a model without this feature, such as an older Teac, Otari, Sony, or Akai 4-track, the monitor mode must be set manually for each track. Tracks that are previously recorded should be placed in sync mode so that further overdubs will come out in time with the original track or tracks. Finally, when all tracks are recorded, repro mode should be selected, which takes the signal from the playback head.

Speakers Vs. Headphones. In almost every case it is preferable to use speakers to monitor what you're doing instead of headphones, both because it's not particularly comfortable to wear 'phones over a long span, and because what you hear is usually more accurately reproduced over speakers.

A pair of high-quality headphones, however, can provide an excellent reference, especially compared to a mediocre set of speakers. There are also times when headphones are necessary in order to record: Speakers will feed back if there's a microphone open nearby, and even if feedback is not caused, the signal from the speakers will leak into the mike, causing unpleasant cancellation and a sloppy ambiance. So make sure to turn down your monitor speakers every time before turning up the microphone, and monitor through headphones.

Lesson Two: Laying Down The First Track

Before you record that first track, remember that you can always do a track over again; there's no pressure to do everything perfectly the first time. That's why you own a multi-track system in the first place, so you can control the pace and setting of your sessions. So relax; the more automatic the mechanical aspects of recording become, the more it's possible to concentrate on the creative side. You have absolutely nothing to lose!

Some Final Details

Of course it's hard to avoid just plunging forward and pressing 'record,' but there are a few final details to take care of. A moment's attention to the monitor mix, counter, and count-off can save frustration down the road.

Record Enable. The *record enable* switch activates the record circuitry for each channel. In order to record you need both to turn on the channel 'record enable' switch, and to hold down the transport's 'record' button while pressing the 'play'

switch. Make sure that it is turned on for each channel you want to record. It sounds silly to be reminded, but it is amazing how many good takes get lost because 'record' was not selected for that track.

Remote Controls And Footswitches. One of the great conveniences of modern life is the punch-in footswitch. It takes the place of the master 'record' button on the tape transport. Hands-free recording can be accomplished by first selecting 'record enable' for the tracks to be recorded. Now when the punch-in footswitch is depressed, the tape transport goes into record; when the switch is clicked again, 'record' is deselected.

This not only makes it easy to record initial tracks: Later on, when you're trying to patch in little corrections that may only cover a few notes or bars, the punch-in footswitch will become indispensable. Make sure that you invest in a mechanically silent model; otherwise when you're using microphones the loud click is sure to be captured on tape.

Some advanced models, such as the AMR Overdubber, not only engage and disengage the record function; a 'rewind' and 'pause' footswitch are added, so that another 'take' can be done without having to put down an instrument or go over to the recorder. Of course, if it's time to record a new channel, you still need to go over to the recorder and change the 'record enable' switches so that you don't write over the track that was just laid down.

Remember The Count-Off. Every composition should have a count-off—where you establish the tempo and beginning of a cut by counting numbers. This makes it far easier to add additional tracks later (overdub), especially if they're supposed to start right on the first beat. Without it there's no telling where the beginning of a composition really is. Don't worry about getting rid of it later, by the way; it can be edited out, or muted.

A two bar count-off is usually best: In the first bar sound off every beat, while in the second, leave out the last beat or two to create a silent buffer zone just before the performance starts. For instance, a count-off might go: "One, two, three, four, One, two, (blank), (blank)." Use an open microphone or the mixer's talkback circuit to record the count-off; make sure the speakers are off. If you're using a metronome or drum machine to keep the beat throughout the song, it's a good idea to have it click or count off (with a side stick for a drum machine click) before the start of the song.

Set The Tape Monitor. Remember that the monitor section of our recorder/mixer or mixing board is listening to the output of the tape recorder (for more detail, see page 40). This output changes according to which mode a particular tape channel is in.

When record mode for a particular track is selected, the input to the recorder (which is what is being recorded) is what we listen to. This output becomes the source for the headphone mix, along with the outputs of the other tape channels. At this stage some adjustment of the headphone mix may be required: Use the tape monitor section to keep things balanced in the headphones or studio monitors.

Here's your 'flight checklist' to run down before you actually press the record button:

1. Set up the monitor mix; use headphones if mikes are on.
2. Select 'record enable' on the track or tracks to be recorded.
3. If using a footswitch or remote, place it in a comfortable spot.
4. Set the tape monitor so you can hear the source you're recording.
4. Use a two-bar count-off.
5. If you're syncing a drum machine or sequencer to tape, be sure to read "Tape Sync Techniques" on page 112.

Start The Recording

The moment of truth has arrived. It's time to put the machine in motion. But in the world of personal recording, remember that in many cases you're not only the performer, but also the producer and recording engineer as well. If your duties as engineer are completely ignored while recording, you may find it impossible to mix and produce your master tape because of recording flaws. So go ahead and get into the music, but stay on top of the machinery and the process of recording. Of course, if your first track is a sync code track, the engineering can have your complete attention!

To start, you simply get the machine

rolling, listen to your countoff, and press 'record' with enough time to spare before your entrance.

Watch Those Levels. Now that recording is underway, it's time to keep an eye on the levels. There's a tendency to get carried away during the heat of a performance. Remember once again that you own the studio; if a track is blown, it's better to start over again and get it right instead of making excuses. If levels are minded, there will be less need to repeat a performance.

Leave Record Mode. There are two steps to coming out of record. The first is to press the 'stop' button. Some professional recorders allow 'record' to be deselected by pressing it a second time, or by pressing 'stop' while holding 'play'—but most decks require that 'stop' be pressed, and 'stop' works to disengage 'record' on all machines.

The second step is to turn off the 'record enable' switch for the channel or channels upon which you're recording. If you're listening back to check if a performance is up to snuff, you *may* want to leave the channel 'record' switch enabled, so that you can easily go back into record. But keep in mind that if you press the master transport 'record' button, the track you've recorded will start to be erased.

Disable 'Record.' Now that you've got a performance you think is worth keeping, remember to turn off the 'record enable' switch for the track just captured. Otherwise, the next time you go into record, this track can be erased as you attempt to record additional tracks.

Time to Listen

If your first track was in fact a sync track, you'll want to ensure that your drum machine or sequencer will in fact sync to the code you've just recorded, as is described on page 112.

Otherwise, there are two things to listen for when you review a track. The first is the quality of the recording, and the second is the caliber of the performance.

Recording Quality. Here you're listening for fundamental errors that will be destructive to the overall sound of your recording. If a track is excessively noisy or distorted, no amount of doctoring in the mix will improve it. On the other hand, if it's slightly dull or needs a more ambient (reverberant) sound, these are minor matters of taste that can be resolved with a little signal processing in the mix. So look for the big, irreparable problems. If a track flunks the recording quality

test, the best thing is to do it over, or repair the section by punching in (page 91).

Performance. Just as a poorly recorded performance can't be fixed by fiddling with it, no amount of trickery will improve a performance that's lacking. Remember that it's *your* studio now, and that there are no time or money constraints to keep you from getting it just the way you want. If the performance doesn't catch the essence of the work you're trying to record, it's your duty as the producer to get it right!

Fix It In The Mix

Some tracks are fatally flawed. For instance, if a track is out of tune, or if there are large sections of poorly performed material it's easier to record over again.

But if there are just a few notes wrong, or if the tone is a little off, there's no need to rehash the same passage until you're sick of it. After all, that's the difference between live and recorded—recording gives you the ability to massage the sound of things and alter them to your satisfaction, while playing live requires that it be right the first time. Neither way is better; each situation requires special skills. So there's no reason to feel bad that things can be fixed afterwards; perhaps it's a higher state of artistic evolution, where more people can achieve perfect performances.

Things that can easily be 'fixed in the mix' include:

● Tone (such as too much bass, or 'not bright enough').
● Ambience (by using reverberation).
● Leakage (if the signal that's leaking in is at a fairly low level).
● Excessive sibilance (smearing of 's' sounds).
● Variations in levels.

Things that can't readily be fixed in the mix include:

● Tracks out of tune (you can use a pitch shifter, but the track is degraded).
● Heavy 'p'—popping of the microphone (aim the mike at the performer's nose—it works!).
● Distortion.
● Noise that is nearly as loud as the signal (low level noise can be 'gated' away).

See Chapter Eight and page 93 for details on how to use various processors to improve your recordings.

Lesson Three: Overdubbing

Now that you've got a track down, it's time to start adding to it. This process is called *overdubbing*. The tape recorder must now do two things at once: play back the tracks that have already been recorded, while recording new information on unused tracks.

Here are the steps involved in overdubbing:

New Assignments. The process we went through to lay down the first track will now be repeated to create the first overdub. First, the new input signal must be routed to the next tape track, or to the track designated for it on the track sheet. Find the next input on the mixer, and make sure that the assignment button for this input channel is routed to the desired track of the recorder. If you're overdubbing the same instrument or mike as was used on the first track, you'll want to:

- Move it to a new input if recording with direct assigns or direct outputs (see page 36), or:
- Reassign the same input to another track by selecting a different output buss.

Reset The Tape Monitor. Remember, the tape monitor section is where the headphone or monitor mix comes from while recording. Some recorders will require that the tape monitor be switched manually from 'input' mode to 'sync' in order to hear back the track just recorded, but most current open-reel and ministudio models do this automatically. The idea is to hear back the tracks already recorded while laying down new ones. This must be done at the record head so that the new tracks line up with the previous ones. If your machine has a 'repro' mode, use this only at mixdown time; all overdubbing should be done in the sync mode. See page 27 for more details.

Set Monitor And Input Levels. There are two sets of levels that need to be adjusted before overdubbing: the input and the tape monitor. First set the input level, because it also affects the tape monitor setting! Remember that you're seeking a gain setting that gets the signal as hot as possible without overloading (saturating) the tape or distorting the mixer. Then make sure that the tape monitor mix is set so that there's a balance between the recorder input (new track) and the one already on tape, so that you or the performer can clearly discern how the new track fits in.

Confirm Which Channel Is In Record. Remember that you were supposed to deselect the last track recorded. If this step was forgotten, here's a last chance to do it before accidentally erasing part of the composition. Equally important is to select the 'record enable' on the track or tracks that are to receive the overdub.

Start Again (from "Start The Recording"). Now the process of recording a track gets repeated. All the same rules apply. The first step is to enter record mode once again by holding down the 'record' transport control and pressing 'play' at the same time. Once the tape is rolling, keep an eye on the meters or overload indicators to make sure that a peak doesn't come along and wipe out the material. When you get to the end, press 'stop' or step on the punch-in footswitch to make sure that the recorder leaves the 'record' mode.

Listen Again. Listen back over the track just recorded, adjusting the tape monitor mix to achieve a balance or blend. Remember when blending that everything doesn't have to be the same level; certain elements of a recording should be expected to be up front. Make sure that if you've recorded one of these parts that the performance and recording are strong enough to support putting the part in the forefront of a mix. If it's a 'take,' deselect the 'record enable' switch for the track just recorded.

The Cyclical Nature Of Further Tracks. The process of overdubbing can continue until all tracks are used up. The exact sequence of steps is followed over again:

1. Assign the new input.
2. Adjust first the input and then the tape monitor levels.
3. Select 'record enable' for the track to be laid down.
4. Roll the tape in 'record' mode.
5. Come out of 'record.'
6. Wind back and listen.
7. Deselect the 'record enable.'

The process is identical whether using four or 48 tracks.

Lesson Four: Punching In

One of the major differences between multi-track work and live performance is that it's possible to repair tracks that might have one section or a few notes that are sour. This isn't cheating—it's using technology and your brains to overcome limitations that have always held back performers. If you're working on your own, the best tool for this purpose is a punch-in footswitch.

How It's Done

To punch in, select the track that needs the repair. Select the 'record enable' for this track so that it is ready to enter record mode, but don't activate the master 'record' switch at the transport. Instead, place the recorder in play mode. Then at the exact moment you need to replace part of the existing track, step on the footswitch to initiate recording. When the end of the defective passage is reached, step on the footswitch once again to leave the record mode. This method allows you to hear the performance up to the punch-in point, and then to hear it again after the questionable section has been replaced.

The same operation can be accom-

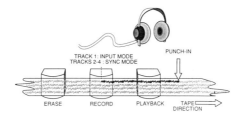

Figure 12.6 A punch in is essentially an overdub that takes place within or on top of an existing track.

plished without a punch-in footswitch on most recorders, but it's difficult if not impossible for the recorder to be controlled by the same person who's performing. On recorders that use solenoid (light touch) controls, you can usually hold down the 'play' button while the transport is running, and then press 'record' when you want to punch-in.

When the end of the punch-in section is reached, the 'stop' button or footswitch should be used to end the recording process. On a few models it is possible to hold down the 'play' button and then touch the 'stop' switch; this has the effect of cancelling record without stopping the machine. You should experiment with this during a 'fool-around' session, and not while in the middle of a meaningful recording, because it may not work on your unit. Mechanical transport controls sometimes allow punch-in by holding 'play' and pressing 'record', but 'stop' must always be pressed to terminate the recording process.

One of the most important considerations when punching in is to carefully pick the 'in' and 'out' points. It is more or less impossible to punch into the middle of sustained material, such as a synthesizer chord. Instead, look for a gap that's long enough to allow the record electronics to 'ramp up.' For most units this is only a few milliseconds, but there are those machines that are slow to go into record. If possible, try to punch in 'on the beat,' so that any minor punch-in noises (clicks, etc.) are less prominent.

To be able to anticipate your machine's ramp-up characteristics, you need to be familiar with your particular machine. Do this by experimenting beforehand, rather than finding out the hard way that you've severed the first word of the second chorus.

If you have a machine that's slow on the punch-in, it's possible to anticipate the punch-in point by just enough time to make every thing fit together—but remember that

if you cut it too close some material can be lost. Before punching in, try a rehearsal, while listening for a gap to jump in on, and a point to bail out.

Lesson Five: Bouncing

When all the tracks of a tape recorder begin to fill up, there are two choices: mix down, or bounce. If everything that needed to get put down has been recorded, there's no particular reason to add more tracks; but more often than not, a few more overdubs will add luster to the work. The way to continue recording is to leave a track or two tracks open, and to pre-mix several track's worth of material onto these open tracks so that new parts can be written over some of the original recording. Transferring these tracks across is called *bouncing*.

How It's Done

Several rules govern the bouncing of tracks. These need to be studied when the track sheet is first laid out. On a 4-track recorder there are not that many choices. Most likely three tracks will be recorded, and then transferred to the fourth so that three more overdubs can be stacked on.

Eight and 16-track options are more numerous. Ideally a stereo image can be preserved when tracks are premixed, so two tracks must be left open rather than one. Bouncing is a form of mixing, and whenever mixing is in progress, the tape tracks that are being mixed need to be directed back into the console.

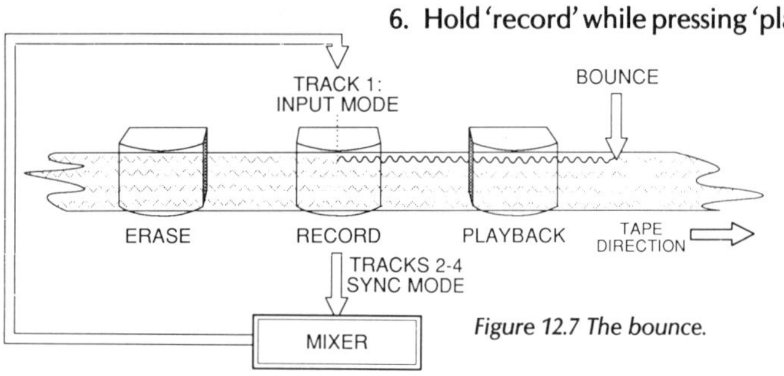

Figure 12.7 The bounce.

If tracks 1, 2, and 3 are to be bounced to track 4, inputs 1, 2, and 3 should be set to 'tape,' or 'line' if no separate tape inputs are available on the mixer and the tape outputs are returned to the mixer's line inputs. Next, the gain should be adjusted for a line level signal. Sending these tracks to the open track is no different than routing any other input source; switch on the channel assignment switch that feeds the input of the open track. If bouncing is done in stereo, two channels will be assigned using odd/even panning (page 88). The 'pan' control will determine where in the left-right panorama a given track will appear. Remember not to place bass-heavy tracks too far away from the center, which can upset the whole mix. Kick drum and bass guitar almost always are panned to the center for just this reason.

Bouncing is mixing and recording at the same time. We've mentioned the mixing part, and have assigned the tape inputs to the outputs that feed the open tracks. Now comes the recording part.

Just as in the overdubbing process, the 'record enable' switch must be selected for any tracks to be recorded, and 'record' must be entered from the transport controls or via a punch-in footswitch.

As with any other recorded track, it is important to rewind after recording and give the pre-mix a very careful listen. After all, once you go back and record over your initial tracks, there's no option to go back and mix it differently. In musical performances, remember that it is often desirable to slightly exaggerate the kick, snare, and bass, because these elements tend to get buried as further tracks are added. Bring them slightly more to the fore than seems natural.

So to do a bounce, or ping-pong tracks:

1. Select 'tape' or 'line' input for all tracks to be bounced.
2. Adjust input gain to line levels.
3. Assign all of the tracks to a buss out that feeds the track to which you want to bounce.
4. If bouncing in stereo, assign all tracks to an odd-even pair of buss outs and set 'pan' controls for a stereo image.
5. Enable 'record' for the bounce track or tracks.
6. Hold 'record' while pressing 'play' on the tape transport controls.
7. Press 'stop' to come out of record at the end of the section or song.

A second tape recorder can also be used to bounce tracks. Instead of mixing to an open track, all tracks are filled up on the multi-track. Then all channels are routed back into the mixer, and are sent to either one or two tracks of a second tape machine. The second machine can be another multi-track, a two-track, a video recorder (especially if equipped with Hi-Fi sound), or even a sampler (if the bounce is short or the sampler has enough memory).

Once these tracks are mixed, they can be fed back onto one or two tracks of a new tape on the multi-track, and more overdubs can be added. This technique has the advantage of preserving all the original tracks, so if a fatal flaw is discovered later on, it is possible to go back and either do the transfer over again or even to replace some of the original tracks. But if you do decide to go

back remember that you'll lose any overdubs you've added after the original transfer. Another drawback of this method is that it adds another tape generation to the whole procedure. See below for more on this topic.

If a second identical multi-track is used, or if a ministudio runs at normal cassette speed, it may be possible to transfer the actual bounce tape back to the first recorder to add more tracks—for example, to remove the tape from the two-channel cassette machine, and place it back into the multi-track ministudio. The transferred tracks will show up on tracks 1 and 2 of the ministudio. This avoids generation loss because the mixed tracks don't need to be recorded once again.

Generation Loss

Every time a track is recorded there are factors which limit the quality of the recording. Noise and distortion are added, even by the finest digital machines. The mechanical variations of the transport (wow and flutter) play a part, and frequency response shortcomings are also incorporated into the audio image on tape. When a track is recorded, and is then bounced or re-recorded on another track, generation loss takes place. This is simply the deterioration in quality caused by all the factors just mentioned, and it is quite noticeable, even on professional machines.

Low-speed and cassette recordings are most susceptible to generation loss. The most audible effects are a loss of high-frequency response and an increase in noise. Transients—quick attacks, such as a snare drum or the pluck of a string—may also become mushy, and bass can become muddy. There's not too much that can be done about it, other than to make as clean a recording as possible. Equalization can also help, by compensating for frequency response loss. But one way to avoid generation loss is to plan tracks carefully, and only do bouncing when necessary.

Sound-on-Sound

Sound-on-sound is the process of mixing a live source with a recorded track while recording both onto a new track. Les Paul used sound-on-sound techniques to create his original multi-layered recordings (see page 8.) Even though multi-track machines have made sound-on-sound obsolete, the technique is still very useful for stretching the number of sources that make up a final recording.

For instance, a vocal part or solo can be added while bouncing tracks. To do this, set up the mixer for a bounce (as described), then bring up one or more additional inputs with whatever line or mike sources desired.

Assign these new inputs to the same tracks that the bounce is going to, and mix them together just like they were one of the tracks already recorded. Adding new material while bouncing or mixing introduces no generation loss, so it's a good way to make a part stand out when there are no more tracks available to preserve it individually.

Ten Tracks From Four. It's possible to get as many as ten signal sources recorded onto four tracks, with no track being more than second generation (original recording plus bounce). Here's how it's done:

1. Record three tracks, then bounce these to the fourth track while adding a live source, using the sound-on-sound technique.
2. Record two tracks, and add a new source while bouncing to the third.
3. Record on one of the two remaining tracks, and add a live overdub while sending it to the open track.
4. This makes the track from which you bounced dispensable—record your final part onto this one.

Keep in mind that with this method you should record the tracks you want the most control over *last*, because the later tracks are combined with progressively fewer other tracks, until the final track is all by itself—which is a great track to put solo and lead vocals on.

Also keep in mind that this method sacrifices mixing flexibility in the name of recording more tracks. A decision needs to be made about which is more important, early on. One final idea: this principle can be applied for part of the recording, without going all the way. For instance you can leave out the live overdubs at any stage, or just bounce once and then fill up the remaining tracks with single sources.

Twenty-Two Tracks From Eight. The method just presented could allow as many as 36 sources to be captured on just 8 tracks of tape. But when working in eight tracks a better recording can be made while still making use of as many as 22 input sources— with some retention of stereo imagery.

To do this, first record six tracks (usually drums, bass, and rhythm instruments), which can be bounced in stereo to tracks seven and eight. Now record five tracks and bounce to six, four tracks and bounce to five, and so on until there are two tracks left. Save these tracks for solo instruments or vocalists, or for any track that you want to have the most possibility of varying in the mix, because these two tracks will have just one signal source on each.

Note that this process doesn't have to be followed to the letter. It's possible to use the sound on sound technique to increase the number of recorded parts (up to the 36 mentioned). Another option is to do less bouncing, but add dimension to the final product by making two bounces in stereo. Here's how it's done:

1. Record six tracks and bounce in stereo to tracks 7 and 8.
2. Record four more tracks and bounce to tracks 5 and 6.
3. Record three tracks and then bounce to track 4.
4. Add two more tracks, which are then mixed on track 3.
5. Add two solo overdubs, each on its own track.

This method, with two stereo bounces, still gets 17 signal sources down on tape!

Lesson Six: Signal Processing In Action

Signal processors are audio modifiers, as we learned in Chapter Eight. They fall into several categories: *equalizers*, which alter tonal balance; *dynamic controllers*, which change volume levels; and *effects*, which is a broad category that covers any device that performs a sonic trick, such as creating ambience (reverberation) or doubling a vocal (delay).

There are times when a signal processor is indispensable, and others when sound modification takes away more than it adds. Here are some guidelines to help determine when and how to apply signal processing.

Recording 'Wet' Or 'Dry'

Effects can be added to a track while it is being recorded, or they can be applied afterwards, either during a bounce or at mix time. There are advantages and disadvantages to recording wet, that is, recording effects along with the original signal. The primary thing in 'wet' recording's favor is that the same effects unit can be used on each individual track, and a different effect can be applied each time. For instance, a digital reverb unit could be used to apply gated reverb sound to a snare drum on one run-through, and plate reverb sound to a vocal overdub. So one effect unit can serve the function of several.

Another big plus is that even if you don't have a mixer with many effect returns, you can still get a big sound out of your recording. So with just one effect and one send and return an entire studio's worth of signal processing can be simulated.

The primary disadvantage of recording wet is that there is a loss of control. You may find yourself applying an effect to a track that sounds absolutely fantastic at the time you do it, but by the time a few more overdubs are added, the effect may be intrusive—or it may be buried by additional tracks. This leaves you in the position of trying to guess how strongly to apply an effect so that it will still be audible later on. If your judgement is off, there's no going back and changing the ratio of wet (effect) to 'dry' (original signal).

How To Record Wet. There are several different ways to record effects along with an original signal. If your console has a channel patch point or 'insert' point (a jack that allows insertion of a signal processor into the signal path of one input channel),

the desired effect can be connected to this point. When the signal processor is used in this manner, the ratio of wet to dry signal will be regulated by the 'mix' or 'effect level' control on the effect. (See page 33 for more information.)

The other way to record wet is to use a line input as an effect return:

1. Connect the effect send of the mixer to the effect's input.
2. Plug the output of the effect into a line input.
3. Set the input selector to 'line.'
4. Assign your dry signal (the source you're

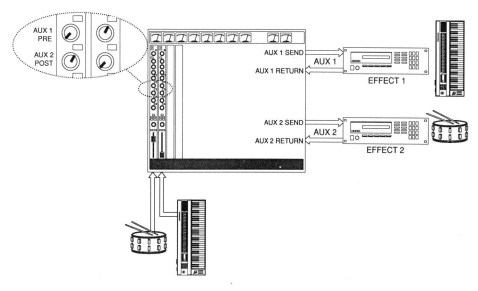

Figure 12.8 Normally, you should use post-fader auxiliary sends as effects sends. That way, when a channel fader is adjusted, its level to the effect is correspondingly adjusted. It's possible to use a pre-fader send, but remember that as we can see above, pre-fader aux sends are not affected by the fader level.

recording) to an output buss.

5. Now assign the effect to the same output buss.

The output buss will feed a tape input, and you should monitor this tape input (as you would normally when recording) to adjust the wet and dry signals for a pleasing mix. For more information on track assignment, see page 37, tape monitoring is discussed on page 40.

How To Monitor Wet While Recording Dry. Even if you don't want to record effects along with the track, it's often desirable to hear effects in the headphone mix or studio monitors. Nearly every vocalist likes to work with some reverberation applied, and most instrumentalists get inspired by tasteful effects.

A handful of consoles, mostly in the upper price ranges, include an 'effects to cue' function that allows an effect to be returned to the headphone cue mix without going to the mix buss or to any of the subgroup (buss) outputs. That's the easy way, but you can monitor wet on almost any unit. Just follow the steps just laid out for recording wet using a line input. The only difference is this: Don't assign the effect to a buss, and don't turn up its input fader. Instead, turn up the 'cue send'—which may also be labeled 'pre-fader auxiliary send'—for the mixer channel that has the effect plugged into it. On in-line monitor mixers such as the Fostex 450, the monitor mix may include a switch labeled 'Tape/Pre/Post'; the 'pre' position will send the console input to the headphones without routing it anywhere else.

Consoles with split monitor sections, such as the Tascam Model 30, and most English consoles, are not as well designed for monitoring wet. You can patch the output of the effect into a 'tape' input and bring it up in the monitor in this way, or you can put an unused tape channel into 'input' mode for monitoring purposes, and combine the output of the effect (that's running through the tape recorder input without being recorded) into the headphone and monitor mix by turning up the spare tape channel. This of course won't work when tracks are used up, since there's no 'spare' tape inputs left. Best of all, use a spare input channel as an effects return, and simply route the input to the stereo mix, as opposed to any of the group buss outputs.

Worst of all for monitoring wet are ministudios, since most have little or no provision for returning an effect into a cue (headphone) mix. The problem is that most of them have a separate tape monitor section, with just four controls, one for each tape track, and no jacks or other points to return an effect. The best solution here is to either record with effects as part of the track, or to get used to recording dry.

Equalization

The obvious application for equalization is to alter the tone of a signal. But there are several other applications that might not be immediately apparent. These include equalizing to reduce noise, and compensating for non-linearity in the response of the recorder.

Poor Man's Noise Reduction. One area of audio that has enjoyed tremendous strides in technology is tape. Newer tapes can handle far more high-frequency energy than tapes of the last decade. One way to use this fact to your advantage is to record your individual tracks brighter than normal, and then decrease the high end back to normal levels in playback. This has the effect of greatly reducing tape hiss.

'Rolling Off' Response. Another noise reduction technique that is remarkably effective is to eliminate frequency response from a recorded track that is irrelevant. For example, if you've used a microphone on a hi-hat, there is no meaningful low frequency energy. So it is possible to 'roll off' the lows—that is, cut them off. Rolling off is accomplished with a shelving type of equalizer (see page 43), but it can also be done with either a graphic or parametric equalizer by figuring out the lowest frequency you need to hear, and then cutting all frequencies below this point.

Rolling off low frequencies eliminates hum and most leakage from bass guitar, kick drums, and toms. High frequencies can also be eliminated from many tracks, which has the benefit of eliminating or greatly reducing tape hiss. A kick drum is a good example; there may be energy in the area of 3 kHz that gives the kick some definition and crispness, but above that there is little or nothing to be heard. Rolling off above 4 kHz will eliminate hiss, as well as leakage from cymbals.

If you don't know what the lowest or highest useful frequencies are for a given track, there's an easy way to determine which frequencies to cut. This is easiest to do with a graphic, but can be done with any EQ. Simply start cutting bands of frequencies. If you're rolling off lows, start with the lowest frequency band. Cut as much as you can without hearing it alter the tone of the track. You'll find on a graphic that the lowest band can almost always be eliminated, and that most instruments other than kick and bass have little or no energy below 100 Hz.

If your mixer is equipped with sweepable (variable-frequency) EQ, set it to the lowest frequency, and set the EQ gain to the cut (counter-clockwise) side. Now start turning the frequency knob so that progressively higher frequencies are cut. Stop when you audibly begin to cut into the sound of the track, and back off the control slightly so you hear no reduction in the low end of the track.

Of course, remember that as a rule, smaller loudspeakers have worse bass response. Consequently, you may find yourself eliminating musical information which *could* be heard on a larger speaker, so proceed with caution.

The same process can be used to roll off highs—with less caution, since quality speakers of all sizes have quite good high frequency response. Noise can be gradually reduced by starting with the top bands of a graphic EQ, or by sweeping frequencies down from the highest rather than up from the lowest.

On some tracks you can reduce both the top and low end. A typical distorted lead guitar tone has no energy below 100 Hz, and very little or none above 8 kHz. By rolling off both the highs and lows a significant amount of noise can be eliminated with no change in tone. Experiment with this on all tracks of your recording when it is time to mix and you'll be pleasantly surprised in the improvement of the overall sound.

Equalizing For The Bounce. Bouncing tracks, as discussed on page 92, is a way to increase the number of signal sources that can be recorded on a multi-track unit. But there are changes in tonal response that take place every time you bounce.

Every tape recorder has a 'head bump' (page 22), which is a rise in the low frequency response. It varies from recorder to recorder both in the amount of low-end boost and in the exact frequency it is centered on, and it changes frequency as you change speed on multi-speed decks. When you lay down a track, the low end is automatically boosted whether or not you use EQ, and this boost is typically between 2 and 3 dB. This isn't all so bad, and in fact a little 'push' on the bottom usually enhances the overall sound.

But when you bounce, another boost takes place, at exactly the same frequencies as before. The result can be a 'tubby' sound to the low end, and this can be made even more noticeable by full-band companding noise reduction systems such as dbx. The solution is to use a peak-and-dip equalizer to reduce the offending frequency band. The offending frequency band is usually centered around 70 to 125 Hz; you want to provide 2 to 3 dB of cut, with about 1 dB of cut in the adjacent bands on a graphic.

The other compensation that should be done when bouncing is to brighten the top end, since each generation of recording robs a little of the highs. Here a simple 'treble' control, which has a shelving action, comes in very handy, or you can use a graphic or parametric to provide a gentle, 2 to 3 dB boost to the entire high end, from about 8 kHz on up. If using a graphic, don't bother boosting any control that has no audible effect other than to increase noise.

Spatial Effects

One of the best ways to increase the spatial sense in a recording is to lay down tracks in stereo, but this is a luxury that can't be indulged in most cases when using a 4- or 8-track machine. So the task of increasing spaciousness is usually accomplished by the use of effects.

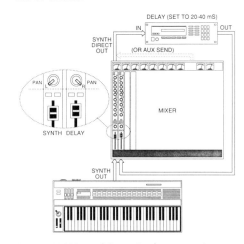

Figure 12.9 Using a delay to simulate stereo. Longer delay times can simulate doubling. Similarly, a signal can be sent to two different EQs: If they're graphic EQs, boosting and cutting alternate bands on each EQ (i.e.: boosting a band on one EQ while cutting the same band on the other EQ) can create 'comb-filter' simulated stereo.

Simulating Stereo. One way to open up the sound of a track in the mix is to simulate stereo by using a digital delay. The effect you're after here is doubling, and it usually requires from 20 to 40 milliseconds of delay time. For the most part you don't need to use modulation, which varies the delay time, but a small amount of modulation applied at a slow speed can add naturalness to the doubling effect. No 'feedback' is used at all.

The key to getting this doubling to open up the stereo image is to use pan controls to place the dry signal and the delayed signal on opposite sides of the mix. This doesn't need to be done with extreme panning, but simply by placing one signal somewhat to the left and the other somewhat to the right. How far apart and out to the sides you go is your decision, but it tends to be annoying to have an important track such as a lead vocal or solo be way off center.

So to simulate stereo with a delay:

1. Use an effect send to route the dry signal into the delay.
2. Return the output of the delay to a signal point with a pan control—either an unused line input or an effect return with pan.
3. Set the delay for 20 to 40 milliseconds of delay, with no feedback and little or no modulation.
4. Pan the dry track towards one side of the mix, and the delay to the other side.

This processing is very effective on vocals, lead instruments, and both keyboard and guitar accompaniment tracks.

Pitch Transposers as Doublers. A very rich doubling effect can be generated by a pitch transposer (also known as a Harmonizer or pitch shifter). Because the doubling is created by pitch shifting, it sounds different than a digital delay to double a signal. To use a pitch transposer as a doubler, select a very small amount of pitch shift. If the shifter has both a 'manual' and 'chromatic' position, you'll want to use the 'manual' knob and adjust it for just a very slight detuning, which is far les than the smallest chormatic interval (a half-step in musical terms). See Figure 8.26.

Stereo Chorusing. A chorus unit can also simulate stereo. The process is identical to the one just described with a digital delay. Some stereo choruses have two 'effected' outputs, so you can bring them back in stereo, pan them left and right, and then have your dry track panned between them, close to the center. Otherwise, bring the effect back so that it's opposite the dry signal.

Beware of Long Decays. Digital reverbs have progressed to the point where studio-quality ambience can be added to any system inexpensively. What's even more surprising is that these low-cost units do a credible job with long decay times, providing the sound of a gymnasium or a cathedral. It's easy to get carried away with the grand wash of sound these reverb settings provide, but they should be used with great caution.

This long-decay reverberation is most useful when there is just one instrument or vocal present, or a very sparse combination of signals. If you apply it to a lead vocal and then later try to mix it in with a rhythm track,

you'll find that the long decay on the vocals results in a mushy overall sound, no matter how 'tight' the rhythm section is. So reserve long decays for special moments, where only a few sonic elements are in the spotlight. Medium and short decay times work far better when all the tracks come together.

How Much Through One Reverb? There's a tendency when mixing to heap reverb on every track. Usually this is done with an effect send, and more or less reverb, using the same reverb setting, is applied to most tracks.

Far from adding to the feeling of a recording, this practice may reduce clarity and muddy up the mix. If you need proof, try listening just to the output of the reverb when four or five different signals are running into it. Usually the sound is somewhat analogous to bashing on garbage can lids. It's far better to get one tasteful reverb setting and apply it judiciously to one or two tracks than to try and enhance all tracks with a little of the same reverb setting. Now that digital reverbs are so inexpensive, consider adding a second or even third unit to cover additional tracks. These add-on units don't need to have many features—just look for one with a reasonable collection of good-sounding presets.

Another consideration is whether to add reverb to a track at all. Certain tracks cry out for reverberation, while others lose far more than they gain. Under most circumstances you won't want to apply reverb to either the kick drum or bass (whether it's an electric bass or synthesizer), because the tightness of the rhythm section will disappear and mush out. On the other hand, it may be hard to conceive of vocals, snare drum, or solo tracks without reverb.

Of course, there are no hard and fast rules; there may be a time when some gated reverb on a kick drum is just what the doctor ordered. Similarly, sometimes *not* using reverb is the perfect 'sonic statement': A dry vocal track may have just the right sparsity or intimacy for a given song. Use your creative judgement, but keep in mind that the ear gets confused if presented with too many spatial cues at once.

Track Thickening. The purpose of ail the signal treatments we've just described is to thicken or add body to a track. Doubling, chorus, and small amounts of pitch shift are all ways to make a track sound more dense.

But keep in mind that sometimes effects that are based on delay (such as all of those just listed) end up making a track sound thinner rather than thicker. This happens because of phase cancellation, and it is especially noticeable when short delay times are used, because the cancellations then take place in the mid and upper frequency ranges. Effects such as flanging and phase shifting should only be used sparingly on most tracks, because they are based on phase cancellation. This is great if you want a rhythm guitar to sound ethereal, but most likely a flanging or phasing effect will destroy a lead track such as a vocal if it is applied for more than just a few bars or one section of a song.

Natural doubling is a perfect alternative, particularly for vocal tracks. The idea is to record a second track, while singing or playing exactly what was recorded in the first track. Being human, we're never able to

duplicate *exactly*, and the small imperfections which result are what serve to thicken the sound. For vocal tracks, it's particularly effective to pan the original and doubled tracks to opposite sides of the mix during mixdown. If you've managed to sing the line with a 'tight' enough double, the results should be most pleasing.

Compression

The control of dynamics is crucial to successful recording. Levels that get out of hand and exceed the signal-handling capability of a recorder or mixer will destroy a recording with distortion. Compression and limiting are the processes used to reduce dynamic range and keep levels under control. The opposite problem is a lack of dynamic range, as is the case when the noise on a track starts to be equal to signals recorded at a low level. Gates and expanders can be used to increase the range between the lowest and highest signal levels.

These functions have been discussed at length, starting on page 55. But there are a host of other applications for both compressor/limiters and expander/gates that go beyond the simple management of dynamics.

Frequency-Dependent Compression. Most compressors now include a *side-chain*, a patch point that allows modification of the compressor's control loop. The complete lowdown on the side-chain can be found on page 58. One application that has been discussed for the side-chain is frequency-dependent gating; see page 58 for the details. The same idea can be applied to compressors, to make them more sensitive in selected frequency bands.

This selective sensitivity comes in very handy when dealing with tracks where certain notes seem to 'run away' or stick out noticeably. This can be caused by a variety of factors. One source is 'hot spots' from the placement of microphones too close to some areas of an instrument. This can be particularly true of the piano or vibes, which are hard to mike uniformly. Another cause can be uneven response of a guitar or bass, or of a speaker system used to amplify them. Regardless of the source, frequency-dependent compression can help to eliminate unevenness.

De-essing is a form of frequency-dependent compression. Here the compressor's side-chain is made sensitive to a fairly narrow band of frequencies that contain most of the energy produced by 's' sounds. You'll find everything you need to know about de-essing on page 58.

Compressing The Whole Mix. Many personal studios now have a stereo compressor as part of the equipment list. The idea of compressing the entire stereo mix doesn't seem so great at first, since you've just spent a huge amount of effort to make sure that everything gets recorded with the most dynamic range possible. But there are times when the energy contained in a mix might overload some signal destinations.

If you're going to apply compression to the mix, be kind to your recording. Only use as much compression as is needed to prevent distortion; any further compression will just serve to make your recording sound lifeless. Compression ratios (on units that allow manual adjustment) should be very gentle, on the order of 2:1, and attack times should be slow. The threshold should be set to affect only peaks and the upper end of the dynamic range—rather than providing constant compression.

Remember also that there's a time-honored way to deal with dynamics, called *gain riding*. There was, after all, a time before there were compressors, and engineers of that era also had a way to deal with levels. They quite simply kept their fingers on the faders, and when something was too loud, they'd turn it down. As soon as the excessive volume was over, they'd turn the channel back up.

This sounds primitive, but there are situations where it makes more sense to ride gain than to compress. If you're working on a track that has just one section where things get out of control, it's better to do a couple of run-throughs and figure out exactly how much to move the faders and how quickly, rather than pass the signal through another set of electronics. Each processing device adds noise, distortion, and phase shift, all of which degrade the signal. If you can take care of a dynamic problem with the simple flick of a wrist, don't bother using a compressor.

Compression And Fade Outs. A compressor that's applied to the whole mix can ruin a fade out. Here's why: If heavy compression is used, a large part of the dynamic range is over the threshold of the compressor, so that compression is happening nearly all the time. As you begin to fade out, the compressor is still working to reduce dynamic range, so that even though you're providing the compressor with less input, the output is still fairly even—after all, it is compressed. It is not until you cross under the threshold point that you get 1 dB of reduction in the output of the compressor for every 1 dB you put in. Moral of the story: don't overcompress the mix or dub!

Gates and Expanders

The functional opposite of a compressor, expanders are used to increase dynamic range. Gates are expanders with a typically fast attack rate and a high degree of gain reduction below the threshold setting (page 57).

Gates and expanders are used to make low-level signals even lower. In this way they can eliminate or reduce noise. But there are other applications that make use of the side-chain or *key input* that extend the usefulness of expander/gates. Let's look at some of the applicable techniques.

Gates For Noise Or Leakage Reduction. This is the most straightforward application of a gate. If you're using an expander with variable controls, set them for a high ratio of expansion (1:8 or greater), use fast release times, and medium-to-fast attack times.

Get an expander/gate with attack, release, and range controls, instead of a simplified unit that just does noise reduction. The modest additional cost is more than made up for by the control over attack, release, and range of gain reduction, all of which are needed to optimize a gate's response.

Frequency-Dependent Gating. This technique uses an equalizer patched into the 'side-chain' jacks of the gate (see page 58). It can be used to make the gate cut off signals in a selected frequency band. One application is to remove the squeak from a bass drum pedal.

Changing Decay Times. Just as a compressor can be used to increase sustain (see page 57), an expander can be used to shorten decay—which is very useful for tightening up the overall 'punch' of tracks. The trick here is to set the 'attack,' 'release,' and 'range' controls to moderate positions so that the effect is not too obvious. The sustained, full-volume signal should be above the threshold of expansion, while the decay portion should fall below the threshold.

Expansion can be used to cut down the ring of a tubby-sounding drum, to tighten up a bass or piano part that was played with too much sustain, or to vary the decay time of spring reverbs that have no control over decay. It can also be used to create 'gated reverb' on a digital reverb that has no 'gated' settings. And even if you have a reverb with 'gated' settings, you might want to use a longer reverb sound and shorten it by expansion for a different tonality.

Exciters and Enhancers

Exciters and enhancers are a relatively new category of signal processing. They use several different processes to alter the harmonic content of a signal in a way that improves clarity and definition. For a complete description, see page 59.

When To Enhance. Should you apply enhancement in the mix, or is it better to enhance individual tracks? The answer is, "Do both." Enhancement can add to many different tracks, lending sparkle to piano, vocal, snare, and even bass guitar tracks—especially when recorded using round-wound strings. It also tends to add clarity and improve the perceived separation between different tracks in the mix. Finally, enhancers really shine when it comes to making 'dubs' or cassette copies. They do a great job of combating the loss of clarity usually associated with generation loss.

Remember that if you apply enhancement to every track and to both the mix and dubs, the result may become over-enhanced. The sound of an over-enhanced tape is too bright, and somewhat brittle. Remember that most enhancers have a control that regulates which frequency band they're active in. If you find that all your enhancement is taking place in the same band, the result will likely be brittle in the final mix. So choose which tracks to enhance carefully, giving preference to elements that you want to stand out. Don't enhance every single track, or the edge that an enhancer offers will be obliterated. And, of course, remember that enhancers may not be for everyone, or for every recording application.

MIDI and Signal Processing

Applications of MIDI control to recording have blossomed. MIDI can be used to automate a mixer, to pull off changes on a reverb that would be impossible by hand, to vary equalization, even to add harmonies where none existed before! Many of the advantages of MIDI are related to its ability to automate functions, such as:

- Muting and level changes.
- EQ changes.
- Effects changes.
- All MIDI instrument parts.

Please note that all the MIDI techniques described require synchronization of the tape recorder to either a sequencer or to software running on a computer that has a MIDI interface. For more details about MIDI and synchronization, see pages 106 and 110.

Lesson Seven: Mixing Down

Mixing down is the process whereby individual tracks become a unified whole. The idea of mixing down is to create a *master tape*, from which additional copies can be generated. These copies can be anything from cassette tapes to phonograph records to compact discs. A master tape is made because it's cumbersome to return to the multi-track tape original every time a copy needs to be made, especially when a mix involves a lot of steps and moves. So the master tape is (in most cases) a stereo mix that combines the individual tracks of a multi-track tape with any additional *virtual tracks* and with signal processing. Virtual tracks, as discussed on page 109, are those added by syncing synthesizer and/or drum machine units to the tape recorder.

Mix time is also the moment of decision. It's time to consider which tracks to keep and which to abandon. It is also quite likely that you'll want to use parts of all tracks even if you don't use an entire track. A rhythm guitar overdub that drones on through an entire song might be just the touch needed for the choruses and the bridge. Another set of decisions surround aesthetic choices, such as what type of effects and signal processing treatments to apply. Luckily, in the surroundings of your own studio it's possible to indulge in some experimentation.

Cleaning Up Tracks

Mixing can be the most enjoyable phase of recording, since the entire work comes to life and takes its final shape during the mix. Sometimes, however, it can be a harrowing experience, especially when you're required to make a lot of 'moves.' A move can be changing the position of a fader, turning on or off a mute, or altering the setting of an effect send knob. There are ways to simplify the mixing process—and one of the best is to remove extraneous noise and unused material from tracks, before the actual mix takes place.

Take the case of a background vocal overdub. In many instances, background vocals are only present during a chorus, or perhaps behind part of a second or third verse. If a performer coughs during a section of the song that doesn't have background vocals, the cough will most likely be recorded—unless you've meticulously punched in at the exact 'in' and 'out' points. Using the punch-in technique discussed on page 91, you can replace any extraneous noises or unused sections with silence. Simply turn the mixer outputs down so no new signal is being fed to the recorder.

Of course you'll need to monitor what you're doing, because you're doing a form of overdubbing, and if you run into the material you mean to keep, it will be destroyed. It is beneficial to map out exactly what you plan to get rid of, track by track, making sure to use the counter to double-check that you're at the point that you should be. If you're relying on the counter, it is crucial that it be set to the correct reference point. If 'zero' is the downbeat of the first measure, make sure that the counter is

still 'zeroed' correctly before punching in.

Also remember that *muting* can be used to cut off the signal from a track without recording over it; this technique is described below.

Stereo Placement

Part of the mixdown decision process is what kind of stereo image to create. You need to figure out where along the panorama from left speaker to right (or left ear to right) you wish each instrument to be placed. This is an area where your creativity can take over, but it's possible to create a stereo image that makes trouble later on, especially in the cutting of phonograph records. A mastering lathe may destroy the lacquer being cut if there's too much off-center energy. It's also possible to cause listener discomfort when things are too unbalanced.

Keep Heavy Elements In The Center. There are a couple of instruments in particular that can throw an entire mix out of kilter: the kick drum, and the bass. It's standard practice to place these sounds in the center—that is, with the 'pan' control straight up, at the middle of its travel. This is done for the reasons mentioned before, namely mastering problems and listener fatigue. Like all rules there can be exceptions, but you'll find that it is uncomfortable to try and listen very long when any heavy sonic element is too far to one side or the other.

That doesn't mean that both kick drum and bass need to be dead center, but it's good to keep them within 10 degrees of the middle, with only a slight spread. Any other 'heavy' tracks should also be reasonably on center, such as synthesizer bass, unless you're deliberately trying to create an effect.

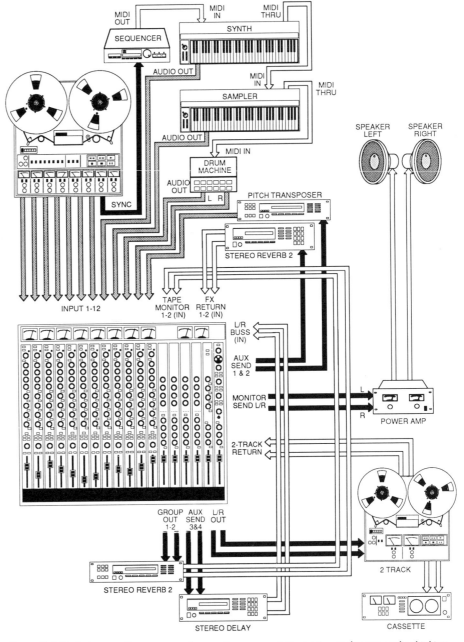

Figure 12.10 Typical connections necessary for a contemporary mixing session. In this case, we're thinking creatively, and are using the group outputs (which are normally unused during a mix) as additional effects sends; we're also using the left/right buss input and two channels of the tape monitor as effects returns.

Beware Of Hard Panning. Another disconcerting situation may result from *hard panning*, which is placing a track all the way to the left or right. As with too many off-center heavy elements, having a track buzzing away in only one ear can easily be tiring (just listen to some of the early Beatle's stereo recordings as evidence).

It's natural to want to create as wide a spatial sense as possible, but it should be done with care. Just keep in mind that it may become annoying to have one of your most important tracks panned way out to the side. The extremes should be reserved for effects (see "Creating Stereo" immediately below) and for lesser enhancement tracks. Hard left and right can also be used to great advantage when you want a track to start out on one side and end up on the other, as might be done at the end of a solo.

Creating Stereo. One way to open up the spatial feeling of a mix is to add stereo depth. Stereo can be created using digital delay, chorus, flanging or reverb. See pages 94 and 95 for descriptions of how these effects can be used to thicken a mono track.

An effect device known as a *stereo synthesizer* may also be used, although delay units are now lower in cost and offer a more dramatic and defined stereo effect.

Mix Rehearsal

It will save both time and energy to rehearse a mixdown several times. The difficulty of a mix is determined by the number of tracks and effects and the number of moves involved—but almost all mixes seem to end up with at least one tricky section. Rather than have to run through a whole mix over again, it makes sense to practice the more difficult passages before rolling the tape on the mix machine.

Cues. Just as a track sheet helped to keep all the tracks and overdubs straightened out, a list of points that require special action during a mix is equally handy. This list is called a *cue sheet*. Committing the changes to paper frees up your mind to work on the mix rather than working to remember. The tape counter is a most useful reference for identifying cue points—just make sure that the zero point has been correctly set each time or you could easily find yourself off by a verse!

Mutes. If you know what you're doing, mutes can be great friends. Here's how they can help. Usually you'll have tracks that aren't active during the entire mix. Mutes allow these tracks to be shut off when they're not needed, which greatly reduces noise. One of the great things about noise is that we humans are fooled by the *masking effect*, whereby a loud sound temporarily reduces our awareness of lower-level sounds such as noise. Thus if a track can be kept muted when no signal is present, the masking effect will take care of noise when a recorded signal is there. So a mix where unused tracks are kept muted will sound cleaner and quieter—in general, far more professional. Mutes may make a mix more complicated, but they're well worth the trouble—be sure to mark them on your cue sheet.

It's possible to perform muting on almost all mixers, even those without a separate 'mute' button. The buss assignment button can serve the same purpose by muting a channel when no outputs are assigned, and even the 'Mic-Line' switch will do in a pinch. It's also possible to simply pull the channel fader all the way down. Make sure that if you're throwing switches to accomplish the mute that the switch is noiseless; otherwise it may interject objectionable clicks into the mix.

Control Changes. Other cues that are important in a mix include changes in level, equalization, effect send level, and pan. If a control change takes place gradually, the cue sheet should include both the starting and ending point. This way it's easier to gauge how rapidly to change a control. Remember that all the tools of a mixer are available for creative alterations during a mix. For instance, it can be very dramatic to gradually boost the amount of reverb at the end of a guitar solo or at the peak of a vocal passage. Sweeping a signal gradually from one side to the other can be equally attention-getting, and tasteful use of the pan control can keep this effect from becoming distracting.

The most common change is in level. It's very common to need to raise and lower tracks during different sections of the mix, and it's generally far more interesting to listen to a mix that features different instruments or combinations of tracks in the foreground as a performance moves from section to section. Careful attention to the cue sheet will make this process much simpler. Once the moves have been defined, it's just a matter of running through the moves until they're down pat.

Using Subgroups: 'Semi-Automation'

One way to simplify mixdowns that involve many tracks and effects is to use *subgroups*. As introduced on page 34, subgroups are the group buss outputs of a mixer. Many mixers allow these 'groups' to be assigned back and panned into the stereo or left-right buss at mix time. In this way, a number of individual tracks can first be assigned to a subgroup, which then allows the entire group to be raised or lowered in the mix by moving the fader for the subgroup rather than the individual faders for each track.

This is particularly useful for drums, especially when they're being added as 'virtual tracks' by using MIDI and sync-to-tape at mix time. Drum machines with individual outputs can have eight or more separate outs—and it's very difficult to try to raise and lower all eight at once and still maintain the correct balance between them. Subgrouping allows us to get the correct balance between the individual drums, and then raise and lower all of them with one, or in the case of stereo, two faders. This makes it easy to get the drums at the right level in the mix without having to move all the individual faders every time. Here are the steps to subgroup:

1. Assign all the tracks or inputs to be grouped into one or two console busses.
2. If two busses are being used for stereo, set the pan control for each input.
3. Assign the subgroup(s) into the stereo or left-right buss, or patch to the 'buss in' points for the stereo (L-R) buss.

4. Use the subgroup fader(s) to mix the grouped tracks into the mix.

Preparing The 2-Track

Our next step is to prepare the 2-track recorder for recording. Any device capable of stereo recording can be used to make a master tape. Most common in professional studios is the half-track recorder, where the full width of a 1/4-inch tape is used to record just two tracks. Advantages of this format include excellent signal-to-noise ratio (compared to other analog recorders) and ease of editing. This comes in handy later on when you might wish to assemble tracks in another order, or to actually rearrange a composition (page 101).

A PCM-encoder with a video deck offers very high-quality masters, as does the DAT format. Alternately, a down-to-earth way to make master recordings of near-digital quality is to use a video recorder with enhanced audio, such as a Beta Hi-Fi or VHS Hi-Fi recorder.

Finally, even the lowly cassette deck is capable of turning out a respectable master for many purposes, and is a mixdown format that nearly everyone already owns. (Refer to page 28 for more in-depth description of these formats.)

Regardless of the format you're using, the steps to mix down are still the same. First of all is routine maintenance. Before a session begins, make sure that heads are clean and that all metal parts are demagnetized. This process naturally differs according to the recorder employed; follow the instructions for cleaning and demagnetization that are part of every owner's manual.

Alignment of the heads and calibration of the recorder are equally important. If you're using an analog cassette or open-reel deck, be sure the machine is calibrated for the proper tape choice (page 5).

Selecting Tape Inputs. Once tape has been mounted on the mixdown machine, the next step is to select the input mode on the mix deck. When the recorder is in this mode, it's normally possible to see the meters moving when the multi-track tape is routed to the mixdown deck's inputs. On professional 3-head decks this is accomplished by pressing a button labelled 'source,' 'input,' or sometimes 'line.'

On many other machines, including 2-head cassette recorders, input mode is selected by putting the deck into record, or to press 'record' and 'pause' if you don't wish the recording to begin. It's best not to leave any recorder in this mode for an excessive amount of time; video recorders can wear out the tape, and audio machines generally aren't that happy about it either. So just use this setting to make sure that the mix machine is receiving signal, and to set levels so that distortion will not take place in the mix.

Selecting The Multi-Track To Repro Mode. The multi-track machine should now be set so that the tape is monitored from the playback or reproduce head. With professional 3-head multi-track recorders (which have a playback head that's distinct from the record head), 'repro' mode should be selected. Two-head machines will automatically be set correctly when all channels are in playback, rather than 'record ready' modes.

Assigning Inputs To The Mix Buss

The process of mixing down requires that all the recorded material on the multi-track machine be blended together into a stereo, two-channel mix. The mixing board that was used to direct the mixer inputs to the tape tracks can now serve its second mixing function, which is to gather together the outputs of the multi-track machine and send them to a pair of outputs for mixing.

With many ministudios it's simply a matter of selecting 'tape' at the inputs; the signals are then routed to the ministudio's stereo outputs.

Most multi-track mixers feed the 2-track via a stereo ('L/R,' or 'mix') output. Some, however, require you to send the inputs to a pair of buss outputs; most people would use busses 1 and 2, though any pair will do. Depending upon the mixer these buss outputs will either serve as the stereo output, or will in turn feed another stereo output.

Assigning and Returning Effects

Almost every recording can use a little spice, and effects are the way to add it. After all channels are assigned and ready to mix, it's time to work on the effects. There are several ways to patch effects into a console. Most obvious is to use a *aux send*, which is an auxiliary buss that picks up the input signal and sends it to an effect.

Most 'effects send' aux busses get their signal after the fader (making them *post-fader*), so that if an input is faded out of a mix, or muted, the effect will be faded or muted as well. A pre-fader send is like an independent mix, so if you use a pre-fader 'cue send' to get into an effect, be aware that turning down the input fader won't affect any pre-fader send's level—though a 'gain' or 'pad' control *will*, because it comes before the send in the signal path.

It's best to use an aux send when more than one input needs to be routed to the same effect. If reverberation needs to be applied to both vocals and drums, an aux send is the way to go. *Channel patching*, on the other hand, puts an effect into the signal path of a single input—by using the channel's *insert* point. This would be ideal if, for instance, delay is only desired on the lead guitar.

There are a couple of additional ways to get into more effects from a mixer. If your console has individual or odd-even assignment switches for the output group busses, it's possible to use those outputs as makeshift effect sends. As an example, you'll typically be using outputs one and two, or the left-right out for the mix. If outputs three and four can be accessed without losing the assignment to the mix, these outputs can be connected to an additional effect. This technique naturally requires a place to return the effect into the mix, such as an unused input, an effect return, or a buss-in jack. (See Figure 12.10.)

In order for an effect to become part of a mix, its output has to be combined back into the buss that's being used to mix down, usually the stereo or left-right buss. Most mixers and ministudios have a provision for this, labeled 'effect return.' A stereo effect return may consist only of a pair of jacks that feed signal back into the mix, or there may be a level control provided. When there's no level control it's necessary to use the

output level control on the effect to get the correct level.

Unfortunately, some effects don't provide such a control; in this case you'll have to adjust the 'send' level to give the correct output. This is not the ideal method for ending up with the best signal-to-noise performance, but if you've set the input gain to the correct range before starting, the level should be just about right without having to reduce or increase the 'send' level too much.

Monaural effect returns often have a pan control so that the output of an effect can be centered in the mix or thrown over to one side or the other. Remember that if you return an effect to one side of a stereo return the signal will only show up in the extreme left or extreme right side of the mix, which can be disconcerting! Use of a simple patching box such as a Boss J-44 or a Peavey Patching Adaptor allows you to *mult* the same signal into both jacks, so that even though there's no stereo panning, at least the effect won't only be on one side. 'Mult' is short for multiply, and a 'mult' is simply a series of jacks that are all connected together so that the same input is available at two or more outputs. A 'y' cord is the simplest form of a 'mult.' (Multing signals together rather than splitting, by the way, should be limited to just two inputs from the same type of source; different levels from sources with different impedances can cause sonic problems when multed together without a mixer.)

Keep in mind that any unused inputs in a mixer can be used for the return of an effect. An effect return is in fact just a line input with very few functions. To use an input as a return, simply plug the output of an effect into the 'line' input. *Caution*: When using inputs as effect returns make sure that the 'send' controls are turned all the way down, to avoid feedback.

You can also bring a number of effects back into a line mixer and then plug the output of the line mixer into effect returns or unused line inputs. For instance, if the outputs of four stereo effects need to be fed into one stereo effect return, a line mixer such as a Tascam Model 1, Rane SM26, Kawai MX8R, or Fostex 2050 can combine the various effect outputs into one stereo mix. The individual level and pan controls can be used to determine relative effect levels, and to place the outputs of the effects in proper left-right perspective. This 'effects submix' can then be handled by one pair of returns.

There are additional jacks that most mixer owners rarely look at which can serve as additional effect returns. Many recorder/mixers not only have effect returns, but they also include a 'L-R buss in' pair of jacks, which also feed the mix buss and are identical to the effect return in function—though lack level and pan controls. If you have the type of board that allows subgroups to be used in the mix (see page 37), you may find that each subgroup also includes a 'buss in' jack—which can be used as yet another effect return.

The majority of English consoles and almost any mixer with a *split monitor* (page 41) have a wealth of effect returns. When the tape outputs are routed into the line inputs, all of the tape monitor inputs are available

for additional effect returns or for the input of virtual tracks. This usually requires a patch bay, although some designs include a switch that places the output of an effect into the tape monitor input jack.

Finally, with some creative thinking, many *in-line monitor* (page 41) consoles can be patched to allow their tape monitor inputs to be used as additional line inputs during mixdown. As with split-monitor consoles, the tape monitor inputs normally feed the stereo output. Since (in most mixdown sessions) the tape recorder outputs are being routed to the channel line inputs rather than the tape monitor inputs, the latter are free to accept other line inputs, such as effects outputs! By simply plugging effects devices—or synced drum machines or anything else that needs additional inputs—into the tape monitor inputs, your mixdown capabilities can be greatly expanded.

Balance

It's time to run through the mix, and get everything in balance. The concept of balance is slightly odd when it comes to mixing multi-track. The goal is not to blend everything to the point of boredom, but rather to figure out how to highlight certain parts of the performance at different places. At the chorus, for example, it might work best for the vocals to be prominent, while the bridge might cry out for the sax part to garner the most attention. So balance means that the tracks that should be in front are clearly audible, but the background tracks should be strong enough to provide a solid foundation for the mix to build on.

One common problem is pushing the lead tracks so far to the front that they lose the support of the other tracks. Even the most searing guitar solo will better captivate the listener when presented against a clearly audible backdrop of additional supporting and driving sounds. Similarly, there may be a temptation to present each supporting track as fully as possible. But if each track is pushed to the 'max,' nothing will have a chance to stand out. Consequently, use restraint when balancing your mix—many times, less is truly more.

Even with 24 or more tracks available, few artists use all tracks at once. The main purpose of all those tracks is to allow more choices in the mix. Each section of the mix should feature a few elements, with the other tracks serving a supporting role. As a basic example, a piano track might be featured as the backup to a vocal during a verse, while strings might swell behind the vocal in a chorus. Don't try and thrust more than two or three parts forward at any one moment; all that will happen is that the listener will become bewildered rather than enchanted.

Another recommendation is that bass be treated with discretion. It might sound impressive to 'goose' the low end of a recording when playing it back over your system, but chances are that all the bass boost will make a recording sound mushy.

The Mix

Now that a reasonable balance between tracks has been achieved, it is time to rehearse the final mix. A rehearsal includes level changes, mute on's and off's, panning

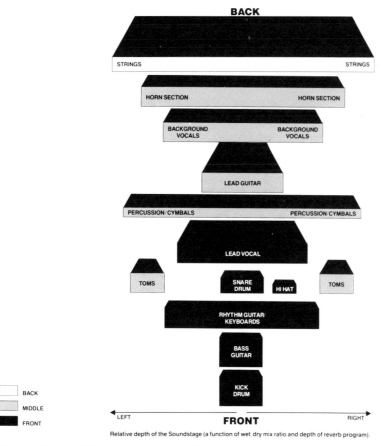

BACK

STRINGS   STRINGS

HORN SECTION   HORN SECTION

BACKGROUND   BACKGROUND
VOCALS   VOCALS

LEAD GUITAR

PERCUSSION/CYMBALS   PERCUSSION/CYMBALS

LEAD VOCAL

TOMS   SNARE   HI HAT   TOMS
                 DRUM

RHYTHM GUITAR/
KEYBOARDS

BASS
GUITAR

KICK
DRUM

□ BACK
▨ MIDDLE
■ FRONT

LEFT ←   FRONT   RIGHT →

Relative depth of the Soundstage (a function of wet/dry mix ratio and depth of reverb program).

Figure 12.11 Left to right balance, and front-to-back depth are two critical elements of the mix. This diagram (from an Alesis Microverb manual) shows us some conventional 'locations' for different instruments. The width of each block represents the left-to-right stereo imaging. The front-to-back dimension of each block represents the relative sense of depth created by different reverb programs (small room, hall, etc.). The height of each block roughly indicates the frequency response of each instrument group. The shading (dark, medium, light) indicates each instrument's front to back placement in the mix, which is dependent upon the wet/dry mix of the reverb, or the level of the reverb returns at the board.

moves, and effect variations. Depending on the complexity of a mix, several run-throughs may be required before all moves can be memorized. Don't get discouraged; if you have to do it ten times, rest assured that you're certainly not the first to whom it has happened. This is why you have your own recording gear—take as much time as you need to get it right!

Once all the moves are rehearsed, put the two-track machine into record, start the multi-track, and make your master recording.

Listening To What You've Got

Knowing *how* to listen to what you've got is as important as laying it down to begin with. Don't rush to accept a flawed mix; most likely you'll be living with the results of the mix for quite a while, and the little things that are wrong will haunt and come to annoy you.

Alternate Monitoring. Using an alternative set of monitors can throw the strong and weak points of a mix into relief. Generally speaking, a mix that sounds good on two different sets of speakers will hold up well on most systems. Monitor speakers go in and out of fashion—one year it's Urei and Auratones, and the next it's Meyer and Yamaha. But too much emphasis is placed on having the same monitors as Mr. Big Producer. All that really matters is to come up with a good reference point, or better yet, two good references.

A set of monitors with extended bass is preferable as a main system; many studios use a smaller pair of speakers located right at

the console as the alternative set. These are called *near-field monitors*. Because they're close to the listener, the coloration of room acoustics is less of a factor. Hopefully this secondary reference will give a good picture of how your mix will sound over small- and medium-sized speakers.

Keep in mind that there are no real rules to tell you which monitors are right and wrong—though as we discussed on page 69, they should be as *accurate* as possible. Any speakers that give you accurate results are worthwhile monitors, even if they happen to be the set already connected to your hi-fi.

One way to check the utility of your monitor speakers is as follows: Make mixes that sound good to you over your monitors, and then play them in a variety of places, such as at a friend's house, in the car, or over a Walkman. If the mix holds up in all these different situations, your monitoring situation is excellent. If not, your monitors may be inaccurate, they may be wired out of phase, or you may just need more mixing experience. Don't be discouraged—it takes a little time before you can create professional-sounding master tapes.

Finally, be sure to monitor the mix at a variety of volumes: A mix that sounds great at high volumes may fall apart when the volume is dropped to a quiet level. In fact, many professional engineers make the mistake of generally monitoring too loud—damaging not only their mixes but in the long run, their hearing as well. A few minutes at high volume makes sense to check your mix, but otherwise, there's no reason why the bulk of your mixing can't take place

at an ample but sane listening level.

Multiple Mixes. It's not uncommon to create multiple mixes of the same song. There are several reasons to do so. First, certain mixes may be more appropriate for particular listeners. Professional artists often create one mix for a pop release, another for an album, and yet a third for release to the dance market. If you're preparing a demo tape, think about what market you're trying to break into, and shape the mix for that reality.

It's also convenient once everything is set up to make another mix—just to have two or more mixes from which to choose. It's a chance to experiment with different things each time; later you can make up your mind which experiment was the most successful. Several mixes can also be combined, using editing, to make a new mix. If you loved the way the verses came out in one take, and are crazy about the choruses in the other they can be spliced together—as we'll learn about on page 101.

Making Dubs

Once the ideal mix is in the can, it's time to make copies, also known as *dubs*. The output from the 2-track machine must be redirected back into the mixing board so that the master tape can be copied onto another 2-track destination, usually a cassette machine. If you're working with a home hi-fi system, this task can be made very simple, since virtually all receivers include some method of hooking up two tape recorders, or at least have circuitry for both an 'aux' input and a tape machine. If your unit has provisions for two tape recorders, treat the output of the console as the 'aux' input, the output from the two-track machine as 'tape 1,' and the cassette machine as 'tape 2.'

If your hi-fi is less sophisticated, bring the 2-track machine back into the console (by using two line inputs if there's no dedicated '2-track return'), and then plug the console into the 'aux' input. Set your dub machine to 'source' if there's a tape/source switch; then set the levels and roll the tape, remembering of course to select 'record' on the dub machine. A pair of headphones can be useful to listen to the quality of the dub without having to re-patch the dub machine into the monitors; just plug right into the headphone jack that's found on the vast majority of cassette units.

Learning for the Next Session

Now it's time to move on to the next session, but it's important to review the work just completed for any insights that might be gleaned. This type of review will lead to better recordings in the future. Analyze the feel of the recording, and see if you've captured what you set out to preserve in the first place. Check the tempo. Was it too fast, too slow, or right on the money?

Pay attention to production values: Did that unique effect really work on the snare drum, or was that the correct microphone for the female vocalist with the wispy voice? It doesn't hurt to tear apart the recording just completed; it's not important to do it over again. Just figure out what is effective and what isn't, and apply the experience on the next go-round.

Lesson Eight: Advanced Session Techniques

Now that we've learned the basics of recording and mixing tracks, let's wrap up the session with some professional techniques you can use in your own studio.

For specialized techniques related to MIDI, synchronization, automation, and more, be sure to turn to Part IV of this book (page 106).

Mixing As You Go

Some mixing boards have a large enough number of inputs so that mixing and tracking can take place at the same time. Consoles with both discrete group outputs and an additional 'L-R' stereo buss are particularly well suited for this purpose. English consoles often follow this design.

If, for instance, 24 inputs are available, along with eight buss outputs, it's possible to bring the output of an 8- or 16-track recorder back to the mixer, while still using the last eight or 16 input channels to send additional sources out to the multi-track recorder. The tape tracks are returned to the line inputs, and are then assigned to the 'L-R' or stereo buss. At the same time, additional mike or line inputs can be sent to outputs 1 through 8.

By monitoring the 'L-R' buss, a stereo mix can be assembled at the same time that tracks are still being laid down; this is 'mixing as you go.' When the last track is finished, the mix may be almost completely done—a few finishing touches can be added as the whole mix is recorded onto the mastering machine.

Editing

There are a number of techniques that combine together to make up the craft of editing. They all involve cutting and leadering the recording (usually the 2-track master) for a number of purposes. One is to separate the selections and to insert the proper amount of blank space between them, which is crucially important if a phonograph record or CD is going to be pressed. Another may be to rearrange, shorten, or lengthen sections of a recording.

For our purposes, by the way, we'll assume that we're editing with an open-reel machine. It is possible to edit with a cassette machine, but the 1/8″ width of the tape makes editing a very cumbersome and difficult process. In addition, some techniques which we'll discuss—such as 'rocking' the tape, are impossible to perform with the average cassette recorder.

Splicing. Splicing is the joining of two pieces of tape with a special adhesive tape. For two pieces of tape to be joined cleanly together, a uniform cut in the tape must be made. A *splicing block* is used for this purpose. It's a piece of metal (or sometimes plastic, which is not recommended) with one or more slots in it that allow a razor blade to be slid across the tape at a fixed angle. The tape itself fits securely into a groove in the block, so it won't slide around while being cut. A grease pencil, available from office supply and stationery shops, is normally used to mark the points to be cut.

White is the most visible color, although red can also do the trick. There's a description of how to mark a point in the tape for cutting just below ("Cutting the 2-Track Master").

While some professional 2-track recorders have built-in splicing scissors, most of us cut tape with a single-edge razor blade. These are available from pro audio suppliers, but can also be found inexpensively at paint stores. However, make sure that the blades are ungreased, since some have a coating that will leave a residue on the tape. Also, discard a blade once it's been used a half-dozen times, because the blade soon becomes dull and it will leave a ragged edge on the cut edge of the tape. Finally, use a demagnetizer and thoroughly demagnetize the razor blade following the procedures and cautions described on page 86. A magnetized blade can cause an audible 'thump' when the splice passes over the play head.

To join together the two pieces of tape, first make the necessary cuts, then put the two ends to be spliced together in the groove that runs the length of the splicing block. Push them together gently, so they just meet and no gap is visible, but not so hard that they begin to pucker up. Now cut a length of splicing tape about 3/4 of an inch long (or slightly shorter). There are a number of ways to do this. One effective method is to take regular masking tape, and pile up three or four layers of it on any flat surface, making a thick strip about a foot long. Now pull the splicing tape off the roll (a regular Scotch tape dispenser will hold it conveniently), press it lightly on the masking tape, and gently slice across it with the razor blade. The extra thickness of the masking tape will prevent you from marring the surface you're working on. You can also use the tape dispenser to cut the splicing tape, although this leaves a more ragged edge.

Next, center the splicing tape over the groove in the splicing block, and over the cut edges of the tape. An easy way to do this is to pick up the cut piece of splicing tape with a corner of the razor blade, since it's far easier to hold on to the blade than to try and

maneuver the splicing tape with your fingers.

Once the splicing tape is positioned correctly, gently press it down, working from one end to the other so that bubbles and wrinkles aren't formed, and taking care that it's centered along the edges of the tape. The best splicing tape for permanent splices is mylar (3M model #67, for example), although acetate (3M model #41) is useful for splices that will be pulled apart later, since it's easier to take off. Acetate is popular in film and advertising work where sections of tape may be assembled and disassembled at various times.

Bear in mind, as you splice tape, that it's an easy matter to re-splice a tape if you've cut too little from the magnetic tape. Should you cut too much, it's a much harder—if not impossible—proposition to try and re-assemble tiny slivers of tape to correct your over-zealous use of the blade.

Leadering. Leader is a plastic or paper tape, the same width as the magnetic tape you're working with, that's inserted between cuts on a tape recording to separate them. In the past it was the convention to use paper leader between cuts and vinyl leader at the ends of the tape, but paper leader is going out of production, so vinyl materials have come to predominate.

Most splicing blocks have more than one angle for tape to be cut at; leader is usually attached with a straight butt splice, that is, with a straight 90-degree cut. Angled cuts are used in the midst of a tape, where a straight splice will cause a noticeable 'pop.' Leadering serves two purposes: It provides a visual reference that shows where you are in a tape; second, it allows you to time the interval between two cuts.

Cutting The 2-Track Master. We mentioned earlier a technique whereby the best parts of several mixes could be assembled into a final mix. For example, choruses can be added or deleted, or verses can switched around to match your heart's desire. Unless you're working in digital audio and have access to a sophisticated video-type editing

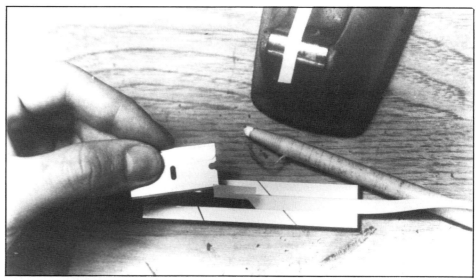

Figure 12.12 Splicing a leader onto the master tape (both are sitting in the splicing block). Note the technique of placing the splicing tape on a corner of the razor.

system—with cut-and-paste editing options (page 127)—the way to do this is by splicing together sections of the different mixes. The technique is quite simple. All that really matters is that there's an open interval of tape somewhere near the transition point.

Let's say we'd like to piece together a final mix of a song, by compiling several different sections of the song—each section being the best mix of that part of the song. The first step is to organize yourself, since it's quite easy to mix up your various tapes. You may prefer to keep each section on separate reels. Otherwise, you may wish to string together the sections on one reel, joining them loosely as if you were joining various pieces of leader tape.

For this example, let's say we've done the latter—that all of our sections are on the same reel, loosely spliced together. Our task is to go in and splice them perfectly, so that the various sections join without any audible 'seams,' and without any changes in the beat.

Play the first mix section up to the point that you wish to cut to a new mix. Stop the recorder. Now drop the tape lifters by engaging the 'cue' control—if your recorder is fitted with one—or just 'rock' the tape across the heads.

Rocking is simply using your hands to turn the reels slowly while the recorder is in 'edit' or 'stop' mode. Your fingers are spread out across the front of the reel, and the reel should turn with just slight energy applied by the hands. If it doesn't, something is wrong, and you shouldn't force it. When plastic reels are used, try and find the type with solid sides, since the reels with cut-outs make it easy to touch and possibly bend the edge of the tape.

While you're rocking, the signal should be audible. It sounds just like you'd expect a tape to sound if it was played back at a fraction of its normal speed. But with a little practice, it's possible to get used to hearing the tape rocked over the heads and to identify exactly where in a mix you're at.

Look for an open gap between beats, where there's no reverberation or sustain carrying over. You'll also want to be aware of timing and keeping the beat. If, for example, you cut immediately following the beat, you'll want to make sure that the following section maintains the same rhythm. One trick is to listen to a steady beat reference, such as a kick or snare drum. By measuring the amount of tape between beats, you'll be able to match up sections which you later splice in so that the same amount of tape transpires between beats over the splice.

A recommended risk-free exercise is to take a song that you're already familiar with—either your own or a commercial recording—and mix it to your 2-track open-reel machine. Set yourself some goals, such as reversing the choruses, or doubling the length of the introduction, and splice away! You'll find that while editing is challenging, once your comfortable handling the blade, the block, and the tape, it's more fun than hard work.

Now mark the tape at this exact point by using a grease pen and making a mark at the center of the playback head. Cut the tape here using an angle cut. Remove the front reel from the recorder, which should contain the performance up to this point.

Thread a second take-up reel; this will be used to hold the unwanted tape that follows the section we just saved, and precedes the *next* mix section. (If your tape recorder has an 'edit' mode, you can put the recorder in play and the machine will 'dump' this unwanted tape; however, a second reel will make the next procedure easier to accomplish.)

Now find the beginning of the second mix. Use the rocking procedure to find the correct point in the recording, and again mark and cut the tape. Now re-mount the first reel of tape on the take-up (right) side, and splice the first part of the first mix to the next part of the second mix. Again, you'll want to listen for your beat reference, and make sure that the same amount of tape passes between beats over the splice as exists in non-spliced passages. Of course, if your rhythm is changing, or you're playing free-time, your splicing talent will have to 'wing' it.

When the second mix is joined to the first, advance the tape to the point where you wish to make another splice, and repeat the process over again.

Although it might sound tedious, this process can actually save a tremendous amount of time in the studio. Instead of having to make a mix that's perfect from beginning to end, each section can be mixed with attention to the most minute detail, and then these sections can be assembled into a mix that's greater than the sum of its parts.

This same concept can be used to advantage if an otherwise good-sounding recording is too short. Figure out which section or sections can be repeated, and then make another master mix of these sections. Use the procedure described above to insert an extra verse or chorus, and your composition is complete, with just a minimum of additional time in the studio!

Similarly, excessive material can be lifted out of the master by editing. Many open-reel 2-track units have a 'dump edit' feature, which allows the supply (left-hand) reel to turn and spill tape even though the take-up (right-hand) reel is not moving. Make a cut at the end of the section you wish to save, right at the beginning of the section to be deleted.

Multi-Track Editing. It's a good idea to insert leader tape between the selections on the multi-track recorder as well. The easiest way to do this is to spin on a piece of leader right after you finish cutting the basics, or at least when the track is finished. This will make it much harder to accidentally rewind too far and record over a finished multi-track performance.

Once in a great while it may be necessary to cut up a multi-track master in the manner just described for 2-track recordings, but it is far better to attempt this maneuver on a 2-track copy, instead of sacrificing the multi-track tape. After all, if you blow it on the multi-track it's back to the drawing board, whereas it's always possible to pull another mix if necessary.

Preparing Your Master Tape

Your *master tape* is the assembled collection of your music. It can be one song, or it can be an album's worth of tunes. While many people prepare a master tape of their work just for their own listening, if you plan to make copies of your work—for friends, demo purposes, or commercial purposes—you'll need to prepare a master tape. From this tape a *mastering lab* can create multiple cassette, LP record, or Compact Disc reproductions.

People create masters on everything from cassette tape to digitally-encoded video cassettes. While many predict that the DAT format may become the next mixdown of choice, for the time being most master tapes are created on half-track open-reel equipment. In this section we'll look at two important details for preparing a master tape. The first is getting the songs in the correct order—which is fairly intrinsic to the purpose of creating a master tape. Secondly, we'll look at 'slating' your master tape with test tones—a very important procedure for any analog master tape destined for a professional mastering lab.

Getting Tracks In Order. If you're submitting your tape to a mastering facility, you'll want to get your songs into the order that they should appear on your album. It helps to have some empty take-up reels around for this purpose. Take an empty reel, and locate your recorder to the beginning of the selection that is to appear first on your master. Make sure that there's a leader before this cut; if none is present, splice it at this point. Cut the tape at this point if it's not physically at the beginning, and remove the take-up reel. Mount an empty reel.

Now play or fast forward through this piece. If the next performance is not the one you want next on your final product, make another cut, and then remove the take-up reel that's now holding your recordings in the order you desire. Again put an empty reel on the take-up side, and locate through the tape until the next cut is found. Of course, if the next take you want is on the section of tape that was previously cut, you'll need instead to remove the supply reel, mount the previous take-up reel on the right side of the recorder, and rewind until you find the cut desired.

Once you're there, the idea is to re-mount the take-up reel that's holding the selections in the right order, splice the next song into sequence, and then fast forward or play up to the next break. 'Post-it' stick-on notes can be very helpful in keeping the various sections of tape straightened out. Make sure to use a sufficient amount of leader tape between cuts so that there's a natural time gap.

Tones. If your sending your master tape to a mastering lab, it should be *slated* with a series of tones. These tones are created by a *tone generator*, which is simply a sine wave oscillator capable of generating tones at preset frequencies. Better consoles have built-in generators. TEAC, Fostex, Loft/Goldline, and others manufacture relatively inexpensive, high-quality outboard generators, designed to plug into a line input of your mixer.

The purpose of tones is to provide a mastering facility or other recording studio with a standardized point of reference. When tones have been correctly recorded, an engineer at another facility can adjust the playback response of their machine to agree with the setting of your recorder. Of course, your tape deck should be calibrated properly and its heads should be aligned, but still there may be some sonic discrepancies between your mixdown machine and the mastering lab's playback machine.

Generally speaking, it's quite sufficient to record just three tones in this order: 1 kHz, 100 Hz, and 10 kHz. Each tone should last for at least one minute. While they should normally be recorded on both channels of the mixdown deck, you may wish to record a preliminary 30 seconds or so of the 1 kHz tone in the *left* channel. When you indicate this in writing along with the tape, the mastering engineer will be sure that your left and right signals aren't crossed.

The 1 kHz tone gives a reference for overall level. If there's a switch for noise reduction, take it out of the circuit to record tones. The 10 kHz tone allows the high end response to be brought into conformity with your recording, while the 100 Hz tone gives the engineer a handle on low-end response. If you have a 15 kHz tone available, you may wish to record it last—it will provide a standard reference for the very high frequency response of your recorder.

The purpose of recording tones is not to get them to all come out at the same level, but rather to show up any tonal biases your equipment might have. So you should disregard how things look at the recorder, and run the tone generator into the mixer. What is most important is to get the same *mixer* meter reading at all three frequencies; most engineers use a reference reading of 0 VU (see page 21).

By recording all three tones with the same mixer reading, if your recorder is misaligned and records the bass tone 3 dB hotter than the mid tone, a competent engineer will be able to compensate at the time your set-up. (You must calibrate the tape deck's input levels, however, so that with the first 1 kHz tone, 0 VU on the mixer equates to 0 VU at the deck.) Once again, watch the meters on the mixer and make the tones of equal value; ignore whether or not the recorder captures them all at the same level.

Make a note of what frequencies were recorded, and the level at which they're supposed to be at on the tape. Make sure

this information is available to the engineer who's charged with the responsibility of mastering your work. If you're going to put tones on a cassette tape, first calibrate to –10 on the meters, since many cassette recorders can't handle a steady 10 kHz tone at 0 VU.

Tones generally appear at the head of the tape, that is, before any recorded material starts. They can be spliced into position if you desire, but it's best to lay them down at the top of a reel of tape, before the session gets rolling. If you *do* splice them in, make sure that you've recorded them on exactly the same machine and type of tape as the music's recorded otherwise the reference will mean nothing to the lab.

*   *   *   *

Now that we've taken ourselves from recording the first track through to the master tape, let's move on to some advanced concepts. As we'll learn, MIDI, synchronization, digital recording, and other such powerful technologies can increase greatly the creative potential for both personal and professional studios.   □

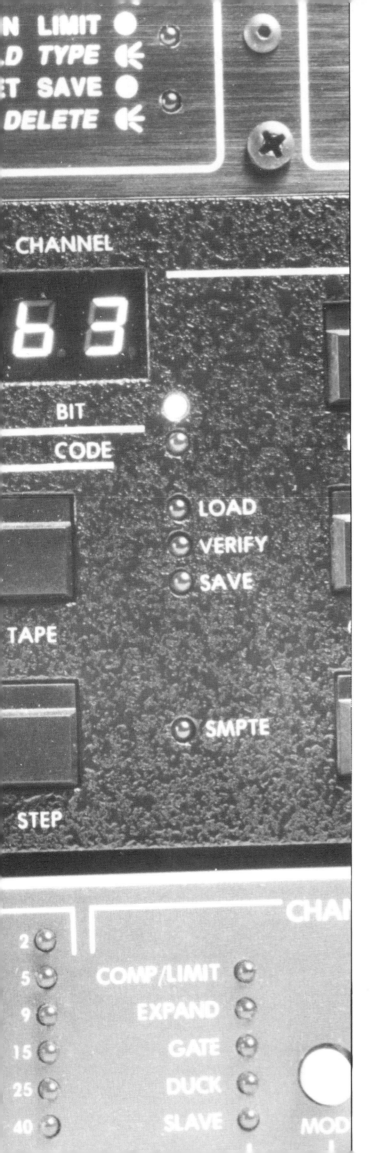

Part IV: Advanced Concepts And Techniques

The lines of distinction between professional and personal recording studios have blurred in recent years. A number of factors have led to this, including the development of MIDI, the preponderance of personal computers, the rising popularity of video, and access to inexpensive, high-performance gear.

MIDI in particular has challenged professionals to learn more about what's happening in personal studios: As we'll discuss next, MIDI can yield recordings that rival those made in world-class studios. For personal recordists, the challenge is to make the most of synchronization, automation, and audio-for-video techniques that have "trickled down" from the professional world.

Finally, as we'll learn in Chapter 16, digital audio will provide a common meeting ground for professional and personal studios—and allow information to be transferred between the two with ease. This amazing power has many implications for how music will be created and recorded in the future. It's also a further mandate, for anyone who's serious about recording, to understand all facets of our craft.

In late 1981, a paper was presented to the Audio Engineering Society during its annual New York City convention. Co-authored by Dave Smith and Chet Wood, respectively the president and design engineer of Sequential Circuits, the paper proposed a standard means of communication between electronic musical instruments. Originally called the Universal Synthesizer Interface (USI), the idea caught the interest of several major manufacturers—including Yamaha, Roland, Korg, and others. Following a year of consultations, the USI specifications evolved into what we now know as *MIDI*—the Musical Instrument Digital Interface.

The first demonstration of MIDI took place in June 1983, when a Sequential Prophet 600 was connected to a Yamaha DX7. Though the demo had its 'bugs,' people were able to get a glimpse at what MIDI could do: By playing notes on the 600, notes would sound on the DX7.

In just a short time, MIDI has developed to a technical sophistication that's light years beyond this simple form of layering sounds. For the home studio, MIDI can mean anything from simple layering, to a complete, self-contained, multi-track recording system for electronic instruments. On its own, such a system can record and play back many tracks of electronic music without ever using tape, by storing musical performances much like a word processor stores correspondence!

Or, as we'll learn, a tapeless MIDI system can be fully integrated with a multi-track tape recorder: MIDI can record and play back all your drum machine and electronic instrument parts, while your tape recorder is kept busy recording 'normal' tracks such as vocals, acoustic guitars, and other instruments which can't be 'MIDI-ized.'

And personal computers are ideal for both data manipulation and storage, which is why they have a high profile in many studios. By installing a MIDI interface and 'booting up' a sequencer program, a personal computer can take charge of recording and playing back synthesizers, samplers, and other instruments in your studio.

For many, MIDI has completely changed the way they make music. Let's take a look at how MIDI works, and what it can do for you in your own studio.

An Overview

You may already be using a MIDI setup, or may be familiar with some of MIDI's basic concepts. If so, feel free to skip ahead to page 107, while we touch on some of those concepts. If you're left with any unanswered questions, please refer to *Using MIDI*, or one of the other MIDI books listed on page 130.

MIDI can perform many functions in the recording studio. In its simplest application, it can allow synthesizers, samplers, and other MIDI instruments, to 'talk' to each other, so that notes played on one synth will sound simultaneously on another. It allows *sequencers*—which are rather like tapeless

tape recorders for MIDI devices—to record and play back songs through MIDI instruments and drum machines. It allows one MIDI device to make *program changes* on another, to change sound parameters or other settings. MIDI can even control reverbs and digital delays, video machines, lighting mixers, and devices that have yet to be invented. But what is MIDI?

MIDI is a 'language,' or communication system between digitally-controlled devices. Since computers, drum machines, and most electronic keyboards are digitally controlled, they can also be outfitted with MIDI *ports*. By connecting MIDI cables (which are 5-pin shielded DIN-type cables) between these ports, information can be shared. It's important to remember that this information is not an audio signal—if you could listen to the output of a MIDI cable, all you'd hear would be buzzing gibberish. Rather, the information is a stream of digital commands, transmitted in *serial* form so that commands fall one after the other.

Digital information consists of *bits*, which are the binary digits of 1 or 0, on or off. In MIDI, each event consists of eight bits, and flows along at 31,250 bits per second—we can call this a *baud rate* of 31.25K.

Devices connected in a MIDI system either transmit, receive, pass along, or ignore these commands, depending upon the setup and the gear being used. By agreement among manufacturers and software engineers, given commands will yield given responses. What kinds of commands are sent through MIDI?

Note commands are perhaps the most common. Different notes of the musical scale are assigned different numbers (there are 128 note numbers), and these numbers

are given different 8-bit MIDI codes, which can be transmitted as digital information. For example, the number 60 represents Middle C. Let's say we hook up two synths, and set them so that one is the transmitter, or *master*, and the other is the receiver, or *slave*. By playing Middle C on the master, the code for note 60 is transmitted to the slave, and we hear the slave play the note simultaneously with the master. Accompanying the note number command are *note on* and *note off* commands, so that the slave knows when to start and stop playing the note.

That's how simple layering of synth sounds takes place. In a similar way, changing the program, or *patch*, of the master synth can perform a program change on the slave synth, so that produces a new tone when played. But so much else can be controlled through MIDI—almost *anything* that can be digitally controlled on a musical instrument or accessory can be controlled through MIDI. For example, 'tempo' knobs on modern drum machines are digital controls; thus MIDI can be used to transmit tempo information between gear, such as sequencers and drum machines.

This leads us to the next important point: Anything that can be digitally controlled can also be digitally stored. The sequencers we described as 'tapeless tape recorders' are digital storage devices: By connecting a synth to a sequencer via MIDI ports and then playing the synth, a musical passage can be recorded by the sequencer—remember, it's recording information such as note numbers and durations, and not actual sound. When the same passage, or sequence, is played back, we'll hear exactly what was recorded.

There are three types of MIDI ports: *in*,

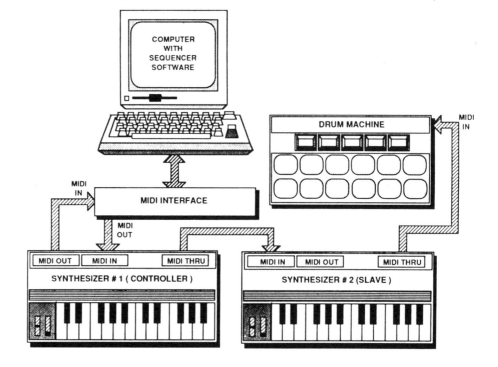

Figure 13.1 A MIDI chain network.

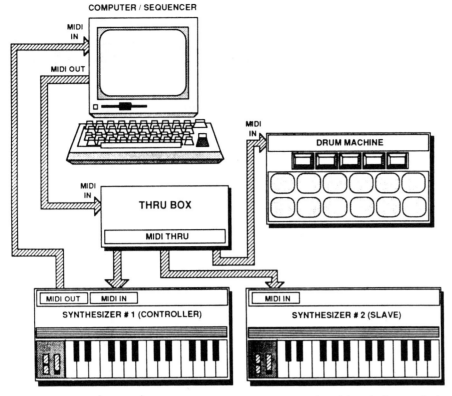

COMPUTER / SEQUENCER

MIDI IN

MIDI OUT

MIDI IN

THRU BOX

MIDI THRU

MIDI IN

DRUM MACHINE

MIDI OUT   MIDI IN

SYNTHESIZER # 1 (CONTROLLER)

MIDI IN

SYNTHESIZER # 2 (SLAVE)

Figure 13.2 A common fallacy is that chaining MIDI instruments can introduce delays; that's not really the case, since practically speaking, MIDI thru ports introduce no delay. Rather, the trouble with successive thru ports is that they can distort MIDI data—which in turn can lead to errors, such as audible delays. The solution? A MIDI 'star' network, utilizing a thru box to distribute MIDI.

out, and *thru*. The in and out ports are self-explanatory. The thru's function, however, is simply to pass along whatever information is coming into a MIDI in port. Let's find out why this is useful.

Let's say we have three MIDI synthesizers, and we designate one as the master controller, and the other two as slaves. The controller can send commands to the first slave by connecting the controller's MIDI out to slave 1's MIDI in. If we connect slave 1's MIDI out to slave 2's MIDI in, however, the second slave will receive its commands from the first slave and not from the controller keyboard. The solution: Connect slave 1's MIDI thru to slave 2's MIDI in. This way the first slave will 'pass along' any commands it receives to the second slave, allowing both synths to be controlled by the master controller. This type of connection is known as a *chain network*, since MIDI devices are chained together, as pictured in Figure 13.1.

Alternately, there are *thru boxes* which will split a MIDI output and route it to several destinations. These allow a *star network* to be configured, as pictured in Figure 13.2. When several devices are chained via MIDI thru ports, the data can become slightly altered, due to very small and inaudible—yet cumulative—data distortion in passing the data from the in ports to the thru ports. When this happens, errors can be introduced. A thru box allows MIDI data to be distributed to several destinations without inducing errors.

This brings us to the next question: How do different MIDI destinations, such as slave synths, know *which* commands are meant for which device? For example, let's say we have a sequencer 'driving' three synths. If one synth is to play the lead melody part, another the chords, and the third the bass line, how does each synth know which part it's supposed to play? Why doesn't each

synth play all three parts? The reason is that the synths can be set to operate on different MIDI *channels*.

There are 16 different MIDI channels over which MIDI information can be sent. The channel concept is best explained by what's become the industry's standard analogy: your own television. Many different stations broadcast into your home on different TV channels, either by high frequency waves or cable. By selecting the channel on your TV, you choose which station's information you receive. Additional TVs in your home can be set to receive the same or different information.

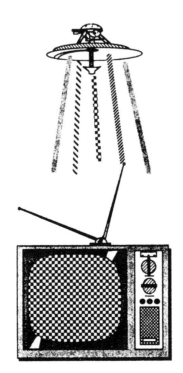

Figure 13.3 Like television transmissions, MIDI information operates on different channels.

MIDI devices operate in a similar way. Anything designed to receive MIDI information, such as a synthesizer, can be set to receive on any one of 16 channels, or to receive all channels at once. And most devices which generate MIDI information can be set to transmit on any or all MIDI channels. In this way, parts recorded on a sequencer can be sent to different destinations: A bass part can be recorded as MIDI channel 1 information and played back through a synth set to receive on channel 1; a lead part as can be recorded as channel 2 information and played back to another instrument set to receive on channel 2, and so on.

Here's a summary of the main points about MIDI:

- It's an open-ended digital communication system.
- MIDI doesn't transmit any actual audio signals. Rather, it transmits digital information such as note values, note on and off commands, an so forth.
- MIDI information can be stored for later playback by sequencers.
- MIDI is transmitted from MIDI out and thru ports, and is received by MIDI in ports.
- There are 16 channels over which MIDI information can be sent. Most devices allow you complete control over which MIDI channels they transmit or receive.

While there's obviously much more to be said about MIDI theory and applications, this much should give you an overview of how MIDI works. Now let's move on to its role in the recording studio.

MIDI And Your Studio

Is MIDI for everyone, even acoustic musicians? Possibly, since MIDI can be used to automate mixing consoles and effects—as we'll be learning more about. Depending upon your needs and applications, MIDI's role in your studio might be anywhere from nonexistent, to incidental, to indispensable.

For example, if you're a singer/guitarist using a 4-track ministudio, MIDI may not be for you. But if all your music is instrumental and electronic—with synthesizers, samplers, and drum machines your instruments—your entire studio can be MIDI-based, and you may have no need whatsoever for a conventional multi-track tape recorder! If you're like many modern musicians, however, who may be using a mix of MIDI-based electronic instruments and 'conventional' instruments (such as electric or acoustic guitars, acoustic drums, and vocal tracks)—MIDI can work in conjunction with your multi-track tape recorder, and offer many new options to your creativity.

Let's look at a 'tapeless' MIDI studio, and then see how such a setup can integrate with a tape-based multi-track studio.

MIDI Instruments. The first order of business is MIDI instruments—the devices which generate sound. The choice of these instruments is ever-increasing, but they fall into one of three main categories:

- Synthesizers, which allow you to create your own sounds from 'scratch,' or offer a wide library of pre-programmed sounds.

- Samplers, which store digital recordings of sounds. Modern samplers such as the Roland S-50 and E-mu Emax can record near-perfect samples of acoustic pianos, drums, as well as sound effects. They also allow you to record your own samples, so just about any sound you hear can be sampled and then played by a keyboard.
- Drum machines, which store samples of drums and other percussive sounds, and usually have a built-in sequencer, to construct complete 'songs' of various drum patterns.

Roland, Ibanez, Synth-Axe, and others offer MIDI guitar controllers. Akai, Yamaha, and several others make MIDI wind controllers, designed for saxophonists and trumpet players. There are vibraphone-like controllers, drum pads, and even accordion- and harmonica-based controllers. Should anyone feel left out, there are several quite effective *pitch-to-MIDI* devices, which can take any input from a microphone or other source—such as a voice, flute, electric guitar, or whatever—and convert it to MIDI.

Drum machines are indispensable for

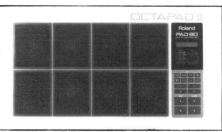

Figure 13.8 Roland Octopad II controller.

nally to a sequencer's clock, so that start, stop, and tempo changes for the two are controlled by the sequencer. If your drum machine and sequencer have a *Song Position Pointer* (SPP) function—as is common on most modern gear—they can be used in perfect synchronization with each other. That is, when the sequencer is cued to start at different measures of a song, the drum machine will shift and play in sync from the same measure numbers. More about this in "Synchronization," starting on page 110.

Many synths and samplers are *multi-timbral*, which means it's possible for them to play more than one sound (patch) at once. The Ensoniq ESQ-1 gained a lot of popularity with personal studios when introduced, since it allows up to eight internal patches to play at once. In this way, multi-timbral synths can be set to play bass, lead, piano, and several other patches all at once. The only limitation is in terms of *voices*—the total number of notes that can sound simultaneously. For example, the ESQ-1 is an *8-voice* instrument, which means that at any given time it can only play eight notes total, whether that's with one patch or all eight.

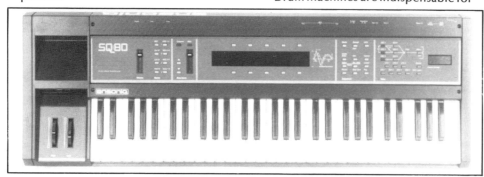

Figure 13.4 The Ensoniq SQ-80 multi-timbral synth/sequencer, with internal disk drive for patch and sequence storage.

Figure 13.5 The Alesis 16-bit HR-16 rhythm computer.

Figure 13.6 E-mu's Emax sampler, with internal hard drive.

Not all synthesizers and samplers have integral keyboards. Thanks to MIDI's ability to transmit note and patch information over different channels, it's possible to have just one master keyboard controlling all your synths and samplers as slaves. This means two things: The master keyboard doesn't have to make its own sounds, and slaves can be rack-mount, keyboardless *sound modules*.

This brings us to the next type of MIDI instrument you'll encounter: the MIDI *master controller*. There are numerous keyboards on the market which don't' generate any sounds on their own. One of these master keyboard controllers is all you need to play all the MIDI instruments in your studio, whether or not they have keyboards of their own. The connections from master to slaves are all through MIDI. Of course, a standard synthesizer with a keyboard can also be used as a master controller; the point is, the controller needn't make its own sounds.

And in fact, your master controller doesn't have to be a keyboard. There is now a broad range of alternate controllers.

most single musician/engineers. Modern machines offer complete tuning, level, panning, and other facilities—giving you many more than just one drum 'kit.' While most agree that there's no substitute for a real drummer when it comes to spontaneity and 'vibes,' a well-programmed drum machine can sound indistinguishable from the real thing.

Sequencers and drum machines have built-in *clocks*, which control tempo settings. These clocks can also be driven by an *external* clock, however, which is essential for making two such devices run in sync. Typically, drum machines are synced exter-

Figure 13.7 Zeta System's Mirror 6 MIDI guitar.

Multi-timbral synths are very useful, especially for smaller studios. Here's why: Let's say you have just one MIDI instrument, such as a synthesizer. If it's 'mono-timbral' (capable of only one patch at a time), you *can* use it to record and play back more than one sequencer track, but all the tracks will have use whatever patch is loaded—and thus sound the same. If it's multi-timbral, however, you can record several different sequencer tracks, and each track can have its own patch.

Sequencers. Synthesizer sequencers have been around since the 1960s, though their applications have flourished since the advent of MIDI. They are available as either stand-alone devices, sometimes called *hardware* sequencers, or they're available as computer programs to run on various personal computers, including the Apple Macintosh and IIGS, the IBM PC and PS/2, and the Atari ST and Mega computers. While most computer-based, or *software* sequencers, require a MIDI interface for the computer, the Atari ST series has MIDI in and out ports built-in.

The distinguishing terms of 'hardware' and 'software' are somewhat misnomers, by the way: All modern sequencers use software programs to do their stuff, though stand-alone sequencers have the software built-in and ready to run, whereas computer-based programs need to be 'loaded' with the appropriate software.

Earlier we described how musical passages can be recorded and played back by a MIDI sequencer. All kinds of digital information can be 'loaded' into a sequencer, including:

- Note numbers and durations.
- The tempo at which the music was played.
- *Aftertouch* (pressure on the keys to introduce vibrato and other effects).
- *Velocity* (the speed at which keys are depressed, which can control dynamics).
- Patch changes.

Of course, multi-track tape recorders

Figure 13.9 The Yamaha C1 PC-compatible computer has MIDI and SMPTE ports.

can record the *sound* of all of these events. Why should we go to the trouble of using a sequencer, which is recording the *data* for all these events, to be replayed by synths and other instruments?

The reasons are plentiful. For one, information recorded in a sequencer is played back directly to MIDI instruments, which in turn generate sound. That means that everything we hear is *first generation*—there's no tape hiss, no added noise, nothing. The sound quality of a MIDI-sequenced passage is even slightly better than if the the same passage were recorded

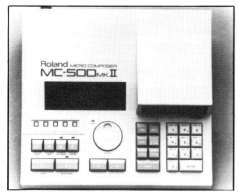

Figure 13.10 Roland's MC500 MkII sequencer.

on a world-class digital tape recorder.

Another big advantage is that we can *edit* what we record. For example, a sequencer's tempo can be sped up or slowed down without altering pitch—that's because we're altering just the speed of the information. Difficult passages can be recorded at a snail's pace, and then replayed quickly to the amazement of your friends and record producers!

Most sequencers allow for much more

elaborate editing, however: Wrong notes can be corrected, timing can be *quantized* so that notes fall 'on beat,' and so forth. It's not even necessary to 'play' the music: Most sequencers offer some type of *step editing*, which allows you to load in notes and durations without playing them in real time. Any of this musical trickery is just about impossible on a tape recorder: Could you imagine stopping and starting the recorder while you recorded a lead synthesizer solo note-by-note?

The advantages go on and on:

- Sequences can be played back through any MIDI instrument—regardless of which instrument originally played the part. Similarly, the patch or sample can be changed during playback: If your brass chords sound better as cellos, no problem!
- Most sequencers offer *looping* and *copy* functions, which allow you to record just one pass of something that is repeated. For example, if the bass part is the same for all four choruses of your song, you only need to record it once, and copy it for the remaining three choruses.
- Typically, sequencers offer unlimited *merging*, which is similar to 'bouncing' tracks together. This way an 8-track sequencer can actually have 12 or more tracks of MIDI information. When MIDI tracks are merged, their MIDI channels are remembered by the sequencer. In this way, one MIDI track can drive two or more synthesizers with different musical parts, through two or more MIDI channels. Since merged tracks can usually be un-merged, 2-track sequencers are still very functional devices, practically allowing 8-track or greater capability.
- Since they don't have to physically move tape around, sequencers are maintenance-free. For the same reason, they can access through their memory any portion of a song in just a matter of seconds; a jump from the introduction to the final chorus of a song is instantaneous.
- Computer-based sequencers offer all sorts of extra power, such as notation printout, simultaneous management of

synthesizer patches (which can be stored as 'libraries' of sound), and more.

Note that effects can't be recorded onto sequencer tracks—with tape, it's possible to record a synth track 'wet' with different settings of reverb, delay or other effects. Sequenced parts, on the other hand, have to be played back through effects if they're to be 'wet' (unless the MIDI instrument has built-in effects).

And here's another sequencing drawback: With tape, one synthesizer can be used to record several different tracks with different sounds. If you want more than one synth sound happening simultaneously with a sequencer, you'll either need a multi-timbral synthesizer (which will be limited to perhaps eight or 16 voices at any one time), or you'll need more than one synth. For this reason, many MIDI studios have a large number of keyboards and sound modules.

Nonetheless, with a sequencer, MIDI instruments can operate as a stand-alone multi-track system. All you need to add is a mixer to accommodate the audio outputs of your synths, along with a monitor system to hear everything. You'll also want effects, and likely a 2-track of some sort for mixdown. In short, a MIDI studio looks a lot like a regular multi-track studio—without a multi-track tape recorder. For most applications, MIDI is far superior to tape for recording MIDI-ized instruments.

Integrating MIDI With Tape. While MIDI does a lot, most of us still need some medium to record non-MIDI parts such as guitars and vocals. Fortunately, the multi-track worlds of MIDI and tape have a common meeting point.

As described in the next chapter, sequencers and drum machines can be *synced-to-tape*, so that they play their parts along with tape tracks. Parts which are synced-to-tape—for most people that means all synth, sampler, and drum machine tracks—are known as *virtual tracks*. The name makes sense: Synced tracks are for most purposes the same as tape tracks.

Let's say you have a 4-track ministudio and synced to it are a drum machine and a sequencer. If you're using the drum machine's stereo outputs and have three synth parts recorded on the sequencer, you have a total of five virtual tracks. Add these to the remaining three tracks on the ministudio (one tape track is used for sync code), and your 4-track recording studio is now a 7-track studio. Of course, if you recorded six synthesizer tracks, you'd be engineering an 11-track session (six synth tracks + two drum machine tracks + three tape tracks).

Thanks to MIDI and the advantages of virtual tracks, many musicians find their tape track requirements are halved from what they would otherwise need.

MIDI Effects. Today, the range of MIDI effects is comprehensive, from reverbs to delays, from compressors to equalizers and even pitch shifters. But these devices don't generate sound on their own—of what use is a MIDI port on, say, a reverb?

MIDI effects are controllable. In Chapter Eight we learned how many new effects allow you to program different 'settings.' A reverb can have up to 64 or more *presets*, each with its own decay time, room algorithm, and so forth. By installing MIDI on a reverb, presets can be changed in the same way patch changes can be changed on synthesizers via MIDI. 'Automating' the presets of a MIDI effect—by recording its patch changes onto a sequencer—can free up your hands during a mixdown, or allow for super-precise preset changes.

MIDI has another role with many effects. Certain units, such as the Lexicon PCM70 allow you to *map* MIDI parameters, so that the actual parameters (not just presets) of an effect can be changed via MIDI. For example, the *modulation wheel* controller of a keyboard, which normally introduces

bar of a MIDI guitar controller) can change mixing consoles. After all, if we can control decay times of a reverb, it's not a much bigger step to control fader levels on a mixer. More about this starting on page 122.

MIDI is also been integrated into the video world. Via a special sync code known as *SMPTE time code*, MIDI-based gear can adapt to almost any video editing or post-production setting. And even in a 'pure' music setting, SMPTE time code has an important role, as does a new code known as *MIDI time code* (MTC). We'll explore this in the next chapter.

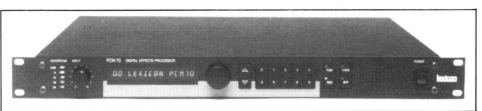

Figure 13.11 Lexicon's powerful PCM70. Aside from programmable reverb, delay, chorusing, and other effects, the PCM70 allows for complete MIDI control of almost any parameter. For instance, a keyboard modulation wheel can be 'mapped' to control reverb decay, or even flange depth.

the 'feedback' amount of a digital delay—introducing more echo repeats. Or a MIDI EQ could be set up, for example, so that striking the keys with increasing velocity could completely change the EQ settings. The sky's the limit!

Other MIDI Applications. One area that holds a lot of promise is MIDI automation of

vibrato and other changes to the sound of the synth, can be 'MIDI-mapped' so that it also changes, via MIDI, the decay time of a reverb. By recording the modulation wheel movements onto a sequencer track, your reverb can have automated decay times.

Similarly, the keyboard's aftertouch (or for that matter, the 'whammy' or tremolo

* * * *

We now know how a MIDI studio with a sequencer and MIDI instruments can stand on its own, and we've explored some of the advantages of MIDI in the recording studio. We've also described how sequenced virtual tracks can augment tape tracks.

But we still need to learn just *how* MIDI gear is 'synced' to a multi-track tape. After all, that's the key to incorporating MIDI into your own studio. In this next chapter we'll learn how that's accomplished, as well as other facets of synchronization. □

CHAPTER 14: SYNCHRONIZATION

In the last chapter we learned that MIDI sequencers can be 'synced' to a tape recorder, to allow tapeless, or 'virtual,' tracks of electronic instruments to start, run, and stop in sync with vocal, guitar, and other tape-based tracks. This technique allows you to expand the practical number of tracks you have well beyond the four, eight, or even 24 *tape* tracks you may have. In this chapter, we're going to learn how that—as well as several other powerful types of synchronization—is accomplished.

Not all musicians or engineers need to know about 'sync,' so this chapter may not be for you. But if you plan to work with:

- MIDI sequencers
- Drum machines
- Video or film (including scoring and sound effects)
- Automated mixing consoles
- Or more than one multi-track tape machine

there's a good chance you'll be working with one or more forms of synchronization.

We're going to start off by looking at *clock* and *MIDI sync*, and how they synchronize devices which can start, run, and stop at their own programmable tempos, such as drum machines and sequencers. We'll then move on to see how these devices can use *tape synchronization*, to run in sync with your multi-track recorder. Next, we'll learn about *SMPTE time code* and its role in synchronization—including the syncing of two or more tape transports, such as a video machine and a multi-track tape recorder. Finally, we'll consider *automation* of mixing consoles and other gear, which is a world very much linked to synchronization.

Clock Synchronization

Here's an exercise in either memory or imagination: Say you're a small child, taking music lessons. Your teacher has an old-time mechanical metronome, and this lesson is about timing. As she winds it, she tells you that she would like you to start playing after the metronome clicks four times. Reading your music, your assignment is to continue playing in perfect tempo with the metronome, until your teacher stop it, at which point you can stop as well. Simple enough, but what does this have to do with synchronization?

This childhood metronome is in fact a 'clock,' telling you when to start the song, what tempo to play, and when to stop. All sequencers and drum machines have internal, electronic clocks designed to perform these same functions. These clocks don't have anything to do with the time of day; rather, they're computerized 'event controllers.'

Here's how they work: MIDI sequencers and drum machines record and play back a string of events, such as notes or drum strikes. These events are recorded sequentially, so that the device's memory knows which events happen in what order. To sound like rhythmic music, however, the device has to record the relative timing of the events. It does this with its internal clock. (Any notes which occur at *exactly* the same time are usually considered the same event, as far as the clock is concerned.)

Instead of ticking every second, music-oriented electronic clocks generate evenly-paced *pulses*. As events are recorded, they're 'time-stamped' with a kind of pulse reference number. That is, when the recording starts and the clock starts running, the

unit keeps track of how many pulses pass between incoming events. Each event—whether it's a MIDI program change, a complete chord, or a snare drum hit—gets stored in memory, complete with its timing reference. When the recording is stopped and the 'play' button is hit, the clock starts and events are played back whenever their 'number' is up.

Since each event is stored in time with a clock pulse, a high rate of pulses need to be generated in order to have good *resolution*. After all, if a pulse is generated only every second, all notes and other events would be separated a second—a fine resolution for a wrist watch, perhaps, but unusable for music.

Clock Rates. Going back to the late '70s—the pre-MIDI days of early drum machines and sequencers—manufacturers realized that clock pulses should relate directly to music. Unless we were working with tempos divisible by 60, such as 60 beats per minute (bpm), it would do no good to have clock pulse rates that had anything to do with seconds.

Consequently, a clock's pulse rate is referenced to quarter notes. For example, Roland, Sequential, Moog, and others settled on a rate of 24 *pulses per quarter note* (ppq). A sequencer or drum machine using this standard will record and play back events with a spacing of 24 clock pulses between each quarter note. Eighth notes are spaced 12 pulses apart, half notes are 48 pulses apart, and if we're recording in 4/4 time, 96 pulses elapse per measure. The 24 ppq standard has a resolution of thirty-second note triplets, which can be spaced at every pulse.

While all sequencers and drum machines

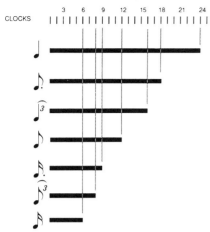

CLOCKS

Figure 14.1 All note durations in a sequencer must be expressed in whole numbers of clocks. Here are the durations of some common rhythm values of 24 pulses per quarter note (ppq). As we can see, we can continue to reduce the number of clocks down to 1 clock, which is equivalent to a thirty-second note triplet in duration. Consequently, we can say that a 24 ppq device has a resolution of thirty-second note triplets. While that's quite high (and 24 ppq is the clock rate at which MIDI operates), some manufacturers design their gear to operate at higher internal clock rates for higher resolution—some go as high as 384 ppq!

have internal clocks, most are able to receive an *external* clock—that is, their tempo can be controlled by another device. By plugging a clock output from a sequencer, for example, into the clock or sync input of a drum machine and then setting the latter device for external sync, the drum machine can be synced to the sequencer, so that it starts, runs, and stops with the sequencer.

When using this type of clock sync, it's important to realize that the two synced devices must be started together from the beginning of a song in order to establish sync. The reason is that ordinary clock sync has no reference to exactly where it is in a song. That is, once the master starts, it only syncs the tempo of the slave. True, it's usually possible to maintain sync by stopping the master in the middle of a song and then continuing from the same spot. But using ordinary clock sync, it's not possible to have the master search ahead or backwards to a certain point and have the slave follow it: Unless the master and slave continue playing from exactly the same point at which they were were stopped, they can only sync together from the beginning of a song. Nonetheless, being able to connect two devices together and have them play in sync is a powerful capability.

Unfortunately, not every manufacturer uses the 24 ppq standard. Other common standards are 48, 96 and even 384 ppq—the latter is Fairlight's standard, and allows for incredibly fine resolution for notes. (Bear in mind that you don't need to be playing notes greater than sixty-fourth note triplets to benefit from high resolution: Since each recorded event is 'time-stamped' with a pulse number, higher resolution allows for more accurate recording of exactly when each event takes place.)

If we use a 24 ppq device to drive a a 48 ppq device, however, the slave will play along at half tempo, since each quarter note lasts for twice as many pulses. And there can be other sync discrepancies, regarding start and stop 'protocol': While most gear starts

when the clock starts, Roland clocks run all the time, and use separate start and stop pulses. And while some gear uses 1/4" connectors for sync, other gear uses miniplugs or 5-pin DIN connectors, which look like MIDI connectors but aren't. The Dr. Click from Garfield Electronics, and other clock translators, can serve as an interface between devices with different clock standards and connectors.

Clock sync applies to the home studio in two important ways. First of all, it helps us better understand MIDI sync, which these days is a more common variation of the clock sync we've been describing. Secondly, by syncing one device to tape—such as a sequencer—clock or MIDI sync can be used in turn to drive drum machines or other slaved devices. Let's take a look at MIDI sync, and then move onto tape sync.

MIDI Synchronization

Most of what we've learned about clock syncing so far applies to syncing devices through MIDI, except for one important point: MIDI sync is a true standard. It allows you to connect most MIDI sequencers and drum machines together via their MIDI ports. In addition to whatever note, patch change, and other data commands are passed through those ports, a 24 ppq MIDI clock standard is used to sync these units together. (Different MIDI devices still have different *internal* clocks—which are often 48 or 96 ppq, for higher resolution when recording events—but 24 ppq is the rate which shows up at their MIDI ports.)

There are several other standards within MIDI sync. When the master device generates a *start* command, all slave units will reset to the beginning of whatever sequence, pattern, or song they're set to play. A *stop* command causes them to stop. And a *continue* command is similar to 'play,' though it doesn't reset the slaves to the beginning after being stopped. In this way, it's possible to connect two devices via MIDI and have them run in sync.

Song Position Pointer. So far, MIDI sync may seem to be nothing more than a standardized type of clock sync. There are two provisions within MIDI, however, that set it far apart from ordinary clock sync. One of these is known as *MIDI Time Code* (MTC), and we'll discuss it further ahead within our description of SMPTE time code. The other is known as the *Song Position Pointer*, or *SPP*, and it works in conjunction with start, stop, continue, and clock information.

MIDI devices equipped with SPP are able to keep track of how many sixteenth-note pulses elapse from the start of a sequence, passage, or song. Let's say you own a sequencer and drum machine, each equipped with SPP. If the drum machine is synced to the sequencer via MIDI, the two can maintain accurate sync, no matter where the sequencer is stopped and restarted. If the sequencer is cued to the 23rd measure of a song and played, the drum machine should also jump to the 23rd measure and start to play. In actual practice, there may a short time lag—so the drum machine mightn't join in until the 24th or 25th measure—but still, this type of sync is a godsend for anyone who has worked with ordinary clock sync, and had to restart songs over and over just to establish sync between

a sequencer and drum machine.

When connecting MIDI devices, remember that only clock-based devices, such as sequencers, drum machines, and automation systems (which we'll learn more about shortly), may be equipped with Song Position Pointer. If introduced after 1985, most of them *should* have SPP, but be sure to check.

Aside from device-to-device MIDI sync, SPP also plays a role in tape synchronization, as we'll learn next.

Tape Synchronization

For some time now we've been extolling the virtues of *sync-to-tape*, or *tape synchronization*—now we get to learn how it's done. This technique allows you to sync a drum machine or sequencer to a multi-track tape recorder, thus augmenting your tape tracks with tapeless 'virtual' tracks from a drum machine or sequencer-driven MIDI instruments.

The Basics. In the preceding pages, we've been learning about clocks, the internal computers which control the timing of various music machines. We've also learned that these clocks can be externally controlled, or synchronized, by another machine's clock.

With tape sync, the external control source is actually a *sync code* that's recorded on one track of a tape recorder. Most devices capable of tape sync will generate a code. This track is recorded, or *striped*, before any other tracks. It's from this *sync track* that drum machines, sequencers, and other devices are driven. If these devices can be synced together without tape—through MIDI or ordinary clock sync—you need to stripe only one sync code to run one device, which in turn will act as the master for other 'syncable' machines in your studio.

Once the code is striped on a single tape track, it becomes the master timing reference. The remaining tracks are free for guitars, vocals, and other non-syncable parts. While these tracks are recorded, the sync code is fed continuously from the tape recorder back to the synced device, which may in turn be driving other devices. This way, you can hear your drum machine or sequencer parts play along with the tape recorder. In fact, you needn't record the sound of any virtual tracks until it's time to mixdown, at which point their audio outputs are mixed with the multi-track tape outputs through your mixer, and sent to the mixdown deck.

The Advantages. Tape sync offers a bunch of advantages over conventionally-recorded tracks. The greatest, of course, is that it gives you extra tracks for all those sources which can't be synced to tape, including all acoustic instruments and vocal tracks, as well as bass and electric guitars.

Here's another advantage: Let's say you've recorded a stereo drum machine pattern on two tracks of a tape—without using tape sync—and have added all the other parts, such as vocals, bass, and guitars. But what if you realize that the syncopation of the snare drum is way off, and that those fancy tom paradiddles just don't make it? Try as you might, there's no way you could hope to have a reprogrammed drum machine part play back in time with the overdubbed parts: It would be well nigh impos-

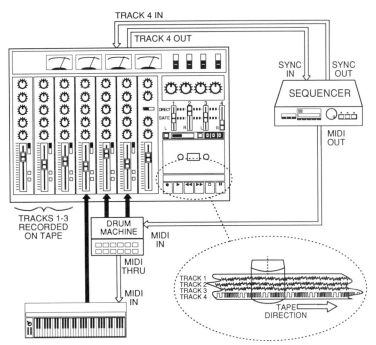

TRACK 4 IN
TRACK 4 OUT
SYNC IN
SYNC OUT
SEQUENCER
MIDI OUT
TRACKS 1-3 RECORDED ON TAPE
DRUM MACHINE
MIDI IN
MIDI THRU
MIDI IN
TRACK 1
TRACK 2
TRACK 3
TRACK 4
TAPE DIRECTION

Figure 14.2 Sync-to-tape in action. Using a single track for code (FSK, 'smart' code, or SMPTE), it's possible to drive an unlimited number of virtual tracks—from drum machines, to samplers, and more. Sync-to-tape offers a tremendous number of advantages over conventional tracking, though it's easy to run out of mixer inputs!

This same story holds true with sequenced parts that are tape synced. Love the way you played that keyboard passage during the chorus, but wish you had played it with a 'brass' patch, rather than the 'strangled cat' sample you chose? No worries: If you've synced your sequencer to tape, instead of having to rerecord the part, you simply change the patch at the keyboard.

In fact, all of the sequencer advantages we listed on page 109—including the fact that virtual tracks don't suffer tape noise or crosstalk problems—apply when you sync instruments to tape.

Are there any disadvantages? A few, perhaps. For one, you do give up a tape track to the sync code, though the number of additional virtual tracks you gain more than offsets the loss. Another is that since your drum machine and MIDI instruments aren't recorded on the tape, you'll need them (or suitable replacement instruments) at hand whenever you want to play back the multi-track tape. If you want to roam to other studios with your tape, you'll probably have to haul your drum machine, sequencer, and synthesizers with you in order to play back the complete recording.

Another disadvantage, of sorts, is that you'll need additional inputs to accommodate the additional tracks you gain. For instance, if all your tracks were tape tracks, a

sible for you to start it at exactly the right split-second. Any tape speed variations would further confound your hopes. If you had you used tape sync, however, it would

be a simple matter to reprogram the drum machine, and use the existing code to drive the new program—in perfect sync with the original.

program, the drum machine's tape sync output jack should be connected to your ministudio or tape recorder (either directly or via the mixer). Some newer ministudios, including the Yamaha MT2X2 and the Tascam Porta Two, have 'dedicated' *sync input* and *output* jacks. These jacks are inputs which bypass the recorder's noise reduction and feed the sync code to an outside track at the correct level. If your ministudio or tape recorder lacks dedicated sync jacks, no problem. You'll want to connect the drum machine's sync output jack to a mixer line input, and then assign that input to the outside track.

Tape Sync Techniques

Syncing your gear to tape should be a straightforward and hassle-free experience. There are some problems you may encounter, however, any of which can cause no end of frustration. If you keep in mind the following points and techniques, you should have no worries.

Plan Against Pitfalls. First of all, when syncing anything to tape, you should use an 'outside track' for the sync code. With a 4-track, that means either track 1 or 4; with an 8-track, track 1 or 8, and so on. By convention, the last track is usually used, so with a 4-track you'd be using track 4.

There's a good reason for using an outside track. Any code—from FSK to 'smart code' to SMPTE—requires snag-free recording and playback. For example, poor quality tapes are prone to drop-outs (losing some oxide coating). Minor drop outs, too small to be heard with a music track, can interrupt the recording or playback of the sync code, causing any synced devices to 'lose sync.' In a similar way, audio tracks adjacent to the code track can interfere with the code. Snare drums, hi-hats, and other percussive parts recorded at too high a level are notorious for this. Consequently, placing the code on an outside track means there's one less adjacent track to cause problems.

While some engineers feel best leaving a blank *guard track* next to the code track, most modern gear has good enough crosstalk specs to let you record a vocal, guitar, or other non-percussive instrument, in the adjacent track.

The code track is best recorded *without* noise reduction. This applies especially to dbx, since most find that Dolby rarely

introduces a problem; dbx, however, can alter the code's signal just enough to render it unreadable during playback.

Finally, before you start, ensure your recorder's heads are freshly cleaned and demagnetized—*this is critical!*

How It's Done. Whether you're using a 24-track and a wall of sequenced synths, or just a ministudio and drum machine, sync techniques with simple or smart sync code remain the same. The techniques employed for SMPTE time code are very similar, but be sure to read "Recording Time Code" on page 115.

Let's say you plan to use a drum machine, a sequencer, a synthesizer, and a sampler, for your virtual tracks. The plan is to sync the drum machine to tape; it will then drive the sequencer, which in turn will play the synth and sampler. You could just as easily, by the way, choose to sync the sequencer to tape, and then sync the drum machine to it. Most people prefer to record and sync the drum tracks first, however, so that they have a rhythmic reference for later tracks.

The first order of business is to program the drum machine. If you're using simple or smart sync (but not SMPTE time code), you need to decide the tempo—or tempo changes—and the total length of the drum program. We can change the actual program at any time, but remember that the code we record starts and stops the machine, and tells it at what tempo to play—once you've striped the sync code, there's no easy way to change tempo. And since sync stops when the code stops, it's consequently a good idea to program the drum sequence slightly longer than you expect it may run, since the sequence can be shortened but not lengthened.

Once you've created this 'template'

Before going any further, make sure that you're using fresh tape, and that any dbx is switched off for the appropriate track. Most modern ministudios should let you do this (again, Dolby is rarely a problem). If you have an older ministudio that doesn't give you this option, such as the Tascam 244, you can either have the machine modified, or you can carry on and try these procedures with care—you should have success, if you're patient enough to try various levels.

And this brings us to the next stage: Start the drum machine. It should start to generate a sync code from its sync output jack. Now set the level of the code so that the tape recorder's input meter reads between '-10' VU and '-3' VU. (You may have to put the track in 'record ready' to see the meter). This level will vary, depending upon the machine you're using. Follow the manufacturer's recommendation. Too little level will not be read back correctly, or may be more prone to slight dropouts. Too much level, and you can cause crosstalk problems on the adjacent track. Once the level is set correctly, stop the drum machine and reset it to the beginning of

12-input mixer would probably be a suitable choice for an 8-track studio. If you had a large number of synced virtual tracks, however, you may need something on the order of 20 or more inputs. For this reason, British-style split-monitor consoles (page 41)—which allow you to use the tape monitor section for additional line inputs during mixdown—are a popular choice with many MIDI-oriented musicians. If you're using a ministudio, you may have to use an outboard submixer to accommodate your virtual tracks.

Finally, as we find out about in "Tape Sync Techniques" (page 112), sync codes are rather frail; slight tape imperfections, improper recording levels, and so forth, can render them unusable. Despite these drawbacks, there are few modern studios that don't take advantage of all that tape sync offers.

There are actually several forms of tape sync. These include:

- *Basic* tape sync.
- *Smart* tape sync.
- *SMPTE* or *MIDI Time Code* sync.

'Basic' (Clock/FSK) Tape Sync. Early tape sync codes would record actual clock pulses to tape. They were replaced by a more reliable code known as an *FSK* code, which stands for *Frequency Shift Keying*. An FSK code consists of two tones, usually around 1000 to 2000 Hz. The code alternates, or shifts, between these two frequencies; the shifting rate is dependent upon the tempo of the song recorded.

While FSK sync allows you to create virtual tracks as well as change MIDI instrument patches and drum machine patterns, it does have some limitations. First of all, whatever the machine's tempo was when the code was recorded will be its tempo when synced to the code. Secondly, you can't lengthen the song without starting from the beginning and re-recording the code. (One way around this is to record a sync track with a drum pattern that's intentionally longer than you expect the song will be. The pattern can later be shortened, so that it stops before the code runs out, to suit the song's length.)

The biggest limitation, however, is that FSK code is quite 'stupid': It knows when to start or stop synced devices, but it doesn't know *where* it is when it's running. This means that if you stop your multi-track recorder in the middle of play back it's necessary to start the *entire* song from the *beginning*—just in order to re-establish sync with your drum machine or sequencer! (In this way, using simple sync codes is much like using ordinary clock sync between devices.)

As you can imagine, this can make for some tedious recording sessions, particularly if you need to keep going over a section near the end of the song, for a solo or some other intricate punch-in. Recording a *reference track* is one way to relieve the tedium (see below).

There is, however, a more elegant solution, as we'll see below.

'Smart' Tape Sync. Wouldn't it be nice if all your virtual tracks could play along with, or chase, your multi-track tape recorder,

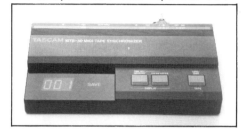

Figure 14.3 Tascam's MTS-30 'smart' sync box allows MIDI devices to sync to tape from anywhere in the song. If you're working in either 4/4 or 3/4 musical time, the MTS-30 will also display the current measure number.

starting and stopping in sync wherever your tape happened to be? It so happens that there are devices, generically known as *'smart' sync boxes*, which can bring this power to any MIDI drum machine or sequencer that's equipped with the Song Position Pointer facility (see page 111). The

---

the program. The sync output level will disappear.

Cue the tape to where you want your recording to start (be sure to leave enough of a leader), and start recording. It's a good idea to let a few seconds pass, after which you should press 'play' on the drum machine. Your meters should tell you that you're recording the sync track. If not, make sure that the machine is recording, check all cable connections, and check your record status switches (some open-reel multi-tracks may have to be set to 'input monitor' in order for the meters to respond to the incoming signal).

While the drum machine is playing back, you can listen to its audio output if you like. Remember that you're just listening to the machine—its audio outputs shouldn't be assigned to any tape tracks at this point. (Actually, you could be recording a 'reference track' as described below, but we won't worry about that for now.)

You probably won't want to monitor the sync track—it will sound like nasty square waves.

Once the drum program is finished, the drum machine will stop, and so will its code output. Now you need to confirm that the recording was a 'take.' Reset the drum machine to the beginning of the program, and also set it for 'external sync-to-tape' mode. Then rewind the recorder to a point a few seconds before the beginning of the code, and disable 'record ready' for the sync track. Connect the code track's output to the 'tape sync input' of the drum machine. You can go directly from a 'tape' or 'sync' output on the recorder to the drum machine, or you can use a direct output from one of the mixer's input channels. If you use a channel, make sure its fader level is up, and that it's set to

receive a signal from the correct tape track. Finally, make sure your mixer is set to listen to the drum machine's audio outputs.

When everything's set, press 'play' on the recorder, making sure the recorder is in 'repro mode' if it's an open-reel machine. In theory, the drum machine should start playing its program as soon as the code starts, and stop when the code stops.

Troubleshooting Tape Sync. If you hear nothing, take a look at the drum machine. Does it read as if it's running, with measure numbers flying by and the 'play' indicator lit?

If so, you have a monitoring problem, and need to check your cables, input switches, and fader levels. If the drum machine's just sitting there looking pretty, however, and set for external sync, you have a code recording or playback problem. Make sure all sync code cables are okay, and try readjusting the playback levels.

If you still have no luck, make a check list of the possible pitfalls we described at the beginning. When all else fails, try the procedure again, perhaps recording the sync tone at a slightly higher record level. It's not uncommon, especially when syncing a device for the first time, to have to try as many as ten different record and playback level settings before it clicks—so don't be discouraged if your first try at sync is unsuccessful!

Once you establish sync, be sure to note the right level settings. And before going any further, remember these points:

- Don't record any sharply percussive tracks adjacent to the sync track.
- Don't bounce any other tracks onto the

sync track.

- The sync track can always be rerecorded before you record any other tracks. Once you've recorded any other parts on the remaining tracks, however, any mishap with the sync track is curtains! A drop out longer than a few milliseconds or an accidental punch-in will mean the end of sync for the song in question. There are elaborate machines, such as the Garfield Dr. Click, that can recreate a sync track, but they're options for the well-financed user, and are not always a guaranteed fix.

Syncing Additional Gear. Now that the drum machine is operating in sync, you can set it to drive your MIDI sequencer. Just place the sequencer in 'external MIDI clock,' connect a MIDI cable from the drum machine's MIDI out to the sequencer's MIDI in, ensure the two are operating on the same MIDI channel, and you should be in business. This way, the tape drives the drum machine, which in turn drives the sequencer, which in turn records and plays back your MIDI instruments.

The Reference Track. Unless you're using smart sync or SMPTE time code—which allow gear to 'chase' the tape—you'll need to start the tape from the top of the song every time you want to reestablish sync.

To avoid this tedious procedure, you may wish to record all your synced devices to a single audio *reference track*. This way you can hear your drum and other parts while you record your other tracks, without having to use sync until mixdown, or until you record over the reference track. (Of course, be sure you don't accidentally record over the sync track!)

pioneer of these is the JL Cooper PPS-1, though similar boxes are available from Tascam and others.

A smart sync box has at least four jacks: A 'MIDI in,' a 'MIDI out,' a 'tape in,' and a 'tape out.' The procedure resembles simple tape sync, though the hook-up is different. The device to be synced is connected via its MIDI ports to the MIDI ports on the smart box. The tape recorder is then connected to the appropriate tape jacks on the box.

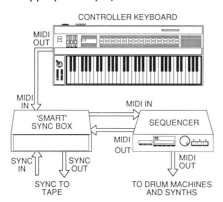

Figure 14.4 A typical smart sync hookup. If the smart sync box has a MIDI merge function, it's possible to overdub new sequencer passages from a controller while the system is synced to tape.

When the MIDI machine is put into play, it sends a MIDI clock and Song Position Pointer message to the smart box. The box then stripes a code on tape which is 'stamped' with location references. This way, when the code is played back into the smart box, it can regenerate both MIDI clock and location information, passing it along to the synced device. And presto—your drum machine or sequencer can follow your tape machine, kicking into play wherever you start your tape. All in all, it's a sensible alternative to recording a reference track or syncing up from the beginning of the song each time you want to record.

But just when you thought your sync-to-tape troubles were over, there are even better alternatives to smart sync boxes!

SMPTE And MIDI Time Code Tape Sync. As we'll be learning next, SMPTE time code is the most sophisticated code available for tape sync. A track striped with SMPTE time code is imprinted with an exact time reference at every point of the tape. In practical terms, this means that synced devices can 'lock up' instantly to your tape recorder, with precision often greater than 1/100th of a second—as opposed to the measure number precision that smart sync boxes provide.

Some musical products, such as the Akai/Linn MPC60, include built-on SMPTE time code generators and readers, so that they can stripe and follow their own time code tracks. Other manufacturers, including Fostex, Yamaha, and others, make SMPTE-to-MIDI converters, which allow MIDI devices with SPP to sync to a time code track.

Finally, a new development is MIDI Time Code (MTC), which—like SPP—is a way of syncing devices and sending timing information through MIDI. Rather than being precise to sixteenth-notes, however, MTC offers precision to the split-second, much like SMPTE time code. We'll learn more about MTC below.

* * * *

Before we find out more about SMPTE and MIDI Time Code sync, let's sum up what we've learned about tape sync:

● With 'simple' tape sync, you have to start the song from the beginning in order to establish sync for your virtual tracks.
● 'Smart' sync boxes will allow your drum machine or sequencer to chase the tape machine with precision to the sixteenth-note.
● SMPTE time code tape sync offers chase-lock sync, but with much greater precision.

SMPTE Time Code And MIDI Applications

SMPTE time code offers the most sophisticated type of synchronization, with much greater resolution than is possible with any other type of code.

If you ever plan to work with video—including any kind of soundtrack or audio-for-video post production (see page 123)— 'SMPTE'-Speak' is a required language. More interested in music than in video? Well, if you've heard of 48-track studios, these are facilities with two 24-track tape recorders perfectly locked in tandem using devices known as SMPTE time code synchronizers. (Actually they're 46-track studios, since time code is recorded on one track of each machine.)

And if you're simply working with MIDI instruments or a drum machine, SMPTE time code can bring a lot of power into your studio. For instance, there are SMPTE-to-MIDI translators, which are similar to smart sync boxes but much more powerful. There are also MIDI Time Code (MTC) translators. MTC is a variant of SMPTE time code, hybrid for transmission through MIDI cables and

ports. It won't be long before most professional drum machines and sequencers have something to do with MTC, if not SMPTE—and the reasons are plentiful.

Using either SMPTE time code or MTC, it's possible to:

● Sync sequenced synthesizers and other virtual tracks to tape with perfect 'chase-lock' accuracy—allowing the virtual tracks to start, play, and stop whenever or wherever the tape does.
● Synchronize two or more audio or video tape machines.
● Perform very sophisticated audio production techniques.

Before we see how SMPTE time code is put to use with MIDI, tape recorders, and audio-for-video production, let's learn a bit more about the code itself.

The Code. If video were never invented, we wouldn't have time code as we know it. Film, after all, has visible, numbered frames. But video tape looks like audio tape, and this presents a number of problems.

For example, when people edit film, it's easy to tell where a reel is in time, just by looking at the frame count printed on the edge of the frame. Since each frame is distinct (there are 24 frames per second in film), it's also easy to see where to make a cut, and to time how long scenes will last. Without visible frames, early video editing was cumbersome, involving lots of cueing the tape, strange dye that would stain the tape where 'video frames' began, and many haphazard cuts. To the rescue was a company called EECO, who developed the first video time code in the mid-1960s, based on a 24-hour clock. By 1969 their code was modified and standardized by the Society of Motion Picture and Television Engineers, and hence become known as SMPTE time code.

SMPTE time code goes by a couple other names, as well. Many people call it just 'SMPTE,' even though, strictly speaking, that's the name of the society and not the code. And in most places outside of North America, it's known as SMPTE/EBU time code, or just EBU—named for the European Broadcasters' Union, which adopted the SMPTE protocol.

Most of us have seen a representation of time code: Have you ever watched a TV monitor and seen a small 'window' with numbers running by? Well, that's known as a window dub, and is one way engineers and editors view the code. But what do those mysterious numbers represent?

Figure 14.5 A 'burned in' window dub display. The Fostex 460 is one of the few recorder/mixers that work with a transport synchronizer.

The early designers of the code decided they needed a 24-hour representation of hours, minutes, seconds, and frames. These different components of the code are represented by a multi-digit string of numbers, which can:

● be created by a time code generator;
● be recorded, or striped, on tape;
● and then be read by a time code reader.

The beauty of this code—as opposed to the FSK or smart sync tones used by many drum machines or sequencers—is that the code's time can be read at any point. Figure 14.5 shows a window dub, with a reading, or *address*, of:

17:26:35:17

This is a reading of "17 hours, 26 minutes, 35 seconds, 17 frames." We all know about hours, minutes, and seconds. What about frames?

As mentioned, film usually is shot at a speed of 24 frames per second (fps). The four frame-count standards used in time code are:

- 24—for some film work.
- 25—the European video standard.
- 29.97—for North American color video.
- 30—the North American black & white video standard.

The 29.97 fps rate is commonly known as *drop-frame*. Drop-frame is a rate that is generated at 30 fps, but actually skips a frame every so often. The full reasons for this are beyond the scope of this book, but here's a simplified explanation: In North America, color video signals have a frequency of 29.97 fps. If a 30 fps generator were to run *without* dropping frames, it would accumulate an error of 3.6 seconds every hour. By dropping two frames every minute (except the 10th minute), a total of 108 frames per hour are dropped—which equals 3.6 seconds. The average resulting rate is 29.97 fps, a perfect match for color video.

This brings us to *subframes*, which are normally not displayed in a window dub, but are usually displayed by time code readers. Subframes are a means of chopping up frames into even smaller portions. One subframe is usually 1/100th of a frame, regardless of the frame rate.

Sometimes, subframes are generated at a rate of 1/80th of a frame, which is known as *bit rate*. The reason? *Bits* are the standard 'alphabet' of computers and other digital gear—each bit being either a '1' (on), or a '0' (off). SMPTE time code is a digital code—a stream of bits—'spelled out' with 80 bits per frame. Aside from registering the current time reading, time code bits are used to describe which frame count is being used, the beginning and end of each frame (known as the *sync word*), and other information.

Since any point on tape can be referenced not only to the second, but also to the frame and subframe, SMPTE time code is very precise—which is necessary for both video and audio work.

Longitudinal Time Code (LTC) vs. Vertical Interval Time Code (VITC). If you use time code exclusively with audio gear, you may not need to know the two different ways in which time code can be recorded and read, and you may wish to skip ahead.

Time code is recorded in one of two ways, either *longitudinally*, or *vertically*. Let's find out what that means.

Longitudinal time code (LTC) is the type of code that is recorded onto audio tape recorders (ATRs). It can also be recorded on one audio track of a video tape recorder (VTR)—most professional VTRs have two or three audio tracks. With either machine, LTC is recorded like an audio track.

LTC is an audible tone, pulsing out bits at either 2000 or 2400 times per second, de-pending upon the frame standard. This frequency of 2000 or 2400 Hz is easily recorded and played back by an ATR (or audio track of a VTR).

When the machine is fast-forwarded, though, the code's frequency will rise above the audio bandwidth of the machine, making it impossible for the code to be read. Also adding to the problem is that in fast wind the tape is usually disengaged from the heads. One solution to enable fast-wind LTC reading is to use a *wideband reader*, which can read very high frequencies. It's also necessary to make sure, either by using a cue lever (on an ATR) or by using a 'fast-scan' mode (on a VTR), that the tape remains against the heads.

When ATRs and VTRs are slowed down, or made to 'crawl,' however—which is common practice when searching to a cue

---

Recording Time Code

Much like FSK and other sync codes (page 113), SMPTE time code is sometimes temperamental. It can be affected by tape dropouts and adjacent percussive tracks. Nonetheless, by its very nature, SMPTE is more dependable than FSK or other sync codes.

For instance, a brief tape dropout on an FSK code track can completely destroy sync with a drum machine or other device. Most time code readers, synchronizers, and SMPTE-responding drum machines and sequencers, however, can 'fill in the gaps' during momentary lapses of code of SMPTE time code. They do this by continuing to run from whatever time they were running at when the code dropped out. When the code returns, they'll make whatever adjustments are necessary to catch up or slow down to the current reading. But despite this inherent advantage, time code must still be treated with respect.

Like FSK, heads must be cleaned and demagnetized before time code is striped onto an outside track. Levels should be in the '–5' to '0' *VU* level, and dbx noise reduction should be bypassed.

Unlike FSK and smart codes, which begin and stop with each song, it's best to start striping time code at the beginning of the tape, and to keep striping the same code all the way to the end of the tape. This way, any given time code address will have just one location on the tape. Since synchronizers and other SMPTE-based devices can be set with variable offset times (page 119), it's fine if a given song starts at the five-minute mark, or wherever. Incidentally, many engineers will sync gear and begin the first song from the "00:01:00:00:00" mark rather than at true zero; this avoids running out of time code when rewinding to the beginning of the tape.

ORIGINAL TIME CODE
SECOND GENERATION
THIRD GENERATION

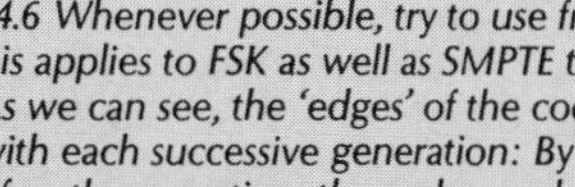

Figure 14.6 Whenever possible, try to use fresh code (this applies to FSK as well as SMPTE time code). As we can see, the 'edges' of the code distort with each successive generation: By the third or fourth generation, the code may become unreadable. Fortunately, most time code readers offer a regeneration function, which will spit out fresh code from old.

The time code itself should always be fresh: Directly copying time code from one tape to another is asking for big trouble. Why? The reason is that copied code, which is entering its second generation of tape, may suffer degeneration. This, at least, can cause occasional lapses of sync; at worst, sync may be impossible.

The easiest way to avoid these problems is to start with freshly-generated code. There are times, however, when transferring audio tracks, that copied tracks must have exactly the same time code readings as the original. In that case, the solution is to *regenerate* the original code, by running it into a time code generator that can spit out a new, identically-timed code.

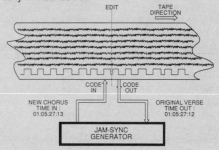

Figure 14.7 If different portions of tape—with different time code readings—are spliced together, the composite tape will be a mish-mash of time code. The solution is to jam-sync, which is a function offered by many higher-quality time code generator/readers. In the above example, jam sync is used to create a continuous code over a newly-spliced chorus.

Regeneration is similar to—but shouldn't be confused with—*jam sync*, which refers most often to a means of generating code in sync with an original LTC or VITC time reading. Jam sync is used by video editors to rewrite, or 'jam,' time code over newly edited portions of video tape. This allows the assembled master tape to have one continuous time code, rather than blocks of tape which jump back and forth to their original time code readings.

When using code, it's important that the generator and reader be set to the proper standard. If you're striping film, 24 is used; 25 is for European Video, 29.97 and 30 are for North American color and black and white video, respectively. While some synchronizers are able to translate different standards, obviously it's best to try and stay consistent.

What if you're using SMPTE for nothing more than syncing sequencers and other audio devices to your multi-track recorder—what frame rate should you use? In fact, it doesn't matter, as long as you pick a frame rate and use it consistently. Most people, however, choose the convention of their part of the world. For North Americans, that's 29.97 fps; for most others it's 25 fps.

point—most time code readers are no longer able to follow LTC, even with a wide-band reader. This brings us to *vertical interval time code*, or VITC (pronounced *vitsee*). This is the type of code recorded by most 3/4" and 1" professional video machines, and is quite different from LTC.

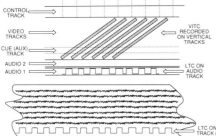

Figure 14.8a, 14.8b The top diagram shows how VITC is recorded vertically on video tape—along with longitudinally recorded LTC. The lower diagram shows an analog multi-track tape, with LTC recorded on track 8. Most musicians working with video can get by fine with just LTC on the video tape, unless they need to maintain perfect sync with the master video tape at all times, such as during slow 'crawls.'

You may know that all VTRs—including the one the one that might be hooked up to your TV—record video information with rotating heads. And the information is recorded vertically: Each time the head scans from top-to-bottom on the tape, it's recording one video frame. (Since the tape is moving, it's actually a diagonal, or *helical* scan, but for our purposes we can think of it as vertical.)

When the heads scan back from the bottom of the frame to the top, they actually don't record or play back any visual information in that area. That gap in visual information is known as the *video blanking interval*, or *color black*. This area, by the way, is what you see when your TV's vertical hold goes kaput, and a black bar starts creeping up your screen.

But while there isn't any stuff in the color black that we're meant to see, lots of information is recorded there, such as color information, and time code, as well. When VITC is read and played back from the VTR, it is done so vertically, as the heads scan back to the head of the frame. And since VITC is *part* of the video information, it must be recorded at the same time the video is recorded.

Though it's a lot more complicated than LTC, VITC offers all kinds of advantages for video people. The biggest advantage is as follows: As we've learned, when VTRs are 'crawling' very slowly, LTC can't be read. But video editors need to make their video machines crawl, or 'shuttle', in order to find precise edit points. Since a VTR's heads are still rotating, the VITC can be read when the tape is barely moving, or even when the picture is frozen.

Video editors enjoy another advantage with VITC: It is perfectly frame-referenced. That is, when a VITC reading says that you're at the beginning of a frame, the actual video is *in fact* at the beginning of a frame. LTC, while it gives frame-precise readings, is not ordinarily adjusted so that the start of an LTC frame reading *exactly* corresponds to the start of the actual video frame (*jam sync* will allow this; see "Recording Time Code" on page 115).

In any event, this explains the differ-ences between VITC and LTC. Remember that conventional multi-track recorders use LTC, and video machines use either LTC or VITC. A translator is necessary to convert VITC into a code that's usable by LTC gear (which includes many synchronizers). And if you wish to 'burn' a window dub of time code into the video, a VITC generator is necessary. For the most part, though, audio people use LTC for scoring and other audio work.

SMPTE-To-MIDI Translation. Earlier we learned about smart sync boxes, such as the J.L. Cooper PPS-1. These are able to stripe a special code on tape, which, when played back, is able to generate Song Position Pointer messages for drum machines and other devices which may recognize them. This way these devices can start sync from the middle of a song, and are able to 'chase' the tape as it's put into play, after being wound in any direction. (Here's an interesting bit of trivia, which you should be able to appreciate by now; Cooper's "PPS" stands for "Poor Person's SMPTE"—it gets this name because while its code isn't smart enough to know where it's at in terms of seconds and frames, it does, at least, know which sixteenth note it's at.)

Originally developed before the advent of the PPS-1 and other smart sync boxes, *SMPTE-to-MIDI translators* are similar devices. Rather than a proprietary smart code, however, they use SMPTE time code, and are able to make a 'translation' between time code and MIDI measure numbers. The Roland SBX-80, the Fostex 4050, and the Garfield Master Beat, are all such translators. Furthermore, many sequencer software programs, such as Passport's Mastertracks and Mark of the Unicorn's Performer, can function as SMPTE-to-MIDI translators. Here's how they work.

As we've learned, SMPTE time code is based on a 24-hour clock, and is broken down to frames and subframes. If we know a song's tempo, time signature, and total number of measures, we can calculate how long—in 24-hour time—a song will run. And if we know this much information about a song it's also possible to make a reverse calculation; that is, to convert 24-hour time to measure numbers.

Here's how that's done. Let's imagine a song running at 120 beats per minute (bpm), with a time signature of 4/4 (four beats per measure), for a total length of 90 measures:

{120 bpm} ÷ {4 beats per measure}
= 30 measures per minute

{90 measures total}
÷ {30 measures per minute}
= 3 minutes total running length

{60 seconds per minute}
÷ {30 measures per minute}
= 2 seconds per measure

Armed with this much information, we—or more to the point, a SMPTE-to-MIDI translator—can convert time to measure numbers, and *vice versa*. For example, we see that the song will run for 3 minutes. That means that if we started a time code generator at "00:00:00:00" at the beginning of the song, by the end of the song it would read "00:03:00:00." At a reading of "00:01:34:00" the song would have just finished playing the 47th measure of the song.

That's the basic logic behind SMPTE-to-MIDI translation: Once a translator is programmed with a song's *tempo map* (its varying or constant time signature and tempo), it can spit out corresponding MIDI Clock and Song Position Pointer information. Assuming synced MIDI devices recognize SPP, full chase-lock to SMPTE time code is possible.

Well, this is all very impressive, but what advantage does this offer us over smart tape sync? After all, smart sync boxes function more or less 'transparently,' since they don't require any pre-programming, and they cost a heck of a lot less than a translator.

It's true, a SMPTE-to-MIDI translator does require some programming and a good chunk of cash, and for many people a smart sync box is a better choice. But there are some real advantages to using SMPTE-to-MIDI translators over smart sync boxes, including:

- SMPTE/EBU time code is universal—any tape striped with it from anywhere on the planet can drive just about any SMPTE-to-MIDI translator—and it's going to be around for a long time. Smart sync box codes are proprietary, however: The box which generates the code is the only box which will read the code (this may change should manufacturers adopt a standard, but many argue that SMPTE already is a standard).

- The same SMPTE time code track that is striped for the translator can be used with synchronizers, video machine, and lots of other gear. If you're using smart sync, and later decide to use the same tape with other gear, you may need to give up two or more tape tracks to codes.

- SMPTE gives you a direct time reading.

- SMPTE-to-MIDI translators allow you to convert a given amount of time to a MIDI tempo, or to a total number of measure numbers. For example, let's say you've created a sequenced instrumental riff that runs for 1 minute, 5 seconds. A producer comes to you and says "You're beautiful, we love it, but it's got to be 1 minute on the nose!" You could fool around with the sequencer's tempo setting, but with a translator there's an elegant alternative: Just program a 'total song time' of "00:01:00:00" and the tempo will speed up (or slow down, if you were under time) to make the song fit the given time to the subframe!

- Since tempo changes can be programmed, it's an easy matter to introduce *retards* or *accelerandi* as desired. Similarly, subtle tempo changes can be programmed, to add a more 'human' feel to virtual tracks. Any or all of these changes can be performed at any time after the code is striped—with smart sync, you're committed to keep the same tempo(s) as you had when the smart code was striped.

- All the other advantages of sync-to-tape, as described on page 111, will apply.

As you can see, that's quite a bit of power. On top of all of this, most SMPTE-to-MIDI converters perform other functions. Fostex's 4050, aside from doing 'ordinary' SMPTE-to-MIDI translation, also has a complete autolocator, designed to work most Fostex tape recorders. It's possible to tell the 4050 to search to a given time code, and not only will the tape recorder search to that time, but all MIDI gear will follow and start at the nearest measure. Or, if you're more musically-minded, you can tell the 4050 to go to, say, measure 19 of your song: Your MIDI gear *and* your tape recorder will search to measure 19! (Tascam's MIDIizer will perform the same function with Tascam gear.) A growing trend will be sequencers, drum machines, and other gear, which respond not only to clock and Song Position Pointer information, but also MIDI Time Code. MTC is in fact a link between the SMPTE and MIDI worlds, allowing time code to be passed between the two worlds.

Figure 14.9 Opcode's Timecode machine will convert SMPTE (LTC) to MIDI Time Code, and vice-versa. When used with a Macintosh computer (via an interface) and the right software, the Timecode machine will function as a full-fledged SMPTE generator and SMPTE-to-MTC reader.

Functionally, MTC operates much like a more precise form of SPP. It's also transparent: Using a SMPTE-to-MTC converter, such as Opcode's Timecode Machine, it's no longer necessary to program tempo and measure information in order to establish sync between SMPTE time code and MIDI devices (of course, the MIDI devices must have MTC implementation). Rather, SMPTE readings can transfer directly to MTC, and be passed through MIDI.

Of course, MTC can also function on its own, as a means of sending extremely precise location information between MIDI devices.

Transport Synchronization

Video tape recorders (VTRs), audio tape recorders (ATRs), film projectors, and even slide projectors and other transports, are commonly synced together for a number of different purposes. Usually three VTRs are synced together for video editing; VTRs are also synced to film projectors to make transfers from film to video.

There are two common types of transport sync with which multi-track engineers should be familiar. The first is sync between two or more audio tape recorders. This allows, for example, two multi-track tape recorders to be linked together to expand the total number of available tracks. Syncing a 2-track to a multi-track also has several uses, as we'll learn.

The other type of transport sync musician/engineers frequently encounter is sync between a VTR and an ATR. This is key to live music video production, as well as modern scoring and sound effects techniques—which are known as *audio-for-video post-production*, or just *a/v post*, techniques.

The heart of any transport sync system is a *synchronizer*. Available from Adams-Smith, Audio Kinetics, Cypher, Fostex, Tascam, and others, a synchronizer is typically a rack-mountable, computerized box, which connects between two or more transports, and an optional remote control. Each manufacturer offers a unique approach to controls and features, the concepts will remain the same though regardless of which system is used.

Synchronizers are, in essence, computers which are able to 'lock' one or more *slave* transports with a *master* transport. At very minimum, the synchronizer compares the time code readings of a master and slave, and adjusts the speed of the slave to match perfectly the speed of the master. In its most elaborate role, a synchronizer can control all transports of all machines—master or slave—and can automate many functions.

Many synchronizers, by the way, include built-in time code reader/generators (normally LTC rather than VITC). Some require a separate reader/generator and/or reader.

ATR-To-ATR Sync. What's the procedure if we want to lock together two 16-track tape recorders, for 30-track recording? (Each machine forfeits one audio track to time code.)

First, time code is striped the length of the tape on track 16 of each machine. Then, one machine is designated 'master' and the other 'slave.' To perform *code-only* sync (see "Code-Only vs. Chase-Lock Sync" on page 118), the synchronizer needs three connections: a time code input from the master, a time code input from the slave, and a cable connection to the *external control*, or

SMPTE port, of the slave. If you want the slave to *chase-lock* to the master, you'll need a connection between the synchronizer and the master's transport, as well. (Most contemporary open-reel recorders—and even a few cassette transports—have an external 'SMPTE port.' If not, they can only be used as masters in a code-only sync arrangement.)

When the connections and some adjustments are made—to match the synchronizer's response to the transport characteristics of the slave (and master, for chase-lock)—the master is put in play. Once the synchronizer begins to read the master's time code, it starts the slave, and compares the slave's time code reading with the master's. It then adjusts the slave's transport until both machines are running in perfect sync, at the same time code reading.

If the two ATRs start quite close in code time, this adjustment is usually a speeding up or slowing down of the slave's capstan motor. If instead they are far apart, the slave will either be fast-forwarded or rewound until it approaches the master's reading, then put in play and capstan-controlled.

Once the two are in sync, an indicator on the synchronizer will light to let you know the mission was successful and the two are perfectly locked—usually to an accuracy within 1/100th of a frame.

And that's it: Two 16-track recorders can now function as a single 30-track. If you have a chase-lock system, you can treat the entire system as if it were one machine.

ATR-To-VTR Sync. In most audio-for-video applications, the VTR is set up as the master. Since most music scoring and sound effects are visually dependent, this arrangement works fine.

If you're scoring music or sound effects for video, you may be watching the visuals with a 3/4" professional video recorder—or you may be using a 1/2" VHS or Beta recorder. With SMPTE time code pre-striped on one of the VTR's audio tracks, the ATR can be code-only synced as a slave, via a synchronizer.

Most 1/2" VTRs lack external control parts—meaning they *must* be used as masters in a code-only sync arrangement. If you have a 3/4" deck, or one of the few professional 1/2" decks that have an appropriate external control port, you can set up chase-lock sync between your VTR and ATR.

ATR-to-ATR Sync Techniques. We've just described syncing two multi-track ATRs, in order to gain additional tracks. But additional tracks aren't the only incentives for using a synchronizer with ATRs. Magnetic tape is a relatively fragile medium, increasingly subject to drop-outs and deterioration with each playing, and particularly with each fast-wind. Here's a popular professional technique, designed to minimize wear on master tapes:

1. Record the 'bed,' or rhythm, tracks on one original master reel.
2. Mix the rhythm tracks down to one or two 'cue' tracks, recording them on a second reel of a second multi-track machine. The original master reel can now be safely put away until mixdown.
3. Using the cue tracks as a guide, the overdubs are recorded on the second reel.
4. Once the overdubs are complete, the

Figure 14.10 The Adams-Smith Zeta-Three is a very powerful SMPTE-to-MIDI translator and transport synchronizer. Shown are two Zeta-Threes and a remote. Each box will provide full chase-lock sync between a master and slave transport plus MIDI gear; the remote can function as a transport controller for the entire system.

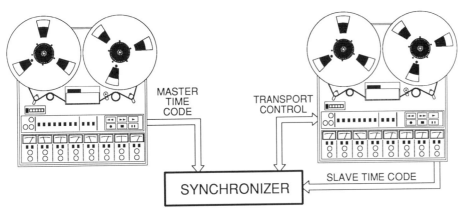

Figure 14.11 Code-only sync. As long as the master and slave are able to provide time code—and the slave can be controlled—limited but useful sync is possible. In fact, anything that will provide code can work as a master: a video tape recorder, a simple cassette player, even the cue track from an industrial slide projector can be used to sync a recorder.

overdub reel is synced together with the original master reel, and the two are mixed down to a 2-track (without the cue tracks, of course).

Since rhythm tracks are usually recorded in just a few passes (whereas overdubs can require dozens or even hundreds of passes), this technique can help avoid potential problems and maintain fidelity.

Some studios perform a similar technique with just one in-house multi-track machine and a syncable 2-track machine with a *center-track* designed to record time code (see Figure 14.12). This type of machine has a third track, between the two audio tracks, designed to record and play back code. By dumping the rhythm tracks to one audio track of the 2-track, overdubs can be recorded one track at a time on the second audio track. As each overdub is a 'take,' it's then bounced back in sync onto the master

multi-track reel.

Another alternative for studios with a single multi-track machine is to bounce the master reel rhythm tracks to a 2-track, and then re-record them onto two tracks of a second multi-track reel—which will serve as the overdub reel. When mixdown time rolls

Figure 14.12 A close-up of a Fostex E-2 headstack. Like some other professional 2-tracks, the E-2 is a 2-track format with a center time code track. Between the two regular audio gaps on the erase, record, and play heads, is a center gap, which is used to record and play back the time code. Center-code machines are compatible for use with regular half-track 2-track tapes.

around, a second multi-track and a synchronizer are rented, the overdub and master reels are synced, and the two are mixed.

Prior to the development of center-code 2-tracks, 4-track machines were the common standard for syncing 2-track information: Tracks 1 and 2 hold the audio, track 3 is blank, and track 4 is the code. The center-code format is perfectly compatible with ordinary half-track tapes.

A center-code 2-track has many sync uses, beyond the 'spare the master reel' technique we just described. For example, sound effects can be stored on 2-track tapes, and can be cued and started by a synchronizer, in order to dump effects to a multi-track recorder at programmed times (see "Event Automation" on page 123). If you've run out of audio tracks on your multi-track, a couple additional tracks can be found by syncing a 2-track to the multi-track.

ATR-to-VTR Sync Techniques. Perhaps the most obvious application for locking an audio tape recorder to a video tape recorder is in live music video production.

As you may know, during a typical live recording, individual performers and their

Code-Only vs. Chase-Lock Sync

There are two basic types of transport sync. The simplest is often known as *code-only* sync; the other is known as *chase-lock* sync. Code-only sync means that the slave follows, via the synchronizer, just the time code from the master: It doesn't follow any of the master's transport cues. That is, if the master kicks into fast forward or rewind, and stops putting out a time code signal, the slave will simply stop and wait for the master to go back into play—whereupon the slave can once again receive time code and be in sync with the master (the slave may have to be wound to a new location to match the master).

With chase-lock sync, the slave follows the master in almost all circumstances. This way, when the master kicks into fast-forward, let's say, so does the slave. As the master begins to slow down to reach its destination, so will the slave (assuming the slave has been fast enough to keep up with the master). And finally, when the master returns to play, the slave will be right there, re-establishing sync within seconds.

Think of it this way: Let's say you (the slave) were driving a car, and following another car (the master). Code-only sync

would be like losing the lead car every time it kicked into high gear. When the lead car once again returned to normal cruising pace, you would be able to see it again and follow once more (though you might have to speed up, or even go into reverse, first). Chase-lock sync, however, would let you stay right on the lead car's tail, regardless of its speed or direction!

Chase-lock is a much faster way of establishing sync, but it's considerably more complicated. With code-only sync, the synchronizer needs just a time code input from each machine, as well as a control cable to the slave's transport. With chase-lock, however, the synchronizer needs all three of these connections, plus a transport cue cable from the master. With this latter connection, the synchronizer knows *which* direction the master is winding and when the master is returning to play.

Some synchronizers—when used with what's known as a *wide-band reader*—actually read and track the master's time code when it's in fast-wind mode. Most synchronizers, however, read *tach pulses*, which are low-voltage pulses typically generated by the electronic tape counter on most ATRs. By knowing which direction the master is heading, and by keeping track of how many tach pulses it generates, synchronizers are able to establish chase-lock sync.

instruments are recorded onto separate tracks. Later, in the studio, those parts can be balanced and processed if necessary (and sometimes eliminated or replaced!), and then mixed down. When a video tape has been made of the performance, the final audio mix must be added to the video.

In order to have lips and hands sync to the music we're hearing, the multi-track or mixed down audio tape has to be locked to the video tape with a synchronizer. Ideally, both the multi-track and video tapes were striped with time code for the recording of the performance. If not, the two can still be synced, by striping each tape with code, locking them with a synchronizer, and then 'tweaking' the synchronizer until the audio perfectly matches the visual image.

Multi-track, center-code 2-track machines, as well as older 4-track machines, are frequently used with VTRs during a/v post. Another a/v post machine you may see in professional studios is a *layback* recorder. This is an audio tape recorder that is designed to hold 1" video tape.

As odd as that sounds, layback machines serve a very useful purpose. Normally, sound tracks are recorded on multi-track recorders synced to 3/4" video 'work' tapes—which are copies of the 1" master video tape. When the sound track is complete, it can be mixed to a normal 2-track recorder, and then transferred at a video production house to the final 1" video tape. The 2-track, though, adds an extra genera-

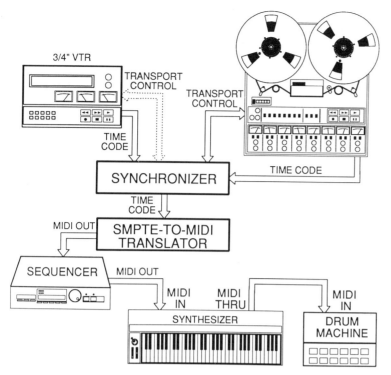

Figure 14.13 A typical musician's audio-for-video production setup, with the VTR as master (it could be a 1/2" deck) and everything else locked to it. If the master deck has an external control port, a control cable from the synchronizer can be used to establish full chase-lock sync. Otherwise, code-only sync is name of the game, but it means that all the synced gear will stop whenever the master is put into a fast wind (or rewind). When the master resumes 'play,' the synced gear will once again have a time code reading from which to establish sync.

tion to the audio. The solution is to record, or 'lay back,' the mixed multi-track audio directly to the 1" video master tape. A lay-back machine doesn't have any rotating video heads; rather it has stationary audio heads which record the linear audio tracks.

For more about a/v post applications, including Foley, scoring, and sound effects work, be sure to see "Audio-For-Video Post Production," below.

Offset And Pre-Roll. Generally, when two ATRs are synced to gain extra tracks, they're synced together at the same time code readings. That is, when the master is at "00:05:12:13," the synced slave is playing along at exactly the same reading.

But what if you need to sync your two transports together at *different* SMPTE time code readings? (This is common for anyone adding music or sound to a pre-striped video tape.) The solution is to use a synchronizer function known as *offset*. Simply, offset allows you to program a precise time

difference between the master and slave time code readings. If you know the exact difference beforehand, most synchronizers allow you to enter the offset directly. Otherwise, by watching or listening to the difference between the master and the slave, you can punch it in on the fly, and then tweak the offset up or down as needed.

(Incidentally, SMPTE time code and MTC-based MIDI sequencers also allow offset values to be stored, which is how *they* deal with time code mismatches.)

Synchronizers also have a function known as *preroll*. This lets you program a 'lead-in' to any point in time. For example, let's say you know that it takes your master and slave about 11 seconds to sync up after a chase. Thus, when searching to a memory location, it takes 11 seconds from when that location is reached to when your transports are synced. By programming an 11 second preroll, the master will stop and go into play 11 seconds before the location time being

sought, allowing the master and slave time enough to get in sync.

Audio-For-Video Post Production

As musical and visual technologies continue to merge, many musicians may find themselves being drawn into video production techniques. Let's find out more about some of the techniques employed.

The idea behind *audio-for-video post production* (a/v post)—also known as *audio sweetening*—is fairly straightforward, though the techniques are very specialized. Most sounds that you hear in any major motion picture or video are dubbed *after* the film has been shot. These dubbed sounds include:

- Special sound effects (screeching tires, explosions, gunshots).
- Ambient noises (footsteps, doors opening, passionate kisses, and other 'ordinary' sounds).
- All music (except in some live music videos).
- Portions of actual dialogue.

Why are these sounds dubbed? Why not record them on-site during the filming? It's easy enough to understand why music should be post-produced; after all, you can't expect composers to score a picture while it's being filmed! But what about sound effects, ambient noises, and portions of dialogue—why not record all these sounds when they actually happen?

The reason is that it's simpler and more effective to add these sounds as part of the post-production process, rather than record them live. On a film set, there are lots of extraneous noises, and it's often difficult to place a microphone. For example, imagine a beach scene, as two lovers stroll along. We watch them at a distance, and while we can't see their lips moving, we hear them talking. We also hear the sound of their feet on the sand, even though there's no microphone on a boom over their heads.

Clearly, in a situation like this, it's far easier to add the footprint noises after the shoot. And the voices? If the actors were clothed, it might be possible for them to wear wireless lavalier (lapel) mikes. But if they were wearing bathing suits, where could you hide the mikes and transmitters, short of surgically implanting them? And if the mood were to be shattered by the sudden appearance of a helicopter, you could get a far more dramatic helicopter sound by recording one up close, and manipulating the sound in the studio before you dubbed it into the film's soundtrack.

To address these situations, a/v post people have created all sorts of interesting techniques to add sound to a film or video.

Let's look at a simple case of modern music scoring. Typically, the composer receives a video tape copy of the film, usually in portions (a tape is used whether the production is a film or a video, since it's a lot easier to work with). These tapes are known as *work tapes*.

Works tapes are 'burned' with a *window dub*—the little window that shows time code running by. As the composer views the tape, music is written with cues and parts related to the timing of the video. While the 'Hollywood standard' timing for film scoring

Figure 14.14 The Fostex 4030 was the first professional synchronizer available for under $2,500. It will sync one master and up to three slaves. The optional 4035 remote offers full transport control of the master and any slave, along with direct programming of offset, pre-roll, and other functions.

has been a type of click/metronome reference that's related to frames and the footage of the film, more and more composers are working to SMPTE time code.

If the composer is creating music on his or her own, the writing is done directly to a MIDI sequencer and/or audio tape recorder that's synced to the video tape recorder. (If it's a sequencer program, the sequencer must respond to SMPTE, or have a SMPTE-to-MIDI translator; if an ATR is used, a synchronizer is necessary at this stage.)

If the composer is writing parts for an orchestra or band, scores are written with click or time code references. Finally, in the studio, the conductor watches the work video and the score, while the musicians are recorded to an ATR in sync with the VTR.

When sound effects are added post-production (filming), they can be added in a few different ways. One way is to lock a multi-track tape recorder to a VTR, and record the effects—from edited tape, sound effects records, and so on—one track at a time. Such sounds can be compiled and spliced together, and assembled into a composite sound effects track.

Background and ambient noises are often recorded as *Foley work*, a technique named for pioneering cinema soundman John Foley. A typical Foley stage is equipped with all kinds of props, such as different types of shoes and surfaces (from cement to sand), doors and frames (complete with squeaky hinges, if needed), folds of cloth (for clothing noises), and so forth.

Foley technicians have the fun job of watching the video while making sounds—footsteps, doors closing, background dialogue, opening bottles, and so forth. Stephen Hart, a sound designer and engineer who worked on the film, *The Unbearable Lightness Of Being*, has confessed that the sound of a farmer slapping a pig was actually Hart slapping his own stomach!

Dialogue is added in a manner known as *ADR*, for automated dialogue replacement; it's also called *looping*. During ADR, the actors watch the work tape, and speak their missing parts, usually onto separate tracks of a synced multi-track recorder.

Sound effects and ambient sounds actually recorded during filming, to be added during post-production, are known as *wild tracks*. These 2-track tapes are often recorded with a portable half-track center-code recorder. While SMPTE is becoming the standard code, some engineers use what's known as *crystal sync*—which is a pulse generator that puts out 50 or 60 pulses per second. Using a device known as a *resolver* (a feature with some synchronizers), the pulse on these tapes can be synced to time code, for transfer to a multi-track recorder. Resolvers are also used when transferring crystal-synced live dialog tracks to the multi-track.

For some interesting thoughts on advanced a/v post techniques, be sure to see the final two chapters of this book.

* * * *

The world of synchronization can bring a tremendous amount of power to the recording studio—whether you're simply syncing a drum machine to your ministudio, or controlling a complex multi-track a/v post facility.

As the complexity of your studio increases, however, you may find that you need some assistance, just to keep everything under control. In this next chapter, we'll learn about some of the tools available to provide that assistance. □

CHAPTER 15: AUTOMATION

Very much linked to synchronization technology is the world of automation—which wouldn't exist without some of the concepts we discussed in the preceding chapter. In the modern recording studio, there are several different types of automation. These include:

- *Console* automation, which offers control of channel levels, muting, and other functions.
- *Effects* automation—the sequencing of effects presets.
- *Event* automation, which usually refers to the preprogrammed playback, or *triggering*, of sounds from a sampler, a tape machine, or any other external device—also known as *edit decision list* automation.

Whatever type, automation exists largely to compensate for the fact that the average engineer has but two hands! For an explanation, let's take a look at console automation.

Console Automation

As we learned in in Chapter Three, 16- and 24-track tape recorders gained popularity in the early 1970s, supplanting 4-and 8-track recorders. Aside from offering new creative options to engineers, however, all those extra tracks posed a new problem: During mixdown, instead of adjusting the levels of four or eight faders, engineers had to juggle up to 24 input faders. Add to that perhaps three to eight effects returns, and it became clear that many 24-track mixdown sessions are jobs well beyond the physical abilities of a single engineer.

Fortunately, the early '70s also saw the introduction of console automation—systems designed to memorize different fader level settings during overdubbing and mixdown. No longer did the engineer have to call in the assistant engineer, the drummer, or studio accountant to help control all the fader levels.

Today, console automation is not just a convenience: With MIDI and other virtual tracks, along with numerous effects returns, some professional sessions have as many as 56 or more channels with which to contend during mixdown! Many personal studios can benefit from automation as well: Take one 8-track tape recorder, add several MIDI-based virtual tracks and drum machine parts, throw in some effects returns, and it's not long before you're dealing with 24 or more channels for mixdown.

Not all automated consoles have the same degree of automation. There are, however, three features found with most automation systems. These include:

- *Fader level control.*
- *Muting.*
- *Grouping.*

Fader Level Control. Perhaps the most liberating function of most automation system is the ability to automate fader levels—so that the faders are able to 'remember' how they're moved by the engineer during a pass of the master multi-track tape. When the tape is played back, the same fader changes are recalled 'hands-off.' This way, an engineer can work on the mixdown over several passes, perhaps mixing the drums on one pass, the vocals on another, and so on.

Most automation systems allow an unlimited number of passes until the mix is perfect. And not even two hands are needed: Critical passages can be mixed one fader at a time.

There are two ways to automate fader levels: with *VCAs*, and with *moving faders*.

Conventional faders are variable resistors, which are designed to let the full voltage of the signal pass when 'wide open,' and attenuate the signal as they're brought down. VCA (for *Voltage-Controlled Amplifier*) automation uses faders which aren't variable resistors; rather they control the voltage output of tiny amplifiers, one for each channel. By recording and playing back these changes relative to time, the mix is automated.

Moving fader automation, on the other hand, actually uses variable resistor faders with little built-in motors; automation takes place by recording fader movements and then having the motors recreate them.

VCA automation is most common, though up until recently VCAs were plagued with audio problems: If they weren't inducing noise and distortion, they were introducing some coloration to the sound. By the mid-1980s, however, quality alternatives appeared on the market, from dbx, B & B, and others.

Moving fader automation has no sonic drawbacks, and though it's generally expensive, it's easy to use, and certainly entertaining—there's nothing quite like seeing several dozen faders moving up and down, as if controlled by the ghost engineers of sessions past!

Let's briefly review some operational differences between VCA and moving fader

Figures 15.1 and 15.2 At left, VCA automation faders from a Mitsubishi Westar console. The right fader can function as a VCA group master. At right, Soundcraft's Twister outboard automation system interfaces between the tape deck and the board. Each Twister module has 8 channels of VCAs.

automation.

Moving fader systems are straightforward: First, the faders are set to *write* mode, which allows you to create new mixes. Then the multi-track tape is played back, and the moves are made. When it's time to listen back—the *read* mode—the faders physically re-create your moves. New channels are automated during another pass by setting them to write mode. When you wish to alter, or *update*, previously mixed channels, just touch the faders and move them as you wish.

Level changes for VCA-based systems are somewhat more tricky. Fader levels are written in the first pass. When you read back your changes, however, the faders don't move at all: The VCA levels—rather than being controlled by the faders themselves—are now being controlled by the automation computer. To automate new channels, passes are also made in write mode.

Here's an important difference between the two systems: With VCA automation, in order to update previously-written channels, it's necessary to make sure that the fader is physically set to its current level reading. This is necessary to avoid a sudden jump in level between the VCA level and the actual fader position. Some systems use 'null' LEDs that illuminate (or go out) when the fader is positioned at the VCA level—at that point you can update and *not* hear a change in level.

More modern systems, on the other hand, offer monitor screens, which visually display the automated VCA levels compared to the current fader position levels.

Muting. With automated *muting*, channels can be programmed to be *live* (turned on) or *muted* (turned off) at different points

in time. By muting tracks whenever they're not delivering music to the mix, additive tape noise can be reduced. Muting also lets you clean up tracks, to get rid of throats being cleared, instruments being tuned, and the like.

Automated muting is offered on virtually all automation systems. Next to the fader is a mute button; when it's engaged during write or update modes, the mutes are remembered. Most systems allow muting information to be written independently of fader levels; that is, updating a channel's mutes won't overwrite the fader levels.

Grouping. On page 34, we learned about subgroups, and how they make mixing easier. *Automated grouping* is a very powerful function: Typically, it allows any fader to become a group fader, with eight or more total groups possible. This way, for instance, four background vocal tracks could have their levels changed by changing the level of one group fader; similarly, they could be muted with one group mute.

All of this is performed by assigning—either with switches or a computer—individual faders to a designated group master.

The group master's mute switch is now the *group mute* switch for whichever channels are assigned to the group. Need to silence all your horns for the verses, but want to bring them in on the choruses? No problem: Just assign the horn faders to a couple groups (two are needed if they're to be mixed in stereo), and mute and unmute those groups as required. Top-grade automation systems will even let you pre-program the exact SMPTE times at which these mutes occur!

SMPTE-Based Automation. Early built-in or drop-in console automation systems,

while a boon to many, were cumbersome and unreliable, and required that two tape tracks be given up to hold automation information. One track would hold the latest pass of information, while the other would have a rather crude, FSK-type sync track.

In the late '70s, SMPTE-based automation became the professional standard, and it appears that it will remain so. The typical SMPTE-based automation system uses a SMPTE time code track to control when the changes occur, and a disk-based storage system for storing the changes. As new passes are recorded, they're saved to disk rather than to a tape track, so that a single SMPTE track is all that one sacrifices to automation. Of course, the SMPTE track can be the same control track that's used for synchronizers, SMPTE-based MIDI instruments, and other devices.

Advanced Console Automation. Some consoles offer more advanced automation features beyond just levels, mutes, and grouping. Some mixers, such as the Harrison Series X, and the Yamaha DMP7 (which we'll be looking at in a moment), allow you to automate all their functions—including effects and equalization.

A step 'in between' is offered by Solid State Logic in their 4000 and 6000 series consoles. Known as 'Total Recall,' SSL's automation system does the standard VCA-based level, muting, and grouping automation. On top of this, Total Recall can take a 'snapshot' of the entire board, including level, EQ, effects send, and other parameters. These snapshots can be stored on disk for later recall.

Figure 15.3 Solid State Logic's Total Recall automation computer will reset all routing and mute switches, automate fader levels, and create mute and fader groups. It will also store and recall a visual display of each module's knob, switch, and fader settings.

When recalled, all routing and bypass switches are reset, and a monitor screen displays the physical settings off all other knobs and controls. Since the screen shows the current settings of these parameters, it's an easy matter to readjust knobs, allowing the perfect replication of a mix's settings. Even though this means some manual re-setting of certain parameters—such as effects send levels—Total Recall nonetheless greatly speeds up setup time, and allows producers and engineers to carry disks between SSL studios world-wide.

Finally, new automation systems can offer quite complex functions. For instance, cutting, pasting, and copying are editing functions with which anyone who uses a word processor is familiar, and allow you to move around various portions of your automation information. Let's say you've just finished several difficult passes of the first chorus. Rather than having to repeat all those moves for the following three choruses, you can copy and paste the changes from the first chorus. If you have any minor changes you'd like to make, you can always update for the individual choruses, but as you can imagine, this save a bunch of work!

Outboard Automation Systems. Console automation comes in a few different ways. Many top-end manufacturers, such as Neve and SSL, include elaborate automation systems as a standard feature, or offer it as a factory-installed option (see "Advanced Console Automation," page 121). Other manufacturers, including Soundtracs, Yamaha, and Allen & Heath Brenell, offer lower-priced consoles with built-in internal routing, muting, and sometimes fader control automation.

Some 'outboard' automation systems, such as those by Digital Creations DiskMix (VCA-based) and GML (moving faders), are designed to 'drop in' to many larger consoles—primarily those which have fader panels which are separate from the actual input modules. Finally, from people such as JL Cooper and MegaMix, come add-on automation systems. These are usually VCA-based, offering level, muting, and grouping facilities.

With each, however, the idea is to insert the VCAs somewhere in each channel's signal path. This can be done by hardwiring them after the faders, by patching them between the multi-track recorder outputs and the mixing channel inputs, or by patching them in the channel inserts (see page 33).

Pointer information. This means that their moves can be stored and driven by a MIDI sequencer. While such MIDI-based systems are a bit more complicated, they do allow you to automate your mix without using tape—though, of course, you can sync the seuquencer to tape.

MIDI Consoles. In 1985, England's Allen & Heath Brenell introduced their CMC series mixers. These mixers—designed for 8-to 24-track work—lack level automation, though they do have programmable routing and muting functions. These changes can be

Figure 15.5 The DMP7, by Yamaha, is a fully programmable digital mixer. It can automate a mix by recalling 'snapshots' of over 200 parameters, from levels (it has moving faders) to internal reverb and EQ settings.

automated to FSK code, SMPTE time code, or they can be externally controlled via MIDI, from a sequencer for instance. Similar mixers are made by Soundtracs, and Studiomaster, to name a few.

Other mixers take the process a good

deal further. Let's look at the Yamaha DMP7, which is similar in some ways to mixers made by Akai, Simmons, and others. The DMP7 is an 8-input, stereo output digital mixer (we'll learn more about 'digital' in the next chapter). Without group outputs and a tape monitor, this mixer is best suited as a submixer or for live performance. Nonetheless, it has some very powerful features, and is surely a portent of future recording mixers.

The DMP7 has an internal memory bank, which stores 'snapshots' of settings of its over 200 parameters. Aside from straight manual mixing facilities, the DMP7 has programmable levels, equalization, reverb, chorus, delay, compression, and much more.

These settings can be recalled manually from the front panel, or they can be recalled as MIDI program changes. That means that these changes can be stored in a sequencer's memory, and automatically recalled as the sequencer plays back a song. High on the entertainment factor, by the way, are the moving faders which the DMP7 uses to play back level changes. The DMP7 is also equipped such that any of its parameters can be altered via MIDI; this allows for external computer-based editing programs to provide another form of automation.

Since what we've just described not only covers levels and mutes, but also effects settings, we've just had a brief introduction to the next section.

Effects Automation

Not long after the introduction of MIDI, signal processors began to materialize that incorporated MIDI ports. These ports—associated with keyboards and drum machines—were first embraced by live performance musicians, who could finally have their reverb, delay, and other effects presets change when their keyboard patches changed. This was done, of course, by sending MIDI program change commands to the devices.

As MIDI sequencers became entrenched in many modern recording studios, it wasn't long before engineers realized something quite significant: By storing and playing back program changes, sequencers allow you to automate MIDI effects.

While reverbs and digital delays—which were the first effects to have presets—were the first to be 'MIDI-ized,' today there are MIDI EQs, compressors, noise gates, pitch transposers, even MIDI-controllable patch bays, lighting systems, and more.

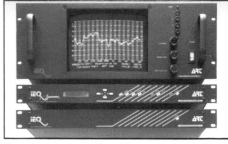

Figure 15.6 Automated equalization is possible by recalling the programmable settings of the ART Intelligent EQ. The IEQ will function as both an analyzer and an EQ; any response curve can be accessed through MIDI or the front panel.

MIDI implementation can go much further than just program changes. Many effects allow their parameters to be changed via MIDI. For example, effects by DigiTech, Lexicon, Korg, and others, allow you to assign internal parameters to external MIDI controllers. In this way, a pitch-bend wheel on a synthesizer can be used to vary the reverb decay time, or the velocity at which the keys of the synth are struck could be set to change the program of a MIDI EQ to brighter-sounding settings! Of course, since pitch bend and velocity information can be stored on a sequencer track—along with program change commands—full automation of the effect is possible.

If a sequencer and a MIDI effect is the only kind of automation gear you own, by the way, here's a trick that may let you automate the levels of your effects: Program

Figure 15.4 Moving faders in action. Shown—mounted in an Amek G2520 mixing console—is the GML moving fader automation system, developed by the well-known engineer/producer George Massenburg. Moving fader systems have been, traditionally, much more expensive than VCA-based systems, though this may change in the future.

Rather than using fader movements to store level changes, some outboard systems have you change channel levels by watching a computer monitor, and moving a mouse up and down for each channel. With actual console faders all the way up, your mouse movements record and play back just VCA level changes. Moving channel levels one-by-one with a mouse can become very tedious, however, so the most popular systems offer fader control, either with drop-in or outboard VCA-controlling faders.

Most of the newer outboard automation systems have internal SMPTE time code generators and readers, and store their moves relative to time code.

Others, however, are designed to be driven by MIDI clock and Song Position

various internal patches of the effect with different output levels (if possible). These various patches can then be sequenced, providing different effects levels throughout the piece. Similarly, MIDI controller #7 (MIDI volume) can be programmed to automate the levels of certain effects, synthesizers, and more.

Event, Or EDL, Automation

Borrowed from the video world, *Edit Decision Lists*, or just *EDLs*, are simple in concept yet very powerful in application: An EDL system allows the user to program when *events* happen in time. EDLs can be stand-alone devices, though more commonly—particularly in audio—they're computer-based software programs.

These 'events' can be any one of a number of varied things. In video, EDL programs are used to start video machines at various points in time—a vital function for constructing difficult scenes with many intricate edits. In audio, EDLs can function as advanced synchronizer editing systems, allowing you to control the start and stop times of different audio machines.

For example, let's say you were piecing together various sounds from 2-track recorders onto a multi-track. An EDL program, controlling your synchronizer system, would let you describe exactly *when* sounds are played back. In addition, many synchronizers have *contact closures*, which are switches that can be set by an EDL to close electronically at a given time. These switches can be modified by a technician to start just about anything—from a turntable, to a video camera, to a coffee machine.

In many ways, a more useful application for our purposes is MIDI-based EDL automation. As you may know, samplers can function not only as musical instruments, but also as 'tapeless' digital recorders capable of playing many different brief and looped (continuous) sounds at once.

For these reasons, samplers have become very popular for the playback of sound effects. As we described on page 119, many sounds are added to video and film *after* the shoot is finished. By storing different door sounds, foot steps, and other ambient sounds on a sampler, an engineer can watch a work video and add appropriate sounds just by playing the appropriate keys —the output of the sampler is recorded to the multi-track. For example, if footsteps are placed on Middle C and C#, depressing

those two keys 'in step' with the actor let's you record the sound of footsteps quite convincingly.

But what if we didn't want to have to play those sounds? What if we were able to program, in time, *when* the sound effects notes are played automatically? The solution is a MIDI-based EDL system.

Digidesign, a music software company, has designed a program named Q-Sheet, and it's designed to work with an Apple Macintosh computer and any Macintosh SMPTE/MIDI interface. As we can see in Figure 15.8, Q-sheet allows you to create lists of when different MIDI notes are played. When the incoming time code reaches the pro-programmed time, the note is played.

So if you know that a door is closed at "01:24:17:22" on the video tape, you can have a door closing sample trigger at exactly the same instant. This is a much easier process than having to play the sampler's notes at exactly the right times. And Q-Sheet can also automate changes, via MIDI, to your effects, MIDI automated mixers, and can start sequencers. In fact, Q-Sheet is like a MIDI sequencer, except it's oriented to controlling different events rather than continuous streams of notes at a given tempo.

Here's a real life scenario, which will make clear the advantage of using an EDL like Q-Sheet, rather than the traditional approach of recording tracks one-by-one with a microphone or effects tapes. Let's say you're in the business of a/v post, have an 8-track tape recorder, and are contracted to provide all the a/v post-production for a stereo video. You might put the music score on tracks 1 and 2, the dialogue on tracks 3 and 4, sound effects on tracks 5 and 6, Foley work on track 7, and the SMPTE time code on track 8. Let's also assume you created this tape with microphones and sound effects libraries, and recorded direct to the 8-track.

All very fine. Now let's say the director comes to you, when you're finished, and says "All right, sounds good—but the video's being re-edited, so the exploding pumpkin happens three seconds earlier. On top of that, the video editor has stretched the pacing of the love scene, so we want more of those smooching noises!"

Your next step would be to go back and re-record the exploding pumpkin effect. For the extended smooching noises, you'd have to take a new tape and lengthen it by adding in more noises. A time-consuming,

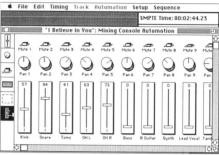

Figures 15.8a, 15.8b Digidesign's Q-Sheet, a Macintosh-based program that brings a lot of a/v post power to studios less well-equipped than the one in Figure 15.7. (It's also extremely useful in any professional studio.) The top screen shows an EDL, or cue list, with sampled sound effects on cue; below is shown a screen that can automate MIDI mixers.

hair-pulling, prospect.

Now imagine if your multi-track recorder were able to *shift* tracks around in time—so that you could advance the exploding pumpkin sound without changing the timing of the music or the dialogue. To do that, you'd need a recorder that allowed you to play back any track at any start time. As far as extending the smooching noises, a recorder that allowed you to repeat sounds over and over would be the answer. In short, you'd need a computer that behaved like a recorder, but didn't use magnetic tape. A sampler, controlled by an EDL program, is such a computer. As we'll learn in the next chapter, there are a number of options available to offer not only extended-time, but also multi-track, tapeless recording.

If you were using Q-Sheet and a high-quality sampler with a reasonable amount of memory, the same requests from your director would take just a few minutes to implement. If the exploding pumpkin sample had been scheduled to trigger when the time code hit "00:47:59:12," all you'd need to do was type in a new start time of "00:47:56:12." And if the smooching noises had been a continuous looping sample, the sample could be set to play for a longer duration of time to match the new, lengthened scene.

*   *   *   *

Like synchronization, automation is a very complex and specialized area of recording that is rapidly evolving. But while these two technologies are becoming more powerful, they're also becoming much more accessible, in terms of cost and 'user-friendliness.'

Another area that's experiencing this kind of evolution is digital audio—something that all of us will ultimately be using to record our music. Let's find out more in the coming chapter. □

Figure 15.7 Robert Berke Sound, of San Francisco, a professional a/v post facility. From left to right we see an Otari MTR-90 16-track, Orban and other signal processing gear, JBL Bi-Radial monitors, an Auditronics production console with BTX/Cypher synchronizer remote, Auratone 5C monitors, BTX/Cypher synchronizers, Otari remotes, Lexicon 200 reverb and other processors, Mitsubishi VTR, and an Otari MTR-12 2-track (the studio has three of them).

The title of this chapter may be an anachronism to some. After all, the digital domain *is* the likely 'final frontier' for audio, at least in terms of how audio is processed and recorded. It won't, however, signal the evolutionary end of recording technology. Rather, it will open doors to endless possibilities. We've seen how dramatically the Compact Disc has changed the reproduction of music. The changes that the digital age will bring to recording are even greater.

In the late-1970s, the first multi-track digital tape recorders began to appear in professional studios. Many observers, citing the meteoric advances made by the computer and electronics industries through the '70s, expected that within a decade, digital recording would be the only game in town. After all, digital recording was initially expensive, but its sonic advantages of no tape hiss or distortion and crystal-clear reproduction were certain to create a fantastic demand for more affordable digital recorders.

A decade later, however—while digital multi-track recorders have proved to be *de rigueur* for any self-proclaiming 'world-class' studio—multi-track *analog* tape recorders also remain popular, even in many professional studios.

A number of factors have led to the delay of the 'digital revolution.' For one, the first digital recorders faced a lot of opposition from seasoned producers and engineers. These people were rather comfortable with analog recorders, and many were accustomed to the slight but audible degrees of distortion they induced—to the point where digital recorders sounded 'cold.' On top of this, some early digital systems did suffer from their own peculiar sonic quirks, though modern systems are generally considered sonically excellent.

There have been other important delay factors, as well. Analog recording has made great leaps since the '70s. Dolby and dbx noise reduction systems have helped reduce tape noise in many professional and personal studios. Four-track cassette multi-trackers, 1/4" 8- and 1/2" 16-track open-reel machines, and more, are innovative formats that work very well in many applications. And Dolby Labs, with its amazing SR noise reduction (page 61), might like us to think that there's no reason for anyone to need a digital recorder.

Along with all of this, both manufacturers and consumers have been spending their respective dollars (or yen) developing and buying such amazing tools as:

- Digital sequencers, drum machines, samplers, and other MIDI-based gear.
- Affordable digital signal processing, such as delays and reverbs.
- Personal computers, to handle many studio chores.

So in fact, the digital revolution *has* been taking place, and the first digital products to reach most studios have been signal processors, MIDI sequencers, digital mixers—such as the Yamaha DMP7—and other such gear. Furthermore, a sequencer is functionally a multi-track digital recorder for MIDI instruments. Samplers are also digital recorders, though they may be limited in terms of time and tracks.

Let's find out more about digital audio—how it's works, what to consider when evaluating digital gear, and some of the options it will bring to the personal and professional studios of the future.

Digital Audio Basics

Whether it's a groove cut in a wax cylinder or magnetic particles rearranged on tape, analog recording works by creating a reproducible 'model' of the sound being recorded. Similarly, all analog audio gear uses varying degrees of electricity to process and transmit audio signals. Whatever the medium—wax, magnetic particles, or electricity—analog audio alters it in such a way that it is directly analogous to the source.

Digital audio—and this applies to digital recording, signal processing, or whatever—works very differently: It analyzes sound and describes it in terms of numbers. These numbers can then be stored as a digital code, altered for level and signal processing, and read back—for ultimate playback.

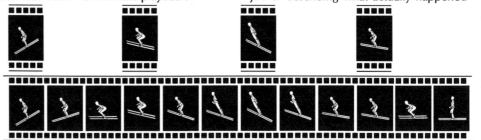

Figure 16.1 'Sampling' a ski jump every three seconds (top) doesn't show us the same story that a 'sampling rate' of every second (bottom) shows us. In a similar way, the sampling rate at which a sound is converted to digital audio has a direct bearing on the quality of audio that we hear.

Since only numbers are stored, altered, and played back, anything that isn't a recognizable number is ignored. For example, digital recordings, even those made with magnetic tape, suffer no tape noise. That's because tape hiss is random magnetic particles, that can be read back by *analog* tape heads (which are looking for any magnetic variations), but mean nothing to a digital recorder's heads.

Sound is converted to digital numbers by taking numeric 'snapshots,' or *samples*, of the sound many thousands of times a second. A digital numeric code is assigned to each sample; as the sound changes, so do the codes. Each sample, incidentally, is like a pulse which registers a value for the audio being sampled. For this reason, digital recording is sometimes known as *PCM* recording, for *Pulse Code Modulation*.

The codes are very important, since they are the digital representations of the sound. This brings us to the next point: Just because something is 'digital' is no guarantee that it's the epitome of audio perfection. After all, there are digital sampling instruments which have poorer frequency response and noise

specs than the average 4-track analog mini-studio. More than anything else, a digital audio device's fidelity depends on two factors:

- How many times per second it takes a 'digital snapshot' of the incoming audio signal; this is known as the *sampling rate*.
- How detailed each 'snapshot' is; this is known as the device's *resolution*, and is expressed in *bits*.

Let's learn more about these two.

Sampling Rate. Imagine you and a friend are sports photographers, assigned to cover a ski jumping event. While your friend's camera is armed with a motor drive, capable of taking one frame a second, your drive has frozen up—leaving you with a manually-wound camera.

After the jump, the two of you thaw out by developing your film. As the images appear on the contact sheets, you compare each others work. Of course, the results are almost predictable: In the 12 seconds or so it took for the gold medalist to complete her jump, you managed to take just four photos, whereas your friend squeezed off a succession of 12 motor-driven shots (Figure 16.1). Clearly, your friend's shots do a much better job of describing what actually happened throughout the winning jump.

And so it's the same story with digital audio. As we know, incoming audio must be sampled—like a series of audio photographs—'x' number of times per second in order to be converted to digital information (Figure 16.2). The more samples per second, the better the description of the incoming audio. What sort of sampling rate is necessary for quality audio?

Well, it may be obvious that a sampling rate of 1 Hz—one sample per second—would be fairly ludicrous. Just as with our ski jump photo shoot, such a system wouldn't 'fill in the blanks,' and would be useless for any musical application. So that tells us, first of all, that we need to sample at a rate fast enough to digitize any possible musical changes in rhythm, level, notes, and so forth. Perhaps a couple thousand times per second would be more than adequate, right?

Wrong. We haven't taken into account the frequency of the sound we're recording. Remember, humans can hear sounds up to 20 kHz. If a cymbal is shimmering at 16 kHz, it's oscillating at 16,000 times per second—

and a sampling rate of 2,000 times per second would simply be unable to create a proper digital 'picture' of that sound. As we can see in Figure 16.3, if we sample a frequency with too low a sampling rate, we wind up with a very odd picture of that frequency. This is known as *aliasing*, and sounds like weird, random pitches. The solution to aliasing is to use a lowpass filter (page 45) to remove any excessively high frequencies.

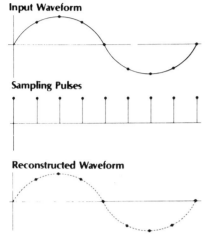

Figure 16.2 An appropriate sampling rate for this frequency. As we can tell, the digital sample is a fine reconstruction of the original waveform.

This leads us to the next logical assumption: The sampling rate needs to be the same frequency as the highest sounds we want to record, right?

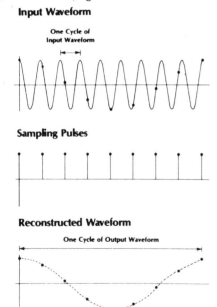

Figure 16.3 This sampling rate is far too infrequent to reconstruct the incoming waveform. Without a high enough sampling rate, the result is known as aliasing, as shown.

Logical, but wrong again. In fact, the sampling rate needs to be at least *twice as high* as the highest audio frequency we wish to record. Figure 16.4 shows an audio signal being sampled; what we see is actually the highest frequency audio signal that we can digitize with the sampling rate shown. If we sampled the audio signal at the *same* sampling rate as its frequency, we would only be sampling each peak, as indicated. With a sampling frequency of twice the audio signal, however, we're able to make a complete sample. The reasoning we've just de-

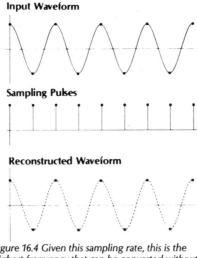

Figure 16.4 Given this sampling rate, this is the highest frequency that can be converted without suffering the dreaded aliasing. The sampling rate must be at least twice the frequency of the audio waveform's frequency, in order to reconstruct all peaks and troughs of the wave.

scribed is often referred to as the *Nyquist theorem*, incidentally, and tells us that if we want 'audiophile' performance of 20 kHz, we need to sample digitally at least 40,000 times per second.

Professional multi-track machines usually have switchable sampling rates of either 44.1 or 48 kHz. Compact Discs are produced with the 44.1 kHz sampling rate, and thus offer a top-end frequency response of 22,050 Hz. Many less-professional sampling instruments have sampling rates of 20 kHz or less, yielding usable—though not great—frequency responses of 10 kHz or less.

A high sampling rate takes up a relatively large amount of memory, which explains why all digital gear doesn't have sampling rates of 40 kHz or higher. In fact, since sampling instruments have limited memory, some allow you to select your own sampling rate. By lowering the rate, you lose high frequency response but gain extra recording time.

Bit-Rate Resolution. Sampling rate is only part of the picture when it comes to digital audio fidelity. To continue with our photographic analogies, let's consider film. Film is covered with light-sensitive particles. Fine-grain film has many more of these particles per frame than does a coarse grain film, and is thus able to take photos with higher resolution.

In digital audio, each sample is described in terms of digital numbers, known as *bits*. Simply, the more bits available to describe a sample, the greater the *audio resolution*.

As you may know, bits—either '1's or '0's—are the language of all things digital. When it comes to digital audio, the number of bits ascribed to each sample has a direct bearing on the dynamic range of the sample. For example, let's say we had a 2-bit digital recorder. That means each sample can have its level described, or *quantized*, to one of four *bit-word* permutations:

00	(Off)
01	(Louder)
10	(Louder still)
11	(Loudest)

As you can surmise from this limited range, a 2-bit system is pretty much useless for music. Much more useful are 8-bit sys-

tems, which gained popularity in the mid-1980s with several affordable sampling instruments, such as the E-mu Emulator II, the Ensoniq Mirage, and others. Eight-bit sampling, with bit words such as "01110001," offers 2^8 level possibilities, for a total of 256 steps. That degree of resolution offers a dynamic range of about 46 dB, which is okay, but not great. Multiplying the number of bits by six, incidentally, gives the approximate dynamic range.

For professional applications, 12-bit sampling is generally considered the minimum, with 4096 levels available, yielding a dynamic range of about 72 dB. While this might be fine for a sampling keyboard or digital reverb, it's still too low for quality digital recording. After all, any analog tape recorder equipped with Dolby C or dbx has a signal-to-noise ratio well above 70 dB.

In a 16-bit device, 65,536 levels can be described, which is equivalent to about 96 dB of dynamic range. With 16-bit digital processing and instruments now commonplace, professional-grade fidelity is both available and affordable.

As far as true digital recorders, there are several 18-and 20-bit systems available, offering extremely good dynamic range. Professional recorders by Mitsubishi, Otari, and others, offer switchable 16- or 20-bit performance. With a dynamic range of 120 dB, there's little need to exceed 20-bit performance.

Error Detection And Correction. When magnetic tape or disks are used as the digital storage medium, drop outs of the magnetic oxide can cause some big problems. In analog recording, a drop out will usually cause a momentary reduction or loss of signal. In digital recording, a drop out can cause all kinds of horrible 'glitches,' since the bits can be misread.

To counteract this, magnetic digital recorders include some form of automatic *error detection* and *correction* circuitry. Different devices use different systems, but the concepts behind all of them are to look for code inconsistencies in playback, and to create average values between the information preceding and following the error.

The ADA Chain. Figure 16.5 shows us a typical analog-to-digital-to-analog signal chain, commonly called an *ADA chain*. When an analog signal enters a digital device, one of the first things it encounters—after level matching switches, balancing amps, gain controls, and so forth—is a lowpass filter (sometimes called the *anti-aliasing filter*). As we just learned, the sampling rate of the device must be twice that of any audio frequencies it will encounter; otherwise, aliasing is possible. The filter removes the possibilities of aliasing.

Following that, the signal meets its moment of truth: the *analog-to-digital converter*, or *ADC*. At this point, the signal is sampled at whatever the 'local' sampling rate happens to be, and is resolved to the local bit rate. From this point on, we're no longer dealing with ordinary audio. Rather, it's just numbers, and we're free to do with them whatever we want.

For example, we can store them, to tape, disk, or in quickly-accessible *RAM* (*Random Access Memory*). That's the basis of digital recording, or for that matter, any sampling

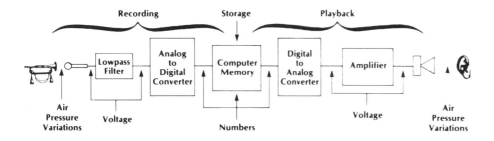

Figure 16.5 The basic components of a typical analog-to-digital-to-analog (ADA) chain. The lowpass filter removes those incoming high frequencies which may cause aliasing.

instrument. If we were designing a digital delay, on the other hand, we would design a circuit which would hold the numbers for user-variable amounts of time, and then spit them out. Similarly, if we were designing a digital reverb, we would create all kinds of interesting mathematical *algorithms*, to 'bounce' those numbers around the walls of simulated concert halls and caverns.

Whatever takes place, the beauty of *this* stage is that everything is numbers. There's no noise being added, since there's nothing in the circuitry which is susceptible to interference. This contrasts to analog gear—its circuits depend upon voltage changes, and noise can enter as stray voltage. Furthermore, digital manipulation offers many more options, in terms of what the sonic outcome will be.

Once the digital signal has been stored and/or manipulated, it can be either be passed along in digital form to a different digital device (as we'll see on page 128), or it can be retrieved for the return to analog. For this step a *digital-to-analog converter (DAC)* is used. The reconversion to analog remains a necessary step in order to pass the signal to another analog device, or to pass it to loudspeakers—after all, at this stage in human evolution we can't *hear* digitally!

Overload. A major difference between analog and digital gear is that digital gear can't accommodate an overloaded input signal. For instance, as you increase input levels, analog gear will gradually begin to distort. Digital gear will remain quiet until you actually overload—at that point the device has run out of numbers and will create some horrific-sounding distortion.

Consequently, many digital devices incorporate automatic limiters before their ADC stage.

Digital Tape Recorders

Through the 1980s the digital multi-track recording market has been dominated by large, very expensive tape recorders, from the Sony *DASH* format, to the Mitsubishi *PD* format, and others. These machines all have 'fixed' headstacks, use 1" magnetic tape, and resemble analog machines in many ways.

To the chagrin of many professionals, DASH-format (*Digital Audio Stationary Head*) machines—by Sony, Studer, and Tascam—are incompatible with PD-format ('*Pro Digi*') machines—by Mitsubishi, Otari, and AEG. For true 'world class' studios, this has often meant buying *both* machines, and has lead to hesitance from many potential digital buyers.

Of course, not all digital recording is multi-track. There are both DASH and PD 2-track machines, designed primarily for

Figure 16.6a, 16.6b The Otari DTR-900 32-track digital tape recorder (left) is similar to the Mitsubishi X-850 32-track. The DTR-900 uses 1" tape and conforms to the 'PD' standard. The Sony PCM-3324 (right) uses 1/2" tape, and records 24 digital tracks in the 'DASH' format.

mixdown and editing. In the mid-'70s, the first digitally recorded analog LPs were produced with a Soundstream digital 2-track tape recorder, though that system was soon to lose ground to a less expensive type of digital 2-track: PCM-encoded video tape.

Figure 16.7 shows a PCM encoder system. Offered by Sony, Nakamichi, and others, PCM encoders receive a stereo analog line or microphone input, and put out a digitally-encoded signal, to be stored on a separate tape. Their digital output is, in fact, a *video* output, even though it contains no video information. Rather it's designed to be recorded on the video tracks of a

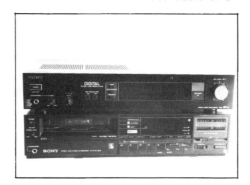

Figure 16.7 The Sony 501 PCM digital encoder, shown sitting on top of a Sony 1/2" Beta video deck. The 501 feeds a video signal to the video deck; encoded in this signal is the PCM audio. Upon playback, the deck's video outputs are routed back to the processor, and the signal is decoded into analog. The 501 operates at either 14- or 16-bit resolution.

video tape recorder (VTR), such as a 1/2" home consumer or 3/4" professional VTR.

When it's time for playback, the video output of the VTR is fed back into the PCM encoder, which in turn has a traditional analog output. Most encoders are switchable between 14- and 16-bit resolution, and usually record at the 44.1 kHz sampling rate.

PCM-encoded VTR recording offers a number of advantages over traditional fixed-head recorders. As we learned on page 116, VTRs use rotating heads. Since the tape is moving in one direction and the heads are rotating in another, an apparent tape transport speed of over 200 ips is achieved. All of this means a very stable transport in a small, inexpensive package—compared to the huge, expensive transports required by fixed-head recording.

Another variation on the rotating head theme is gaining ground, however, offering all the advantages of PCM-encoded VTRs and then some. The variation is *DAT* recording—initially known as *R-DAT*, for *Rotary-head Digital Audio Tape*—and we had our introduction to these machines back on page 29.

The DAT format has 16-bit resolution, and professional machines will offer sampling rates switchable between 48, 44.1, and

Figure 16.8 One of the first DAT recorders to be marketed, the Tascam DA-50. DAT recorders may very well be the mixdown format of choice through the 1990's.

32 kHz. Though the current spec is 2-track only, some observers are confident that multi-track DATs are inevitable. Others suggest that the rotating head format of DAT

Figure 16.9 When introduced in 1988 at $35,000, Akai's DR1200 12-track digital recorder was half the dollar-per-track cost of other digital tape recorders. The A-DAM (Akai Digital Audio Multi-track) uses 8mm video tape, for 17 minutes of recording with professional specs. The transport is at left.

will make multi-track punch-ins an engineering nightmare—but there's no challenge design engineers like better than for something to be branded impossible!

Akai has put forth yet another digital recording format: In 1987 they unveiled a 12-track digital recorder which uses 8 mm *video* tape, costing about as much as a quality analog 24-track machine. This isn't the first time Akai has gone out on a limb with its own format, as their 12-track analog cassette recorders (page 27) prove.

So while it's clear that digital recording is the wave of the future, what remains unclear is which, if any, tape format will be the standard. Some feel that tape may be bypassed altogether. Tape can stretch, requires complex, expensive transports, and is generally prone to all kinds of physical horrors. For these reasons, 'tapeless recording' is an option growing in popularity.

Digital Audio Workstations And Tapeless Recording

Samplers, which we've already described as digital recorders, were the first of the 'tapeless recorders' to hit the market. Digitalized music and sounds can be recorded directly into their computer-based memories, and be stored to a floppy or hard disk. Most conventional samplers, though, are

Figure 16.11 From Surrey, England, hails the Digital Audio Research SoundStation II—another digital audio workstation. This device can be configured to record from two to eight tracks of audio, at several hours total recording time. Aside from such features as track shifting, time compression, and so forth, audio in the SoundStation II can be edited by touching the screen!

limited to several minutes of recording at best—in order to achieve longer recording times, extremely large amounts of memory are required.

For example, the typical sampling key-

board may have between 2 to 4 *megabytes*—meaning that it can store between 2 to 4 million bits of digital information. New England Digital, the makers of the Synclavier digital music production system, produce a sampling-style system known as their *Direct-To-Disk* recorder. It's a computer-based recording system, and as the name suggests, records directly to hard magnetic disks. These systems can have up to 16-tracks, with total recording times of over two hours. This is accomplished with hard disks capable of storing up to 8 *gigabytes* (8 trillion bits) of information! Other manufacturers—including Fairlight, Lexicon, AMS, and WaveFrame—have followed suit with similar tapeless, high-power recording systems, known as *digital audio workstations* (DAWs).

DAWs are in fact much more than just tapeless tape recorders. The impetus for their development was the growing sophistication of a/v post production, as we discussed on page 119. Traditional a/v post was

so relatively cumbersome that Lucasfilm—the makers of Star Wars and other hit films—commissioned the development of the Sound Droid. While it was a commercial failure, the Sound Droid laid the groundwork for many of today's DAWs, with such features as:

- Complete sync to video, film, and audio tape recorders.
- Multi-track disk-based digital recording.
- Built-in digital signal processing and mixing.
- Full editing capabilities.

Editing power is really the key to DAWs. You may recall our 'exploding pumpkin' challenge from page 123, where our producer asked us to shift that sound back in time by three seconds.

By assigning individual tracks their own SMPTE-referenced start and stop points, we can assume complete control over all musical and audio events.

Does this sound very video-oriented? Well, it is, but there are some very important features which will ultimately 'trickle down' to purely musical applications. For example, most DAWs offer *cut*, *paste*, and *copy* facilities. Imagine being able to transfer musical passages around in time with ease (*i.e.*: no razor blades or additional tape recorders):

Figure 16.10 WaveFrame's AudioFrame digital audio workstation (DAW) is controlled by an IBM PS/2 computer. The AudioFrame is designed to be fully modular, so that digital processing, MIDI, mixing, and other modules can be added as needed. The system can operate on its own, as a tapeless recorder, or it can operate with a keyboard, to behave more like a conventional sampler.

With a DAW, deleting or adding extra choruses is just a matter of listening and punching the right buttons!

The advantages of digital tapeless recording go on and on. We mentioned internal signal processing and mixing. Since these features are digital, it's a relatively simple design matter to automate them. In short, the potential power of the DAW is far greater than one could realize with any tape-based multi-track recorder.

The Future Of Personal Recording

From our discussions of *digital* audio workstations, *digital* audio busses, and *digital* audio in general, it may seem as if analog audio's days are numbered, so to speak. Does this mean that the analog studio sitting in front of you is soon to be obsolete?

Definitely not, in many significant ways. For one, analog synthesis remains a very viable way of generating sound—it seems that every new digital synth has at least one preset that attempts to duplicate the now ancient and analog Minimoog. And as we've pointed out, modern noise reduction

Figure 16.12 The CompuSonics DSP1000 digital audio disk recorder uses WORM (write once, read many) optical disks. Down the road will be affordable disk recorders that can re-write disks, much the same way that we can re-record over audio tape. Those who own Compact Disc players already know that optical disks have many advantages over tape: They won't stretch, can't be demagnetized, and allow almost-instant access to any location on the disk.

systems can yield excellent results. Furthermore, there are many professional analog mixing consoles with specs as good as digital gear.

Still, the writing is on the wall: Digital is

on its way. What else can we expect?

Consolidation and compatibility are two most welcome trends—of which both digital audio workstations and the digital audio bus are representative. Like DAWs, the studios of the future will have fully integrated recording and signal processing systems, and complete edit decision lists.

Mixers and recording devices, especially for the personal studio, will integrate. Perhaps the ministudio of the future will be a 16-track digital device, complete with built-in digital reverb and sound synthesis on every channel. Yamaha's DMP7 digital mixer (page 122) is a step in this direction— just add a hard disk drive for recording and storage and some tiny synthesis and drum machine integrated circuits—and you have a concept of our future ministudio.

As far as storage and recording, magnetic disk recording isn't necessarily the last word in digital recording. After all, floppy and hard disks are still magnetic, and thus are prone to accidental erasure and other traumas. One alternative is digital *optical* storage. This format has proven itself with the Compact Disc. While not indestructible, CDs are quite hardy, and are able to store lots of information in a very small and portable disk.

But while it's fairly easy to record once on an optical disk, creating a disk that can be rerecorded many times is an engineering challenge that has yet to be surmounted. Conventional optical disks, after all, are known as *WORM* disks—for *Write Once, Read Many* times. Before optical storage can truly come of age, an affordable, rerecordable system must be developed. For this reason, audio may turn to other forms of storage, such as organic memory—a system being explored by the computer industry which actually uses living microscopic organisms to store huge amounts of digital information.

While music will always exist for its own sake, the integration of audio and video technologies will continue. Some professional tape machines, for example, already include internal synchronizers for quick and easy connection to other audio or video gear.

Human interfaces will also evolve. For example, it's now possible to interface just about any instrument into a MIDI system. However you'd like to control a synthesizer—with a guitar, with drums, with your

The Digital Audio Buss

Traditional equipment interconnection has been with conductive cabling, carrying actual audio signals. This includes all normal guitar cables, multi-track 'snakes,' mike cables, and so forth.

In 1983, a new kind of cable began to appear in recording studios. The MIDI cable, used to connect sequencers, synthesizers, and other such gear, transmits no analog audio data whatsoever. Rather, it transmits digital information, which in turn can make synthesizers play and drum machines stay in sync. Similarly, before long, the *digital audio buss* will be used to connect most digital audio devices of the future.

Here's the story. In order to connect the audio signals of two digital devices, such as a reverb and delay, the traditional approach has been to use their standard *analog* inputs and outputs. As we saw in Figure 16.5, the ADA chain takes an incoming analog signal, converts it to digital information, and then reconverts it to analog for output. Unfortunately, each analog stage adds some degree of unwelcome noise and distortion.

As we know, ultimately the digital signal must be converted when we want to hear it. But wouldn't it make sense if there was a way—when passing audio information between digital gear—to keep the audio in the *digital* domain, rather than converting back and forth?

That is precisely the idea behind the digital audio bus. In 1986 the Audio Engineering Society (AES) and the European Broadcaster's Union (EBU) adopted their guidelines for a standard means of transmitting two channels of digital data between equipment: the AES/EBU buss.

And in 1988, Sony, Mitsubishi, Neve, and Solid State Logic, put forth proposals for MADI—a Multi-channel Audio Digital

Interface. The MADI spec supports up to 56 audio channels.

While the standard digital transmission cable is a multi-pin conductive cable, rather like a computer printer cable, this too is starting to change. In 1987 Roland introduced two new digital products, a reverb and an equalizer, which sport *fiber-optic* digital interconnections. These two devices can be completely connected with just one thin cable that transmits the digital information on a beam of light.

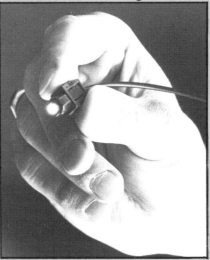

Figure 16.13 Music on a beam of light! This fiber-optic cable can carry two channels of audio information between digital devices equipped with an optical AES/EBU digital buss.

The fiber-optic digital audio buss makes sense. Cabling costs and intricacies can be kept to a minimum, and ground loops are avoided— since there's no chassis ground between optically-linked devices. On top of this, fiber-optic technology, as proved with new telecommunications systems, is capable of transmitting *lots* of information over very long distances for relatively little money. Our studios of the future may well depend upon fiber-optic digital audio transmission, not only for interconnecting our own gear, but perhaps to interconnect with any other studio on the planet!

hands waving wildly in the air (Figure 16.14) —it's possible!

For a glimpse of possible human interfaces, we should look to the computer industry. Many personal computers now offer a *mouse* for selecting items on a screen. Most DAWs also offer a mouse or some similar interface, such as a flywheel or

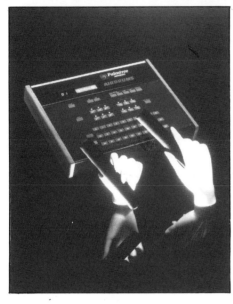

Figures 16.14a, 16.14b Name your interface. If you're a woodwind or trumpet player (top), you too can join the MIDI/digital revolution with the Akai EWI (Electronic Wind Instrument) or EVI (Electronic Valve Instrument) controllers. They're shown with the EWV2000 synthesizer module. Are you most musically inspired while waving your hands wildly in the air? The Palmtree AirDrums allow you send MIDI commands with a flick of the wrist. No matter the instrument, almost every musician can enjoy equal access to today's technology.

tracking ball, for selecting parameters and options. And as Apple computers have shown us, many people are happier dealing with pictographic icons rather than computer codes. Again, this should also translate to the studio.

Incorporating all the power of MIDI, digital audio, and personal computers, we may be able to look forward to the complete 'studio in a box.' By simply customizing our

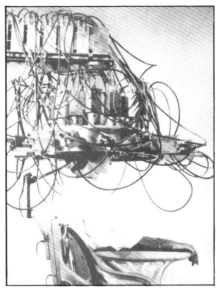

Figure 16.15 Who knows—seriously—what the future of multi-track recording will be? The meteoric advances multi-tracking has enjoyed in its first 35 years may well lead us to the point where we need only to think of the music we want to hear.

own boxes, we could have complete sound generation, recording, and editing facilities, all driven by our own interface choices. Want your zither to drive your sound generators? No problem. Want to be able to wear a fingertip sensory controller, rather than have to push buttons? No problem.

But what about the respective roles of personal and professional studios? If the quality and diversity of what we can create in our own living rooms continues to improve, will there still be work for the professional studio?

Absolutely. Let's not forget that one of the greatest joys of music is creating with

others. Professional studios offer us the facilities to come together with others. And certainly, the expertise found in a professional environment will still be appreciated. If anything, however, the lines of distinction will blur in many directions. The first example of this 'blurring' has been with MIDI.

And we have yet to realize the power of the digital audio buss (described on page 128). Imagine, when all digital information can be transmitted by fiber-optic cable (or some other miracle), that personal studios may serve as 'satellites' to professional studios, which may serve as 'hubs.' This concept first came to light after Stevie Wonder and Quincy Jones performed a transcontinental recording session, using a digitally-encoded transmission via satellite in Earth orbit. Unfortunately, that procedure has some major problems: Travelling at the speed of light, the signal is still delayed by several seconds, which means that while overdubs are possible, it's impossible to 'jam' with someone else.

With the digital audio buss, however, transmission can take place directly—without significant delay—rather than via a signal beamed to outer space and back. Thus long-distance recording sessions may well become easier and more commonplace. Perhaps there will come a time when you want to use the latest, most expensive digital reverb. Rather than buying one, or even renting one, you may be able to tie into it digitally via your telephone line. Just dial up the local pro studio and get 'on line!' With the same technology, you could phone in your part (something which can be done now with a sequencing program and a modem), or record a duet with your long-distance partner.

You get the picture. The future of recording holds an unlimited number of possibilities. And while it's true that *music*—rather than technology for technology's sake—is the ultimate purpose of recording, of this book, and of the instruments we play, technology *has* opened many musical doors. Just as the invention of the piano and the guitar brought about new creative directions, our modern-day multi-track tools may let many of us realize our most visionary musical dreams. □

Brent Hurtig. Following a brief phase of intensive "air guitar," Brent started guitar instruction when he was 12 years of age, in Winnipeg, Canada. Several years later, he twice won regional competitions in classical guitar, and attended the Banff Centre of the Arts. In 1977—while teaching guitar at a Winnipeg music shop—he pestered the engineers of its basement 8-track studio until they kindly showed him the ropes. After a year of improving his studio tan, Brent attended Brandeis University near Boston, where he studied sociology and served for three years as the technical director of WBRS-FM. Before graduating, he also studied electronic music, and taught at a summer program at Wellesley College. Drawn to San Francisco, he spent several years designing and selling recording and broadcast systems, before heading overseas as a consultant to studios and manufacturers. He has been with GPI Publications since 1987, serving as editor of *Synthesizers And Computers* and several other books. Brent is currently editor of GPI's *Home Recording* newsletter and is a regular contributor to *Keyboard* magazine.

J.D. Sharp (contributor, Chapter Twelve). Hailing from Washington, D.C., J.D. studied English at the University of Wisconsin before touring as a keyboardist from 1968 to 1974 with several rock bands. In 1974, he co-founded Bananas At Large, a professional audio and music store in San Rafael, California. Intrigued from his first sight of a Minimoog synthesizer, J.D. soon entangled himself in patch cords and oscillators. In following years, he owned a 24-track recording studio, and was widely acknowledged as one of the first retailers to recognize the enormous potential of MIDI. Currently—aside from serving as president for Bananas and as a manufacturers' consultant—he is an "addicted" computer programmer and desk-top publisher. J.D. is a regular contributor to GPI's *Home Recording* newsletter.

ACKNOWLEDGEMENTS

For historical accuracy in the development of multi-track recording, I thank Les Paul for his informative (and thoroughly entertaining) recollections. As the reader will learn in Chapter Three, we have Mr. Paul to thank for his foresight and determination in bringing multi-track recording to fruition. I'm also indebted to Jim Hillbun and Peter Hammar of the Ampex Museum.

A number of people provided assistance in a variety of ways, from technical documentation to providing equipment, from the outline of the book to reading the manuscript. They include: David Maxson and Steve Riggs (WCRB-FM); Mark Cohen and Bob Hunt (Fostex USA); David Roudebush, Bryan Lanser, Sally Saubolle (Otari USA); Sue Jones and Heather Penn (Amek/TAC); Bill Threlkeld (JBL/Soundcraft/UREI); Bruce Griffen and Larry Winter (Rane); Bill Mohrhoff and Susan Rubalcava (Tascam); Alan Wald (Alesis); Dane Butcher (Symetrix); John Delantoni and Bob Orban (Orban); John Sugnet (Zeta Systems); Jim Chen and Jeff Davies (A.I.C. Sales); Jerry Long, Mike Raskovsky, and Rolf Hartley (Bananas At Large); Andy Wild, Noel Bell, Jane Swadling (Solid State Logic), Lee Bartolomei (Digital Audio Research); Peter Gotcher (Digidesign); Dean Stubbs (DOD); Dick Begley (Tradepower/Fostex Australia); Mark Terry (New England Digital); Barbi Clarke (Roland USA); Leo de Gar Kulka (College of Recording Arts); Spencer Taylor (Spectral Music); Jaime Byrd (GML); Guitar Center (San Jose, CA); Jim Hatlo, Dominic Milano, Mark Vail, Ted Greenwald, Don Menn (GPI); Sandy Feldstein, David Black, and Patrick Wilson (Alfred Publishing); Brian Trankle and Lynn Martin (Brian Trankle & Assoc.); Larry and Madeline Petersen (LP Marketing); John Frigaard and Barbara Richardson (JND); Don Otomo (Radon Assoc.); Gama Contreras (Techline); Lance Schmidt (Peavey); Wane Fuday (Future Sales); Denny Handa; Frank Hubach; Jim Coe; Jeff Cooper; Yogi Kloss; Richard and Bob Denischuk; Michael Heath; Bruce Penner; Harold Shapero; Erica Lopez; Andrea Albi; Warren Sirota; George Wagner; Tim Fluharty; Barbara Popolow; Tom Lavin; Stephen Hart; Andy Widders-Ellis; Bradley Wait; Terry Collins; Warren Hukill. Thanks go to all of you, and any of those I may have missed.

A big tip of the hat to J.D. Sharp, whose lessons grace Chapter Twelve of this book. I'm also very grateful to all in the Books, Production, and Typesetting divisions of GPI for their efforts, especially Rick Eberly for his illustrations, and Alan Rinzler for his editorial guidance and the opportunity to write this book.

Finally, the encouragement of my family and friends will be treasured always.

Brent Hurtig

RECOMMENDED READING

Acoustic Techniques For Home And Studio, by F. Alton Everest, TAB Books, Blue Ridge Summit, PA 17214.

The Art of Electronic Music, compiled and with commentary by Tom Darter, edited by Greg Armbruster, A Morrow/Quill/GPI Book, from GPI Publications, 20085 Stevens Creek, Cupertino, CA 95014.

Audio Production Techniques For Video, by David Miles Huber, Howard Sams, 4300 West 62nd St., Indianapolis, IN 46268.

Beginning Synthesizer, by Helen Casabona and David Frederick, a volume in the *Keyboard* (magazine) library for electronic musicians. An Alfred Publishing/GPI Book, from GPI Publications.

Building A Recording Studio, by Jeff Cooper, Synergy Group Inc., 4766 Park Grenada, Ste. 106, Calabasas, CA 91302.

CAMEO Dictionary Of Creative Audio Terms, The, by CAMEO (Creative Audio And Music Electronics Organization), Framingham, MA 01701.

The Complete Synthesizer, by Dave Crombie, Omnibus Press, London.

Computer Music Journal (quarterly), The MIT Press, Cambridge, MA 02142.

The Development And Practice Of Electronic Music, by Jon Appleton and Ronald Perera, Prentice-Hall.

Electronic Music, 2nd edition, by Allen Strange, Wm. C. Brown Company, 135 S. Locust St., Dubuque, IA 52001.

Electronic Music Circuit Guidebook, by Brice Ward, TAB Books, Blue Ridge Summit, PA 17214.

Electronic Music Production, by Alan Douglas, TAB Books.

Electronic Musical Instruments, by Norman Crowhust, TAB Books.

Electronic Musician (magazine), Mix Publications, 6400 Hollis St., Ste. 12, Emeryville, CA 94608.

Electronmusic, by Robert De Voe, EML, Vernon, CT 06066.

Elementi di Informatica Musicale, by Goffredo Haus, Gruppo Editoriale Jackson, Milano, Italy.

The Evolution Of Electronic Music, by David Ernst, Schirmer Books, 866 Third Ave., New York, NY 10022.

Experimenting With Electronic Music, by Robert Brown and Mark Olsen, TAB Books.

Foundations Of Computer Music, edited by Curtis Roads and John Strawn, The MIT Press.

Guitar Player (magazine), GPI Publications.

Home Recording (newsletter), GPI Publications.

Home Recording For Musicians, by Craig Anderton, Music Sales, 24 E. 22nd St., New York, NY 10010.

Home & Studio Recording (magazine), 7361 Topanga Cyn. Blvd., Canoga Park, CA 91303.

The IMA Bulletin (newsletter), International MIDI Association, 12439 Magnolia Blvd., Suite 104, North Hollywood, CA 91607.

Keyboard (magazine), GPI Publications.

The Microphone Handbook, by John Eargle, Sagamore Publishing, 1120 Old Country Road, Plainview, NY 11803.

Microphones—How They Work And How To Use Them, by Martin Clifford, TAB Books.

Mix (magazine), Mix Publications.

MIDI For Musicians, by Craig Anderton, Music Sales Corp., Chester, N.Y. 10918.

Mind Over MIDI, compiled by the editors of *Keyboard* (magazine), a volume in the Keyboard Synthesizer Library, a Hal Leonard Publishing/GPI Book from GPI Publications.

Modern Recording Techniques, by Robert Runstein and David Miles Huber, Howard W. Sams and Co., Inc.

Multi-Track Primer, The, by Dick Rosmini, TEAC Production Products, 7733 Telegraph Road, Montebello, CA 90640.

Multi-Track Recording, compiled from the pages of *Keyboard* (magazine) and edited by Dominic Milano. A volume in the Keyboard Synthesizer Library, a Hal Leonard Publishing/GPI Book from GPI Publications.

Nueva Generacion De Instrumentos Musicales Electronicos, by Juan Bermudez Costa, 7, Spain.

Recording Engineer/Producer (magazine), 1850 Whitley St., Ste. 220, Hollywood, CA 90028.

Recording Studio Handbook, The, by John Woram, Elar Publishing Co., 1120 Old Country Road, Plainview, NY 11803.

Studio Sound (magazine), Link House, Dingwall Ave., Croydon CR92TA, England.

Synthesis, by Herbert Deutsch, Alfred Publishing, 15335 Morrison St., Sherman Oaks, CA 91413.

The Synthesizer (four-volume set), published by Roland, Box 22289, Los Angeles, CA 90040.

Synthesizers And Computers, compiled from the pages of *Keyboard* (magazine) and edited by Brent Hurtig, a volume in the Keyboard Synthesizer Library, a Hal Leonard Publishing/GPI Book from GPI Publications.

Synthesizers Basics, compiled from the pages of *Keyboard* (magazine) and edited by Brent Hurtig, a volume in the Keyboard Synthesizer Library, a Hal Leonard Publishing/GPI Book from GPI Publications.

Synthesizer Technique, compiled by the editors of *Keyboard* (magazine), a volume in the Keyboard Synthesizer Library, a Hal Leonard Publishing/GPI Book from GPI Publications.

The Technique Of Electronic Music, by Thomas Wells and Eric Vogel, Sterling Swift Publishing, Box 188, Manchaca, TX 78652.

The Technology Of Computer Music, by Max Mathews, The MIT Press.

Using MIDI, by Helen Casabona and David Frederick, a volume in the *Keyboard* (magazine) library for electronic musicians, an Alfred Publishing/GPI Book, from GPI Publications.

From GPI Books

SYNTHESIZER BASICS (Revised)

A valuable collection of articles from the pages of *Keyboard* magazine covering all facets of electronic music. Includes chapters on: perspectives on synthesizers, understanding synthesis, MIDI, sound systems and components, and recording electronic music. Also included are hardware and software manufacturers' addresses, recommended books, and a complete glossary. Contributors include: Helen Casabona, Ted Greenwald, Bryan Lanser, Dominic Milano, Bob Moog, Bobby Nathan, Tom Rhea, and the staff of *Keyboard* magazine.
ISBN 0-88188-552-5 $14.95   From Hal Leonard Publishing.

SYNTHESIZERS AND COMPUTERS (Revised)

A comprehensive overview, useful for beginners or seasoned pros, or anyone interested in the future of music. Includes discussions of digital audio, synthesis, sampling, MIDI, choosing software and interface hardware, and choosing the right computer. Also included is a section on Programming Your Own Software—which leads the reader step-by-step into the world of writing music software, and covers many insider's programming tips. From the pages of *Keyboard* magazine, with articles by Steve De Furia, Dominic Milano, Jim Aikin, Ted Greenwald, Jim Cooper, Bob Moog, Craig Anderton, and other leading experts.
ISBN 0-88188-716-1 $14.95   From Hal Leonard Publishing.

SYNTHESIZER PROGRAMMING

Don't be satisfied with factory presets! Get the most out of your instrument, whether it's a battered Minimoog or the latest digital dream machine. You can create your own unique sound with the concrete and understandable information in this practical introduction to programming and synthesis. With contributions by Wendy Carlos, Bo Tomlyn, and the editors and staff of *Keyboard* magazine. Includes specific guidelines for the DX7, Oberheim Xpander, CZ-101, Roland JX8P, and JX10.
ISBN 0-88188-550-9 $14.95   From Hal Leonard Publishing.

SYNTHESIZER TECHNIQUE (Revised)

How to utilize all the technical and creative potential of today's synthesizers, with discussions of Recreating Timbres; Pitch-Bending, Modulation and Expression; Lead Synthesizer; Soloing and Orchestration. Hands-on practical advice and instruction by leading practitioners, including Bob Moog, Tom Coster, George Duke, Roger Powell, and others. Diagrams, illustrations, and musical examples throughout. Edited from the pages of *Keyboard* magazine.
ISBN 0-88188-290-9 $14.95   From Hal Leonard Publishing.

MULTI-TRACK RECORDING

Information on the latest home and studio recording techniques and equipment, edited from the pages of *Keyboard* magazine by Dominic Milano. Includes chapters on Getting Started, Outboard Gear, Synchronization, Keyboard Recording, and Advanced Techniques And Technical Change. With contributions by Bobby Nathan, Bryan Lanser, Dave Frederick and the staff of *Keyboard* magazine.
ISBN 0-88188-552-5 $14.95   From Hal Leonard Publishing.

THE ART OF ELECTRONIC MUSIC

The creative and technical development of an authentic musical revolution, from the Theremin Electrical Symphony to today's most advanced synthesizers. Scientific origins, the evolution of hardware, the greatest artists—including Tangerine Dream, Vangelis, Keith Emerson, Wendy Carlos, Jan Hammer, Kraftwerk, Brian Eno, Thomas Dolby, and others—in stories, interviews, illustrations, analysis, and practical musical technique. From the pages of *Keyboard* magazine, and with a foreword by Bob Moog.
ISBN 0-688-03106-4 $15.95   From Wm. Morrow & Co.

BEGINNING SYNTHESIZER

A step-by-step guide to understanding and playing synthesizers with discussions of how to use and edit presets and performance controls. A comprehensive, easy-to-understand, musical approach, with hands-on lessons in a variety of styles, including rock, pop, classical, jazz, techno-pop, blues, and more.
ISBN 0-88284-353-2 $12.95   From Alfred Publishing. Item Number 2606.

BEGINNING SYNTHESIZER is also available in a two-volume set of shorter Special Focus Guides, including:
Playing Synthesizers: A Beginner's Guide To Effective Techinque
ISBN 0-88284-362-1 $8.95   Item Number 4110.
Programming Synthesizers: A Beginner's Guide To Editing Preset Sounds
ISBN 0-88284-363-X $8.95   Item Number 4121.
All from Alfred Publishing.

MIND OVER MIDI

A comprehensive and practical introduction to this crucial new technology, including: What MIDI Does, Data Transmission Tutorial, Channels, Modes, Controllers, Computers, Interfaces, Software, Sequencers, Accessories, SMPTE & MIDI, MIDI systems, and more. Edited by Dominic Milano from the pages of *Keyboard* magazine.
ISBN 0-88188-551-7 $14.95   From Hal Leonard Publishing Corp.

USING MIDI

The first comprehensive, practical guide to the application of Musical Instrument Digital Interface in performance, composition, and recording, including: basic MIDI theory, using MIDI performance controls, channels and modes, sequencers, MIDI synchronization, using MIDI effects, MIDI and computers, alternate MIDI controllers, and more. A definitive and essential tutorial.
ISBN 0-88282-354-0 $14.95   From Alfred Publishing. Item Number 2607.

USING MIDI is also available in a three-volume set of shorter Special Focus Guides, including:
What Is MIDI?: Basic Theory And Concepts
ISBN 0-88284-364-8 $8.95   Item Number 4126
Basic MIDI Applications: Sequencers, Drum Machines, And Keyboards
ISBN 0-88284-365-6 $8.95   Item Number 4139
Advanced MIDI Applications: Computers, Time Codes, And Beyond
ISBN 0-88284-365-6 $8.95   Item Number 4143
All from Alfred Publishing.

BASIC GUITAR (Revised)

Chet Atkins, Arnie Berle, Paul Chasman, Dan Crary, Rik Emmett, Brad Gillis, Edward Van Halen, John Hammond, Bill Keith, Steve Morse, Arlen Roth, Mike Seeger, and other distinguished players and writers present a comprehensive, practical introduction to the technique and art of playing guitar. Edited from the pages of *Guitar Player* and *Frets* magazines by Helen Casabona, with a foreword by Les Paul.
ISBN 0-88188-906-7 $14.95   From Hal Leonard Publishing Corp.

ROCK GUITAR

B.B. King, Lee Ritenour, Jeff Baxter, Larry Coryell, Arlen Roth, Rik Emmett, Jimmy Stewart, Bruce Bergman, Rick Derringer, Jim Aikin, and other outstanding working guitar players and teachers present a comprehensive approach to learning and performing the different styles of contemporary rock guitar. Edited by Jon Sievert from the pages of *Guitar Player* magazine.
73999-00689-00294   ISBN 0-88188-294-1 $9.95

ELECTRIC BASS GUITAR

Carol Kaye, Chuck Rainey, Stanley Clarke, Herb Mickman, Jeff Berlin, Michael Brooks, Andy West, Ken Smith, and other outstanding working bassists and bass teachers present a definitive approach to the theory, practice, and performance of electric bass guitar. Edited by Jon Sievert from the pages of *Guitar Player* magazine, with a foreword by Jeff Berlin.
73999-00689-00292   ISBN 0-88188-292-5 $9.95

THE GUITAR PLAYER BOOK

The most comprehensive book on guitar ever produced, from the pages of America's foremost magazine for professional and amateur guitarists. Any style, any level, whether player or fan—this is the book. Includes definitive articles on all the important artists who have given the guitar its life and expression, plus design, instructions, equipment, accessories, and technique. Edited from the pages of *Guitar Player* magazine.
ISBN 0-394-62490-4 $11.95

NEW DIRECTIONS IN MODERN GUITAR

A wealth of insight into the styles and techniques of guitarists who have moved into the vanguard of contemporary music. Artists such as Adrian Belew, Robert Fripp, Stanley Jordan, acoustic wizard Michael Hedges, and bassist Jaco Pastorius are covered in depth—with interviews, instructive musical examples, and an analysis of their playing and equipment. Edited by Helen Casabona from the pages of *Guitar Player* and *Frets* magazines.
ISBN 0-88188-423-5 $14.95

To subscribe to *Keyboard*, *Guitar Player*, or *Frets*, write to magazine name, Subscription Department, P.O. Box 2110, Cupertino, CA 95015

All prices subject to change without notice.